OTHER VOICES

Other Voices

Readings in Spanish Philosophy

edited by

JOHN R. WELCH

University of Notre Dame Press
Notre Dame, Indiana

Library of Congress Cataloging-in-Publication Data

Other voices : readings in Spanish philosophy / edited by John R. Welch.
p. cm.
Selections in English translated from Arabic, Hebrew, Latin, or Spanish
originals.
Includes bibliographical references.
ISBN-13: 978-0-268-04419-0 (pbk. : alk. paper)
ISBN-10: 0-268-04419-8 (pbk. : alk. paper)
1. Philosophy, Spanish.   I. Welch, John R.
B4561.O84   2010
196'.1—dc22

                          2010008785

To my parents, the first voices

Contents

Preface

Rainer Maria Rilke once spent most of a night lying awake beneath the great Sphinx. Later, in describing his quest for insight into the world's particulars, he recounted the culminating experience of that night:

> Behind the great projecting crown on the Sphinx's head, an owl had flown up and had slowly, indescribably *audibly* in the pure depths of the night, brushed the face with her faint flight: and now, upon my hearing, which had grown very acute in the hours-long nocturnal silence, the outline of that cheek was (as though by a miracle) inscribed.[1]

This encounter between the owl and the Sphinx belonged to Rilke in a special sense; he was its sole human participant, its only witness. But the encounter has become ours as well, thanks to Rilke's text. Yet it is not ours in the same sense. The owl that Rilke saw was a particular, brief and barely present. The owl that we see through Rilke is a type; it persists because it is profoundly symbolic. Rilke's owl is the owl of Athena, who speaks the world with the sweep of its wings.

Athena has more than one owl, and they speak with more than one voice. Because they cannot all be heard at once, philosophers develop selective listening habits to help them cope. English-speaking philosophers are generally attuned to the German and French philosophical traditions, for instance, but not to the Spanish. I first became aware of this when not a single Spanish philosopher was so much as mentioned in my graduate courses in philosophy in the United States. The same pattern is repeated in the culture at large. Why, for example, does someone with the vivid and near-local appeal of Bartolomé de Las Casas remain almost completely unknown to native English speakers in North America? This cultural lopsidedness was the target of Robert Caponigri's anthology of contemporary Spanish philosophy:

The presentation of an anthology of contemporary Spanish philosophy to the English language reading public requires justification for a singular reason: such a presentation should need no justification. Knowledge of Spanish speculative thought, as indeed of Spanish culture in all its forms and dimensions, should in the normal course of things constitute an integral part of the cultural formation of every Western mind. . . .

Such, however, is manifestly not the case. What has, as a matter of history, developed is a situation of absence, of alienation, between Spanish culture and that Western European culture of which historically and spiritually it forms so integral an element. . . .

. . . [T]his situation of absence . . . is a process whose origins may be traced, without doubt, to the Counter-Reformation in its cultural, religious, and political aspects alike, a process which by slow and corrosive stages advanced through the centuries.[2]

That Caponigri may be right about the causes of this "situation of absence" is suggested by the relative prominence of Thomas Aquinas and Francisco Suárez in English-language philosophy. Both are Scholastic thinkers, and their contributions to philosophy are at least roughly comparable. Yet pre-Reformation Aquinas is mainstream; Counter-Reformation Suárez is not. Whatever the causes, however, the effects endure. Spanish philosophy has been little heard in English for quite some time.

To facilitate the hearing of these voices is the purpose of this anthology. Unlike the Caponigri volume, it is not dedicated to contemporary philosophy. Rather, it attempts to represent the high points of nearly two millennia of Spanish philosophy, from Seneca to Ortega y Gasset.[3] While the anthology's contents are conveniently described as Spanish, it should be remembered that the word "Spain" and its cognates have distinct though overlapping senses. On the one hand, "Spain" is a place name derived from *Hispania,* the Latin term for the entire Iberian peninsula. But "Spain" also designates the nation that currently occupies the greater part of this peninsula. The first six of the thirteen works excerpted here are Spanish in the first sense, because written by thinkers from the Iberian peninsula, but not Spanish in the second, for they antedate the Spanish nation. In addition, Seneca, Quintilian, Moses

Maimonides, and Juan Luis Vives are Spanish philosophers in much the same sense that Ludwig Wittgenstein is an Austrian philosopher. They were born in Spain, they lived in Spain, but they left Spain. Hence much (or, in Seneca's case, all) of their philosophical work was carried out elsewhere.

A volume of this modest size is bound to have lacunae. But even if the number of pages were to be quadrupled, philosophers of unquestionable stature would still have to be excluded. Those who have been included would be on the short list of anyone knowledgeable about the Spanish philosophical tradition. Still, some knowledgeable persons might have chosen different philosophers from the same list, while others might have added philosophers to the ones I have chosen. To those who might have chosen different philosophers, I simply point to the prominence of this volume's representatives in standard synopses of the Spanish philosophical tradition.[4] To those who would have added philosophers, I can only say that this anthology emphasizes breadth, not depth. Since the aim is to provide an overview of a bimillenary tradition, figures whom a deeper inquiry would take in must regrettably be left out.

The manuscript that became this book could not have matured without the help of a diverse group of people. Rosa Montero piqued my interest in Spanish culture while we were both visiting professors at Wellesley College. Javier Muguerza humored me during the early, formative stages of the work. Theodore Vitali facilitated my stay at the Frost campus of Saint Louis University in many ways, great and small. John P. Doyle was unstinting with his knowledge of Suárez and Latin expertise. My colleagues Francisco García-Serrano, Renzo Llorente, and Anna Barbero offered invaluable advice on sticky parts of the manuscript. Julie Arata Heringer at Saint Louis University's Madrid campus; Ron Crown at Saint Louis University's Frost campus; Manuel Oliva Hernández, Cristina Arbós Ayuso, and their staff at the Universidad Complutense in Madrid; and Ana María Jiménez and her staff at the Instituto de Filosofía in Madrid were unfailingly helpful in locating essential documents. Frank Reale, S.J., rector of Saint Louis University's Madrid campus, and Paul Vita, academic dean at the same institution, provided humane leadership and imparted support and encouragement during a difficult period. Charles Van Hof and Rebecca R. DeBoer, my editors at the University of Notre Dame Press, were liberal with their time and professional talents. Margaret Gloster, also of the University of Notre Dame Press, was a font of creative ideas for the cover. My wife Cristina talked me through some obscure patches of the Benito Jerónimo Feijóo selection, and my son Guillermo graciously donated his scanning expertise. For assistance in making the voices of this anthology a little less alien, less other, my heartfelt thanks to all.

One

ROMAN SPAIN

Carthage began to expand its position on the Iberian peninsula late in the third century B.C. When Hannibal attacked the Iberian city of Saguntum in 219, the Romans responded by invading the peninsula. Although they forced the Carthaginians out, the peninsula's inhabitants were not entirely subdued until two centuries later. The country was rugged. The Romans lacked an overall strategy. And the native Iberian, Celtiberian, and Lusitanian tribes were fiercely refractory. The Celtiberian city of Numantia defied a Roman siege for eight months until, reduced at last to cannibalism, many of its inhabitants chose suicide over submission. By 19 B.C., however, the peninsula in its entirety had become *Hispania*—Roman Spain.

Roman occupation brought Roman culture, particularly the cultivation of rhetoric as the capstone of higher education. Both Seneca and Quintilian, this volume's representatives of the period, were trained as rhetoricians, though their rhetorical pursuits eventually developed in a philosophical direction. Roman philosophers in general were more practically oriented than their Greek counterparts, and Seneca and Quintilian illustrate the trend. Although Seneca occasionally theorizes in the speculative Greek manner, his philosophy more often takes a vital, practical turn. Both of these tendencies are found in his *Epistulae morales*, excerpted here. Quintilian's *Institutio oratoria*, also excerpted, seconds this decidedly practical approach to philosophy, including Quintilian's distinctively Roman view of the orator as philosopher.

SENECA

The Roman province of Baetica had its capital at Cordoba, where Lucius Annaeus Seneca (often called Seneca the Younger) was born into a distinguished family around 4 B.C. Externally, Seneca's life was a dizzying series of ups and downs. His father, Seneca the rhetorician, took him to Rome as a boy to be educated in rhetoric and philosophy, but illness curtailed the young man's studies, forcing his removal to Egypt. Returning to Rome in A.D. 31, he rose to prominence in the Senate but aroused the jealousy of the emperor Caligula, who was dissuaded from killing him by the argument that ill health would soon do him in. In 41, the first year of Claudius' reign, Seneca was accused of adultery with the emperor's niece and exiled to the island of Corsica. Recalled to Rome in 49, he became tutor to the future emperor Nero. When Claudius was poisoned in 54, Nero acceded to the throne, Seneca to the power behind it. Together with the army officer Burrus, Seneca was responsible for the successful government of Nero's first five years, marked by the absence of capital punishment and bloody contests, by reduced taxes, and by the provision for civil suits against masters by slaves. By 62, however, Seneca's influence was gone. He retired to his estates, bequeathing his enormous fortune to Nero, and devoted himself to philosophy. In 65, having been charged with participation in the conspiracy of Piso, he obeyed Nero's order to commit suicide.[1]

Although Seneca wrote tragedy, satire, and poetry, he is represented here as a philosopher, the greatest figure of the late Stoa. His philosophical writings include dialogues, moral essays, a treatise on nature, and letters. The following selections are taken from the *Epistulae morales* (Moral Letters), written during Seneca's final retirement. Nominally addressed to his old friend Lucilius, procurator of Sicily, the 124 letters were probably meant for publication from the start. They have been recognized as essays in all but name since at least the time of Francis Bacon.[2] In them Seneca emphasizes the harshness of life (Letter 107) and proposes philosophy as a means of self-defense (Letter 18). Appropriating the Stoic distinctions between matter and reason, body and soul, he locates freedom in the ascendancy of soul over body. To achieve this ascendancy, he recommends following nature (Letters 41, 107), thereby ridding the soul progressively of its diseases and passions. Anyone who manages to complete this process is a Stoic sage, able to "take things philosophically" come what may. Unsurprisingly, perhaps, this ideal has been criticized as inhuman.[3] Readers who care to reflect on the justice of the charge may consult Seneca's observations on death (Letter 63). Similarly, those curious about his humanity may want to weigh his remarks on slavery (Letter 47).

The freshness of Seneca's philosophical writing still strikes readers nearly two thousand years later. There is certainly more than one reason for this, but the primary one is probably its straightforward practicality. Although Seneca occasionally indulges in "less deserving," more theoretical topics,[4] theory is kept on a short leash and is strictly subservient to practical ends. Philosophy, as he understands it, is the enlightened pursuit of happiness; it consists not so much in words as in actions. Seneca offers vivid examples of these philosophical actions in Letter 18.

Moral Letters

Philosophy as Self-Defense

Letter XVIII

It is the month of December, and yet the whole city is in a sweat! Festivity at state expense is given unrestricted license. Everywhere there echoes the noise of preparations on a massive scale. It all suggests that the Saturnalia[1] holidays are different from the ordinary working day, when the difference is really nonexistent—so much so in fact that the man who said that December used to be a month but is now a year was, in my opinion, not far wide of the mark!

If I had you with me I should enjoy consulting you and finding out what course you think we should follow: should we make no alteration in our daily habits, or should we take off our togas—time was when a change from formal wear would come about only during periods of grave political upheaval, whereas with us it happens for holidays' and pleasure's sake!—and have dinner parties with a note of gaiety about them, to avoid giving the impression that we disagree with the ways of those around us? If I know you as well as I think I do and you had to give a decision in the matter, you would say that we should be neither altogether like nor altogether unlike the festive-hatted crowd. But perhaps this is the very season when we should be keeping the soul under

From *Letters from a Stoic* by Seneca, selected and translated with an introduction by Robin Campbell (Penguin Classics, 1969). Copyright © Robin Alexander Campbell, 1969. Reproduced by permission of Penguin Books Ltd.

strict control, making it unique in abstaining from pleasure just when the crowd are all on pleasure bent. If the soul succeeds in avoiding either heading or being carried away in the direction of the temptations that lead people into extravagant living, no surer proof of its strength of purpose can be vouchsafed it. Remaining dry and sober takes a good deal more strength of will when everyone about one is puking drunk; it takes a more developed sense of fitness, on the other hand, not to make of oneself a person apart, to be neither indistinguishable from those about one nor conspicuous by one's difference, to do the same things but not in quite the same manner. For a holiday can be celebrated without extravagant festivity.

Still, my determination to put your moral strength of purpose to the test is such that I propose to give even you the following direction found in great men's teaching: set aside now and then a number of days during which you will be content with the plainest of food, and very little of it, and with rough, coarse clothing, and will ask yourself, "Is this what one used to dread?" It is in times of security that the spirit should be preparing itself to deal with difficult times; while fortune is bestowing favors on it then is the time for it to be strengthened against her rebuffs. In the midst of peace the soldier carries out maneuvers, throws up earthworks against a nonexistent enemy and tires himself out with unnecessary toil in order to be equal to it when it is necessary. If you want a man to keep his head when the crisis comes you must give him some training before it comes. This was the aim of the men[2] who once every month pretended they were poor, bringing themselves face to face with want, to prevent their ever being terrified by a situation which they had frequently rehearsed.

You must not at this point imagine that I mean meals like Timon's or "the poor man's room" or anything else to which the extravagance of wealth resorts to amuse away its tedium. That pallet must be a real one, and the same applies to your smock, and your bread must be hard and grimy. Endure all this for three or four days at a time, sometimes more, so that it is a genuine trial and not an amusement. At the end of it, believe me, Lucilius, you will revel in being sated for a penny, and will come to see that security from care is not dependent on fortune—for even when she is angry she will always let us have what is enough for our needs.

There is no reason, mind you, why you should suppose yourself to be performing a considerable feat in doing this—you will only be doing something done by thousands upon thousands of slaves and paupers. But take credit on one account, that you will be doing it of your own free choice—and finding it no more difficult to endure on a permanent basis than to try out once in a while. We should be practicing with a dummy target, getting to be at home with poverty so that fortune cannot catch us unprepared. We shall be easier in our minds when rich if we have come to realize how far from burdensome it is to be poor. The great hedonist teacher Epicurus used to observe certain periods during which he would be niggardly in satisfying his hunger, with the object of seeing to what extent, if at all, one thereby fell short of attaining full and complete pleasure, and whether it was worth going to much trouble to make the deficit good. At least so he says in the letter he wrote to Polyaenus in the year Charinus was in office. He boasts in it indeed that he is managing to feed himself for less than a halfpenny whereas Metrodorus, not yet having made such good progress, needs a whole halfpenny! Do you think such fare can do no more than fill a person up? It can fill him with pleasure as well, and not the kind of insubstantial, fleeting pleasure that needs constant renewal but a pleasure which is sure and lasting. Barley porridge, or a crust of barley bread, and water do not make a very cheerful diet, but nothing gives one keener pleasure than the ability to derive pleasure even from that—and the feeling of having arrived at something which one cannot be deprived of by any unjust stroke of fortune. Prison rations are more generous: the man in the condemned cell is not so scantily fed as that by the executioner; to reduce oneself, then, of one's own free choice to a diet that no man has any real call to be apprehensive about even if he is sentenced to death, that is an act of real spiritual greatness. To do this is truly to forestall the blows of fortune. So, my dear Lucilius, start following these men's practice and appoint certain days on which to give up everything and make yourself at home with next to nothing. Start cultivating a relationship with poverty.

> Dear guest, be bold enough to pay no heed
> To riches, and so make yourself, like him,
> Worthy of a god.[3]

For no one is worthy of a god unless he has paid no heed to riches. I am not, mind you, against your possessing them, but I want to ensure that you possess them without tremors; and this you will only achieve in one way, by convincing yourself that you can live a happy life even without them, and by always regarding them as being on the point of vanishing.

But it's time I started folding up this letter. "Not till you've settled your account," you say. Well, I'll refer you to Epicurus for payment. "Anger carried to excess begets madness." How true this is you're bound to know, having had both slaves and enemies. It is a passion, though, which flares up against all types of people. It is born of love as well as hate, and is as liable to arise in the course of sport or jesting as in affairs of a serious kind. The factor that counts is not the importance of the cause from which it springs but the kind of personality it lands in, in the same way as with fire what matters is not the fierceness of the flame but where it catches—solid objects may resist the fiercest flame while, conversely, dry and inflammable matter will nurse a mere spark into a conflagration. It is true, my dear Lucilius. The outcome of violent anger is a mental raving, and therefore anger is to be avoided not for the sake of moderation but for the sake of sanity.

Letter XLI

You are doing the finest possible thing and acting in your best interests if, as you say in your letter, you are persevering in your efforts to acquire a sound understanding. This is something it is foolish to pray for when you can win it from your own self. There is no need to raise our hands to heaven; there is no need to implore the temple warden to allow us close to the ear of some graven image, as though this increased the chances of our being heard. God is near you, is with you, is inside you. Yes, Lucilius, there resides within us a divine spirit, which guards us and watches us in the evil and the good we do. As we treat him, so will he treat us. No man, indeed, is good without God—is any one capable of rising above fortune unless he has help from God? He it is that prompts us to noble and exalted endeavors. In each and every good man

A god (what god we are uncertain) dwells.[4]

If you have ever come on a dense wood of ancient trees that have risen to an exceptional height, shutting out all sight of the sky with one thick screen of branches upon another, the loftiness of the forest, the seclusion of the spot, your sense of wonderment at finding so deep and unbroken a gloom out of doors, will persuade you of the presence of a deity. Any cave in which the rocks have been eroded deep into the mountain resting on it, its hollowing out into a cavern of impressive extent not produced by the labors of men but the result of processes of nature, will strike into your soul some kind of inkling of the divine. We venerate the sources of important streams; places where a mighty river bursts suddenly from hiding are provided with altars; hot springs are objects of worship; the darkness or unfathomable depth of pools has made their waters sacred. And if you come across a man who is never alarmed by dangers, never affected by cravings, happy in adversity, calm in the midst of storm, viewing mankind from a higher level and the gods from their own, is it not likely that a feeling will find its way into you of veneration for him? Is it not likely that you will say to yourself, "Here is a thing which is too great, too sublime for anyone to regard it as being in the same sort of category as that puny body it inhabits." Into that body there has descended a divine power. The soul that is elevated and well regulated, that passes through any experience as if it counted for comparatively little, that smiles at all the things we fear or pray for, is impelled by a force that comes from heaven. A thing of that soul's height cannot stand without the prop of a deity. Hence the greater part of it is situated where it descends from; in the same way as the sun's rays touch the earth but are really situated at the point from which they emanate, a soul possessed of greatness and holiness, which has been sent down into this world in order that we may gain a nearer knowledge of the divine, associates with us, certainly, but never loses contact with its source. On that source it depends; that is the direction in which its eyes turn, and the direction it strives to climb in; the manner in which it takes part in our affairs is that of a superior being.

What, then, is this soul? Something which has a luster that is due to no quality other than its own. Could anything be more stupid than to praise a person for something that is not his? Or more crazy than admiring things which in a single moment can be transferred to another? It is not a golden bit that makes one horse superior to others. Sending a lion into the arena with his mane gilded, tired by the handling he has been given in the process of being forced to submit to this embellishment, is a very different thing from sending in a wild one with his spirit unbroken. Bold in attack, as nature meant him to be, in all his unkempt beauty, a beast whose glory it is that none can look on him without fear, he stands higher in people's eyes than the other, docile, gold-leaf coated creature.

No one should feel pride in anything that is not his own. We praise a vine if it loads its branches with fruit and bends its very props to the ground with the weight it carries: would any one prefer the famous vine that had gold grapes and leaves hanging on it? Fruitfulness is the vine's peculiar virtue. So, too, in a man praise is due only to what is his very own. Suppose he has a beautiful home and a handsome collection of servants, a lot of land under cultivation and a lot of money out at interest; not one of these things can be said to be in him—they are just things around him. Praise in him what can neither be given nor snatched away, what is peculiarly a man's.

You ask what that is? It is his spirit, and the perfection of his reason in that spirit. For man is a rational animal. Man's ideal state is realized when he has fulfilled the purpose for which he was born. And what is it that reason demands of him? Something very easy—that he live in accordance with his own nature. Yet this is turned into something difficult by the madness that is universal among men; we push one another into vices. And how can people be called back to spiritual well-being when no one is trying to hold them back and the crowd is urging them on?

Letter XLVII

I'm glad to hear, from these people who've been visiting you, that you live on friendly terms with your slaves. It is just what one expects of an enlightened, cultivated person like yourself. "They're slaves," people say. No. They're human beings. "They're slaves." But they share the same roof as ourselves. "They're slaves." No, they're friends, humble friends. "They're slaves." Strictly speaking they're our fellow-slaves, if you once reflect that fortune has as much power over us as over them.

This is why I laugh at those people who think it degrading for a man to eat with his slave. Why do they think it degrading? Only because the most arrogant of conventions has decreed that the master of the house be surrounded at his dinner by a crowd of slaves, who have to stand around while he eats more than he can hold, loading an already distended belly in his monstrous greed until it proves incapable any longer of performing the function of a belly, at which point he expends more effort in vomiting everything up than he did in forcing it down. And all this time the poor slaves are forbidden to move their lips to speak, let alone to eat. The slightest murmur is checked with a stick; not even accidental sounds like a cough, or a sneeze, or a hiccup are let off a beating. All night long they go on standing about, dumb and hungry, paying grievously for any interruption.

The result is that slaves who cannot talk before his face talk about him behind his back. The slaves of former days, however, whose mouths were not sealed up like this, who were able to make conversation not only in the presence of their master but actually with him, were ready to bare their necks to the executioner for him, to divert on to themselves any danger that threatened him; they talked at dinner but under torture they kept their mouths shut. It is just this high-handed treatment which is responsible for the frequently heard saying, "You've as many enemies as you've slaves." They are not our enemies when we acquire them; we make them so.

For the moment I pass over other instances of our harsh and inhuman behavior, the way we abuse them as if they were beasts of burden instead of human beings, the way for example, from the time we take our places on the dinner couches, one of them mops up the spittle and another stationed at the foot of the couch collects up the "leavings" of the drunken diners. Another carves the costly game birds, slicing off choice pieces from the breast and rump with the unerring strokes of a trained hand—unhappy man, to exist for the one and only purpose of carving a fat bird in the proper style—although the person who learns the technique from sheer necessity is not quite so much to be pitied as the person who gives demonstrations of it for pleasure's sake. Another, the one who serves the wine, is got up like a girl and engaged in a struggle with his years; he cannot get away from his boyhood, but is dragged back to it all the time; although he already has the figure of a soldier, he is kept free of hair by having it rubbed away or pulled out by the roots. His sleepless night is divided between his master's drunkenness and sexual pleasures, boy at the table, man in the bedroom. Another, who has the privilege of rating each guest's character, has to go on standing where he is, poor fellow, and watch to see whose powers of flattery and absence of restraint in appetite or speech are to secure them an invitation for the following day. Add to these the caterers with their highly developed knowledge of their master's palate, the men who know the flavors that will sharpen his appetite, know what will appeal to his eyes, what novelties can tempt his stomach when it is becoming queasy, what dishes he will push aside with the eventual coming of sheet satiety, what he will have a craving for on that particular day.

These are the people with whom a master cannot tolerate the thought of taking his dinner, assuming that to sit down at the same table with one of his slaves would seriously impair his dignity. "The very idea!" he says. Yet have a look at the number of masters he has from the ranks of these very slaves.[5] Take Callistus' one-time master. I saw him once actually standing waiting at Callistus' door and refused admission while others were going inside, the very master who had attached a price-ticket to the man and put him up for sale along with other rejects from his household staff. There's a slave who has paid his master back—one who was pushed into the first lot, too, the batch on which the auctioneer is merely trying out his voice! Now it was the slave's turn to strike his master off his list, to decide that *he*'s not the sort of person he wants in *his* house. Callistus' master sold him, yes, and look how much it cost him!

How about reflecting that the person you call your slave traces his origin back to the same stock as yourself, has the same good sky above him, breathes as you do, lives as you do, dies as you do? It is as easy for you to see in him a free-born man as for him to see a slave in you. Remember the Varus disaster: many a man of the most distinguished ancestry, who was doing his military service as the first step on the road to a seat in the Senate, was brought low by fortune, condemned by her to look after a steading, for example, or a flock of sheep. Now think contemptuously of these people's lot in life, in whose very place, for all your contempt, you could suddenly find yourself.

I don't want to involve myself in an endless topic of debate by discussing the treatment of slaves, towards whom we Romans are exceptionally arrogant, harsh and insulting. But the essence of the advice I'd like to give is this: treat your inferiors in the way in which you would

like to be treated by your own superiors. And whenever it strikes you
how much power you have over your slave, let it also strike you that
your own master has just as much power over you. "I haven't got a master," you say. You're young yet; there's always the chance that you'll
have one. Have you forgotten the age at which Hecuba became a slave,
or Croesus, or the mother of Darius, or Plato, or Diogenes? Be kind
and courteous in your dealings with a slave; bring him into your discussions and conversations and your company generally. And if at this
point all those people who have been spoilt by luxury raise an outcry
protesting, as they will, "There couldn't be anything more degrading,
anything more disgraceful," let me just say that these are the very persons I will catch on occasion kissing the hand of someone else's slave.

Don't you notice, too, how our ancestors took away all odium from
the master's position and all that seemed insulting or degrading in the
lot of the slave by calling the master "father of the household" and
speaking of the slaves as "members of the household" (something which
survives to this day in the mime)? They instituted, too, a holiday on
which master and slave were to eat together, not as the only day this
could happen, of course, but as one on which it was always to happen.
And in the household they allowed the slaves to hold official positions
and to exercise some jurisdiction in it; in fact they regarded the household as a miniature republic.

"Do you mean to say," comes the retort, "that I'm to have each and
every one of my slaves sitting at the table with me?" Not at all, any
more than you're to invite to it everybody who isn't a slave. You're
quite mistaken, though, if you imagine that I'd bar from the table certain slaves on the grounds of the relatively menial or dirty nature of
their work—that muleteer, for example, or that cowhand. I propose to
value them according to their character, not their jobs. Each man has a
character of his own choosing; it is chance or fate that decides his choice
of job. Have some of them dine with you because they deserve it, others
in order to make them so deserving. For if there's anything typical of
the slave about them as a result of the low company they're used to living in, it will be rubbed off through association with men of better
breeding.

You needn't, my dear Lucilius, look for friends only in the City or
the Senate; if you keep your eyes open, you'll find them in your own
home. Good material often lies idle for want of someone to make use of

it; just give it a trial. A man who examines the saddle and bridle and not the animal itself when he is out to buy a horse is a fool; similarly, only an absolute fool values a man according to his clothes, or according to his social position, which after all is only something that we wear like clothing.

"He's a slave." But he may have the spirit of a free man. "He's a slave." But is that really to count against him? Show me a man who isn't a slave; one is a slave to sex, another to money, another to ambition; all are slaves to hope or fear. I could show you a man who has been a Consul who is a slave to his "little old woman," a millionaire who is the slave of a little girl in domestic service. I could show you some highly aristocratic young men who are utter slaves to stage artistes. And there's no state of slavery more disgraceful than one which is self-imposed. So you needn't allow yourself to be deterred by the snobbish people I've been talking about from showing good humor towards your slaves instead of adopting an attitude of arrogant superiority towards them. Have them respect you rather than fear you.

Here, just because I've said they "should respect a master rather than fear him," someone will tell us that I'm now inviting slaves to proclaim their freedom and bringing about their employers' overthrow. "Are slaves to pay their 'respects' like dependent followers or early morning callers? That's what he means, I suppose." Anyone saying this forgets that what is enough for a god, in the shape of worship, cannot be too little for a master. To be really respected is to be loved; and love and fear will not mix. That's why I think you're absolutely right in not wishing to be feared by your slaves, and in confining your lashings to verbal ones; as instruments of correction, beatings are for animals only. Besides, what annoys us does not necessarily do us any harm; but we masters are apt to be robbed of our senses by mere passing fancies, to the point where our anger is called out by anything which fails to answer to our will. We assume the mental attitudes of tyrants. For they too forget their own strength and the helplessness of others and grow white-hot with fury as if they had received an injury, when all the time they are quite immune from any such danger through the sheer exaltedness of their position. Nor indeed are they unaware of this; but it does not stop them seizing an opportunity of finding fault with an inferior and maltreating him for it; they receive an injury by way of excuse to do one themselves.

But I won't keep you any longer; you don't need exhortation. It is a mark of a good way of life that, among other things, it satisfies and abides; bad behavior, constantly changing, not for the better, simply into different forms, has none of this stability.

Letter LXIII

I am very sorry to hear of your friend Flaccus' death. Still, I would not have you grieve unduly over it. I can scarcely venture to demand that you should not grieve at all—and yet I am convinced that it is better that way. But who will ever be granted that strength of character, unless he be a man already lifted far out of fortune's reach? Even he will feel a twinge of pain when a thing like this happens—but only a twinge. As for us, we can be pardoned for having given way to tears so long as they have not run down in excessive quantities and we have checked them for ourselves. When one has lost a friend one's eyes should be neither dry nor streaming. Tears, yes, there should be, but not lamentation. Can you find the rule I am laying down a harsh one when the greatest of Greek poets has restricted to a single day, no more, a person's right to cry—in the passage where he tells us that even Niobe remembered to eat?[6] Would you like to know what lies behind extravagant weeping and wailing? In our tears we are trying to find means of proving that we feel the loss. We are not being governed by our grief but parading it. No one ever goes into mourning for the benefit merely of himself. Oh, the miserable folly of it all—that there should be an element of ostentation in grief!

"Come now," you will be asking, "are you saying that I should forget a person who has been a friend?" Well, you are not proposing to keep him very long in your memory if his memory is to last just as long as your grief. At any moment something or other will happen that will turn that long face of yours into a smiling one. I do not see very much time going by before the sense of loss is mitigated and even the keenest sorrowings settle down. Your face will cease to be its present picture of sadness as soon as you take your eyes off yourself. At the moment you are keeping a watch on your grief—but even as you do it is fading away, and the keener it is the quicker it is in stopping.

Let us see to it that the recollection of those we have lost becomes a pleasure to us. Nobody really cares to cast his mind back to something which he is never going to think of without pain. Inevitable as it is that the names of persons who were dear to us and are now lost should cause us a gnawing sort of pain when we think of them, that pain is not without a pleasure of its own. As my teacher Attalus used to say, "In the pleasure we find in the memory of departed friends there is a resemblance to the way in which certain bitter fruits are agreeable or the very acidity of an exceedingly old wine has its attraction. But after a certain interval all that pained us is obliterated and the enjoyment comes to us unalloyed." If we are to believe him, "Thinking of friends who are alive and well is like feasting on cakes and honey. Recalling those who are gone is pleasant but not without a touch of sourness. Who would deny, though, that even acid things like this with a harshness in their taste do stimulate the palate?" Personally I do not agree with him there. Thinking of departed friends is to me something sweet and mellow. For when I had them with me it was with the feeling that I was going to lose them, and now that I have lost them I keep the feeling that I have them with me still.

So, my dear Lucilius, behave in keeping with your usual fair-mindedness and stop misinterpreting the kindness of fortune. She has given as well as taken away. Let us therefore go all out to make the most of friends, since no one can tell how long we shall have the opportunity. Let us just think how often we leave them behind when we are setting out on some long journey or other, or how often we fail to see them when we are staying in the same area, and we shall realize that we have lost all too much time while they are still alive. Can you stand people who treat their friends with complete neglect and then mourn them to distraction, never caring about anyone unless they have lost him? And the reason they lament them so extravagantly then is that they are afraid people may wonder whether they did care; they are looking for belated means of demonstrating their devotion. If we have other friends, we are hardly kind or appreciative of them if they count for so very little when it comes to consoling us for the one we have buried. If we have no other friends, we have done ourselves a greater injury than fortune has done us: she has deprived us of a single friend but we have deprived ourselves of every friend we have failed to make. A person, moreover, who has not been able to care about more than one friend cannot have cared even about that one too much. Supposing someone lost his one and only shirt in a robbery, would you not think him an utter idiot if he chose to bewail his loss rather than look about him for some means of keeping out the cold and find something to put over his shoulders? You have buried someone you loved. Now look for someone to love. It is better to make good the loss of a friend than to cry over him.

What I am about to go on to say is, I know, a commonplace, but I am not going to omit it merely because every one has said it. Even a person who has not deliberately put an end to his grief finds an end to it in the passing of time. And merely growing weary of sorrowing is quite shameful as a means of curing sorrow in the case of an enlightened man. I should prefer to see you abandoning grief than it abandoning you. Much as you may wish to, you will not be able to keep it up for very long, so give it up as early as possible. For women our forefathers fixed the period of mourning at a year with the intention, not that women should continue mourning as long as that, but that they should not go on any longer: for men no period is prescribed at all because none would be decent. Yet out of all the pathetic females you know of who were only dragged away from the graveside, or even torn from the body itself, with the greatest of difficulty, can you show me one whose tears lasted for a whole month? Nothing makes itself unpopular quite so quickly as a person's grief. When it is fresh it attracts people to its side, finds someone to offer it consolation; but if it is perpetuated it becomes an object of ridicule—deservedly, too, for it is either feigned or foolish.

And all this comes to you from me, the very man who wept for Annaeus Serenus, that dearest of friends to me, so unrestrainedly that I must needs be included—though this is the last thing I should want—among examples of men who have been defeated by grief! Nevertheless I condemn today the way I behaved then. I realize now that my sorrowing in the way I did was mainly due to the fact that I had never considered the possibility of his dying before me. That he was younger than I was, a good deal younger too, was all that ever occurred to me—as if fate paid any regard to seniority! So let us bear it constantly in mind that those we are fond of are just as liable to death as we are ourselves. What I should have said before was, "My friend Serenus is younger than I am, but what difference does that make? He should die later than me, but it is quite possible he will die before me." It was just because I did not do so that fortune caught me unprepared with that sudden blow. Now I bear it in mind not only that all things are liable to death but that that liability is governed by no set rules. Whatever can happen at any time can happen today. Let us reflect then, my dearest Lucilius, that we ourselves shall not be long in reaching the place we mourn his having reached. Perhaps, too, if only there is truth in the story told by sages and some welcoming abode awaits us, he whom we suppose to be dead and gone has merely been sent on ahead.

Letter CVII

Where's that moral insight of yours? Where's that acuteness of perception? Or magnanimity? Does something as trivial as that upset you? Your slaves have seen your absorption in business as their chance to run away. So be it, you have been let down by friends—for by all means let them keep the name we mistakenly bestowed on them and be called such just to heighten their disgrace; but the fact is that your affairs have been freed for good and all of a number of people on whom all your trouble was being wasted and who considered you insufferable to anyone but yourself. There's nothing unusual or surprising about it all. To be put out by this sort of thing is as ridiculous as grumbling about being spattered in the street or getting dirty where it's muddy. One has to accept life on the same terms as the public baths, or crowds, or travel. Things will get thrown at you and things will hit you. Life's no soft affair. It's a long road you've started on: you can't but expect to have slips and knocks and falls, and get tired, and openly wish—a lie—for death. At one place you will part from a companion, at another bury one, and be afraid of one at another. These are the kind of things you'll come up against all along this rugged journey. Wanting to die? Let the personality be made ready to face everything; let it be made to realize that it has come to terrain on which thunder and lightning play, terrain on which

> Grief and vengeful Care have set their couch,
> And pallid Sickness dwells, and drear Old Age.[7]

This is the company in which you must live out your days. Escape them you cannot, scorn them you can. And scorn them you will if by constant reflection you have anticipated future happenings. Everyone faces up more bravely to a thing for which he has long prepared himself, sufferings, even, being withstood if they have been trained for in advance. Those who are unprepared, on the other hand, are panic-stricken by the most insignificant happenings. We must see to it that nothing takes us by surprise. And since it is invariably unfamiliarity that makes a thing more formidable than it really is, this habit of continual reflection will ensure that no form of adversity finds you a complete beginner.

"I've been deserted by my slaves!" Others have been plundered, incriminated, set upon, betrayed, beaten up, attacked with poison or with calumny—mention anything you like, it has happened to plenty of people. A vast variety of missiles are launched with us as their target. Some are planted in our flesh already, some are hurtling towards us at this very moment, others merely grazing us in passing on their way to other targets. Let's not be taken aback by any of the things we're born to, things no one need complain at for the simple reason that they're the same for everybody. Yes, the same for everybody; for even if a man does escape something, it was a thing which he might have suffered. The fairness of a law does not consist in its effect being actually felt by all alike, but in its having been laid down for all alike. Let's get this sense of justice firmly into our heads and pay up without grumbling the taxes arising from our mortal state. Winter brings in the cold, and we have to shiver; summer brings back the heat and we have to swelter. Bad weather tries the health and we have to be ill. Somewhere or other we are going to have encounters with wild beasts, and with man, too—more dangerous than all those beasts. Floods will rob us of one thing, fire of another. These are conditions of our existence which we cannot change. What we can do is adopt a noble spirit, such a spirit as befits a good man, so that we may bear up bravely under all that fortune sends us and bring our wills into tune with nature's; reversals, after all, are the means by which nature regulates this visible realm of hers: clear skies follow cloudy; after the calm comes the storm; the winds take turns to blow; day succeeds night; while part of the heavens is in the ascendant, another is sinking. It is by means of opposites that eternity endures.

This is the law to which our minds are needing to be reconciled. This is the law they should be following and obeying. They should assume that whatever happens was bound to happen and refrain from railing at nature. One can do nothing better than endure what cannot be cured and attend uncomplainingly the God at whose instance all things come about. It is a poor soldier that follows his commander grumbling. So let us receive our orders readily and cheerfully, and not desert the ranks along the march—the march of this glorious fabric of creation in which everything we shall suffer is a strand. And let us address Jupiter, whose guiding hand directs this mighty work, in the way our own Cleanthes did, in some most expressive lines which I may perhaps be pardoned for translating in view of the example set here by that master of expressiveness, Cicero. If you like them, so much the better; if not, you will at least know that I was following Cicero's example.

> Lead me, Master of the soaring vault
> Of Heaven, lead me, Father, where you will.
> I stand here prompt and eager to obey.
> And ev'n suppose I were unwilling, still
> I should attend you and know suffering,
> Dishonorably and grumbling, when I might
> Have done so and been good as well. For Fate
> The willing leads, the unwilling drags along.[8]

Let us speak and live like that. Let fate find us ready and eager. Here is your noble spirit—the one which has put itself in the hands of fate; on the other side we have the puny degenerate spirit which struggles, and which sees nothing right in the way the universe is ordered, and would rather reform the gods than reform itself.

QUINTILIAN

Marcus Fabius Quintilianus was born around A.D. 35 in Calagurris (modern Calahorra, in northeastern Spain), then part of the Roman province of Hispania Tarraconensis. Quintilian, like Seneca, was the son of a prominent rhetorician who practiced in Rome and arranged for his son to study there. Once his education was complete, Quintilian returned to Spain to teach rhetoric. But the governor of Hispania Tarraconensis recalled him to Rome in 68. He appeared as an advocate in the courts and embarked on a highly successful career as a teacher. The first rhetorician to set up a public school, he was paid a salary by the state. The Emperor Domitian entrusted him with the education of his heirs, and he was awarded the title of honorary consul. Quintilian married late in life and fathered two sons. But after his wife had died at age nineteen, then his younger son at age five, and finally the older, "my little Quintilian," at age nine, he confessed he had no desire to go on living.[1] He died sometime after the year 96.

Quintilian is remembered chiefly for his *Institutio oratoria* (Oratorical Training). Published late in life and grounded in twenty years of teaching experience, it presents his program for the formation of an ideal orator. The philosophical interest of this program springs from the sharp debate over rhetoric pursued by philosophers and rhetoricians over the preceding centuries. Why debate about rhetoric? The ancient world was rhetorical. Far more so than today, its movers and shakers roused people to act through formal public speech. Philosophy, by contrast, was "a relatively minor element in the total Greek [and Roman] culture, never competitive with rhetoric either in the number of its practitioners or in its immediate social effects."[2] That philosophy appears so prominent to us against the backdrop of ancient Greece, for example, is an illusion created by cultural distance.

Hence when Plato skewered rhetoric in the *Gorgias*, defining it as a form of flattery, as a pseudo-art acquired as a knack rather than knowledge, he was taking on the dominant cultural form of his day.[3] Nevertheless, he pointed the way to a genuine, knowledge-based rhetoric in the *Phaedrus*, arguing that a rhetorician worthy of the name should have knowledge of the subject, the kinds of discourse, the varieties of soul, and the aptness of different types of discourse to each sort of soul.[4] Although Plato apparently never developed this proposal, Aristotle did; his treatise on the subject treats rhetorical persuasion as a type of demonstration and describes the various species of discourse and character in detail.[5]

The empire of rhetoric struck back, however, in the pages of Cicero's *De oratore*, where Socrates and Plato are maligned for shattering the original unity of rhetoric and philosophy, thus severing eloquence from wisdom.[6] This Ciceronian critique undergirds Quintilian's rhetorical ideal: the orator as philosopher. The following selections, taken from Books 1 and 12 of *Institutio oratoria*, develop this ideal. Note Quintilian's distinctive, provocative take on the traditional view of philosophy as the love of wisdom.

Although rhetoric as such has disappeared almost completely from the university curriculum, the ancient controversy over it is as relevant as ever. What Plato objected to was not rhetoric in all its forms, but rhetoric in the debased form of sophistry, a perversion of the word that transforms it from an instrument of communication to an instrument of power. Sophistry is manipulation, and manipulation is a permanent temptation. Nietzsche's insight still bites: "The era of the sophists—our time!"[7]

Institutio oratoria

The Orator as Philosopher

Book I

Preface

Having at length, after twenty years devoted to the training of the
young, obtained leisure for study, I was asked by certain of my friends
to write something on the art of speaking. For a long time I resisted
their entreaties, since I was well aware that some of the most distinguished Greek and Roman writers had bequeathed to posterity a number of works dealing with this subject, to the composition of which they
had devoted the utmost care. This seemed to me to be an admirable excuse for my refusal, but served merely to increase their enthusiasm.
They urged that previous writers on the subject had expressed different
and at times contradictory opinions, between which it was very difficult

---

Reprinted by permission of the publishers and the Trustees of the Loeb Classical
Library from *The Institutio Oratoria of Quintilian*, vols. 1 and 4, Loeb Classical Library ® Vols. 124 and 127, translated by H. E. Butler (Cambridge, Mass.: Harvard
University Press, 1920, 1922). The Loeb Classical Library ® is a registered trade-
mark of the President and Fellows of Harvard College.

to choose. They thought therefore that they were justified in imposing on me the task, if not of discovering original views, at least of passing definite judgment on those expressed by my predecessors. I was moved to comply not so much because I felt confidence that I was equal to the task, as because I had a certain compunction about refusing. The subject proved more extensive than I had first imagined; but finally I volunteered to shoulder a task which was on a far larger scale than that which I was originally asked to undertake. I wished on the one hand to oblige my very good friends beyond their requests, and on the other to avoid the beaten track and the necessity of treading where others had gone before. For almost all others who have written on the art of oratory have started with the assumption that their readers were perfect in all other branches of education and that their own task was merely to put the finishing touches to their rhetorical training; this is due to the fact that they either despised the preliminary stages of education or thought that they were not their concern, since the duties of the different branches of education are distinct one from another, or else, and this is nearer the truth, because they had no hope of making a remunerative display of their talent in dealing with subjects, which, although necessary, are far from being showy: just as in architecture it is the superstructure and not the foundations which attracts the eye. I on the other hand hold that the art of oratory includes all that is essential for the training of an orator, and that it is impossible to reach the summit in any subject unless we have first passed through all the elementary stages. I shall not therefore refuse to stoop to the consideration of those minor details, neglect of which may result in there being no opportunity for more important things, and propose to mold the studies of my orator from infancy, on the assumption that his whole education has been entrusted to my charge. This work I dedicate to you, Marcellus Victorius. You have been the truest of friends to me and you have shown a passionate enthusiasm for literature. But good as these reasons are, they are not the only reasons that lead me to regard you as especially worthy of such a pledge of our mutual affection. There is also the consideration that this book should prove of service in the education of your son Geta, who, young though he is, already shows clear promise of real talent. It has been my design to lead my reader from the very cradle of speech through all the stages of education which can be of any service to our budding orator till we have reached the very summit of the art. I have been all the more desirous of so doing because two books on the art of rhetoric are at present circulating under my name, although never published by me or composed for such a purpose. One is a two days' lecture which was taken down by the boys who were my audience. The other consists of such notes as my good pupils succeeded in taking down from a course of lectures on a somewhat more extensive scale: I appreciate their kindness, but they showed an excess of enthusiasm and a certain lack of discretion in doing my utterances the honor of publication. Consequently in the present work although some passages remain the same, you will find many alterations and still more additions, while the whole theme will be treated with greater system and with as great perfection as lies within my power.

My aim, then, is the education of the perfect orator. The first essential for such a one is that he should be a good man, and consequently we demand of him not merely the possession of exceptional gifts of speech, but of all the excellences of character as well. For I will not admit that the principles of upright and honorable living should, as some have held, be regarded as the peculiar concern of philosophy. The man who can really play his part as a citizen and is capable of meeting the demands both of public and private business, the man who can guide a state by his counsels, give it a firm basis by his legislation and purge its vices by his decisions as a judge, is assuredly no other than the orator of our quest. Wherefore, although I admit I shall make use of certain of the principles laid down in philosophical textbooks, I would insist that such principles have a just claim to form part of the subject-matter of this work and do actually belong to the art of oratory. I shall frequently be compelled to speak of such virtues as courage, justice, self-control; in fact scarcely a case comes up in which some one of these virtues is not involved; every one of them requires illustration and consequently makes a demand on the imagination and eloquence of the pleader. I ask you then, can there be any doubt that, wherever imaginative power and amplitude of diction are required, the orator has a specially important part to play? These two branches of knowledge were, as Cicero has clearly shown,[1] so closely united, not merely in theory but in practice, that the same men were regarded as uniting the qualifications of orator and philosopher. Subsequently this single branch of study split up into its component parts, and thanks to the indolence of its professors was regarded as consisting of several distinct subjects. As soon as speaking became a means of livelihood and the practice of making an evil use of the blessings of eloquence came into vogue, those who had a reputation for eloquence ceased to study moral philosophy, and ethics, thus abandoned by the orators, became the prey of weaker intellects. As a consequence certain persons, disdaining the toil of learning to speak well, returned to the task of forming character and establishing rules of life and kept to themselves what is, if we *must* make a division, the better part of philosophy, but presumptuously laid claim to the sole possession of the title of philosopher, a distinction which neither the greatest generals nor the most famous statesmen and administrators have ever dared to claim for themselves. For they preferred the performance to the promise of great deeds. I am ready to admit that many of the old philosophers inculcated the most excellent principles and practiced what they preached. But in our own day the name of philosopher has too often been the mask for the worst vices. For their attempt has not been to win the name of philosopher by virtue and the earnest search for wisdom; instead they have sought to disguise the depravity of their characters by the assumption of a stern and austere mien accompanied by the wearing of a garb differing from that of their fellow men. Now as a matter of fact we all of us frequently handle those themes which philosophy claims for its own. Who, short of being an utter villain, does not speak of justice, equity and virtue? Who (and even common country-folk are no exception) does not make some inquiry into the causes of natural phenomena? As for the special uses and distinctions of words, they should be a subject of study common to all who give any thought to the meaning of language. But it is surely the orator who will have the greatest mastery of all such departments of knowledge and the greatest power to express it in words. And if ever he had reached perfection, there would be no need to go to the schools of philosophy for the precepts of virtue. As things stand, it is occasionally necessary to have recourse to those authors who have, as I said above, usurped the better part of the art of oratory after its desertion by the orators and to demand back what is ours by right, not with a view to appropriating their discoveries, but to show them that they have appropriated what in truth belonged to others. Let our ideal orator then be such as to have a genuine title to the name of philosopher: it is not sufficient that he should be blameless in point of character (for I cannot agree with those who hold this opinion): he must also be a thorough master of the science and the art of speaking, to an extent that perhaps no orator has yet attained. Still we must none the less follow the ideal, as was done by not a few of the ancients, who, though they refused to admit that the perfect sage had yet been found, none the less handed down precepts of wisdom for the use of posterity. Perfect eloquence is assuredly a reality, which is not beyond the reach of human intellect. Even if we fail to reach it, those whose aspirations are highest will attain to greater heights than those who abandon themselves to premature despair of ever reaching the goal and halt at the very foot of the ascent.

I have therefore all the juster claim to indulgence, if I refuse to pass by those minor details which are none the less essential to my task. My first book will be concerned with the education preliminary to the duties of the teacher of rhetoric. My second will deal with the rudiments of the schools of rhetoric and with problems connected with the essence of rhetoric itself. The next five will be concerned with Invention, in which I include Arrangement. The four following will be assigned to Eloquence, under which head I include Memory and Delivery. Finally there will be one book in which our complete orator will be delineated; as far as my feeble powers permit, I shall discuss his character, the rules which should guide him in undertaking, studying and pleading cases, the style of his eloquence, the time at which he should cease to plead cases and the studies to which he should devote himself after such cessation. In the course of these discussions I shall deal in its proper place with the method of teaching by which students will acquire not merely a knowledge of those things to which the name of art is restricted by certain theorists, and will not only come to understand the laws of rhetoric, but will acquire that which will increase their powers of speech and nourish their eloquence. For as a rule the result of the dry textbooks on the art of rhetoric is that by straining after excessive subtlety they impair and cripple all the nobler elements of style, exhaust the life-blood of the imagination and leave but the bare bones, which, while it is right and necessary that they should exist and be bound each to each by their respective ligaments, require a covering of flesh as well. I shall therefore avoid the precedent set by the majority and shall not restrict myself to this narrow conception of my theme, but shall include in my twelve books a brief demonstration of everything which may seem likely to contribute to the education of an orator. For if I were to attempt to say all that might be said on each subject, the book would never be finished.

There is however one point which I must emphasize before I begin, which is this. Without natural gifts technical rules are useless. Consequently the student who is devoid of talent will derive no more profit from this work than barren soil from a treatise on agriculture. There are, it is true, other natural aids, such as the possession of a good voice and robust lungs, sound health, powers of endurance and grace, and if these are possessed only to a moderate extent, they may be improved by methodical training. In some cases, however, these gifts are lacking to such an extent that their absence is fatal to all such advantages as talent and study can confer, while, similarly, they are of no profit in themselves unless cultivated by skillful teaching, persistent study and continuous and extensive practice in writing, reading and speaking.

Book XII

Introduction

I now come to what is by far the most arduous portion of the task which I have set myself to perform. Indeed had I fully realized the difficulties when I first designed this work, I should have considered betimes whether my strength was sufficient to support the load that now weighs upon me so heavily. But to begin with, I felt how shameful it would be to fail to perform what I had promised, and later, despite the fact that my labor became more and more arduous at almost every stage, the fear of stultifying what I had already written sustained my courage through every difficulty. Consequently even now, though the burden that oppresses me is greater than ever, the end is in sight and I am resolved to faint by the wayside rather than despair. But the fact that I began with comparatively trivial details deceived me. Subsequently I was lured still further on my voyage by the temptations of the favoring breeze that filled my sails; but the rules which I was then concerned to give were still of a familiar kind and had been already treated by most writers of rhetorical textbooks: thus far I seemed to myself to be still in sight of shore and I had the company of many who had ventured to entrust themselves to the self-same winds. But presently when I entered on the task of setting forth a theory of eloquence which had been but newly discovered and rarely essayed, I found but few that had ventured so far from harbor. And finally now that the ideal orator, whom it was my design to mold, has been dismissed by his masters and is either proceeding on his way borne onward by his own impetus, or seeking still mightier assistance from the innermost shrine of wisdom, I begin to feel how far I have been swept into the great deep. Now there is

"Nothing before and nothing behind but the sky and the Ocean."[2]

One only can I discern in all the boundless waste of waters, Marcus Tullius Cicero, and even he, though the ship in which he entered these seas is of such size and so well found, begins to lessen sail and to row a slower stroke, and is content to speak merely of the kind of speech to be employed by the perfect orator. But my temerity is such that I shall essay to form my orator's character and to teach him his duties. Thus I have no predecessor to guide my steps and must press far, far on, as my theme may demand. Still an honorable ambition is always deserving of approval, and it is all the less hazardous to dare greatly, when forgiveness is assured us if we fail.

Chapter I

The orator then, whom I am concerned to form, shall be the orator as defined by Marcus Cato, "a good man, skilled in speaking."[3] But above all he must possess the quality which Cato places first and which is in the very nature of things the greatest and most important, that is, he must be a good man. This is essential not merely on account of the fact that, if the powers of eloquence serve only to lend arms to crime, there can be nothing more pernicious than eloquence to public and private welfare alike, while I myself, who have labored to the best of my ability to contribute something of value to oratory, shall have rendered the worst of services to mankind, if I forge these weapons not for a soldier, but for a robber. But why speak of myself? Nature herself will have proved not a mother, but a stepmother with regard to what we deem her greatest gift to man, the gift that distinguishes us from other living things, if she devised the power of speech to be the accomplice of crime, the foe to innocency and the enemy of truth. For it had been better for men to be born dumb and devoid of reason than to turn the gifts of providence to their mutual destruction. But this conviction of mine goes further. For I do not merely assert that the ideal orator should be a good man, but I affirm that no man can be an orator unless he is a good man. For it is impossible to regard those men as gifted with intelligence who on being offered the choice between the two paths of virtue and of vice choose the latter, nor can we allow them prudence, when by the unforeseen issue of their own actions they render themselves liable not merely to the heaviest penalties of the laws, but to the inevitable torment of an evil conscience. But if the view that a bad man is necessarily a fool is not merely held by philosophers, but is the universal belief of ordinary men, the fool will most assuredly never become an orator. To this must be added the fact that the mind will not find leisure even for the study of the noblest of tasks, unless it first be free from vice. The reasons for this are, first, that vileness and virtue cannot jointly inhabit in the selfsame heart and that it is as impossible for one and the same mind to harbor good and evil thoughts as it is for one man to be at once both good and evil: and secondly, that if the intelligence is to be concentrated on such a vast subject as eloquence it must be free from all other distractions, among which must be included even those preoccupations which are free from blame. For it is only when it is free and self-possessed, with nothing to divert it or lure it elsewhere, that it will fix its attention solely on that goal, the attainment of which is the object of its preparations. If on the other hand inordinate care for the development of our estates, excess of anxiety over household affairs, passionate devotion to hunting or the sacrifice of whole days to the shows of the theater, rob our studies of much of the time that is their due (for every moment that is given to other things involves a loss of time for study), what, think you, will be the results of desire, avarice, and envy, which waken such violent thoughts within our souls that they disturb our very slumbers and our dreams? There is nothing so preoccupied, so distracted, so rent and torn by so many and such varied passions as an evil mind. For when it cherishes some dark design, it is tormented with hope, care and anguish of spirit, and even when it has accomplished its criminal purpose, it is racked by anxiety, remorse and the fear of all manner of punishments. Amid such passions as these what room is there for literature or any virtuous pursuit? You might as well look for fruit in land that is choked with thorns and brambles. Well then, I ask you, is not simplicity of life essential if we are to be able to endure the toil entailed by study? What can we hope to get from lust or luxury? Is not the desire to win praise one of the strongest stimulants to a passion for literature? But does that mean that we are to suppose that praise is an object of concern to bad men? Surely every one of my readers must by now have realized that oratory is in the main concerned with the treatment of what is just and honorable? Can a bad and unjust man speak on such themes as the dignity of the subject demands? Nay, even if we exclude the most important aspects of the question now before us, and make the impossible concession that the best and worst of men may have the same talent, industry and learning, we are still confronted by the question as to which of the two is entitled to be called the better orator. The answer is surely clear enough: it will be he who is the better man. Consequently, the bad man and the perfect orator can never be identical. For nothing is perfect, if there exists something else that is better. However, as I do not wish to appear to adopt the practice dear to the Socratics of framing answers to my own questions, let me assume the existence of a man so obstinately blind to the truth as to venture to maintain that a bad man equipped with the same talents, industry and learning will be not a whit inferior to the good man as an orator; and let me show that he too is mad. There is one point at any rate which no one will question, namely, that the aim of every speech is to convince the judge that the case which it puts forward is true and honorable. Well then, which will do this best, the good man or the bad? The good man will without doubt more often say what is true and honorable. But even supposing that his duty should, as I shall show may sometimes happen, lead him to make statements which are false, his words are still certain to carry greater weight with his audience. On the other hand bad men, in their contempt for public opinion and their ignorance of what is right, sometimes drop their mask unawares, and are impudent in the statement of their case and shameless in their assertions. Further, in their attempt to achieve the impossible they display an unseemly persistency and unavailing energy. For in lawsuits no less than in the ordinary paths of life, they cherish depraved expectations. But it often happens that even when they tell the truth they fail to win belief, and the mere fact that such a man is its advocate is regarded as an indication of the badness of the case.

I must now proceed to deal with the objections which common opinion is practically unanimous in bringing against this view. Was not Demosthenes an orator? And yet we are told that he was a bad man. Was not Cicero an orator? And yet there are many who have found fault with his character as well. What am I to answer? My reply will be highly unpopular and I must first attempt to conciliate my audience. I do not consider that Demosthenes deserves the serious reflections that have been made upon his character to such an extent that I am bound to believe all the charges amassed against him by his enemies; for my reading tells me that his public policy was of the noblest and his end most glorious. Again, I cannot see that the aims of Cicero were in any portion of his career other than such as may become an excellent citizen. As evidence I would cite the fact that his behavior as consul was magnificent and his administration of his province a model of integrity, while he refused to become one of the twenty commissioners,[4] and in the grievous civil wars which afflicted his generation beyond all others, neither hope nor fear ever deterred him from giving his support to the better party, that is to say, to the interests of the common weal. Some, it is true, regard him as lacking in courage. The best answer to these critics is to be found in his own words, to the effect that he was timid not in confronting peril, but in anticipating it. And this he proved also by the manner of his death, in meeting which he displayed a singular fortitude. But even if these two men lacked the perfection of virtue, I will reply to those who ask if they were orators, in the manner in which the Stoics would reply, if asked whether Zeno, Cleanthes or Chrysippus himself were wise men. I shall say that they were great men deserving our veneration, but that they did not attain to that which is the highest perfection of man's nature. For did not Pythagoras desire that he should not be called a wise man, like the sages who preceded him, but rather a student of wisdom?[5] But for my own part, conforming to the language of every day, I have said time and again, and shall continue to say, that Cicero was a perfect orator, just as in ordinary speech we call our friends good and sensible men, although neither of these titles can really be given to any save to him that has attained to perfect wisdom. But if I am called upon to speak strictly and in accordance with the most rigid laws of truth, I shall proclaim that I seek to find that same perfect orator whom Cicero also sought to discover. For while I admit that he stood on the loftiest pinnacle of eloquence, and can discover scarcely a single deficiency in him, although I might perhaps discover certain superfluities which I think he would have pruned away (for the general view of the learned is that he possessed many virtues and a few faults, and he himself[6] states that he has succeeded in suppressing much of his youthful exuberance), none the less, in view of the fact that, although he had by no means a low opinion of himself, he never claimed to be the perfect sage, and, had he been granted longer life and less troubled conditions for the composition of his works, would doubtless have spoken better still, I shall not lay myself open to the charge of ungenerous criticism, if I say that I believe that he failed actually to achieve that perfection to the attainment of which none have approached more nearly, and indeed had I felt otherwise in this connection, I might have defended my point with greater boldness and freedom.[7] Marcus Antonius declared that he had seen no man who was genuinely eloquent (and to be eloquent is a far less achievement than to be an orator), while Cicero himself has failed to find his orator in actual life and merely imagines and strives to depict the ideal. Shall I then be afraid to say that in the eternity of time that is yet to be, something more perfect may be found than has yet existed? I say nothing of those critics who will not allow sufficient credit even for eloquence to Cicero and Demosthenes, although Cicero himself does not regard Demosthenes as flawless, but asserts that he sometimes nods,[8] while even Cicero fails to satisfy Brutus and Calvus (at any rate they criticized his style to his face), or to win the complete approval of either of the Asinii, who in various passages attack the faults of his oratory in language which is positively hostile.

However, let us fly in the face of nature and assume that a bad man has been discovered who is endowed with the highest eloquence. I shall none the less deny that he is an orator. For I should not allow that every man who has shown himself ready with his hands was necessarily a brave man, because true courage cannot be conceived of without the accompaniment of virtue. Surely the advocate who is called to defend the

accused requires to be a man of honor, honor which greed cannot corrupt, influence seduce, or fear dismay. Shall we then dignify the traitor,
the deserter, the turncoat with the sacred name of orator? But if the
quality which is usually termed goodness is to be found even in quite ordinary advocates, why should not the orator, who has not yet existed,
but may still be born, be no less perfect in character than in excellence of
speech? It is no hack-advocate, no hireling pleader, nor yet, to use no
harsher term, a serviceable attorney of the class generally known as *cau-
sidici,* that I am seeking to form, but rather a man who to extraordinary
natural gifts has added a thorough mastery of all the fairest branches of
knowledge, a man sent by heaven to be the blessing of mankind, one to
whom all history can find no parallel, uniquely perfect in every detail
and utterly noble alike in thought and speech. How small a portion of all
these abilities will be required for the defense of the innocent, the re-
pression of crime or the support of truth against falsehood in suits involving questions of money? It is true that our supreme orator will bear
his part in such tasks, but his powers will be displayed with brighter
splendor in greater matters than these, when he is called upon to direct
the counsels of the senate and guide the people from the paths of error
to better things. Was not this the man conceived by Virgil and described
as quelling a riot when torches and stones have begun to fly:[9]

> "Then, if before their eyes some statesman grave
> Stand forth, with virtue and high service crowned,
> Straight are they dumb and stand intent to hear."

Here then we have one who is before all else a good man, and it is only
after this that the poet adds that he is skilled in speaking:

> "His words their minds control, their passions soothe."

Again, will not this same man, whom we are striving to form, if in time
of war he be called upon to inspire his soldiers with courage for the fray,
draw for his eloquence on the innermost precepts of philosophy? For
how can men who stand upon the verge of battle banish all the crowding
fears of hardship, pain and death from their minds, unless those fears be
replaced by the sense of the duty that they owe their country, by cour-

age and the lively image of a soldier's honor? And assuredly the man who will best inspire such feelings in others is he who has first inspired them in himself. For however we strive to conceal it, insincerity will always betray itself, and there was never in any man so great eloquence as would not begin to stumble and hesitate so soon as his words ran counter to his inmost thoughts. Now a bad man cannot help speaking things other than he feels. On the other hand, the good will never be at a loss for honorable words or fail to find matter full of virtue for utterance, since among his virtues practical wisdom will be one. And even though his imagination lacks artifice to lend it charm, its own nature will be ornament enough, for if honor dictate the words, we shall find eloquence there as well. Therefore, let those that are young, or rather let all of us, whatever our age, since it is never too late to resolve to follow what is right, strive with all our hearts and devote all our efforts to the pursuit of virtue and eloquence; and perchance it may be granted to us to attain to the perfection that we seek. For since nature does not forbid the attainment of either, why should not someone succeed in attaining both together? And why should not each of us hope to be that happy man? But if our powers are inadequate to such achievement, we shall still be the better for the double effort in proportion to the distance which we have advanced toward either goal. At any rate let us banish from our hearts the delusion that eloquence, the fairest of all things, can be combined with vice. The power of speaking is even to be accounted an evil when it is found in evil men; for it makes its possessors yet worse than they were before.

I think I hear certain persons (for there will always be some who had rather be eloquent than good) asking, "Why then is there so much art in connection with eloquence? Why have you talked so much of 'glosses,'[10] the methods of defense to be employed in difficult cases, and sometimes even of actual confession of guilt, unless it is the case that the power and force of speech at times triumphs over truth itself? For a good man will only plead good cases, and those might safely be left to truth to support without the aid of learning." Now, though my reply to these critics will in the first place be a defense of my own work, it will also explain what I consider to be the duty of a good man on occasions when circumstances have caused him to undertake the defense of the guilty. For it is by no means useless to consider how at times we should speak in defense of falsehood or even of injustice, if only for this reason, that such an investigation will enable us to detect and defeat them with the greater ease, just as the physician who has a thorough knowledge of all that can injure the health will be all the more skillful in the prescription of remedies. For the Academicians, although they will argue on either side of a question, do not thereby commit themselves to taking one of these two views as their guide in life to the exclusion of the other, while the famous Carneades, who is said to have spoken at Rome in the presence of Cato the Censor, and to have argued against justice with no less vigor than he had argued for justice on the preceding day, was not himself an unjust man. But the nature of virtue is revealed by vice, its opposite, justice becomes yet more manifest from the contemplation of injustice, and there are many other things that are proved by their contraries. Consequently the schemes of his adversaries should be no less well known to the orator than those of the enemy to a commander in the field. But it is even true, although at first sight it seems hard to believe, that there may be sound reason why at times a good man who is appearing for the defense should attempt to conceal the truth from the judge. If any of my readers is surprised at my making such a statement (although this opinion is not of my own invention, but is derived from those whom antiquity regarded as the greatest teachers of wisdom), I would have him reflect that there are many things which are made honorable or the reverse not by the nature of the facts, but by the causes from which they spring. For if to slay a man is often a virtue and to put one's own children to death is at times the noblest of deeds, and if it is permissible in the public interest to do deeds yet more horrible to relate than these, we should assuredly take into consideration not solely and simply what is the nature of the case which the good man undertakes to defend, but what is his reason and what his purpose in so doing. And first of all everyone must allow, what even the sternest of the Stoics admit, that the good man will sometimes tell a lie, and further that he will sometimes do so for comparatively trivial reasons; for example we tell countless lies to sick children for their good and make many promises to them which we do not intend to perform. And there is clearly far more justification for lying when it is a question of diverting an assassin from his victim or deceiving an enemy to save our country. Consequently a practice which is at times reprehensible even in slaves, may on other occasions be praiseworthy even in a wise man. If this be granted, I can see that there will be many possible emergencies such as to justify an orator in undertaking cases of a kind which, in the absence of any honorable reason, he would have refused to touch. In saying this I do not mean that we should be ready under any circumstances to defend our father, brother or friend when in peril (since I hold that we should be guided by stricter rules in such matters), although such contingencies may well cause us no little perplexity, when we have to decide between the rival claims of justice and natural affection. But let us put the problem beyond all question of doubt. Suppose a man to have plotted against a tyrant and to be accused of having done so. Which of the two will the orator, as defined by us, desire to save? And if he undertakes the defense of the accused, will he not employ falsehood with no less readiness than the advocate who is defending a bad case before a jury? Again, suppose that the judge is likely to condemn acts which were rightly done, unless we can convince him that they were never done. Is not this another case where the orator will not shrink even from lies, if so he may save one who is not merely innocent, but a praiseworthy citizen? Again, suppose that we realize that certain acts are just in themselves, though prejudicial to the state under existing circumstances. Shall we not then employ methods of speaking which, despite the excellence of their intention, bear a close resemblance to fraud? Further, no one will hesitate for a moment to hold the view that it is in the interests of the commonwealth that guilty persons should be acquitted rather than punished, if it be possible thereby to convert them to a better state of mind, a possibility which is generally conceded. If then it is clear to an orator that a man who is guilty of the offenses laid to his charge will become a good man, will he not strive to secure his acquittal? Imagine for example that a skillful commander, without whose aid the state cannot hope to crush its enemies, is laboring under a charge which is obviously true: will not the common interest irresistibly summon our orator to defend him? We know at any rate that Fabricius publicly voted for and secured the election to the consulate of Cornelius Rufinus, despite the fact that he was a bad citizen and his personal enemy, merely because he knew that he was a capable general and the state was threatened with war.[11] And when certain persons expressed their surprise at his conduct, he replied that he had rather be robbed by a fellow-citizen than be sold as a slave by the enemy. Well then, had

Fabricius been an orator, would he not have defended Rufinus against a charge of peculation, even though his guilt were as clear as day? I might produce many other similar examples, but one of them taken at random is enough. For my purpose is not to assert that such tasks will often be incumbent on the orator whom I desire to form, but merely to show that, in the event of his being compelled to take such action, it will not invalidate our definition of an orator as a "good man, skilled in speaking." And it is necessary also both to teach and learn how to establish difficult cases by proof. For often even the best cases have a resemblance to bad, and the charges which tell heavily against an innocent person frequently have a strong resemblance to the truth. Consequently, the same methods of defense have to be employed that would be used if he were guilty. Further, there are countless elements which are common to both good cases and bad, such as oral and documentary evidence, suspicions and opinions, all of which have to be established or disposed of in the same way, whether they be true or merely resemble the truth. Therefore, while maintaining his integrity of purpose, the orator will modify his pleading to suit the circumstances.

Chapter II

Since then the orator is a good man, and such goodness cannot be conceived as existing apart from virtue, virtue, despite the fact that it is in part derived from certain natural impulses, will require to be perfected by instruction. The orator must above all things devote his attention to the formation of moral character and must acquire a complete knowledge of all that is just and honorable. For without this knowledge no one can be either a good man or skilled in speaking, unless indeed we agree with those who regard morality as intuitive and as owing nothing to instruction: indeed they go so far as to acknowledge that handicrafts, not excluding even those which are most despised among them, can only be acquired by the result of teaching, whereas virtue, which of all gifts to man is that which makes him most near akin to the immortal gods, comes to him without search or effort, as a natural concomitant of birth. But can the man who does not know what abstinence is, claim to be truly abstinent? or brave, if he has never purged his soul of the fears of pain, death and superstition? or just, if he has never, in language approaching that of philosophy, discussed the nature of virtue and justice, or of the laws that have been given to mankind by nature or established among individual peoples and nations? What a contempt it argues for such themes to regard them as being so easy of comprehension! However, I pass this by; for I am sure that no one with the least smattering of literary culture will have the slightest hesitation in agreeing with me. I will proceed to my next point, that no one will achieve sufficient skill even in speaking, unless he makes a thorough study of all the workings of nature and forms his character on the precepts of philosophy and the dictates of reason. For it is with good cause that Lucius Crassus, in the third book of [Cicero's] *De oratore*,[12] affirms that all that is said concerning equity, justice, truth and the good, and their opposites, forms part of the studies of an orator, and that the philosophers, when they exert their powers of speaking to defend these virtues, are using the weapons of rhetoric, not their own. But he also confesses that the knowledge of these subjects must be sought from the philosophers for the reason that, in his opinion, philosophy has more effective possession of them. And it is for the same reason that Cicero in several of his books and letters proclaims that eloquence has its fountainhead in the most secret springs of wisdom, and that consequently for a considerable time the instructors of morals and of eloquence were identical. Accordingly this exhortation of mine must not be taken to mean that I wish the orator to be a philosopher, since there is no other way of life that is further removed from the duties of a statesman and the tasks of an orator. For what philosopher has ever been a frequent speaker in the courts or won renown in public assemblies? Nay, what philosopher has ever taken a prominent part in the government of the state, which forms the most frequent theme of their instructions? None the less I desire that he, whose character I am seeking to mold, should be a "wise man" in the Roman sense, that is, one who reveals himself as a true statesman, not in the discussions of the study, but in the actual practice and experience of life. But inasmuch as the study of philosophy has been deserted by those who have turned to the pursuit of eloquence, and since philosophy no longer moves in its true sphere of action and in the broad daylight of the forum, but has retired first to porches and gymnasia and finally to the gatherings of the schools, all that is essential for an orator, and yet is not taught by the professors of eloquence, must undoubtedly be sought from those persons in whose possession it has remained. The authors who have discoursed on the nature of virtue must be read through and through, that the life of the orator may be wedded to the knowledge of things human and divine. But how much greater and fairer would such subjects appear if those who taught them were also those who could give them most eloquent expression! O that the day may dawn when the perfect orator of our heart's desire shall claim for his own possession that science that has lost the affection of mankind through the arrogance of its claims and the vices of some that have brought disgrace upon its virtues, and shall restore it to its place in the domain of eloquence, as though he had been victorious in a trial for the restoration of stolen goods! And since philosophy falls into three divisions, physics, ethics and dialectic, which, I ask you, of these departments is not closely connected with the task of the orator?

Let us reverse the order just given and deal first with the third department which is entirely concerned with words. If it be true that to know the properties of each word, to clear away ambiguities, to unravel perplexities, to distinguish between truth and falsehood, to prove or to refute as may be desired, all form part of the functions of an orator, who is there that can doubt the truth of my contention? I grant that we shall not have to employ dialectic with such minute attention to detail when we are pleading in the courts as when we are engaged in philosophical debate, since the orator's duty is not merely to instruct, but also to move and delight his audience; and to succeed in doing this he needs a strength, impetuosity and grace as well. For oratory is like a river: the current is stronger when it flows within deep banks and with a mighty flood, than when the waters are shallow and broken by the pebbles that bar their way. And just as the trainers of the wrestling school do not impart the various *throws* to their pupils that those who have learnt them may make use of all of them in actual wrestling matches (for weight and strength and wind count for more than these), but that they may have a store from which to draw one or two of such tricks, as occasion may offer; even so the science of dialectic, or if you prefer it of disputation, while it is often useful in definition, inference, differentiation, resolution of ambiguity, distinction and classification, as also in luring on or entangling our opponents, yet if it claim to assume the entire direction of the struggles of the forum, will merely stand in the way of arts superior to itself and by its very subtlety will exhaust the strength that has been pared down to suit its limitations. As a result you will find that certain persons who show astonishing skill in philosophical debate, as soon as they quit the sphere of their quibbles, are as helpless in any case that demands more serious pleading as those small animals which, though nimble enough in a confined space, are easily captured in an open field.

Proceeding to moral philosophy or ethics, we may note that it at any rate is entirely suited to the orator. For vast as is the variety of cases (since in them, as I have pointed out in previous books, we seek to discover certain points by conjecture,[13] reach our conclusions in others by means of definition,[14] dispose of others on legal grounds[15] or by raising the question of competence,[16] while other points are established by syllogism[17] and others involve contradictions[18] or are diversely interpreted owing to some ambiguity of language),[19] there is scarcely a single one which does not at some point or another involve the discussion of equity and virtue, while there are also, as everyone knows, not a few which turn entirely on questions of quality. Again in deliberative assemblies how can we advise a policy without raising the question of what is honorable? Nay, even the third department of oratory, which is concerned with the tasks of praise and denunciation, must without a doubt deal with questions of right and wrong. For the orator will assuredly have much to say on such topics as justice, fortitude, abstinence, self-control and piety. But the good man, who has come to the knowledge of these things not by mere hearsay, as though they were just words and names for his tongue to employ, but has grasped the meaning of virtue and acquired a true feeling for it, will never be perplexed when he has to think out a problem, but will speak out truly what he knows. Since, however, *general* questions are always more important than special (for the particular is contained in the universal, while the universal is never to be regarded as something superimposed on the particular), everyone will readily admit that the studies of which we are speaking are preeminently concerned with general questions. Further, since there are numerous points which require to be determined by appropriate and concise definitions (hence the *definitive basis*[20] of cases), it is surely desirable that the orator should be instructed in such things by those who have devoted special attention to the subject. Again, does not every question of law turn either on the precise meaning of words, the discussion of equity, or conjecture as to the intention—subjects which in part encroach on the domain of dialectic and in part on that of ethics? Consequently all oratory involves a natural admixture of all these philosophic elements—at least, that is to say, all oratory that is worthy of the name. For mere garrulity that is ignorant of all such learning must needs go astray, since its guides are either nonexistent or false.

Physics[21] on the other hand is far richer than the other branches of philosophy, if viewed from the standpoint of providing exercise in speaking, in proportion as a loftier inspiration is required to speak of things divine than of things human; and further it includes within its scope the whole of ethics, which as we have shown[22] are essential to the very existence of oratory. For, if the world is governed by providence, it will certainly be the duty of all good men to bear their part in the administration of the state. If the origin of our souls be divine, we must win our way towards virtue and abjure the service of the lusts of our earthly body. Are not these themes which the orator will frequently be called upon to handle? Again there are questions concerned with auguries and oracles or any other religious topic (all of them subjects that have often given rise to the most important debates in the senate) on which the orator will have to discourse, if he is also to be the statesman we would have him be. And finally, how can we conceive of any real eloquence at all proceeding from a man who is ignorant of all that is best in the world? If our reason did not make these facts obvious, we should still be led by historical examples to believe their truth. For Pericles, whose eloquence, despite the fact that it has left no visible record for posterity, was none the less, if we may believe the historians and that free-speaking tribe, the old comic poets, endowed with almost incredible force, is known to have been a pupil of the physicist Anaxagoras, while Demosthenes, greatest of all the orators of Greece, sat at the feet of Plato. As for Cicero, he has often proclaimed[23] the fact that he owed less to the schools of rhetoric than to the walks of Academe: nor would he ever have developed such amazing fertility of talent, had he bounded his genius by the limits of the forum and not by the frontiers of nature herself.

But this leads me to another question as to which school of philosophy is like to prove of most service to oratory, although there are only a few that can be said to contend for this honor. For in the first place Epicurus banishes us from his presence without more ado, since he bids all his followers to fly from learning in the swiftest ship that they can find. Nor would Aristippus, who regards the highest good as consisting in physical pleasure, be likely to exhort us to the toils entailed by our study. And what part can Pyrrho have in the work that is before us? For he will have doubts as to whether there exist judges to address, accused to defend, or a senate where he can be called upon to speak his opinion. Some authorities hold that the Academy will be the most useful school, on the ground that its habit of disputing on both sides of a question approaches most nearly to the actual practice of the courts. And by way of proof they add the fact that this school has produced speakers highly renowned for their eloquence. The Peripatetics also make it their boast that they have a form of study which is near akin to oratory. For it was with them in the main that originated the practice of declaiming on general questions[24] by way of exercise. The Stoics, though driven to admit that, generally speaking, their teachers have been deficient both in fullness and charm of eloquence, still contend that no men can prove more acutely or draw conclusions with greater subtlety than themselves. But all these arguments take place within their own circle, for, as though they were tied by some solemn oath or held fast in the bonds of some superstitious belief, they consider that it is a crime to abandon a conviction once formed. On the other hand, there is no need for an orator to swear allegiance to any one philosophic code. For he has a greater and nobler aim, to which he directs all his efforts with as much zeal as if he were a candidate for office, since he is to be made perfect not only in the glory of a virtuous life, but in that of eloquence as well. He will consequently select as his models of eloquence all the greatest masters of oratory, and will choose the noblest precepts and the most direct road to virtue as the means for the formation of an upright character. He will neglect no form of exercise, but will devote special attention to those which are of the highest and fairest nature. For what subject can be found more fully adapted to a rich and weighty eloquence than the topics of virtue, politics, providence, the origin of the soul and friendship? The themes which tend to elevate mind and language alike are questions such as what things are truly good, what means there are of assuaging fear, restraining the passions and lifting us and the soul that came from heaven clear of the delusions of the common herd.

But it is desirable that we should not restrict our study to the precepts of philosophy alone. It is still more important that we should know and ponder continually all the noblest sayings and deeds that have been handed down to us from ancient times. And assuredly we shall nowhere find a larger or more remarkable store of these than in the records of our own country. Who will teach courage, justice, loyalty, self-control, simplicity, and contempt of grief and pain better than men like Fabricius, Curius, Regulus, Decius, Mucius and countless others? For if the Greeks bear away the palm for moral precepts, Rome can produce more striking examples of moral performance, which is a far greater thing. But the man who does not believe that it is enough to fix his eyes merely on his own age and his own transitory life, but regards the space allotted for an honorable life and the course in which glory's race is run as conditioned solely by the memory of posterity, will not rest content with a mere knowledge of the events of history. No, it is from the thought of posterity that he must inspire his soul with justice and derive that freedom of spirit which it is his duty to display when he pleads in the courts or gives counsel in the senate. No man will ever be the consummate orator of whom we are in quest unless he has both the knowledge and the courage to speak in accordance with the promptings of honor.

Two

VISIGOTHIC SPAIN

The Visigoths, a Germanic tribe displaced by the Huns in 376, stunned the Western empire by sacking Rome in 410. With the Romans tied up by the Visigothic threat, the Vandals, Suebi, and Alani were able to invade the Iberian peninsula. The Visigoths then established their own Iberian beachhead in 415. Soon thereafter they became *federati,* allies of the Romans against other barbarian tribes. After helping the Romans defend Gaul against Attila and the Huns, the Visigoths took advantage of deteriorating imperial control and appropriated territory in southern Gaul and Hispania. When the Franks defeated them at Vouillé in 507, the Visigoths withdrew to Iberia, founded their capital at Toledo, and eventually took control of the entire peninsula.

The Visigoths had been Arian Christians since the late fourth century, but they converted to Catholicism at the Third Council of Toledo in 589. A leading participant in this council was Leander, the archbishop of Seville. Leander's younger brother Isidore, who succeeded him as archbishop of Seville, is the most prominent Visigothic thinker. His encyclopedia *Etymologiae,* which attempted to preserve the heritage of the ancient world, is excerpted below. As a work of reference, it was never meant to be an original philosophical treatise. But it appears here to serve a double purpose: to represent the Visigothic moment in Spain and to contextualize later selections by Ibn Rushd, Maimonides, Vives, Vitoria, Las Casas, and Suárez.

ISIDORE OF SEVILLE

Isidore of Seville lived during a period of Gothic ascendancy on the Iberian peninsula. At the time of his birth around 562, Iberia was divided among three ethnic groups. The Visigoths occupied a swath through the southwest, center, and northeast; the Suebi, the northwest; and the Byzantines, the southeast. But by Isidore's death in 636, two of these groups had been overrun. The peninsula had become Visigothic Spain.

Isidore's birthplace is uncertain—possibly Cartagena, probably Seville. He was most likely educated in the episcopal school of Seville, where his older brother Leander was archbishop. After Leander's death between 600 and 602, Isidore succeeded to his brother's chair. He presided over the Second Council of Seville in 619 and the Fourth Council of Toledo in 633. The latter obliged each of the sixty-six bishops attending from Iberia and Gaul to establish a diocesan school and stressed their collective mission to teach the people, for "ignorance is the mother of all errors."[1]

The Toledan Council's attempt to forge a united front against ignorance is symptomatic of the early Middle Ages in general and Isidore in particular. Although Isidore wrote a great deal, one manuscript stands out as indispensable to the age: his twenty-volume encyclopedia *Etymologiae* (Etymologies).[2] The work is a concerted attempt to gather up the pieces of antiquity, shattered by the barbarian invasions, and preserve them against the prevailing darkness. Isidore organized the encyclopedia thematically, but it was divided into volumes by his friend Braulio, bishop of Zaragoza, after the author's death.[3] It is represented here not because of its originality but because of its enormous influence. One particularly energetic scholar located 1,096 extant manuscripts of the *Etymologiae* dating from the eighth to the sixteenth centuries (and two more dating from the seventeenth).[4] According to one estimate, there were some five thousand copies in existence.[5] It was the standard reference work of the Middle Ages.

Why the emphasis on etymologies? Knowing the origin of a word helps not only to understand the word but to understand things, Isidore claimed.[6] The first point is hardly controversial, but not so the second. Consider two views of naming. One is that the name is an arbitrary sign; a rose by any other name would smell as sweet. But Isidore, like Plato in the *Cratylus,* held that the name in its original form *captures* the thing by expressing its essence.[7] An etymology that succeeds in recovering an original name thereby illuminates that which is named.

The excerpts from the *Etymologiae* are from Books 2 and 5. The material from Book 2 on rhetoric and dialectic is background for this volume's texts by Ibn Rushd, Maimonides, and Vives; likewise for Book 5's trichotomy of human law and the texts by Vitoria, Las Casas, and Suárez. As the reader would expect, Isidore's presentation is cut-and-dried, but some sections of the *Etymologiae* are unintentionally poignant. Notable instances are the sections on the syllogism (not included here).[8] Isidore's discussion emphasizes rhetorical and dialectical syllogisms without a single reference to the demonstrative syllogism, which was of central importance in the theology and philosophy of the High Middle Ages. This lacuna reflects the loss of Aristotle's logical treatises (except for the *Categories* and *On Interpretation*) to the Latin West, a loss that was not repaired until the twelfth century. Isidore's chapter on the dialectical syllogism follows two chapters (also not included here) on the known Aristotelian logical works and cites Apuleius' *On Interpretation* instead of Aristotle's *Prior Analytics.*

Etymologies

Rhetoric, Dialectic, Philosophy, and Law

Book 2. On Rhetoric and Dialectic

Chapter 1. On rhetoric and its name

Rhetoric is the art of speaking well on civil questions; eloquence is fluency meant to persuade about the just and the good. The word "rhetoric" comes from the Greek term ῥητορίζειν [rhētorizein], that is, fluency of speech, for among the Greeks ῥῆσις [rhēsis] means "speech" and ῥήτωρ [rhētōr] "public speaker" or "orator." Rhetoric is connected to the art of grammar. For with grammar we learn the art of speaking correctly; with rhetoric, how to express what we have learned.

Chapter 2. On the inventors of the art of rhetoric

This discipline was invented by the Greeks, by Gorgias, Aristotle, and Hermagoras, and translated into Latin by Cicero, evidently, and Quintilian, but in such abundance and variety that even though the reader

---

Translated for this volume by John R. Welch.

admires it at first glance, it is impossible to grasp as a whole. For while the reader has the manuscript in hand, the sequence of words seems to be retained in memory, but once the manuscript is put aside, all recollection vanishes. Perfect knowledge of this discipline makes the orator.

Chapter 3. On the name of the orator and the parts of rhetoric

The orator is a good man, skilled in speaking.[1] A man's goodness consists of nature, character, and accomplishments [*artibus*]. Skill in speaking consists of studied eloquence in five areas: invention, arrangement, style, memory, and delivery,[2] together with the purpose of rhetoric, which is to persuade. Skill in speaking also consists of nature, learning, and experience.[3] Nature, that is, talent; learning, knowledge; and experience, constant practice. We expect to find these qualities not only in the orator but in any effective practitioner [*artifice*].

Chapter 22. On dialectic

Dialectic is the discipline devised to explain the causes of things. It is the area of philosophy called "logic," that is, the rational capacity to define, inquire, and explain. It teaches how argumentation can distinguish between truth and falsehood in many types of questions. Certain early philosophers used it in discussion, though it was still not structured as a formal discipline. Aristotle later systematized the content of this study, calling it "dialectic" because it concerns argumentation about things said. For λεκτόν [lekton] in Greek means "something said." Thus dialectic came after the discipline of rhetoric, for many things are common to both.

Chapter 23. On the difference between the arts of dialectic and rhetoric

In the nine books of *Disciplines*, Varro distinguished dialectic and rhetoric with the following comparison: "Dialectic and rhetoric are like a man's closed fist and open palm: dialectic contracts words; rhetoric expands them." Though dialectic provides sharper explanations, rhetoric is more eloquent in advancing an agenda. Dialectic occasionally enters the schools, while rhetoric continually goes to the forum. Dialectic seeks very few followers, but rhetoric frequently seeks entire peoples. Prior to treating the *Isagoge*,[4] philosophers usually provide a definition of philosophy in order to facilitate the explanation of matters pertaining to it.

Chapter 24. On the definition of philosophy

Philosophy is knowledge of things human and divine, allied to the pursuit of right living. It has two branches: knowledge and opinion. Knowledge is characterized by certain reasoning about a thing; opinion, by reasoning about a thing that is still uncertain and not firmly grounded, such as whether the sun is the size it appears to be or is larger than the whole earth, or whether the moon is spherical or concave, or whether the stars are fixed in the sky or move freely through the air, or how large is the sky and what it is made of, or whether it remains quiet and motionless or rotates at incredible speed, or how thick is the earth, or on what foundations it remains suspended and balanced.

The very name of philosophy means "love of wisdom," for in Greek φιλο- [philo-] means "love" and σοφία [sophia] means "wisdom." Philosophy is divided into three parts: the first is natural philosophy ("physics" in Greek), which investigates nature; the second is moral philosophy ("ethics" in Greek), whose subject is morals; and the third is rational philosophy ("logic" in Greek), which concerns ways of seeking the truth about the causes of things or the conduct of life. Accordingly, physics searches for causes; ethics for right living; and logic for rational understanding.

The first to pursue physics among the Greeks was Thales of Miletus, one of the seven sages. He, before anyone else, rationally contemplated the causes of the heavens and the powers of natural things. Plato later divided physics into four branches: arithmetic, geometry, music, and astronomy.

Socrates first established ethics to correct and order conduct, and he devoted all his energy to the examination of right living, dividing it into four virtues of the soul: prudence, justice, fortitude, and temperance. Prudence permits good and evil to be distinguished in affairs. Fortitude lets adversity be borne with equanimity. Temperance allows lust and desire to be controlled. Justice employs right judgment to distribute to each his own.

Plato added logic, known as rational philosophy, which he used to analyze the causes of things and of conduct and to rationally investigate their capabilities. He divided logic into dialectic and rhetoric. "Logic" means "rational," for among the Greeks λόγος [logos] means both "word" and "reason."

Of course, the Holy Scriptures also consist of these three branches of philosophy. For they customarily discuss nature, as in Genesis and Ecclesiastes; or conduct, as in Proverbs and scattered parts of the other books; or logic, in virtue of which our writers vindicate theology, as in the Song of Songs and the Gospels.[5]

Also, certain scholars define the term "philosophy" and its parts as follows: "philosophy is probable knowledge of divine and human affairs, insofar as humanly possible." Alternatively: "philosophy is the art of arts and the science of sciences." Again: "philosophy is meditation on death," which is more fitting for Christians, who have trampled on worldly ambition and live a disciplined way of life in imitation of their future home.

Others have defined philosophical reason as compounded of two parts: the first is speculative; the second, practical. Speculative philosophy is divided into three branches: the first is natural; the second, theoretical; the third, divine. Theoretical philosophy has four subdivisions: first, arithmetic; second, music; third, geometry; fourth, astronomy. Practical philosophy has three branches: first, moral; second, economic; third, civil.

In speculative philosophy we pass beyond the visible and contemplate something of the divine and celestial. Since such objects transcend corporeal vision, we can consider them only with the mind. The natural branch of speculative philosophy discusses the nature of each thing, since nothing arises contrary to nature in life; each thing has the uses assigned to it by the Creator, unless perhaps the will of God reveals some miracle. The divine branch undertakes the deepest examination of God's ineffable nature or creatures that are spiritual to some degree.

The theoretical branch is the science of abstract quantity. Abstract quantity is separated from matter or other accidents by the intellect and treated by reason alone, such as the concepts of equality, inequality, or others of this sort. Theoretical philosophy has four species: arithmetic, geometry, music, and astronomy. Arithmetic is the discipline that studies numerical quantity in itself. Geometry is the discipline that treats static magnitudes and forms. Music is the discipline that discourses about numbers in special relationships: those that are discovered in sound. Astronomy is the discipline that contemplates the paths of the heavenly bodies and all the constellations, and rationally investigates the situation of the stars both among themselves and in relation to the earth.

Finally, practical philosophy explains proposed courses of action with reference to their workings. It has three parts: moral, economic, and civil. Morality seeks an honorable way of life and establishes practices leading to virtue. Economics wisely regulates the organization of domestic affairs. Civil philosophy administers what is useful to the entire community.

Book 5. On Laws and Time

Chapter 2. On divine and human laws

All laws [*leges*] are either divine or human. Divine laws are based on nature, while human laws are based on customs.[6] Hence human laws differ, since different laws please different peoples. Divine law is right [*fas*]; human law is legal [*ius*]. To cross another's property is right, but it is not legal.[7]

Chapter 4. Natural law

Law [*ius*] can be natural or civil or of nations. Natural law [*ius naturale*] is common to all peoples; it holds everywhere due to natural instinct, not ordinance. For example, the union of man and woman, the begetting and raising of children, the communal possession of all things, the same liberty for all, and the right to things obtained from the sky, the earth, and the sea. Likewise, the restitution of goods or money given in trust, and the use of force to repulse violence. This, or whatever is similar to this, is never unjust [*iniustum*] but natural and equitable.

Chapter 5. Civil law

Civil law [*ius civile*] is the law that each populace or city has set up for itself for human and divine reasons.

Chapter 6. The law of nations

The law of nations [*ius gentium*] concerns the occupation of settlements, buildings, fortifications, wars, prisoners, slaves, repatriations, peace treaties, truces, the inviolability of ambassadors, and the prohibition of marriage with foreigners. It is called the law of nations because it holds in almost all nations.

Three

THE HIGH MIDDLE AGES

For nearly eight hundred years, Iberian territory was under Muslim control. At the request of a Visigothic faction seeking allies, a force of Berber, Syrian, and Yemeni Muslims crossed the Strait of Gibraltar in 711. They defeated the Visigothic ruler Rodrigo (Roderic) at the battle of Guadalete that same year. Taking advantage of the resultant power vacuum and offering favorable terms, they marched north and took Toledo, the Visigothic capital. By 716 they had overrun almost the entire peninsula. The beginning of the Christian reconquest is traditionally dated from the battle of Covadonga in Asturias around 722, but the frontier between Christian north and Muslim south shifted very slowly. After a long siege, Toledo fell to Christian forces in 1085.

This is a convenient, if ultimately arbitrary, date to mark the beginning of the High Middle Ages in Spain. The Muslim civilization of the Iberian peninsula had been highly developed from the start. To cite one instance, Abu 'l-Qāsim (Albucasis), physician to Abd ar-Rahman III, the ruler of Cordoba from 912 to 961, wrote what became the standard European text on surgery for several centuries. With the fall of Toledo, a windfall of Greek, Arabic, and Hebrew manuscripts on philosophy, medicine, mathematics, astronomy, and other sciences passed into the hands of Christian and Jewish scholars. Toledo became the site of a school of translation charged with rendering these manuscripts into Latin. Scholars such as Domingo Gundisalvo, a Christian, and Juan Hispano (Ibn Daud), Gundisalvo's Jewish teacher of Arabic, secured for the school an international reputation. After 1085, then, Spain is distinguished by the florescence of three cultures: Muslim, Jewish, and Christian.

Among the Spanish Muslims of the period are Ibn Bājja (Avempace), who synthesized the ideals of Aristotelian contemplation and Neoplatonic ascent, and Ibn Rushd (Averroës), the greatest Arabic-speaking philosopher of the Middle Ages. Spain's Jewish culture produced Solomon ibn Gabirol, an outstanding Neoplatonic philosopher and poet, and Moses Maimonides, the paragon of medieval Jewish thinkers. Prominent Christian philosophers include Peter of Spain, whose *Summulae logicales* was a widely disseminated logic text, and Ramón Llull, perhaps the most original medieval theorist of all.

The texts chosen here for this period reflect the three cultures of medieval Spain. Ibn Rushd's *Faṣl al-Maqāl* upholds the compatibility of Islamic faith and Aristotelian reason. Moses Maimonides' *Dalālat al-ḥā'irīn* is addressed to Jews beset with philosophically motivated religious doubts. And Ramón Llull's *Ars brevis* attempts to attract Muslims and Jews to Christianity through the irenic means of reason.

IBN RUSHD (AVERROËS)

In the first part of the twelfth century, the city of Cordoba was part of the Muslim empire of three Berber tribes known as the Almoravids. There Ibn Rushd, whose name became Latinized as Averroës, was born around 1126. Well educated in Islamic scripture and law, medicine, and philosophy, he was an up-and-coming scholar when the Almoravids were overthrown by North African Muslim rivals, the Almohads, beginning in 1145. By 1153 he was in Marrakesh, Morocco, where he became acquainted with the first Almohad caliph. In Marrakesh again in 1169, he was presented to the first caliph's son, now the Almohad ruler. Although this meeting was probably the decisive event of Ibn Rushd's professional life, it did not begin well. The caliph asked a question that Ibn Rushd feared to answer: Is the world eternal or not? Noting Ibn Rushd's discomfort, the caliph answered the question himself, redirected the conversation, and sent the scholar away with gifts. Soon after, the caliph requested Ibn Rushd to provide a correct interpretation of Aristotle's philosophy. As a result, Ibn Rushd wrote commentaries on most of Aristotle's works during the years 1169 to 1195, thereby earning the epithet "the Commentator." The same caliph appointed him chief judge of Seville in 1169 and of Cordoba in 1171, and he became the caliph's physician in 1182. Although his patron died in 1184, Ibn Rushd remained in favor until 1195, when he was banished to Lucena, a village near Cordoba, possibly because of religious controversy. Restored to favor shortly thereafter, he died in Marrakesh in 1198.

Medieval thinkers, whether Muslim, Jewish, or Christian, were acutely sensitive to the relations between faith and reason. Reason reinforced faith at crucial points; Aristotle's inferences to an Unmoved Mover, for example, were taken to demonstrate the existence of God.[1] But there were well-known points of conflict as well. In *Tahāfut al-Falāsifah* (The Incoherence of the Philosophers), Ibn Rushd's predecessor Algazali had identified three articles of Islamic faith that were flatly contradicted by Aristotelian reason: the resurrection of the body, divine knowledge of particulars, and the creation of the world.[2] Denial of these teachings, Algazali insisted, made one an infidel—hence Ibn Rushd's fear at the caliph's question about the world's eternity.

Ibn Rushd's response to Algazali survives in three works: *Tahāfut al-Tahāfut* (The Incoherence of the Incoherence), a direct rebuttal of Algazali's treatise; *Manāhij* (Examination of the Methods of Proof Concerning the Doctrines of Religion); and *Faṣl al-Maqāl* (The Decisive Treatise, Determining the Nature of the Connection between Religion and Philosophy). This last work is included in its entirety below. In it Ibn Rushd proposes different canons of interpretation for different groups within the Muslim community, and offers exegeses of the inconsistencies identified by Algazali. These exegeses show considerable sensitivity, even by contemporary standards, to linguistic nuance. As a good Aristotelian, Ibn Rushd relies heavily on the distinction between demonstrative and nondemonstrative reasoning, and as a good Muslim, he takes it for granted that it is sometimes necessary to interpret scripture allegorically.

The reader may wish to keep the following details in mind. Abū Ḥāmid is known in the West as Algazali, Ibn Sīnā as Avicenna, and Abū Naṣr as Alfarabi. The Muʿtazilites and Ashʿarites were theologians who applied philosophical analysis to scripture. The discussion of life after death presupposes Ibn Rushd's interpretation of Aristotle's concept of the active intellect: there is a single active intellect, which is the same for all human beings, and immortality is therefore impersonal rather than personal.[3] Finally, the chapter divisions, summaries, and interpolations provided by the translator are set off in brackets, and bracketed numbers such as [LIX, 2] refer to passages of the *Qur'ān*.

The Decisive Treatise, Determining the Nature of the Connection between Religion and Philosophy

[What is the attitude of the Law to philosophy?]

Thus spoke the lawyer, *imām*, judge, and unique scholar, Abul Walīd Muḥammad Ibn Aḥmad Ibn Rushd:

Praise be to God with all due praise, and a prayer for Muḥammad His chosen servant and apostle. The purpose of this treatise is to examine, from the standpoint of the study of the Law, whether the study of philosophy and logic is allowed by the Law, or prohibited, or commanded—either by way of recommendation or as obligatory.

[Chapter One]
[The Law Makes Philosophic Studies Obligatory]

[If teleological study of the world is philosophy, and if the Law commands such a study, then the Law commands philosophy.]

From *Averroes on the Harmony of Religion and Philosophy*, translated by George F. Hourani (Cambridge: E. J. W. Gibb Memorial Trust, 1961). Excerpts are reprinted by consent of the Trustees of the E. J. W. Gibb Memorial Trust.

59

We say: If the activity of "philosophy" is nothing more than study of existing beings and reflection on them as indications of the Artisan, i.e. inasmuch as they are products of art (for beings only indicate the Artisan through our knowledge of the art in them, and the more perfect this knowledge is, the more perfect the knowledge of the Artisan becomes), and if the Law has encouraged and urged reflection on beings, then it is clear that what this name signifies is either obligatory or recommended by the Law.

[The Law commands such a study.]

That the Law summons to reflection on beings, and the pursuit of knowledge about them, by the intellect is clear from several verses of the Book of God, Blessed and Exalted, such as the saying of the Exalted, "Reflect, you have vision" [LIX, 2]: this is textual authority for the obligation to use intellectual reasoning, or a combination of intellectual and legal reasoning. Another example is His saying, "Have they not studied the kingdom of the heavens and the earth, and whatever things God has created?" [VIII, 185]: this is a text urging the study of the totality of beings. Again, God the Exalted has taught that one of those whom He singularly honored by this knowledge was Abraham, peace on him, for the Exalted said, "So we made Abraham see the kingdom of the heavens and the earth, that he might be" [and so on to the end of the verse] [VI, 75]. The Exalted also said, "Do they not observe the camels, how they have been created, and the sky, how it has been raised up?" [LXXXVIII, 17–18], and He said, "and they give thought to the creation of the heavens and the earth" [III, 191], and so on in countless other verses.

[This study must be conducted in the best manner, by demonstrative reasoning.]

Since it has now been established that the Law has rendered obligatory the study of beings by the intellect, and reflection on them, and since reflection is nothing more than inference and drawing out of the unknown from the known, and since this is reasoning or at any rate done by reasoning, therefore we are under an obligation to carry on our study of beings by intellectual reasoning. It is further evident that this manner of study, to which the Law summons and urges, is the most perfect kind of study using the most perfect kind of reasoning; and this is the kind called "demonstration."

[To master this instrument the religious thinker must make a preliminary study of logic, just as the lawyer must study legal reasoning. This is no more heretical in the one case than in the other. And logic must be learned from the ancient masters, regardless of the fact that they were not Muslims.]

The Law, then, has urged us to have demonstrative knowledge of God the Exalted and all the beings of His creation. But it is preferable and even necessary for anyone, who wants to understand God the Exalted and the other beings demonstratively, to have first understood the kinds of demonstration and their conditions [of validity], and in what respects demonstrative reasoning differs from dialectical, rhetorical and fallacious reasoning. But this is not possible unless he has previously learned what reasoning as such is, and how many kinds it has, and which of them are valid and which invalid. This in turn is not possible unless he has previously learned the parts of reasoning, of which it is composed, i.e. the premises and their kinds. Therefore he who believes in the Law, and obeys its command to study beings, ought prior to his study to gain a knowledge of these things, which have the same place in theoretical studies as instruments have in practical activities.

For just as the lawyer infers from the Divine command to him to acquire knowledge of the legal categories that he is under obligation to know the various kinds of legal syllogisms, and which are valid and which invalid, in the same way he who would know [God] ought to infer from the command to study beings that he is under obligation to acquire a knowledge of intellectual reasoning and its kinds. Indeed it is more fitting for him to do so, for if the lawyer infers from the saying of the Exalted, "Reflect, you who have vision," the obligation to acquire a knowledge of legal reasoning, how much more fitting and proper that he who would know God should infer from it the obligation to acquire a knowledge of intellectual reasoning!

It cannot be objected: "This kind of study of intellectual reasoning is a heretical innovation since it did not exist among the first believers." For the study of legal reasoning and its kinds is also something which has been discovered since the first believers, yet it is not considered to be a heretical innovation. So the objector should believe the same about the study of intellectual reasoning. (For this there is a reason, which it is not the place to mention here.) But most [masters] of this religion support intellectual reasoning, except a small group of gross literalists, who can be refuted by [sacred] texts.

Since it has now been established that there is an obligation of the Law to study intellectual reasoning and its kinds, just as there is an obligation to study legal reasoning, it is clear that, if none of our predecessors had formerly examined intellectual reasoning and its kinds, we should be obliged to undertake such an examination from the beginning, and that each succeeding scholar would have to seek help in that task from his predecessor in order that knowledge of the subject might be completed. For it is difficult or impossible for one man to find out by himself and from the beginning all that he needs of that subject, as it is difficult for one man to discover all the knowledge that he needs of the kinds of legal reasoning; indeed this is even truer of knowledge of intellectual reasoning.

But if someone other than ourselves has already examined that subject, it is clear that we ought to seek help towards our goal from what has been said by such a predecessor on the subject, regardless of whether this other one shares our religion or not. For when a valid sacrifice is performed with a certain instrument, no account is taken, in judging the validity of the sacrifice, of whether the instrument belongs to one who shares our religion or to one who does not, so long as it fulfills the conditions for validity. By "those who do not share our religion" I refer to those ancients who studied these matters before Islam. So if such is the case, and everything that is required in the study of the subject of intellectual syllogisms has already been examined in the most perfect manner by the ancients, presumably we ought to lay hands on their books in order to study what they said about that subject; and if it is all correct we should accept it from them, while if there is anything incorrect in it, we should draw attention to that.

[After logic we must proceed to philosophy proper. Here too we have to learn from our predecessors, just as in mathematics and law. Thus it is wrong to forbid the study of ancient philosophy. Harm from it is accidental, like harm from taking medicine, drinking water, or studying law.]

When we have finished with this sort of study and acquired the instruments by whose aid we are able to reflect on beings and the indications of art in them (for he who does not understand the art does not understand the product of art, and he who does not understand the product of art does not understand the Artisan), then we ought to begin the examination of beings in the order and manner we have learned from the art of demonstrative syllogisms.

And again it is clear that in the study of beings this aim can be fulfilled by us perfectly only through successive examinations of them by one man after another, the later ones seeking the help of the earlier in that task, on the model of what has happened in the mathematical sciences. For if we suppose that the art of geometry did not exist in this age of ours, and likewise the art of astronomy, and a single person wanted to ascertain by himself the sizes of the heavenly bodies, their shapes, and their distances from each other, that would not be possible for him— e.g. to know the proportion of the sun to the earth or other facts about the sizes of the stars—even though he were the most intelligent of men by nature, unless by a revelation or something resembling revelation. Indeed if he were told that the sun is about 150 or 160 times as great as the earth, he would think this statement madness on the part of the speaker, although this is a fact which has been demonstrated in astronomy so surely that no one who has mastered that science doubts it.

But what calls even more strongly for comparison with the art of mathematics in this respect is the art of the principles of law; and the study of law itself was completed only over a long period of time. And if someone today wanted to find out by himself all the arguments which have been discovered by the theorists of the legal schools on controversial questions, about which debate has taken place between them in most countries of Islam (except the West), he would deserve to be ridiculed, because such a task is impossible for him, apart from the fact that the work has been done already. Moreover, this is a situation that is self-evident not in the scientific arts alone but also in the practical arts; for there is not one of them which a single man can construct by himself. Then how can he do it with the art of arts, philosophy? If this is so, then whenever we find in the works of our predecessors of former nations a theory about beings and a reflection on them conforming to what the conditions of demonstration require, we ought to study what they said about the matter and what they affirmed in their books. And we should accept from them gladly and gratefully whatever in these books accords with the truth, and draw attention to and warn against what does not accord with the truth, at the same time excusing them.

From this it is evident that the study of the books of the ancients is obligatory by Law, since their aim and purpose in their books is just the purpose to which the Law has urged us, and that whoever forbids the study of them to anyone who is fit to study them, i.e. anyone who unites two qualities, (1) natural intelligence and (2) religious integrity and moral virtue, is blocking people from the door by which the Law summons them to knowledge of God, the door of theoretical study which leads to the truest knowledge of Him; and such an act is the extreme of ignorance and estrangement from God the Exalted.

And if someone errs or stumbles in the study of these books owing to a deficiency in his natural capacity, or bad organization of his study of them, or being dominated by his passions, or not finding a teacher to guide him to an understanding of their contents, or a combination of all or more than one of these causes, it does not follow that one should forbid them to anyone who is qualified to study them. For this manner of harm which arises owing to them is something that is attached to them by accident, not by essence; and when a thing is beneficial by its nature and essence, it ought not to be shunned because of something harmful contained in it by accident. This was the thought of the Prophet, peace on him, on the occasion when he ordered a man to give his brother honey to drink for his diarrhea, and the diarrhea increased after he had given him the honey: when the man complained to him about it, he said, "God spoke the truth; it was your brother's stomach that lied." We can even say that a man who prevents a qualified person from studying books of philosophy, because some of the most vicious people may be thought to have gone astray through their study of them, is like a man who prevents a thirsty person from drinking cool, fresh water until he dies of thirst, because some people have choked to death on it. For death from water by choking is an accidental matter, but death by thirst is essential and necessary.

Moreover, this accidental effect of this art is a thing which may also occur accidentally from the other arts. To how many lawyers has law been a cause of lack of piety and immersion in this world! Indeed we find most lawyers in this state, although their art by its essence calls for nothing but practical virtue. Thus it is not strange if the same thing that occurs accidentally in the art which calls for practical virtue should occur accidentally in the art which calls for intellectual virtue.

[For every Muslim the Law has provided a way to truth suitable to his nature, through demonstrative, dialectical or rhetorical methods.]

Since all this is now established, and since we, the Muslim community, hold that this divine religion of ours is true, and that it is this religion which incites and summons us to the happiness that consists in the knowledge of God, Mighty and Majestic, and of His creation, that [end] is appointed for every Muslim by the method of assent which his temperament and nature require. For the natures of men are on different levels with respect to [their paths to] assent. One of them comes to assent through demonstration; another comes to assent through dialectical arguments, just as firmly as the demonstrative man through demonstration, since his nature does not contain any greater capacity; while another comes to assent through rhetorical arguments, again just as firmly as the demonstrative man through demonstrative arguments.

Thus since this divine religion of ours has summoned people by these three methods, assent to it has extended to everyone, except him who stubbornly denies it with his tongue or him for whom no method of summons to God the Exalted has been appointed in religion owing to his own neglect of such matters. It was for this purpose that the Prophet, peace on him, was sent with a special mission to "the white man and the black man" alike; I mean because his religion embraces all the methods of summons to God the Exalted. This is clearly expressed in the saying of God the Exalted, "Summon to the way of your Lord by wisdom and by good preaching, and debate with them in the most effective manner" [XVI, 125].

[Chapter Two]
[Philosophy Contains Nothing Opposed to Islam]

[Demonstrative truth and scriptural truth cannot conflict.]

Now since this religion is true and summons to the study which leads to knowledge of the Truth, we the Muslim community know definitely that demonstrative study does not lead to [conclusions] conflicting with what Scripture has given us; for truth does not oppose truth but accords with it and bears witness to it.

[If the apparent meaning of Scripture conflicts with demonstrative conclusions it must be interpreted allegorically, i.e. metaphorically.]

This being so, whenever demonstrative study leads to any manner of knowledge about any being, that being is inevitably either unmentioned or mentioned in Scripture. If it is unmentioned there is no contradiction, and it is in the same case as an act whose category is unmentioned, so that the lawyer has to infer it by reasoning from Scripture. If Scripture speaks about it, the apparent meaning of the words inevitably either accords or conflicts with the conclusions of demonstration about it. If this [apparent meaning] accords there is no argument. If it conflicts there is a call for allegorical interpretation of it. The meaning of "allegorical interpretation" is: extension of the significance of an expression from real to metaphorical significance, without forsaking therein the standard metaphorical practices of Arabic, such as calling a thing by the name of something resembling it or a cause or consequence or accompaniment of it, or other things such as are enumerated in accounts of the kinds of metaphorical speech.

[If the lawyer can do this, the religious thinker certainly can. Indeed these allegorical interpretations always receive confirmation from the apparent meaning of other passages of Scripture.]

Now if the lawyer does this in many decisions of religious law, with how much more right is it done by the possessor of demonstrative knowledge! For the lawyer has at his disposition only reasoning based on opinion, while he who would know [God] [has at his disposition] reasoning based on certainty. So we affirm definitely that whenever the conclusion of a demonstration is in conflict with the apparent meaning of Scripture, that apparent meaning admits of allegorical interpretation according to the rules for such interpretation in Arabic. This proposition is questioned by no Muslim and doubted by no believer. But its certainty is immensely increased for those who have had close dealings with this idea and put it to the test, and made it their aim to reconcile the assertions of intellect and tradition. Indeed we may say that whenever a statement in Scripture conflicts in its apparent meaning with a conclusion of demonstration, if Scripture is considered carefully, and the rest of its contents searched page by page, there will invariably be found among the expressions of Scripture something which in its apparent meaning bears witness to that allegorical interpretation or comes close to bearing witness.

[All Muslims accept the principle of allegorical interpretation; they only disagree about the extent of its application.]

In the light of this idea the Muslims are unanimous in holding that it is not obligatory either to take all the expressions of Scripture in their apparent meaning or to extend them all from their apparent meaning by allegorical interpretation. They disagree [only] over which of them should and which should not be so interpreted: the Ash'arites for instance give an allegorical interpretation to the verse about God's directing Himself [II, 29] and the Tradition about His descent, while the Hanbalites take them in their apparent meaning.

[The double meaning has been given to suit people's diverse intelligence. The apparent contradictions are meant to stimulate the learned to deeper study.]

The reason why we have received a Scripture with both an apparent and an inner meaning lies in the diversity of people's natural capacities and the difference of their innate dispositions with regard to assent. The reason why we have received in Scripture texts whose apparent meanings contradict each other is in order to draw the attention of those who are well grounded in science to the interpretation which reconciles them. This is the idea referred to in the words received from the Exalted, "He it is who has sent down to you the Book, containing certain verses clear and definite" [and so on] down to the words "those who are well grounded in science" [III, 7].

[In interpreting texts allegorically we must never violate Islamic consensus, when it is certain. But to establish it with certainty with regard to theoretical texts is impossible, because there have always been scholars who would not divulge their interpretation of such texts.]

It may be objected: "There are some things in Scripture which the Muslims have unanimously agreed to take in their apparent meaning, others [which they have agreed] to interpret allegorically, and others about which they have disagreed; is it permissible, then, that demonstration should lead to interpreting allegorically what they have agreed to take in its apparent meaning, or to taking in its apparent meaning what they have agreed to interpret allegorically?" We reply: If unanimous agreement is established by a method which is certain, such [a result] is not sound; but if [the existence of] agreement on those things is a matter of opinion, then it may be sound. This is why Abū Ḥāmid, Abul-Maʿālī, and other leaders of thought said that no one should be definitely called an unbeliever for violating unanimity on a point of interpretation in matters like these.

That unanimity on theoretical matters is never determined with certainty, as it can be on practical matters, may be shown to you by the fact that it is not possible for unanimity to be determined on any question at any period unless that period is strictly limited by us, and all the scholars existing in that period are known to us (i.e. known as individuals and in their total number), and the doctrine of each of them on the question has been handed down to us on unassailable authority, and, in addition to all this, unless we are sure that the scholars existing at the time were in agreement that there is not both an apparent and an inner meaning in Scripture, that knowledge of any question ought not to be kept secret from anyone, and that there is only one way for people to understand Scripture. But it is recorded in Tradition that many of the first believers used to hold that Scripture has both an apparent and an inner meaning, and that the inner meaning ought not to be learned by anyone who is not a man of learning in this field and who is incapable of understanding it. Thus, for example, Bukhārī reports a saying of 'Alī Ibn Abī Ṭālib, may God be pleased with him, "Speak to people about what they know. Do you want God and His Prophet to be accused of lying?" Other examples of the same kind are reported about a group of early believers. So how can it possibly be conceived that a unanimous agreement can have been handed down to us about a single theoretical question, when we know definitely that not a single period has been without scholars who held that there are things in Scripture whose true meaning should not be learned by all people?

The situation is different in practical matters: everyone holds that the truth about these should be disclosed to all people alike, and to establish the occurrence of unanimity about them we consider it sufficient that the question [at issue] should have been widely discussed and that no report of controversy about it should have been handed down to us. This is enough to establish the occurrence of unanimity on matters of practice, but on matters of doctrine the case is different.

[Ghazālī's charge of unbelief against Fārābī and Ibn Sīnā, for asserting the world's eternity and God's ignorance of particulars and denying bodily resurrection, is only tentative, not definite.]

You may object: "If we ought not to call a man an unbeliever for violating unanimity in cases of allegorical interpretation, because no unanimity is conceivable in such cases, what do you say about the Muslim philosophers, like Abū Naṣr and Ibn Sīnā? For Abū Ḥāmid called them both definitely unbelievers in the book of his known as *The disintegration* [*The disintegration of the philosophers*], on three counts: their assertions of the pre-eternity of the world and that God the Exalted does not know particulars" (may He be Exalted far above that [ignorance]!), "and their allegorical interpretation of the passages concerning the resurrection of bodies and states of existence in the next life."

We answer: It is apparent from what he said on the subject that his calling them both unbelievers on these counts was not definite, since he made it clear in *The book of the distinction* that calling people unbelievers for violating unanimity can only be tentative.

[Such a charge cannot be definite, because there has never been a consensus against allegorical interpretation. The *Qur'ān* itself indicates that it has inner meanings which it is the special function of the demonstrative class to understand.]

Moreover, it is evident from what we have said that a unanimous agreement cannot be established in questions of this kind, because of the reports that many of the early believers of the first generation, as well as others, have said that there are allegorical interpretations which ought not to be expressed except to those who are qualified to receive allegories. These are "those who are well grounded in science"; for we prefer to place the stop after the words of God the Exalted "and those who are well grounded in science" [III, 7], because if the scholars did not understand allegorical interpretation, there would be no superiority in their assent which would oblige them to a belief in Him not found among the unlearned. God has described them as those who believe in Him, and this can only be taken to refer to the belief which is based on demonstration; and this [belief] only occurs together with the science of allegorical interpretation. For the unlearned believers are those whose belief in Him is not based on demonstration; and if this belief which God has attributed to the scholars is peculiar to them, it must come through demonstration, and if it comes through demonstration it only occurs together with the science of allegorical interpretation. For God the Exalted has informed us that those [verses] have an allegorical interpretation which is the truth, and demonstration can only be of the truth. That being the case, it is not possible for general unanimity to be established about allegorical interpretations, which God has made peculiar to scholars. This is self-evident to any fair-minded person.

[Besides, Ghazālī was mistaken in ascribing to the Peripatetics the opinion that God does not know particulars. Their view is that His knowledge of both particulars and universals differs from ours, in being the cause, not an effect, of the object known. They even hold that God sends premonitions in dreams of particular events.]

In addition to all this we hold that Abū Ḥāmid was mistaken about the Peripatetic philosophers, in ascribing to them the assertion that God,

Holy and Exalted, does not know particulars at all. In reality they hold that God the Exalted knows them in a way which is not of the same kind as our way of knowing them. For our knowledge of them is an effect of the object known, originated when it comes into existence and changing when it changes; whereas Glorious God's Knowledge of existence is the opposite of this: it is the cause of the object known, which is existent being. Thus to suppose the two kinds of knowledge similar to each other is to identify the essences and properties of opposite things, and that is the extreme of ignorance. And if the name of "knowledge" is predicated of both originated and eternal knowledge, it is predicated by sheer homonymy, as many names are predicated of opposite things: e.g. *jalal* of great and small, *ṣarīm* of light and darkness. Thus there exists no definition embracing both kinds of knowledge at once, as the theologians of our time imagine. We have devoted a separate essay to this question, impelled by one of our friends.

But how can anyone imagine that the Peripatetics say that God the Glorious does not know particulars with His eternal Knowledge, when they hold that true visions include premonitions of particular events due to occur in future time, and that this warning foreknowledge comes to people in their sleep from the eternal Knowledge which orders and rules the universe? Moreover, it is not only particulars which they say God does not know in the manner in which we know them, but universals as well; for the universals known to us are also effects of the nature of existent being, while with His Knowledge the reverse is true. Thus the conclusion to which demonstration leads is that His Knowledge transcends qualification as "universal" or "particular." Consequently there is no point in disputing about this question, i.e. whether to call them unbelievers or not.

[On the question of the world, the ancient philosophers agree with the Ash'arites that it is originated and coeval with time. The Peripatetics only disagree with the Ash'arites and the Platonists in holding that past time is infinite. This difference is insufficient to justify a charge of unbelief.]

Concerning the question whether the world is pre-eternal or came into existence, the disagreement between the Ash'arite theologians and the ancient philosophers is in my view almost resolvable into a disagreement about naming, especially in the case of certain of the ancients. For they agree that there are three classes of beings: two extremes and one intermediate between the extremes. They agree also about naming the extremes; but they disagree about the intermediate class.

[1] One extreme is a being which is brought into existence from something other than itself and by something, i.e. by an efficient cause and from some matter; and it, i.e. its existence, is preceded by time. This is the status of bodies whose generation is apprehended by sense, e.g. the generation of water, air, earth, animals, plants, and so on. All alike, ancients and Ash'arites, agree in naming this class of beings "originated." [2] The opposite extreme to this is a being which is not made from or by anything and not preceded by time; and here too all members of both schools agree in naming it "pre-eternal." This being is apprehended by demonstration; it is God, Blessed and Exalted, Who is the Maker, Giver of being and Sustainer of the universe; may He be praised and His Power exalted!

[3] The class of being which is between these two extremes is that which is not made from anything and not preceded by time, but which is brought into existence by something, i.e. by an agent. This is the world as a whole. Now they all agree on the presence of these three characters in the world. For the theologians admit that time does not precede it, or rather this is a necessary consequence for them since time according to them is something which accompanies motion and bodies. They also agree with the ancients in the view that future time is infinite and likewise future being. They only disagree about past time and past being: the theologians hold that it is finite (this is the doctrine of Plato and his followers), while Aristotle and his school hold that it is infinite, as is the case with future time.

Thus it is clear that [3] this last being bears a resemblance both to [1] the being which is really generated and to [2] the pre-eternal Being. So those who are more impressed with its resemblance to the pre-eternal than its resemblance to the originated name it "pre-eternal," while those who are more impressed with its resemblance to the originated name it "originated." But in truth it is neither really originated nor really pre-eternal, since the really originated is necessarily perishable and the really pre-eternal has no cause. Some—Plato and his followers—name it "originated and coeval with time," because time according to them is finite in the past.

Thus the doctrines about the world are not so very far apart from each other that some of them should be called irreligious and others not. For this to happen, opinions must be divergent in the extreme, i.e. contraries such as the theologians suppose to exist on this question; i.e. [they hold] that the names "pre-eternity" and "coming into existence" as applied to the world as a whole are contraries. But it is now clear from what we have said that this is not the case.

[Anyhow, the apparent meaning of Scripture is that there was a being and time before God created the present being and time. Thus the theologians' interpretation is allegorical and does not command unanimous agreement.]

Over and above all this, these opinions about the world do not conform to the apparent meaning of Scripture. For if the apparent meaning of Scripture is searched, it will be evident from the verses which give us information about the bringing into existence of the world that its form really is originated, but that being itself and time extend continuously at both extremes, i.e. without interruption. Thus the words of God the Exalted, "He it is Who created the heavens and the earth in six days, and His throne was on the water" [XI, 7], taken in their apparent meaning imply that there was a being before this present being, namely the throne and the water, and a time before this time, i.e. the one which is joined to the form of this being, namely the number of the movement of the celestial sphere. And the words of the Exalted, "On the day when the earth shall be changed into other than earth, and the heavens as well" [XIV, 48], also in their apparent meaning imply that there will be a second being after this being. And the words of the Exalted, "Then He directed Himself towards the sky, and it was smoke" [XLI, 11], in their apparent meaning imply that the heavens were created from something.

Thus the theologians too in their statements about the world do not conform to the apparent meaning of Scripture but interpret it allegorically. For it is not stated in Scripture that God was existing with absolutely nothing else: a text to this effect is nowhere to be found. Then how is it conceivable that the theologians' allegorical interpretation of these verses could meet with unanimous agreement, when the apparent meaning of Scripture which we have mentioned about the existence of the world has been accepted by a school of philosophers!

[On such difficult questions, error committed by a qualified judge of his subject is excused by God, while error by an unqualified person is not excused.]

It seems that those who disagree on the interpretation of these difficult questions earn merit if they are in the right and will be excused [by God] if they are in error. For assent to a thing as a result of an indication [of it] arising in the soul is something compulsory, not voluntary: i.e. it is not for us [to choose] not to assent or to assent, as it is to stand up or not to stand up. And since free choice is a condition of obligation, a man who assents to an error as a result of a consideration that has occurred to him is excused, if he is a scholar. This is why the Prophet, peace on him, said, "If the judge after exerting his mind makes a right decision, he will have a double reward; and if he makes a wrong decision he will [still] have a single reward." And what judge is more important than he who makes judgments about being, that it is thus or not thus? These judges are the scholars, specially chosen by God for [the task of] allegorical interpretation, and this error which is forgivable according to the Law is only such error as proceeds from scholars when they study the difficult matters which the Law obliges them to study.

But error proceeding from any other class of people is sheer sin, equally whether it relates to theoretical or to practical matters. For just as the judge who is ignorant of the [Prophet's] way of life is not excused if he makes an error in judgment, so he who makes judgments about beings without having the proper qualifications for [such] judgments is not excused but is either a sinner or an unbeliever. And if he who would judge what is allowed and forbidden is required to combine in himself the qualifications for exercise of personal judgment, namely knowledge of the principles [of law] and knowledge of how to draw inferences from those principles by reasoning, how much more properly is he who would make judgments about beings required to be qualified, i.e. to know the primary intellectual principles and the way to draw inferences from them!

[Texts of Scripture fall into three kinds with respect to the excusability of error. [1] Texts which must be taken in their apparent meaning by everyone. Since the meaning can be understood plainly by demonstrative, dialectical and rhetorical methods alike, no one is excused for the error of interpreting these texts allegorically. [2] Texts which must be taken in their apparent meaning by the lower classes and interpreted allegorically by the demonstrative class. It is inexcusable for the lower classes to interpret them allegorically or for the demonstrative class to take them in their apparent meaning. [3] Texts whose classification under the previous headings is uncertain. Error in this matter by the demonstrative class is excused.]

In general, error about Scripture is of two types: either error which is excused to one who is a qualified student of that matter in which the error occurs (as the skillful doctor is excused if he commits an error in the art of medicine and the skillful judge if he gives an erroneous judgment), but not excused to one who is not qualified in that subject; or error which is not excused to any person whatever, and which is unbelief if it concerns the principles of religion, or heresy if it concerns something subordinate to the principles.

This [latter] error is that which occurs about [1] matters, knowledge of which is provided by all the different methods of indication, so that knowledge of the matter in question is in this way possible for everyone. Examples are acknowledgement of God, Blessed and Exalted, of the prophetic missions, and of happiness and misery in the next life; for these three principles are attainable by the three classes of indication, by which everyone without exception can come to assent to what he is obliged to know: I mean the rhetorical, dialectical and demonstrative indications. So whoever denies such a thing, when it is one of the principles of the Law, is an unbeliever, who persists in defiance with his tongue though not with his heart, or neglects to expose himself to learning the indication of its truth. For if he belongs to the demonstrative class of men, a way has been provided for him to assent to it, by demonstration; if he belongs to the dialectical class, the way is by dialectic; and if he belongs to the class [which is convinced] by preaching, the way for him is by preaching. With this in view the Prophet, peace on him, said, "I have been ordered to fight people until they say 'There is no god but

God' and believe in me"; he means, by any of the three methods of attaining belief that suits them.

[2] With regard to things which by reason of their recondite character are only knowable by demonstration, God has been gracious to those of his servants who have no access to demonstration, on account of their natures, habits or lack of facilities for education: He has coined for them images and likenesses of these things, and summoned them to assent to those images, since it is possible for assent to those images to come about through the indications common to all men, i.e. the dialectical and rhetorical indications. This is the reason why Scripture is divided into apparent and inner meanings: the apparent meaning consists of those images which are coined to stand for those ideas, while the inner meaning is those ideas [themselves], which are clear only to the demonstrative class. These are the four or five classes of beings mentioned by Abū Ḥāmid in *The book of the distinction*.

[1] But when it happens, as we said, that we know the thing itself by the three methods, we do not need to coin images of it, and it remains true in its apparent meaning, not admitting allegorical interpretation. If an apparent text of this kind refers to principles, anyone who interprets it allegorically is an unbeliever, e.g. anyone who thinks that there is no happiness or misery in the next life, and that the only purpose of this teaching is that men should be safeguarded from each other in their bodily and sensible lives, that it is but a practical device, and that man has no other goal than his sensible existence.

If this is established, it will have become clear to you from what we have said that there are [1] apparent texts of Scripture which it is not permitted to interpret allegorically; to do so on fundamentals is unbelief, on subordinate matters, heresy. There are also [2] apparent texts which have to be interpreted allegorically by men of the demonstrative class; for such men to take them in their apparent meaning is unbelief, while for those who are not of the demonstrative class to interpret them allegorically and take them out of their apparent meaning is unbelief or heresy on their part.

Of this [latter] class are the verse about God's directing Himself and the Tradition about His descent. That is why the Prophet, peace on him, said in the case of the black woman, when she told him that God was in the sky, "Free her, for she is a believer." This was because she was not of the demonstrative class; and the reason for his decision was that the class of people to whom assent comes only through the imagination, i.e. who do not assent to a thing except in so far as they can imagine it, find it difficult to assent to the existence of a being which is unrelated to any imaginable thing. This applies as well to those who understand from the relation stated merely [that God has] a place; these are people who have advanced a little in their thought beyond the position of the first class, [by rejecting] belief in corporeality. Thus the [proper] answer to them with regard to such passages is that they belong to the ambiguous texts, and that the stop is to be placed after the words of God the Exalted, "And no one knows the interpretation thereof except God" [III, 7]. The demonstrative class, while agreeing unanimously that this class of text must be interpreted allegorically, may disagree about the interpretation, according to the level of each one's knowledge of demonstration.

There is also [3] a third class of Scriptural texts falling uncertainly between the other two classes, on which there is doubt. One group of those who devote themselves to theoretical study attach them to the apparent texts which it is not permitted to interpret allegorically, others attach them to the texts with inner meanings which scholars are not permitted to take in their apparent meanings. This [divergence of opinions] is due to the difficulty and ambiguity of this class of text. Anyone who commits an error about this class is excused, I mean any scholar.

[The texts about the future life fall into [3], since demonstrative scholars do not agree whether to take them in their apparent meaning or interpret them allegorically. Either is permissible. But it is inexcusable to deny the fact of a future life altogether.]

If it is asked, "Since it is clear that Scriptural texts in this respect fall into three grades, to which of these three grades, according to you, do the descriptions of the future life and its states belong?", we reply: The position clearly is that this matter belongs to the class [3] about which there is disagreement. For we find a group of those who claim an affinity with demonstration saying that it is obligatory to take these passages in their apparent meaning, because there is no demonstration leading to the impossibility of the apparent meaning in them—this is the view of the

Ash'arites; while another group of those who devote themselves to demonstration interpret these passages allegorically, and these people give the most diverse interpretations of them. In this class must be counted Abū Ḥāmid and many of the Ṣūfīs; some of them combine the two interpretations of the passages, as Abū Ḥāmid does in some of his books.

So it is likely that a scholar who commits an error in this matter is excused, while one who is correct receives thanks or a reward: that is, if he acknowledges the existence [of a future life] and merely gives a certain sort of allegorical interpretation, i.e. of the mode of the future life not of its existence, provided that the interpretation given does not lead to denial of its existence. In this matter only the negation of existence is unbelief, because it concerns one of the principles of religion and one of those points to which assent is attainable through the three methods common to "the white man and the black man."

[The unlearned classes must take such texts in their apparent meaning. It is unbelief for the learned to set down allegorical interpretations in popular writings. By doing this Ghazālī caused confusion among the people. Demonstrative books should be banned to the unqualified, but not to the learned.]

But anyone who is not a man of learning is obliged to take these passages in their apparent meaning, and allegorical interpretation of them is for him unbelief because it *leads to* unbelief. That is why we hold that, for anyone whose duty it is to believe in the apparent meaning, allegorical interpretation is unbelief, because it leads to unbelief. Anyone of the interpretative class who discloses such [an interpretation] to him is summoning him to unbelief, and he who summons to unbelief is an unbeliever.

Therefore allegorical interpretations ought to be set down only in demonstrative books, because if they are in demonstrative books they are encountered by no one but men of the demonstrative class. But if they are set down in other than demonstrative books and one deals with them by poetical, rhetorical or dialectical methods, as Abū Ḥāmid does, then he commits an offense against the Law and against philosophy, even though the fellow intended nothing but good. For by this procedure he wanted to increase the number of learned men, but in fact he increased the number of the corrupted not of the learned! As a result, one group came to slander philosophy, another to slander religion, and another to reconcile the [first] two [groups]. It seems that this [last] was one of his objects in his books; an indication that he wanted by this [procedure] to arouse minds is that he adhered to no one doctrine in his books but was an Ash'arite with the Ash'arites, a Ṣūfī with the Ṣūfīs and a philosopher with the philosophers, so that he was like the man in the verse:

"One day a Yamanī, if I meet a man of Yaman,
And if I meet a Ma'addī, I'm an 'Adnānī."

The *imāms* of the Muslims ought to forbid those of his books which contain learned matter to all save the learned, just as they ought to forbid demonstrative books to those who are not capable of understanding them. But the damage done to people by demonstrative books is lighter, because for the most part only persons of superior natural intelligence become acquainted with demonstrative books, and this class of persons is only misled through lack of practical virtue, unorganized reading, and tackling them without a teacher. On the other hand their total prohibition obstructs the purpose to which the Law summons, because it is a wrong to the best class of people and the best class of beings. For to do justice to the best class of beings demands that they should be known profoundly, by persons equipped to know them profoundly, and these are the best class of people; and the greater the value of the being, the greater is the injury towards it, which consists of ignorance of it. Thus the Exalted has said, "Associating [other gods] with God is indeed a great wrong" [XXXI, 12].

[We have only discussed these questions in a popular work because they were already being publicly discussed.]

This is as much as we see fit to affirm in this field of study, i.e. the correspondence between religion and philosophy and the rules for allegorical interpretation in religion. If it were not for the publicity given to the matter and to these questions which we have discussed, we should not have permitted ourselves to write a word on the subject; and we should not have had to make excuses for doing so to the interpretative scholars, because the proper place to discuss these questions is in demonstrative books. God is the Guide and helps us to follow the right course!

[Chapter Three]
[Philosophical Interpretations of Scripture Should Not Be Taught to the
Majority. The Law Provides Other Methods of Instructing Them.]

[The purpose of Scripture is to teach true theoretical and practical science and right practice and attitudes.]

You ought to know that the purpose of Scripture is simply to teach true science and right practice. True science is knowledge of God, Blessed and Exalted, and the other beings as they really are, and especially of noble beings, and knowledge of happiness and misery in the next life. Right practice consists in performing the acts which bring happiness and avoiding the acts which bring misery; and it is knowledge of these acts that is called "practical science." They fall into two divisions: (1) outward bodily acts; the science of these is called "jurisprudence"; and (2) acts of the soul such as gratitude, patience and other moral attitudes which the Law enjoins or forbids; the science of these is called "asceticism" or "the sciences of the future life." To these Abū Ḥāmid turned his attention in his book: as people had given up this sort [of act] and become immersed in the other sort, and as this sort [2] involves the greater fear of God, which is the cause of happiness, he called his book *"The revival of the sciences of religion."* But we have digressed from our subject, so let us return to it.

[Scripture teaches concepts both directly and by symbols, and uses demonstrative, dialectical and rhetorical arguments. Dialectical and rhetorical arguments are prevalent because the main aim of Scripture is to teach the majority. In these arguments concepts are indicated directly or by symbols, in various combinations in premises and conclusion.]

We say: The purpose of Scripture is to teach true science and right practice; and teaching is of two classes, [of] concepts and [of] judgments, as the logicians have shown. Now the methods available to men of [arriving at] judgments are three: demonstrative, dialectical and rhetorical; and the methods of forming concepts are two: either [conceiving] the object itself or [conceiving] a symbol of it. But not everyone has the natural ability to take in demonstrations, or [even] dialectical arguments, let alone demonstrative arguments which are so hard to learn and need so much time [even] for those who are qualified to learn them. Therefore, since it is the purpose of Scripture simply to teach everyone, Scripture has to contain every method of [bringing about] judgments of assent and every method of forming concepts.

Now some of the methods of assent comprehend the majority of people, i.e. the occurrence of assent as a result of them [is comprehensive]: these are the rhetorical and the dialectical [methods]—and the rhetorical is more comprehensive than the dialectical. Another method is peculiar to a smaller number of people: this is the demonstrative. Therefore, since the primary purpose of Scripture is to take care of the majority (without neglecting to arouse the élite), the prevailing methods of expression in religion are the common methods by which the majority comes to form concepts and judgments.

These [common] methods in religion are of four classes:

One of them occurs where the method is common, yet specialized in two respects: i.e. where it is certain in its concepts and judgments, in spite of being rhetorical or dialectical. These syllogisms are those whose premises, in spite of being based on accepted ideas or on opinions, are accidentally certain, and whose conclusions are accidentally to be taken in their direct meaning without symbolization. Scriptural texts of this class have no allegorical interpretations, and anyone who denies them or interprets them allegorically is an unbeliever.

The second class occurs where the premises, in spite of being based on accepted ideas or on opinions, are certain, and where the conclusions are symbols for the things which it was intended to conclude. [Texts of] this [class], i.e. their conclusions, admit of allegorical interpretation.

The third is the reverse of this: it occurs where the conclusions are the very things which it was intended to conclude, while the premises are based on accepted ideas or on opinions without being accidentally certain. [Texts of] this [class] also, i.e. their conclusions, do not admit of allegorical interpretation, but their premises may do so.

The fourth [class] occurs where the premises are based on accepted ideas or opinions, without being accidentally certain, and where the conclusions are symbols for what it was intended to conclude. In these cases the duty of the élite is to interpret them allegorically, while the duty of the masses is to take them in their apparent meaning.

[Where symbols are used, each class of men, demonstrative, dialectical and rhetorical, must try to understand the inner meaning symbolized or rest content with the apparent meaning, according to their capacities.]

In general, everything in these [texts] which admits of allegorical interpretation can only be understood by demonstration. The duty of the élite here is to apply such interpretation; while the duty of the masses is to take them in their apparent meaning in both respects, i.e. in concept and judgment, since their natural capacity does not allow more than that.

But there may occur to students of Scripture allegorical interpretations due to the superiority of one of the common methods over another in [bringing about] assent, i.e. when the indication contained in the allegorical interpretation is more persuasive than the indication contained in the apparent meaning. Such interpretations are popular; and [the making of them] is possibly a duty for those whose powers of theoretical understanding have attained the dialectical level. To this sort belong some of the interpretations of the Ash'arites and Mu'tazilites—though the Mu'tazilites are generally sounder in their statements. The masses on the other hand, who are incapable of more than rhetorical arguments, have the duty of taking these [texts] in their apparent meaning, and they are not permitted to know such interpretations at all.

Thus people in relation to Scripture fall into three classes:

One class is those who are not people of interpretation at all: these are the rhetorical class. They are the overwhelming mass, for no man of sound intellect is exempted from this kind of assent.

Another class is the people of dialectical interpretation: these are the dialecticians, either by nature alone or by nature and habit.

Another class is the people of certain interpretation: these are the demonstrative class, by nature and training, i.e. in the art of philosophy. This interpretation ought not to be expressed to the dialectical class, let alone to the masses.

[To explain the inner meaning to people unable to understand it is to destroy their belief in the apparent meaning without putting anything in its place. The result is unbelief in learners and teachers. It is best for the learned to profess ignorance, quoting the *Qur'ān* on the limitations of man's understanding.]

When something of these allegorical interpretations is expressed to anyone unfit to receive them—especially demonstrative interpretations because of their remoteness from common knowledge—both he who expresses it and he to whom it is expressed are led into unbelief. The reason for that [in the case of the latter] is that allegorical interpretation comprises two things, rejection of the apparent meaning and affirmation of the allegorical one; so that if the apparent meaning is rejected in the mind of someone who can only grasp apparent meanings, without the allegorical meaning being affirmed in his mind, the result is unbelief, if it [the text in question] concerns the principles of religion.

Allegorical interpretations, then, ought not to be expressed to the masses nor set down in rhetorical or dialectical books, i.e. books containing arguments of these two sorts, as was done by Abū Ḥāmid. They should [not] be expressed to this class; and with regard to an apparent text, when there is a [self-evident] doubt whether it is apparent to everyone and whether knowledge of its interpretation is impossible for them, they should be told that it is ambiguous and [its meaning] known by no one except God; and that the stop should be put here in the sentence of the Exalted, "And no one knows the interpretation thereof except God" [III, 7]. The same kind of answer should also be given to a question about abstruse matters, which there is no way for the masses to understand; just as the Exalted has answered in His saying, "And they will ask you about the Spirit. Say, 'The Spirit is by the command of my Lord; you have been given only a little knowledge'" [XVII, 85].

[Certain people have injured the masses particularly, by giving them allegorical interpretations which are false. These people are exactly analogous to bad medical advisers. The true doctor is related to bodily health in the same way as the Legislator to spiritual health, which the *Qur'ān* teaches us to pursue. The true allegory is "the deposit" mentioned in the *Qur'ān*.]

As for the man who expresses these allegories to unqualified persons, he is an unbeliever on account of his summoning people to unbelief. This is contrary to the summons of the Legislator, especially when they are false allegories concerning the principles of religion, as has happened in the case of a group of people of our time. For we have seen some of them thinking that they were being philosophic and that they perceived, with their remarkable wisdom, things which conflict with Scripture in every respect, i.e. [in passages] which do not admit of allegorical interpretation; and that it was obligatory to express these things to the masses. But by expressing those false beliefs to the masses they have been a cause of perdition to the masses and themselves, in this world and the next.

The relation between the aim of these people and the aim of the Legislator [can be illustrated by] a parable, of a man who goes to a skillful doctor. [This doctor's] aim is to preserve the health and cure the diseases of all the people, by prescribing for them rules which can be commonly accepted, about the necessity of using the things which will preserve their health and cure their diseases, and avoiding the opposite things. He is unable to make them all doctors, because a doctor is one who knows by demonstrative methods the things which preserve health and cure disease. Now this [man whom we have mentioned] goes out to the people and tells them, "These methods prescribed by this doctor for you are not right"; and he sets out to discredit them, so that they are rejected by the people. Or he says, "They have allegorical interpretations"; but the people neither understand these nor assent to them in practice. Well, do you think that people in this condition will do any of the things which are useful for preserving health and curing disease, or that this man who has persuaded them to reject what they formerly believed in will now be able to use those [things] with them, I mean for preserving health? No, he will be unable to use those [things] with them, nor will they use them, and so they will all perish.

This [is what will happen] if he expresses to them true allegories about those matters, because of their inability to understand them; let alone if he expresses to them false allegories, because this will lead them to think that there are no such things as health which ought to be preserved and disease which ought to be cured—let alone that there are things which preserve health and cure disease. It is the same when someone expresses allegories to the masses, and to those who are not qualified to understand them, in the sphere of Scripture; thus he makes it appear false and turns people away from it; and he who turns people away from Scripture is an unbeliever.

Indeed this comparison is certain, not poetic as one might suppose. It presents a true analogy, in that the relation of the doctor to the health of bodies is [the same as] the relation of the Legislator to the health of souls: i.e. the doctor is he who seeks to preserve the health of bodies when it exists and to restore it when it is lost, while the Legislator is he who desires this [end] for the health of souls. This health is what is called "fear of God." The precious Book has told us to seek it by acts conformable to the Law, in several verses. Thus the Exalted has said, "Fasting has been prescribed for you, as it was prescribed for those who were before you; perhaps you will fear God" [II, 183]. Again the Exalted has said, "Their flesh and their blood shall not touch God, but your fear shall touch him" [XXII, 37]; "Prayer prevents immorality and transgression" [XXIX, 45]; and other verses to the same effect contained in the precious Book. Through knowledge of Scripture and practice according to Scripture the Legislator aims solely at this health; and it is from this health that happiness in the future life follows, just as misery in the future life follows from its opposite.

From this it will be clear to you that true allegories ought not to be set down in popular books, let alone false ones. The true allegory is the deposit which man was charged to hold and which he held, and from which all beings shied away, i.e. that which is mentioned in the words of the Exalted, "We offered the deposit to the heavens, the earth and the mountains," [and so on to the end of] the verse [XXXIII, 72].

[It was due to the wrong use of allegorical interpretation by the Mu'tazilites and Ash'arites that hostile sects arose in Islam.]

It was due to allegorical interpretations—especially the false ones—and the supposition that such interpretations of Scripture ought to be expressed to everyone, that the sects of Islam arose, with the result that each one accused the others of unbelief or heresy. Thus the Mu'tazilites interpreted many verses and Traditions allegorically, and expressed their interpretations to the masses, and the Ash'arites did the same, although they used such interpretations less frequently. In consequence they threw people into hatred, mutual detestation and wars, tore the Scriptures to shreds, and completely divided people.

In addition to all this, in the methods which they followed to establish their interpretations they neither went along with the masses nor with the élite: not with the masses, because their methods were [more] obscure than the methods common to the majority, and not with the élite, because if these methods are inspected they are found deficient in the conditions [required] for demonstration, as will be understood after the slightest inspection by anyone acquainted with the conditions of demonstration. Further, many of the principles on which the Ash'arites based their knowledge are sophistical, for they deny many necessary truths such as the permanence of accidents, the action of things on other things, the existence of necessary causes for effects, of substantial forms, and of secondary causes.

And their theorists wronged the Muslims in this sense, that a sect of Ash'arites called an unbeliever anyone who did not attain knowledge of the existence of the Glorious Creator by the methods laid down by them in their books for attaining this knowledge. But in truth it is they who are the unbelievers and in error! From this point they proceeded to disagree, one group saying "The primary obligation is theoretical study," another group saying "It is belief"; i.e. [this happened] because they did not know which are the methods common to everyone, through whose doors the Law has summoned all people [to enter]; they supposed that there was only one method. Thus they mistook the aim of the Legislator, and were both themselves in error and led others into error.

[The proper methods for teaching the people are indicated in the *Qur'ān*, as the early Muslims knew. The popular portions of the Book are miraculous in providing for the needs of every class of mind. We intend to make a study of its teachings at the apparent level, and thus help to remedy the grievous harm done by ignorant partisans of philosophy and religion.]

It may be asked: "If these methods followed by the Ash'arites and other theorists are not the common methods by which the Legislator has aimed to teach the masses, and by which alone it is possible to teach them, then what are those [common] methods in this religion of ours?" We reply: They are exclusively the methods set down in the precious Book. For if the precious Book is inspected, there will be found in it the three methods that are available for all the people, [namely] the common methods for the instruction of the majority of the people and the special method. And if their merits are inspected, it becomes apparent that no better common methods for the instruction of the masses can be found than the methods mentioned in it.

Thus whoever tampers with them, by making an allegorical interpretation not apparent in itself, or [at least] not more apparent to everyone than they are (and that [greater apparency] is something nonexistent), is rejecting their wisdom and rejecting their intended effects in procuring human happiness. This is very apparent from [a comparison of] the condition of the first believers with the condition of those who came after them. For the first believers arrived at perfect virtue and fear of God only by using these sayings [of Scripture] without interpreting them allegorically; and anyone of them who did find out an allegorical interpretation did not think fit to express it [to others]. But when those who came after them used allegorical interpretation, their fear of God grew less, their dissensions increased, their love for one another was removed, and they became divided into sects.

So whoever wishes to remove this heresy from religion should direct his attention to the precious Book, and glean from it the indications present [in it] concerning everything in turn that it obliges us to believe, and exercise his judgment in looking at its apparent meaning as well as he is able, without interpreting any of it allegorically, except where the allegorical meaning is apparent in itself, i.e. commonly apparent to everyone. For if the sayings set down in Scripture for the instruction of the people are inspected, it seems that in mastering their meaning one arrives at a point, beyond which none but a man of the demonstrative class can extract from their apparent wording a meaning which is not apparent in them. This property is not found in any other sayings.

For those religious sayings in the precious Book which are expressed to everyone have three properties that indicate their miraculous character: (1) There exist none more completely persuasive and convincing to everyone than they. (2) Their meaning admits naturally of mastery, up to a point beyond which their allegorical interpretation (when they are of a kind to have such an interpretation) can only be found out by the demonstrative class. (3) They contain means of drawing the attention of the people of truth to the true allegorical meaning. This [character] is not found in the doctrines of the Ashʿarites nor in those of the Muʿtazilites, i.e. their interpretations do not admit of mastery nor contain [means of] drawing attention to the truth, nor are they true; and this is why heresies have multiplied.

It is our desire to devote our time to this object and achieve it effectively, and if God grants us a respite of life we shall work steadily towards it in so far as this is made possible for us; and it may be that that work will serve as a starting point for our successors. For our soul is in the utmost sorrow and pain by reason of the evil fancies and perverted beliefs which have infiltrated this religion, and particularly such [afflictions] as have happened to it at the hands of people who claim an affinity with philosophy. For injuries from a friend are more severe than injuries from an enemy. I refer to the fact that philosophy is the friend and milk-sister of religion; thus injuries from people related to philosophy are the severest injuries [to religion]—apart from the enmity, hatred and quarrels which such [injuries] stir up between the two, which are companions by nature and lovers by essence and instinct. It has also been injured by a host of ignorant friends who claim an affinity with it: these are the sects which exist within it. But God directs all men aright and helps everyone to love Him; He unites their hearts in the fear of Him, and removes from them hatred and loathing by His grace and His mercy!

Indeed God has already removed many of these ills, ignorant ideas and misleading practices, by means of this triumphant rule. By it He has opened a way to many benefits, especially to the class of persons who have trodden the path of study and sought to know the truth. This [He has done] by summoning the masses to a middle way of knowing God the Glorious, [a way] which is raised above the low level of the followers of authority but is below the turbulence of the theologians; and by drawing the attention of the élite to their obligation to make a thorough study of the principles of religion. God is the Giver of success and the Guide by His Goodness.

MOSES MAIMONIDES

Moses Maimonides, a contemporary of Ibn Rushd, was born as Moses ben Maimon to a Jewish family in Cordoba (also the birthplace of Seneca and Ibn Rushd) in 1135. Although Cordoba was part of the Muslim regime of the Almoravids, Jews were permitted to practice their faith openly, and Maimonides' early years were undisturbed on that account. He studied Jewish scripture and law, the sciences, and philosophy under the tutelage of his father. Before he was quite thirteen, however, the peace was shattered by the Almohads, who captured Cordoba from the Almoravids in 1148. Cordoban Jews were issued an ultimatum: convert to Islam or leave. Maimonides' family lived publicly as Muslims but privately as Jews for some eleven years before finally emigrating to Fez, Morocco, also under the Almohads, about 1159. When a rabbi with whom Maimonides had studied was executed there as a practicing Jew in 1165, the Maimons relocated to Palestine. But the region was economically depressed, and the family moved directly on to Egypt, where Jews were permitted freedom of worship. Even so, Jews who had converted to Islam and relapsed to Judaism could be put to death; Maimonides was accused but found innocent on the grounds that he had never really become a Muslim. To earn a living, he took up the practice of medicine; his reputation grew to the point that he became the physician of Saladin, the sultan who conquered Jerusalem and withstood Richard the Lion-Hearted in the Third Crusade. Maimonides also became a leader of the Jewish community, internationally known for his rabbinic learning, and eventually the head (*Nagid*) of all Egyptian Jews. He died in Cairo in 1204.

Maimonides wrote on legal, medical, logical, philosophical, and religious topics. His major works are the *Kitāb al-Sirāj* (Book of Illumination), a commentary on the Mishnah written in Arabic; the *Mishne Torah* (The Torah Reviewed), a magisterial codification of Jewish law written in Hebrew; and *Dalālat al-ḥā'irīn* (The Guide of the Perplexed), a work on philosophy and religious belief. Although *The Guide of the Perplexed* was conceived by a Jew for Jews on topics of Jewish interest, it was nonetheless written in Arabic—one indication of the dominance of the Muslim culture at the time.

The *Guide,* composed in Egypt during the years 1176 to 1191, was a response to particular personal need. A young man by the name of Joseph ben Judah had come a great distance to study with Maimonides. An excellent student, gifted in logic and mathematics, Joseph became perplexed in the course of his studies, apparently through contact with Muslim theologians. He was particularly unsettled by doubts about the interpretation of certain passages in scripture. Maimonides observed that someone who, like Joseph, is both a faithful Jew and a critical reasoner confronts a stark and painful alternative:

> [E]ither he follows his reason and rejects those expressions as he understands them: then he will think that he is rejecting the dogmas of our religion. Or else he continues to accept them in the way he has been taught and refuses to be guided by his reason. He thus brusquely turns his back on his own reason, and yet he cannot help feeling that his faith has been gravely impaired. He will continue to hold those fanciful beliefs although they inspire him with uneasiness and disgust, and be continuously sick at heart and utterly bewildered in his mind.[1]

To offer a solution to Joseph's dilemma, Maimonides wrote the *Guide.*

The title may suggest that this is an elementary work. It is not. Maimonides explicitly warns the reader not to expect a systematic exposition of scientific and metaphysical truths. Only outlines of these truths, he says, will appear in the *Guide.* "Even so, these outlines will not appear in our treatise in their proper order or set out continuously, but scattered and mixed with other subjects which we desire to expound. For I want the Truths to flash forth for a moment and then to disappear."[2] Deep truths can only be communicated in "vague similes and riddles"; hence "[t]he exposition of all these things is . . . clothed in words with several meanings, so that the vulgar can take them, according to their lights, in one sense, while the perfect and educated man will take them in quite a different sense."[3] Unsurprisingly, the work has been very variously interpreted.[4]

The following passages are from Book 2 of the *Guide*. Selections from the introductory propositions and the first chapter sketch Aristotelian demonstrations of the existence, incorporeality, and unity of God. The remaining chapters show Maimonides, like Ibn Rushd, grappling with the clash between the Aristotelian thesis that the world is eternal and the scriptural tenet that it was created—a precursor of certain issues in contemporary cosmology. Note in particular the clear division of labor between chapters 17 and 18, on the one hand, and chapters 19 and 22, on the other. The work of the former is to show merely that Aristotle did not demonstrate the world's eternity, while that of the latter is to establish the greater probability of the creation view. This latter task is complicated considerably by Maimonides' unwitting attribution to Aristotle of an emanation doctrine that Aristotle did not hold.[5]

The Guide of the Perplexed

God and the World's Creation

BOOK II

Propositions

xviii. Everything that emerges from potentiality to actuality must do so because of something else which is outside the thing itself. If the cause of its emergence were within the thing itself, and there were no restraining cause, that thing would at no time be potential, but always actual.

xix. Everything for whose existence there is a cause is, as far as its essence is concerned, of possible existence; for if its causes are present it will exist, but if they are not present, or nonexistent, or there has been a change in their relation to that thing by which they call it into existence, then the thing does not exist.

xx. If a thing is, as far as its essence is concerned, of necessary existence, then its existence can in no way and under no circumstances have a cause.[1]

From Moses Maimonides, *The Guide of the Perplexed*, edited by Julius Guttmann, translated by Chaim Rabin. Copyright © 1995 by Hackett Publishing Company, Inc. Reprinted by permission of Hackett Publishing Company, Inc. All rights reserved.

xxi. If a thing is composed of two items, and that composition is the indispensable cause of its existence as it is, then it is not of necessary existence in its essence, since its existence depends upon the existence of its two parts and upon their being put together.

xxii. Every body is necessarily composed of two items and necessarily substrate to accidents. The two items that constitute it are its matter and its form. The accidents to which it is substrate are quantity, shape, and position.[2]

xxiii. Everything that is potential and has in its essence an element of possibility may at some time not exist in actuality.

xxiv. Everything that is something potentially must needs be possessed of matter, because possibility always applies to matter.

Chapter I

The third philosophical argument in this connection is taken from the writings of Aristotle, though he propounded it in quite a different context. It runs as follows:

There is no doubt concerning the existence of some things, viz. those perceived by the senses. To these one of three cases must apply—there being no others possible: either nothing is subject to generation[3] and corruption, or everything is subject to them, or some things are permanent and others are transitory. The first alternative is obviously absurd, because we can constantly observe things coming into being and ceasing to be. The second alternative is also absurd, as will appear after some reflection: if everything were subject to generation and corruption, then every single thing would be liable to cease. As you know, however, in a species that which is possible must necessarily come to pass. It is therefore unavoidable that existing things should perish. If all are destroyed, it is absurd that anything should exist, since no one would remain in existence so as to bring other things into existence. It would therefore necessarily follow that nothing at all exists. However, we can observe that things exist, and we ourselves exist. From this consideration it results that if there exist, as we are aware, things that come into being and perish, then there must also exist some being that neither comes into being nor perishes. That unborn and imperishable being cannot be thought of as liable to perish. It must exist by necessity, not by possibility.[4]

It has also been said that its existence by necessity may refer either to itself or to its cause. If so, its existence or nonexistence may be possible as far as its essence is concerned, but necessary as far as its cause is concerned. Thus its cause would be the one that exists by necessity, as has been shown in the nineteenth proposition. It is thus proven that there must of necessity be some being that exists by necessity with regard to its own self. If this being did not exist, no being at all would exist, neither one subject to generation and corruption nor one not subject to them—if, as Aristotle says, there were such a thing as the latter, not subject to generation and corruption because it is caused by a cause which exists by necessity. This is a proof which admits of no doubt, no rejection, and no counterargument, except by those who have no idea of the technique of philosophical demonstration.

We add on our part that in the case of anything existing by necessity with regard to its own self it must necessarily be admitted that its existence has no cause, as has been said in the twentieth proposition. Nor can there be in it any plurality of notions in any respect, as has been said in the twenty-first proposition. It follows that it is neither a body nor a force in a body, cf. the twenty-second proposition. From this consideration it is proven that there is a being existing of necessity with regard to its own self, that it is the one whose existence has no cause, and which is not compound and therefore neither a body nor a force in a body. That is God—Whose Name is exalted. It is likewise easy to demonstrate that it is absurd to think that existence necessary with regard to their own selves can be found in two beings. In that case the generic quality of necessary existence would be a notion superadded to the essence of each one of the two, and neither of them would exist by necessity through its essence alone, but through that property, the generic quality of necessary existence, which is found both in that thing and in other things. It can be shown in a number of ways that duality is not possible in a thing that exists of necessity, neither through the existence of equals nor that of antagonists. The reason for all this is the absolute non-compositeness and absolute perfection which allows nothing of its own kind to exist apart from itself and the absence of cause from every point of view. Thus there is no possibility of a plurality (of things existing by necessity).[5]

A fourth argument, again philosophical. It is well known that we constantly witness things, which hitherto existed potentially, emerging into actual existence. Everything that passes from potentiality to actuality must have done so by virtue of a factor outside itself, as we have said in the eighteenth proposition. It is obvious that that factor was at first a potential cause for the emergence of that thing and then became an actual cause. The cause for its power remaining potential in the past may be sought either in some impediment within itself, or the fact that there was at first some connection missing between it and the thing it subsequently brought into actuality, and only when that connection became established it actually could cause the emergence of that thing. Each of these two cases necessarily requires a factor causing its emergence or removing the impediment. The same considerations apply concerning the second factor of emergence or the factor removing the impediment. But this chain cannot go on forever. We must necessarily arrive in the end at a factor of emergence which exists perpetually in one condition and in which nothing is potential. I mean that nothing in its essence must be potential, for if something in its essence existed only possibly it might cease to exist at times, as has been explained in the twenty-third proposition. It is absurd to think that such a thing could be material; it must be incorporeal, as has been shown in the twenty-fourth proposition. That incorporeal being which does not admit of any possibility, but is essentially existent, is God. It has been made clear above that He is not a body. He is therefore One, as has been shown in the sixteenth proposition.[6]

All these are methods of demonstrating the existence of One God who is neither a body nor a force in a body, without denying that the world is uncreated.

Here is another method to demonstrate the inadmissibility of belief in a bodily God and the necessity of belief in unity. If there were two Gods, there would necessarily be one property common to both, namely that property by which each of them would deserve the name God. There would also necessarily be one property in each by which they would be distinct from each other and be two. Either each of them may have a property not possessed by the other. Then each of them would be composed of two properties, so that neither would be a first cause and therefore exist by necessity with regard to his own self, but each of them would have causes, as has been shown in the nineteenth proposition. Or the differentiating property is found only in one of the two; then the one having the two properties would not exist by necessity with regard to his own self.

Another method of proving the unity of God. It has been definitely proved by demonstration that the whole universe of existing things is like one organism in which everything hangs together, and that the force of the sphere circulates within this lower matter and shapes it.[7] If this is accepted as true, it would be absurd to believe that one God is in charge of one part of this universe and the other in charge of another part, since these parts hang together. Therefore, if the universe were divided between them, they would either have to act at different times or would constantly act together, in such a way that no act would come about unless both participate in it.

The idea that the two Gods act at different times is absurd for a variety of reasons. Let us assume that during the time that the one acts it would be possible for the other to act. What is the cause then that the one acts and the other is inactive? If again we assume that during the time that one acts the other is restrained from acting, then there must be another cause which makes it possible for the one to act and impossible for the other—since time is not differentiated in any way and the field of action is one in which everything hangs together, as we have explained. Furthermore, both of them would be subject to time, since their activity is timebound. Also each of them would at the time of his activity emerge from potentiality to actuality; this would presuppose a factor causing their emergence into actuality. More than that, the essence of both of them would include the element of possibility.

The alternative, that both of them act constantly on everything that exists, so that neither acts without the other, is also absurd, as I shall show. Wherever we have an entity of such a kind that an action can only come about through all of its parts, it is not possible for one of its constituents to be considered an effective cause in itself, nor can any of them be a first cause of that action, but the first cause is the junction of the parts of that entity. It has been proved that a thing which exists by necessity cannot possibly have a cause. Furthermore, the junction of the parts of an entity is an event, and thus in need of a cause in its turn, namely the cause that brings about the junction. If the cause effecting the junction of that entity, through which alone any act can come about, is one, then there can be no doubt that it is God. If the cause effecting the junction of this entity is again compound, then the same principles must be applied to that second entity as to the first. We shall necessarily arrive in the end at a single cause for the existence of the one universe, whichever view we take and whether we assume it to have been created after nonexistence or consider its existence an eternal necessity. This argumentation has also shown that the fact that the whole universe is one points to the cause of its existence being one.[8]

Chapter XIII

The views of people with regard to the problem whether the world is without beginning or created—having regard only to the opinion of those who believe that a God exists—are of three kinds:

The first view, which is the one held by those who believe in the Law of Moses, is that the whole world—I mean everything that exists, apart from God Himself—was brought into existence by God after having been completely and absolutely devoid of existence. They hold that only God alone existed and nothing beside Him, neither angel nor sphere nor anything that is within the sphere. Then He brought into existence all existing things, as they are, by His will and volition, and not from anything. Time itself, according to them, is one of the things created, since time is consequent upon movement and movement is an accident of that which moves; the thing that moves, and upon the movement of which time is consequent, was created and came into being, not having existed before.

When we say that God *was* before the world was created, where the word "was" implies time; and likewise all the associations in our mind when we think of the infinite duration of His existence before the creation of the world—all this is assumed time or imagined time, not true time. There can be no doubt that time is an accident. In our system it is just one of the created accidents such as blackness and whiteness. It does not belong to the class of qualities, though, but is an inherent accident of movement, as will be clear to anyone who has understood what Aristotle said in explanation of the true nature of time.

We shall here discuss a subject which is not strictly part of the matter with which we are dealing, but has some bearing on it. The analysis of the concept of time has presented difficulties to most thinkers, so much so that they became bewildered as to whether it had any real existence or not, as happened to Galen and others. The reason for this is that it is an accident of an accident. Those accidents that have a primary existence in bodies, such as colors and tastes, can be understood without further ado, and their purport can easily be realized. Those accidents, however, that have accidents as their substrate, such as brilliancy in colors and curvedness and roundness in lines, are very hard to grasp. This is especially so when on top of this the substrate accident is not permanently in one state but changes from one state to another. Then the concept becomes even more difficult to grasp. With time the two things come together. It is an accident pursuant to motion, which itself is an accident of the thing that moves. Motion is not like blackness or whiteness which are permanent states, but it is the very nature and essence of motion that it does not persist in one state even for a single moment. This is one of the reasons why the nature of time is so difficult to investigate.

What I want to make clear is that time in our system is a created thing that has come into being like all other accidents as well as the substances which are the substrates of these accidents. Therefore the creation of the world by God cannot have taken place in a temporal beginning, as time itself was one of the things created. You must give very careful consideration to this matter, so as to be ready to deal with the objections which are impossible to avoid for anyone who is not aware of this point. If you admit the possibility of time having existed before the world, you will be led into accepting the belief that the world is uncreated, for time is an accident and must needs have a substrate. Thus something would of necessity have existed before this present world existed. That, however, is just the view from which we try to get away.[9]

This then, is the first view. It is, without any doubt, the one on which the Law of Moses is based. It comes in importance immediately after the dogma of the unity of God—make no mistake about that. It was our father Abraham himself who first proclaimed this view, having arrived at it by speculation. For this reason he would call upon *the name of the Lord the God of the World* (Genesis 21:33),[10] after he had put this view clearly into words by speaking of *the Maker*[11] *of heaven and earth* (Genesis 14:22).

The second view is the one held by all the philosophers of whom we have heard or which we have read. They say that it is absurd to believe that God should bring forth something from nothing. In their opinion it is also not possible for a thing to pass away into nothing. This means it is not possible for a thing possessing matter and form to come into being after this matter had been completely devoid of existence. To describe God as having the power to accomplish this is in their opinion the same as to describe him as having the power to unite two opposites at the same time, or to create His own equal or to become a body or to create a rectangle with the diagonal equal to its side, and similar impossibilities.[12]

We can deduce from their arguments that they mean: just as there is no lack of power imputed to God in the fact that God does not create impossibilities—because the impossible has a permanent character which is not produced by anyone and therefore cannot be changed—so there is no lack of power imputed to God if He is not thought to be able to bring forth something from nothing, since this belongs to the category of impossibilities. They therefore hold that there is some matter in existence, having no beginning just as God has no beginning, that God does not exist without it, nor it without God. They do not hold that its existence is of the same rank as the existence of God, but they think Him to be the cause of its existence. It would be to Him in the relation of, say, the clay to the potter or the iron to the ironworker. This is the matter from which He creates whatever He wills, forming it one time into heaven and earth and another time into something else. Those who follow this opinion believe that the heaven, too, has come into being and is liable to perish, but that it did not come into being from nothing and will not perish into nothing. As the individual living beings come into being and perish out of existing matter and into existing matter, so the heaven comes into being and perishes, and its coming into being and ceasing to be takes place in the same way as that of other existing things.

The people of this class are divided into various sects, the number and opinions of which it would be useless to mention in this treatise. The general and fundamental tenet of this sect, however, is as I have described it to you. It is also the belief of Plato. We find that Aristotle reports of him in the *Physics* (VIII.1, 251a17) that he, Plato, believed that the heaven had come into being and was liable to perish. You can find this opinion clearly expressed in the *Timaeus* (38bc). However,

Plato did not hold the same belief as we (Jews), as some people think who cannot analyze opinions and do not think precisely, and therefore imagine that our view is the same as his. This is not so. We believe that the heaven came into being, not out of another thing, but out of absolute nonexistence. He believes it to have been brought into existence and being out of another thing. This, then, is the second view.

The third view is that of Aristotle, of his followers and commentators. He says the same as the followers of the sect just mentioned, namely that a thing composed of matter can never be brought forth out of no matter. He goes beyond this, however, and says that the heaven does not fall under the laws of generation and corruption in any way. To put his view briefly, he claims that this universe as a whole, such as it is, never ceased and never will cease to be as it is. The one permanent thing which is not subject to generation and corruption, namely heaven, will always be so. Time and motion are eternal and continuous, having neither come into being nor being liable to cease. Things that come into being and perish, namely those beneath the lunar sphere, will not cease to be so. That means that primary matter essentially neither comes into being nor perishes, but the forms follow each other in it: it divests itself of one form and clothes itself in another. This whole order both in the higher and the lower regions cannot be upset or stopped, or any innovation made in it other than those implied in its own nature, nor does anything ever happen within it that is in any way contrary to the laws of nature. He also says—though not in so many words, but it can be deduced from his opinions—that he considers it impossible that God should in any way change His will or exercise any fresh volition. True, all this universe as it is was brought into being by God's will, but not made out of nonexistence. Just as it is impossible that God should cease to be or that His essence should change, so he thinks it impossible that He should change His will or exercise any new volition. The conclusion is thus forced upon us that this universe, just as it is now, has been so forever and will be so in the most distant future.

This is a brief but adequate presentation of the various views. They are the views of those who accept the existence of God in this world as proven. Others know nothing of the existence of God, but pretend that things come into being and perish by purely accidental aggregation and separation, and that there is no one to guide and arrange their existence. Such are, according to Alexander, Epicure and his school, among others. There is no point for us in expounding the views of those sects since the existence of God is definitely proven, and it is useless to discuss the views of people who base themselves on a proposition the opposite of which is evident. It is also useless for us to undertake an investigation into the truth of the views of the second school of thought, who believe heaven to be created but transitory, since they accept the idea of something uncreated. In our opinion there is no difference between one who holds that heaven must necessarily have originated out of something else, or will perish and pass into something else, and the belief of Aristotle that it neither came into being nor is liable to perish.[13] The aim of everyone who follows the Law of Moses and Abraham, or any similar outlook, is to believe that there is nothing whatsoever uncreated and co-existent with God, and that the production of existent things from non-existence on the part of God is not impossible, but—according to some thinkers—even necessary. Now that we have established the various views I shall proceed to explain and summarize the arguments of Aristotle for his view and the reasons that led him to it.

Chapter XIV

Aristotle maintains that motion neither comes into being nor ceases to be. He refers to motion in an absolute sense. He argues that even if we assume motion to have come into being we must admit that everything that comes into being is preceded by motion, namely its own emergence into reality and its coming into being after it had not been. Motion must thus have been preexistent, namely the motion by which this latter motion came into being. That former motion must necessarily be uncreated, or the sequence would be continued indefinitely.[14] Following from this thesis he further maintains that time neither came into being nor is liable to cease, because time is pursuant to motion and inherent in it. There is no motion except in time, and time cannot be conceived except through motion, as has been shown. This is one of the methods by which he establishes the eternity of the world.

Another proof of his is by maintaining that the prime matter which is common to the four elements cannot have come into being or be liable to perish. Were we to assume that prime matter came into being at some time, we should have to admit that there was some matter from which it originated, and also that the matter which thus originated possessed form, since this is what constitutes "coming into being." Our axiom, however, is that prime matter is matter not possessing form. It must thus necessarily be considered not to have come into being out of another thing and therefore to be eternal and imperishable. This again implies that the world is uncreated.[15]

These are the essential methods used by Aristotle to establish the eternity of the world by basing his argument on the structure of the world itself. There are, however, other methods, mentioned by those who came after him. They deduced these proofs from his philosophical system so as to establish the eternity of the world while accepting the existence of God.

One of these is as follows: Assuming that God brought the world into existence out of nonexistence, we would have to admit that God was before the creation of the world a Doer only potentially: after He had created it He became a Doer in actuality. Thus God would have emerged from potentiality into actuality, and there would be a factor of possibility within Him. He would then require some cause to cause Him to pass from potentiality into actuality. This is very difficult, and is an objection which demands from every intelligent person an effort of thought, so as to dispose of it and to demonstrate its hidden inconsistencies.

Another method starts from the fact that if an effective cause acts at one time and does not act at another, this is due to supervening causes restraining or furthering its action from without or within. Thus restraining factors would have obliged God to refrain from doing what He willed, and the conducive factors would have imposed upon Him to will what He did not will before. The Creator, may His name be glorified, is not affected by the appearance or cessation of factors that would make Him change His will, hinder Him, or restrain Him. There is thus no reason to think that He should have acted at one time and not acted at another time. His activity is perpetually actual, just as He perpetually exists in actuality.[16]

Chapter XVI

In this chapter I shall explain what my own view on this problem is, leaving for later the arguments for what I am trying to prove. I should like to add that I am not satisfied with the arguments that have been produced by those Mutakallimun [Muslim dialecticians] who claim to have proved that the world was created. I do not deceive myself by calling sophistic arguments proofs. If a man claims to have produced proof regarding some problem by means of sophistic arguments, this does not strengthen my faith in that thesis, but weakens it and provokes opposition to it, because when the inadequacy of the arguments becomes apparent, one's mind becomes unwilling to admit the truth of the statement for which these arguments are adduced. It would in such a case have been better had the matter for which no proof is available remained open, or had one of the two contradictory opinions concerning it been accepted by dint of tradition. I have expounded the methods the Mutakallimun employ to establish that the world is created, and have pointed out the weak spots in their arguments. Similarly I consider all the arguments of Aristotle and his school for the eternity of the world not as decisive proofs, but as assertions open to grave doubts, as you will learn later on.[17]

What I want to say is that there is no inherent improbability in the belief that the world was created, which belief I have shown to be the intent of our Law. All the philosophical arguments from which it appears that the matter is otherwise—as we have mentioned—can be shown to be invalid and without convincing force. Once this point is conceded to me, and thus the problem whether the world is created or not is completely open, I accept the traditional solution of it as it is given by prophecy. Prophecy provides an answer to problems which speculation is unable to solve. We shall later show that prophecy need not be rejected even according to the view of those who believe in an uncreated world.

When I have demonstrated the possibility of our proposed view, I shall proceed to show its superiority over other views by speculative argument, too—I mean the superiority of the view that the world is created over the view that it is eternal—and shall demonstrate that though we may not get rid of some discomfort in admitting that it is created, we experience much greater discomfort in admitting that it is eternal. I shall now proceed to develop the methods by which the arguments of all those who argue for the eternity of the world can be invalidated.

Chapter XVII

Whenever a created thing comes into being after it had not been—though its matter may have existed and only divested itself of one form and taken another—its nature after its creation, completion, and permanent establishment differs from its nature at the moment when it came into being and began to emerge from potentiality to actuality, and this again differs from its nature before it was set in motion to emerge into actuality.

For example, the nature of the female sperm, while it is still blood in the blood-vessels, differs from its nature at the moment of conception, when it meets with the male sperm and is set in motion. Again, its nature at that moment is different from that of the complete organism after birth. There is no justification whatsoever for arguing from the nature a thing possesses when it has come into being, is complete, and has become established in its most perfect state, about the nature the same thing had when it was moving towards coming into being. Neither can one argue from its circumstances at the moment of its being set in motion about its circumstances before it was set in motion. Whenever you err in this respect, and advance arguments derived from the nature of the actual thing about the nature of the same thing while in potentiality, grave doubts will arise in your mind, and things that necessarily exist will appear absurd to you, while absurd things will appear necessary. Taking our example, assume that a man of very perfect physical habitus had been born and his mother died after feeding him for a few months. Then the father charged himself with the entire upbringing of that babe on a desert island, so that it grew up and reached the age of discretion without ever having seen a woman or the female of any other species of animal. One day he would ask one of the men about him: "how do we exist and in what circumstances have we come into being." Then the man he asked would reply: "every one among us came into being in the abdomen of an individual of our own species and like to ourselves, but female, and of such-and-such appearance. Each one of us was small of body when in the abdomen, and would develop and be nourished and grow little by little, being alive, until he would reach a certain size. Then an outlet would be opened for him on the lower side of the body, through which he would pass outside. Then he continues growing until he becomes as you see us." That orphan youth can hardly help asking: "But when that individual among us was small in the womb, being alive, moving, and growing—did he then eat and drink and breathe through his mouth and nose, and relieve his bowels?" On receiving a negative reply to this he would no doubt rashly call his interlocutor a liar and prove that all these simple truths are impossible, deriving his arguments from observation of the perfect and established being. He would say: "If you stop anyone of us breathing for a short while, he will die and his movements will cease. How can one imagine that one of us can be inside a thick-walled vessel enclosed within a body for months, and still go on living and moving? If one of us swallowed a bird, that bird would die immediately it came into his stomach, how much more so in the lower abdomen? If anyone of us would not eat food and drink water through his mouth for a few days, he would certainly die. How then can an individual remain alive for months without eating and drinking? If you pierced the abdomen of one of us he would die after some days. How can one maintain that the navel of that embryo was open? How is it possible that he did not open his eyes or stretch out his arms or straighten his legs, although all his limbs were sound and not affected in any way, as you say?" Thus the whole pattern of life would prove to him that it was not possible for man to come into being in that manner.

Now, dear reader, consider this parable carefully and try to understand it. You will see that this is precisely our situation with regard to Aristotle. We, the followers of Moses and Abraham, believe that the world came into being in a certain fashion, and that certain things arose from certain others, and certain things were created after certain others. Aristotle contradicts us, deriving his arguments from the nature of the established, completed, actual universe. We are assuring him that its state after its establishment and completion does not in the least resemble its state when it came into being, and that it was brought into existence after absolute nonexistence. What arguments then need we bring against anything he says? Such arguments are necessary for those who claim that the nature of this universe, as established, points to it having been created. I have told you clearly enough that I make no such claims.[18]

I shall now mention Aristotle's essential arguments and show you that they do not affect our position at all, since we maintain that the entire world was created by God out of nonexistence, and that He brought it into being in such a way that it emerged as perfect as you see it now.

Aristotle says that primary matter is eternal. He proceeds to bring arguments for this from things that come into being and perish, and to demonstrate that the primary matter cannot have come into being. This is perfectly correct. We, too, do not claim that primary matter came into being as man comes into being from sperm or perishes as man perishes by turning into dust. We claim that God brought it into existence from nothing in exactly the state in which it is now, namely that everything comes into being out of primary matter and that everything that came out of it perishes and turns back into it, and that it is never found devoid of form, that it is the ultimate background of generation and corruption and does not come into being as the things that come from it, or perish as the things that turn back into it. We say it is created *ex nihilo* and that if He who made it out of nothing wishes so, He can again make it vanish completely and absolutely.

We say the same about motion. He argues from the nature of motion that it can neither have come into being nor cease. This is correct. We assert that once motion had come into existence possessing the nature with which it is now established, it is unimaginable that it should as a whole come into being or cease totally, in the same way as individual movements come into being or cease. In an analogous manner we must treat all that is connected with the nature of motion.

The same applies to his statement concerning circular motion having no beginning (*Physics* VIII.9). This is correct once the spherical body performing a circular motion has come into existence: no beginning of this motion can be imagined.

You are well advised to get a firm hold of this argument. It is a high wall I have built round the Law, a wall that surrounds it on all sides and keeps away from it stones, whoever it may be that throws them. Should Aristotle, or rather those who adopt his views, attempt to argue with us, and say: "If the existing universe gives us no clue, how do you know that it has come into being and that there was another nature which brought it into being?"—then we shall reply: "This proof is not incumbent on us for our purposes. Our purpose at the moment is not to establish that the world is created, but to prove that it might be created, and that our assertion cannot be proved false by arguments drawn from the nature of the existing universe. About the latter we do not dispute." Now that the possibility of our assertion is established, as we have shown, we shall return to demonstrate the greater probability of the view that the world is created.

At this stage our opponents have only one thing left, and that is to find some arguments proving it impossible that the world was created, not taken from the nature of the universe but from what our reason tells us about God. Such are indeed the three arguments I have mentioned before, in which they argue the eternity of the world by starting from God. I shall show you in the next chapter how the weakness of these arguments can be demonstrated, so much so that they lose any value as arguments.

Chapter XVIII

The first argument they mention and with which we have to deal is their assertion that we are forced to admit God would have passed from potentiality to actuality, since He would have acted at one time and not acted at another. It is very easy to see how this objection can be refuted. This qualification only applies to something composed of matter, admitting of possibility, and form. There is no doubt that such a body, when it acts in its form after having been inactive, proves to have contained something potential which passed into actuality, and we must seek the factor which caused it to do so. This principle has been proved only with regard to material bodies. Anything that is not a body and contains no matter has no element of possibility inherent in its essence in any way. All its properties are perpetually actual, and our qualification does not apply to it. It is not precluded from acting at one time and not acting at another; this cannot be considered in the case of the incorporeal as change or as transition from potentiality to actuality.

As an instructive instance of this we may adduce the Active Intelligence, as described by Aristotle and his school. It is incorporeal and may be active at one time and inactive at another, as has been proved by Alfarabi in his treatise *De intellectu et intellectis.* He has there a passage which I shall quote here: "it is obvious that the Active Intelligence is not always active, but is active at one time and inactive at another." What he says is evidently true. While this is the case, no one would say that the Active Intelligence changes, nor that it was potentially active and has become actual when it acts at any given moment in a manner in which it has not acted before. The reason is that there is no relation or any similarity whatsoever between the corporeal and the incorporeal either at the time of activity or at the time of refraining from activity. The word "action" is used of the material forms and of the incorporeal only by way of homonymy. Therefore, when the incorporeal does not at any given time act in the same way as it acts afterwards, there is no need to assume that it has passed from potentiality to actuality, as we find it to be the case with things consisting of forms combined with matter.

According to the second argument, the world must be considered as uncreated because no encouraging, supervening, or restraining factors can be admitted in the case of God. This objection is difficult to dispose of, and the answer is of a subtle nature. Follow therefore attentively. It must be fully realized that every agent gifted with will carries out his actions by reason of something. If he acts at one time and does not act at another, this must necessarily be by reason of restraining or supervening factors. For example, a man wants to have a house, but does not build it because of some restraining factors. Thus the materials may not be available, or they may be available but cannot be given the proper shape because of lack of tools. Sometimes both materials and tools may be available, and still he does not build because he does not want to do so, being able to manage without shelter. When, however, further factors supervene, such as heat or cold which force him to seek shelter, then he will want to build. It is thus clear that supervening factors may change the will and restraining factors may counter the will, with the result that he does not act according to it. All this is true where actions take place by reason of something outside the will itself. When, on the other hand, action has no other purpose in any way but to conform with an act of will, such will does not require any motives. Although there may be nothing to stop the person whose will it is, yet it is not necessary for that person to act perpetually, there being no external purpose by reason of which he should act, so that it should be necessary to act whenever there are no obstacles in the way of achieving that purpose. In our case action is dependent on nothing but will.

It might be objected: all this is true, but is not the fact that He wills at one time and does not will at another to be taken as a change? To this we can reply in the negative. The nature and essence of will is in the fact that one is free to will or not to will. If this will is exercised by a material being, which implies that that being seeks with it an exterior purpose, then the will is changed in accordance with restraining and supervening causes. The will of the incorporeal, however, which is in no way influenced by anything other than itself, does not change. The fact that He wills something now and something else tomorrow does not constitute a change in His essence and hence does not require an outside cause, just as the fact that He acts or does not act does not constitute a change, as we have just proved. It will be proved later on that our will and the will of the incorporeal are both called by that name only by way of homonymy, and there is no similarity between the two kinds of will. Thus this objection, too, has been disposed of. It is demonstrated that this argument does not prove us necessarily wrong, which is what we have set out to show.[19]

Aristotle also mentions certain things on which all nations in ancient times agreed, such as the idea that the angels are in heaven or that God is in heaven. Similar ideas are also expressed in biblical passages, if we take these in their literal meaning. These are not arguments for the eternity of heaven, as he wants them to be. These things have been said to draw our attention to the fact that the existence of heaven indicates to us the existence of incorporeal intelligences, namely spiritual beings and angels, and they again indicate to us the existence of God, who moves and controls them, as we shall show later on. We also shall demonstrate that there is no argument that indicates, according to our system, the existence of the Maker as clearly as that provided by the heavens. These indicate also according to the view of the philosophers—as we have said before—the existence of Him who moves them as well as the fact that He is not a body nor a force in a body.

Having demonstrated to you that our assertion is at least possible and not an impossibility, as say those who proclaim that the world is uncreated, I shall retrace my steps and prove in the next chapters that our view is the more acceptable on speculative grounds, as well as showing up the inherent absurdity of Aristotle's view.

Chapter XIX

Enough of the views of Aristotle and all those who hold that the world is uncreated, will be clear to you by now to enable you to realize that he considers that this universe proceeds from the Creator by way of necessity and that God is a cause and the universe something caused: their relation is thus automatic.[20] As it cannot be said of God why or how He exists just so, I mean in Unity and incorporeality, so one cannot say of the world as a whole why and how it exists just so. All this inevitably exists as it is: the cause and the thing caused by it. There is no possibility of their not both existing or being any different from what they are. According to this view, therefore, it necessarily follows that everything should always have the same nature and no thing should ever change its nature in any way whatsoever. According to this view any change in the nature of any existing thing is an impossibility. All these things, therefore, cannot be due to the design of one who chose and willed that they be thus. Had they been due to the intention of anyone they would not have existed thus before the act of intention had taken place.

According to our view, on the other hand, it is obvious that they are there by intention, not by necessity. It is possible that He who intended can change them and have another intention, though not just any intention, because there is a permanent category of the impossible which cannot be set aside, as we shall show. My purpose in this chapter is to demonstrate to you with arguments almost amounting to proof that this universe of ours indicates to us that it is necessarily due to intention.

Chapter XXII

There is a theorem on which Aristotle and everyone who calls himself a philosopher are agreed, that from a simple thing only one simple thing can result by necessity. If a thing is compound, then things will result from it in the same number as the simple elements from which it is composed. For example, in fire there is a compound of two qualities, heat and dryness; the result is that it heats through its heat and dries through its dryness. Similarly, when a thing is composed of matter and form, certain things result from it owing to its matter and certain other things owing to its form—assuming the thing to be of multiple composition. In accordance with this theorem Aristotle says that only one single simple intelligence derives directly from God, and nothing else.[21]

A second theorem is that not any chance thing can result from any other chance thing, but there must always be some relationship between the cause and its effect. Even in the case of accidents not just any accident can derive from any other chance accident, such as a quantity from a quality or vice versa. Similarly no form can result from matter, nor any matter from form.

A third theorem is that whenever a doer acts by intention and will, not by natural force, many different actions may emanate from him.

A fourth theorem states that if a whole is composed of different substances juxtaposed, it deserves the name of compound more truly than a whole composed of different substances in mixture. For example a bone or muscle or vein or nerve is simpler than the whole of the hand or foot, which are composed of nerves, muscles, veins, and bones. This is too obvious to waste any more words on it.

After these prefatory remarks I shall deal with Aristotle's assertion that the first intelligence is the cause of the second, and this the cause of the third. In this way, even if their number came to thousands, the last intelligence would still, without any doubt, be simple. Whence, then, does the composite character originate which is, on Aristotle's own assertion, found necessarily in the things existing around us? Let us concede to Aristotle his whole theory that the further the intelligences are removed from the first, the more compound their functions become, because of the greater number of intelligibles apprehended by them. Even if we concede to him this wild guess, we must still ask how the intelligences came to be a cause from which the spheres resulted, and what relationship is there between matter and the incorporeal which contains no matter whatsoever. But suppose even that we concede to him that each sphere has as its cause an intelligence in the manner described, that intelligence may be described as compound since it apprehends both itself and other things. Thus it is, so to say, composed of two things.

From one of these two the next intelligence below it results, from the other the sphere. One must then ask: if the sphere is supposed to have resulted from that one simple idea, how can a sphere have resulted from it, since a sphere is composed of two kinds of matter and two kinds of form, viz. the matter and form of the sphere itself and the matter and form of the star fixed to it? If everything existed by mechanical necessity, we would definitely require for this compound a compound cause, from one part of which the body of the sphere and from the other part of which the body of the star would result. This would be true if the matter of all stars were one and the same. It is, however, likely that the substance of the bright stars differs from that of the non-luminous stars: as is well known, each body is composed of matter and form peculiar to itself.

It must be clear to you by now that these things cannot possibly be consistently viewed as having arisen from mechanical necessity, as he says. It is similar with the differences in the movements of the spheres: it does not correspond to the manner in which these are arranged underneath each other to such an extent as to justify the claim that there is any mechanical necessity in it. We have spoken about this before.[22]

There is, however, another point which upsets all that is established as natural law when applied to the condition of the spheres. Since the matter of all spheres is one and the same, why is the result not that the form of one sphere is transferred to the matter of another sphere, as happens beneath the lunar sphere as a consequence of the adaptability of matter? Why does this particular form remain permanently in that particular matter, when the same matter is common to all? My God, the next thing is that someone will make out a case that the matter of each sphere is different from that of the next. In that case the form of the motion would not be any indication of the matter (of which the moving body is composed).[23] This is contrary to all principles.

Furthermore, since the matter of all stars is one and the same, by what are they individually distinguished? Is it by their forms or by accidents? In either case it would be necessary for those forms or accidents to be transferable and to apply to each of them in turn, lest the adaptability of matter cease to operate. It thus becomes clear to you that when we speak of the matter of the spheres or of the stars, this does not imply the same meaning as the matter around us. It is mere homonymy. Every one of the heavenly bodies that exist has an existence of a distinctive kind which it does not share with anything else. If so, how comes it that there is some analogy, in so far as all spheres turn and all stars are permanent?

If, on the other hand, we believe all this to be due to the design of someone who made it and imparted to it its distinctive character as directed by His wisdom that passes comprehension, none of these problems affect us. They only affect those who claim that all this exists by virtue of mechanical necessity, not by a personal will. That latter view does not conform with the order of the universe, and no convincing reason or proof has ever been advanced for it. Withal some very weighty contradictions attach to it. One is that God, whom every sensible person acknowledges to be perfect from every possible point of view, is thought of as merely existing by the side of all existing things without any initiative. If He wanted to do so much as to lengthen the wing of a fly or shorten the leg of a caterpillar, He could not do it. Still, Aristotle would say that God does not want such things, and that it is absurd for Him to want things different from what they are. This does not exactly mean emphasizing the perfection of God; rather it implies that He has some shortcomings.[24]

I know that many zealous partisans will accuse me on account of these statements either of having imperfectly understood what they say or of intentional distortion. Nonetheless I shall not for this reason refrain from stating briefly what I have grasped and understood, however insufficient it be. In brief, therefore, I admit that all Aristotle says concerning the universe between the sphere of the moon and the center of the earth is undoubtedly true. Only those will differ from him there who either have not understood him, or who want to defend their prejudices, or have been misguided by them into denying observable facts. On the other hand all Aristotle's description of the part of the universe situated beyond the sphere of the moon is in the nature of guess and conjecture, with few exceptions, leave alone what he has to say on the order of the intelligences and some of the metaphysical theories he holds, which contain the greatest improbabilities and most obvious contradictions, evident to people of all faiths, as well as spreading wicked falsehoods for which he gives no proof.

Do not criticize me for having set out the doubts attaching to Aristotle's view. You may ask whether we have any right to reject a view and maintain the opposite because of mere doubts. The case is not like that at all. We are only treating this philosopher as his followers told us to treat him. Alexander makes it clear that in all cases where conclusive proof is not possible, the two extreme and incompatible solutions must be applied and after investigating what doubts attach to each of the two opposites, the solution must be adopted which carries less doubt with it. This is the method which Alexander says he employs with regard to all those views enunciated by Aristotle about metaphysical matters which are not proven. Indeed, all those who lived after Aristotle are constantly saying that Aristotle's views on this subject raise less doubts than any other possible views. This is what we did. Once we became convinced that this problem—whether the heavens have come into being or are eternal—allows of no proof for either of the contradictory solutions, and have set out the doubts attaching to both views, we have shown you that the assumption of eternity raises more doubts and is less compatible with the beliefs that ought to be held with regard to God. Quite apart from this, the view that the world was created is the one held by our father Abraham and our prophet Moses, peace be upon them.

Chapter XXV

It should be clearly understood that our reason for rejecting the eternity of the world is not to be sought in any text of the Torah which says that the world is created. The passages which indicate that the world is created are no more numerous than those that indicate that God is a body. The method of allegorical interpretation is no less possible or permissible in the matter of the world being created than in any other. We would have been able to explain it allegorically just as we did when we denied corporeality.[25] Perhaps it would have been even much easier. We would in any case not have lacked the capacity to explain those texts allegorically and establish the eternity of the world just as we explained those other texts allegorically and denied that God was a body. If we have not done this and do not believe in it, this is for two reasons: one is that it is conclusively proved that God is not a body. We must of necessity explain allegorically all those passages the literal sense of which is contradicted by evidential proof, so that we are conscious that they must be allegorically interpreted. The eternity of the world is not conclusively proved. It is therefore wrong to reject the texts and interpret them allegorically because of preference for a view the opposite of which might be shown to be preferable for a variety of reasons. This is one reason; the other is that our belief that God is not a body does not destroy in our eyes any of the ordinances of our Law or belie the statements of any prophet. There is nothing contrary to Scripture in it, except that the ignorant think it is. As we have explained, there is no contradiction, but this is the real intention of the text. If, on the other hand, we believed in the eternity of the world according to the principles laid down by Aristotle—that the world exists by necessity, that the nature of no thing ever changes and that nothing ever deviates from its customary behavior—this would destroy the Law from its very foundation and belie automatically every miracle, and make void all hopes and fears the Law seeks to inspire, unless, of course, one chooses to interpret the miracles as well allegorically, as did the *Batiniyya* sect among the Moslems. In this way we would end up in some kind of idle prattling.

RAMÓN LLULL

Ramón Llull was born in 1232 or 1233 on the Balearic island of Majorca, which had been recovered from the Muslims some three years earlier by Jaime (James) I of Aragon. Llull grew up at the royal court of Majorca, where he absorbed the traditions of knighthood, became something of a troubadour, and even wrote a manual of chivalry. Around the age of thirty he was well-to-do, married, the father of two children, and admittedly "licentious" and "worldly."[1] One night, while intent on composing a song "to a lady whom he loved with a foolish love," he saw a vision of Christ on the cross.[2] Each time he tried to complete the song, the vision returned. What did it mean? After much vacillation, Llull decided that it meant he should devote his life to sharing his faith. Realizing, however, that his meager education afforded few resources for colloquy with cultivated Muslims and Jews, he devoted the next decade to the mastery of Arabic and Latin and the acquisition of medical, astronomical, philosophical, and theological learning. In 1274, on Majorca's Mount Randa, he experienced a vision that provided the kernel of his grand project, the *Ars magna* ("Great Art"), referred to in this introduction as "the Art."[3] The vision touched off the hyperactivity that marked the rest of his life. Crisscrossing the Mediterranean, expounding the Art wherever he went, he was in northern Africa on three occasions; Paris three (perhaps four) times; Rome, Genoa, Montpellier, Barcelona, and Majorca repeatedly; Cyprus, Armenia Minor, Vienna, Naples, Pisa,

Messina, Lyon, Marseille, and possibly Jerusalem at least once. He produced at least 265 works ranging over medical, astronomical, philosophical, theological, and fictional themes in Latin, Arabic, and Catalan. Llull was the first scholar to write on philosophical and theological topics in a Romance language. He appears to have died as a member of the Third Order of St. Francis in 1316.[4]

As an Augustinian Neoplatonist, Llull identified the Neoplatonic One with the Christian God and conceived individual things to be exemplars of their divine source. This exemplarist thinking is captured visually in the First and Second Figures from Part 2 of the work entitled *Ars brevis* (Brief Art), whose prologue and first six parts are excerpted below. The First Figure represents God as Alpha, the source of the Llullian dignities (the principal facets of the divine nature that extend their influence through all of nature, like Platonic Forms). The Second Figure expresses the exemplarist intuition in relational form; the central "T" is the Trinity, the origin of the triangles BCD, EFG, and HIK. Each triangle stands for a triple of rudimentary relations instantiated in the world: difference, concordance, and contrariety; beginning, middle, and end; majority, equality, and minority.

The key to the following selection from the *Ars brevis* is the "Alphabet" in Part 1. It contains six columns, the first two of which are based on the First and Second Figures. The third column lists the basic kinds of questions recognized by Llull; the fourth, the fundamental ontological categories; the fifth and sixth, the primary virtues and vices. The letters "BCDEFGHIK" at the extreme left of the Alphabet are variables in a limited sense, for each can take one of the six terms to its right as a value. To understand why the variables' values are so limited is to understand much about the Art. Llull believed that the columns of the Alphabet were like girders of the globe, describing the world's basic structure, and that Muslims, Jews, and Christians would all see them as such. The Alphabet, therefore, could serve as an ecumenical starting point for discussion.

Llull claimed that this initial agreement could resolve disagreements among Muslims, Christians, and Jews. How? Just as letters in an alphabet combine to form words, the words in Llull's conceptual alphabet can be combined to form sentences. If all such combinations could be found, Llull believed one could then winnow the true sentences from the false.

The result, the wheat, would contain the most general truths about the world—the definitive philosophy.

Llull showed considerable ingenuity in carrying out the combinatorial part of his project. The Fourth Figure from the *Ars brevis,* for instance, is a mechanical device for finding ternary combinations of the Alphabet's variables. In early versions of the manuscript, the two inner circles were cut out and joined to the center of the outer circle by a thread knotted at both ends, making it possible for the inner circles to be turned.[5]

Llull's work retains philosophical interest as an early statement of conceptual atomism, the theory that the majority of concepts are compounds formed from a small number of conceptual atoms. Conceptual atomism can be developed in two directions. Llull worked synthetically, combining conceptual atoms into molecules, and Leibniz followed suit: "a kind of alphabet of human thoughts can be worked out and . . . *everything can be discovered and judged by a comparison of the letters of the alphabet and an analysis of the words made from them.*"[6] By contrast, early analytic philosophy (Frege's analysis of number, Russell's theory of definite descriptions, Wittgenstein's simple and complex signs, the positivist reduction program) all evolved as attempts to decompose conceptual molecules into their constituent atoms.

Ars brevis

A Philosophical Calculator

Prologue

We have written this *Ars brevis* so that the *Ars magna* may be more easily understood. For once the former is understood, the latter, along with the other Arts, can be easily understood and learned.

The subject of this Art is the answering of all questions, assuming that one can identify them by name.[1]

This book is divided into thirteen parts, just like the *Ars magna*.[2]

The first part concerns the Alphabet. The second, the Figures. The third, the Definitions. The fourth, the Rules. The fifth, the Table. The sixth, the Evacuation of the Third Figure. The seventh, the Multiplication of the Fourth Figure. The eighth, the Mixture of Principles and Rules. The ninth, the Nine Subjects. The tenth, Application. The eleventh, Questions. The twelfth, Habituation. The thirteenth, the way the Art should be taught.

And now we will begin by discussing the first part.

Part I, Which Treats of the Alphabet of this Art

We have employed an alphabet in this Art so that it can be used to make figures, as well as to mix principles and rules for the purpose of investigating the truth. For, as a result of any one letter having many meanings, the intellect becomes more general in its reception of the things signified, as well as in acquiring knowledge. And this alphabet must be learned by heart, for otherwise the artist will not be able to make proper use of this Art.

The Alphabet

B   signifies goodness, difference, whether?, God, justice, and avarice.
C   signifies greatness, concordance, what?, angel, prudence, and gluttony.
D   signifies eternity or duration,[3] contrariety, of what?, heaven, fortitude, and lust.
E   signifies power, beginning, why?, man, temperance, and pride.
F   signifies wisdom, middle, how much?, imaginative, faith, and accidie.
G   signifies will, end, of what kind?, sensitive, hope, and envy.
H   signifies virtue, majority, when?, vegetative, charity, and ire.
I   signifies truth, equality, where?, elementative, patience, and lying.
K   signifies glory, minority, how and with what?, instrumentative, pity, and inconstancy.

The Alphabet of the *Ars Brevis*

	Fig. A	*Fig. T*	*Questions and Rules*[4]	*Subjects*	*Virtues*	*Vices*
B	goodness	difference	whether?	God	justice	avarice
C	greatness	concordance	what?	angel	prudence	gluttony
D	eternity*	contrariety	of what?	heaven	fortitude	lust
E	power	beginning	why?	man	temperance	pride
F	wisdom	middle	how much?	imaginative	faith	accidie
G	will	end	of what kind?	sensitive	hope	envy
H	virtue	majority	when?	vegetative	charity	ire
I	truth	equality	where?	elementative	patience	lying
K	glory	minority	how? and with what?	instrumentative	pity	inconstancy

* or duration

Part II, Which Treats of the Four Figures

1. The First Figure, Denoted by A

This Part is divided into four sections, one for each of the four figures. The First Figure is that of A, and it contains nine principles, to wit, goodness, greatness, etc., and nine letters, to wit, B, C, D, E, etc. This figure is circular to show that any subject can become a predicate and vice versa, as when one says, "goodness is great," "greatness is good," and so on. In this figure, moreover, the artist seeks the natural conjunction between subject and predicate,[5] as well as their relative disposition and proportion, so that he can find the middle term and thus reach a conclusion.

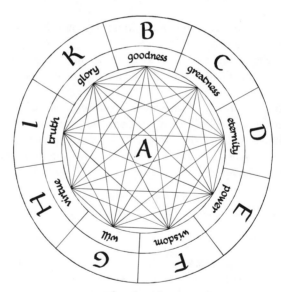

The First Figure

Each principle, taken by itself, is completely general, as when one says "goodness" or "greatness." However, as soon as one principle is applied to[6] another, then it is subordinate, as when we say "great goodness." And when some principle is applied to a singular thing, then it is completely particular, as when we say "Peter's goodness is great." And thus the intellect has a ladder for ascending and descending; as, for instance, descending from a completely general principle to one neither

completely general nor completely particular, and from a principle neither completely general nor completely particular to one that is completely particular. And in a similar fashion one can discuss the ascent of
this ladder.

Everything that exists is implicit in the principles of this figure, for
everything is either good or great, etc., as God and angels, which are
good, great, etc. Therefore, whatever exists is reducible to the above-
mentioned principles.

2. The Second Figure, Denoted by T

The Second Figure goes under the name of T, and it contains three triangles, each of which is general and all-embracing.

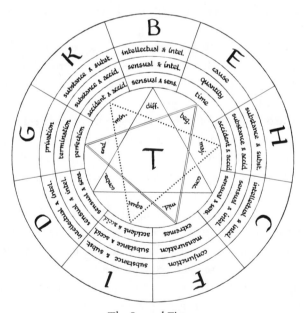

The Second Figure

1. The first triangle consists of difference, concordance and contrariety, and it comprises everything which exists, according to its category.
For everything which exists is either in difference, concordance or contrariety, and outside of these principles nothing can be found.

One must know, moreover, that each angle of this triangle has three species. For there is a difference between sensual and sensual, as for instance between a stone and a tree. There is also a difference between the sensual and the intellectual, as for instance between body and soul. And there is furthermore a difference between intellectual and intellectual, as between soul and God, between the soul and an angel, between one angel and another, or between God and an angel. And the same can be said for concordance and contrariety, each in its own way. And this difference existing in each angle of this triangle is the ladder by which the intellect ascends and descends, so that it can find the natural middle term between subject and predicate, with which middle term it can reach a conclusion. And the same is true for the ladder of concordance and contrariety, each in its own way.

2. The second triangle consists of beginning, middle, and end, and it comprises everything that exists. For everything that exists is either in beginning, middle, or end, and outside of these principles nothing can be found.

The word "cause" written in the angle of "beginning" stands for the efficient, material, formal, and final cause. The words "quantity" and "time" refer to the other predicaments, and to those things that can be reduced to them.[7]

The angle of "middle" contains three species of middle. First there is the conjunctive middle, which exists between subject and predicate, as when we say, "man is an animal." For between man and animal there are middle terms, such as their life and body, without which man would not be an animal. Then there is the middle of mensuration, which refers to the act existing between the doer and the doable, like loving between the lover and the lovable. And then there is the middle between extremes, like a line between two points. And this angle of "middle" acts as a general ladder with respect to the intellect.

The angle of "end" also contains three species. The first is the end of privation, which refers to a privative state and to those things that are in the past. The second species is the end of termination, which refers to the extremities, like the two points that terminate a line, or like the lover and beloved in relation to loving. The third species is the end of perfection, which refers to ultimate purpose, like man, who exists to multiply his species, and to understand, love, and remember God, and so forth. This angle also acts as a general ladder with respect to the intellect.

3. The third triangle is made up of majority, equality, and minority, and it is general and all-embracing in its way. For whatever exists is either in majority, equality, or minority. Majority has three species. The first is when there exists majority between substance and substance, as, for instance, the substance of heaven, which is greater than the substance of fire. The second species is when there exists majority between substance and accident, like a substance that is greater than its quantity; for substance exists of itself, which is something no accident does. The third species is when there exists majority between accident and accident, like understanding, which is greater than seeing, and seeing than running. And what we have said about majority applies equally to minority, since they are correlative to one another.

The angle of equality has three species. The first is when things are substantially equal, like Peter and Martin, who are equal in substance. The second species is when substance and accident are regarded as equal to one another, such as substance and its quantity. The third species is when there is equality between accident and accident, like understanding and loving, which are equal in their object. And this angle is a ladder by which the intellect can ascend and descend, as was said of the other triangles. And when the intellect ascends to general objects, then it itself becomes general; and when it descends to particulars, then it itself becomes particular.

The Figure T serves the First Figure, for through difference one can distinguish between goodness and goodness, between goodness and greatness, etc. And by joining this figure to the first, the intellect acquires knowledge. And because this figure is general, therefore the intellect becomes general.

3. The Third Figure

The Third Figure is a composite of the first and second; for the letter B that appears in it stands for the B that is in both the first and second figures; and similarly for the other letters.

This one consists of 36 compartments,[8] as can be seen in the illustration. Each compartment has many different meanings as a result of the two letters it contains. Thus the compartment of B C has many different meanings as a result of B C, and similarly the compartment of B D has many different meanings as a result of B D, and so on.[9] And this should be clear from the alphabet we gave above.

BC	CD	DE	EF	FG	GH	HI	IK
BD	CE	DF	EG	FH	GI	HK	
BE	CF	DG	EH	FI	GK		
BF	CG	DH	EI	FK			
BG	CH	DI	EK				
BH	CI	DK					
BI	CK						
BK							

The Third Figure

Each compartment contains two letters, and these represent subject and predicate, between which the artist seeks the middle term that will join them, like goodness and greatness that are joined through concordance, and similarly for other terms. With this middle term the artist tries to reach a conclusion and state a proposition.

This figure is meant to show that any principle can be attributed to any of the others: thus to B we can attribute C, D, etc., and to C we can attribute B, D, etc., as can be seen from the illustration. This is so that the intellect may know each principle in terms of all the others, and be enabled to deduce many arguments from a single proposition.

To give an example with "goodness," we make it into a subject and use the other principles as predicates, giving:

goodness is different

goodness is great   goodness is concordant

goodness is enduring   goodness is contrary

goodness is powerful   goodness is beginning

goodness is knowable   goodness is mediating

goodness is lovable   goodness is ending

goodness is virtuous   goodness is magnifying

goodness is true   goodness is equalizing

goodness is glorious   goodness is lessening

What we have said of goodness can be applied equally well to the other principles, each in its own way.

This figure is very general, and by using it the intellect is made very general in acquiring knowledge.

It is a condition of this figure that one compartment not be contrary to another, but that they be concordant in their conclusion. Thus the compartment of B C should not be contrary to that of B D, and so on for the others. With such a condition, the intellect is conditioned to the acquisition of knowledge.

4. The Fourth Figure

The Fourth Figure has three circles, the outermost of which is fixed and the two inside ones of which are mobile, as appears in the illustration. The middle circle revolves on top of the outer fixed circle, so that, for instance, C can be put opposite B. The innermost circle revolves on the middle circle, so that, for instance, D can be put opposite C. And in this way 9 compartments are formed at a time, one being B C D, another C D E, and so on. After that, E of the smaller circle can be put opposite C of the middle one, with which another 9 compartments are formed. When all the letters of the smallest circle have been brought opposite B on the largest circle and C on the middle circle, then C is the middle term between B and D, since B and D are related to one another through the meanings of C. And the same is true of the other compartments. And thus by means of these compartments, one may seek out necessary conclusions and find them.

After that, we can bring all the letters opposite the B of the largest circle and D of the middle circle, and so on for all the letters of the middle and smallest circle, by rotating them, with the B of the largest circle remaining immobile, until we arrive at a position with B on the largest circle, I on the middle one, and K on the innermost; and this will make a total of 252 compartments.[10]

This figure is more general than the third, because in each compartment of this figure there are three letters, whereas in each compartment of the Third Figure there are only two. Thus the intellect is rendered more general as a result of the Fourth Figure than as a result of the Third.[11]

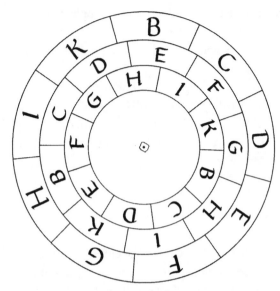

The Fourth Figure

The condition of the Fourth Figure is that the intellect must apply to a proposition those letters that are most applicable to it. And once the compartment has been formed from three letters, it must grasp the meanings of the letters, keeping in mind the agreement between subject and predicate and avoiding disagreement. And with this condition, the intellect can acquire knowledge by means of the Fourth Figure, and can form many arguments toward a single conclusion.

So much for the four figures, which the artist must learn by heart, for without them he cannot use or practice this Art.

Part III, Which Treats of Definitions of the Principles

In this Art, the principles thereof are defined, so that they may be known by said definitions, and so that one may use them, affirming or denying in such a way that the definitions remain unimpaired. With such conditions, the intellect acquires knowledge, discovers middle terms, and dispels ignorance, which is its enemy.

1. Goodness is that thing by reason of which good does good.[12]
2. Greatness is that by reason of which goodness, duration, etc. are great.
3. Eternity or duration is that by reason of which goodness, etc. endure.
4. Power is that by reason of which goodness, etc. can exist and act.
5. Wisdom is that by reason of which the wise man understands.
6. Will is that by reason of which goodness, greatness, etc. are lovable or desirable.
7. Virtue is the origin of the union of goodness, greatness, and the other principles.[13]
8. Truth is that which is true concerning goodness, greatness, etc.
9. Glory is that bliss in which goodness, greatness, etc. come to rest.
10. Difference is that by reason of which goodness, etc. are clearly distinguishable from one another.
11. Concordance is that by reason of which goodness, etc. accord in one or in several things.
12. Contrariety is the mutual opposition of certain things as a result of different goals.
13. Beginning is that which is found in everything where there is any question of priority.
14. Middle is the subject through which end influences beginning, and beginning reinfluences end, and thus it participates in the nature of both.
15. End is that in which beginning comes to rest.
16. Majority is the image of the immensity of goodness, greatness, etc.
17. Equality is the subject in which the end of concordance, goodness, etc. comes to rest.
18. Minority is the thing close to nothingness.

So much for definitions of the principles, which must be learned by heart; for without knowing these definitions, the Art is unteachable.

Part IV, Which Treats of Rules

The rules of this Art consist of ten general questions, to which all other possible questions can be reduced. They are the following:

B. Whether a thing is.   G. Of what kind is it?

C. What is it?   H. When is it?

D. Of what is it?   I. Where is it?

E. Why is it?   K-1. How is it?

F. How much is it?   K-2. With what is it?[14]

Each of these questions is divisible into various species.

B. "Whether" has three species, to wit, dubitative, affirmative and negative, so that, from the outset, the intellect assumes either side to be possible, and does not bind itself to believing, which is not as natural to it as is understanding. And thus it must take that side with which it has the greatest understanding, which side must be that of truth.

C. "What?" has four species:

1. The first is definitional, as when one asks, What is the intellect? To which one must reply that it is that power whose function it is to understand.

2. The second species is when one asks, What does the intellect have coessentially in itself?[15] To which one must reply that it has its correlatives, that is to say, intellective, intelligible, and understanding, without which it could not exist, and would, moreover, be idle and lack nature, purpose, and repose.

3. The third species is when one asks, What is the intellect in something other than itself? To which one must reply that it is good when understanding in goodness, great when understanding in greatness, etc.; and grammatical in grammar, logical in logic, rhetorical in rhetoric, etc.

4. The fourth species is when one asks, What does a thing have in another thing? As when one asks, What does the intellect have in another thing? To which one must reply, In knowledge understanding and in faith belief.

D. The rule "Of what?" has three species:

1. The first is the original meaning, as when one says, Of what is the intellect? To which one must reply, Of itself, since it is not naturally derived from some other general thing.

2. The second species is when one inquires specifically, What is a thing composed of? As when one asks, What is the intellect composed of? To which one must reply that it is composed of its own specific matter and form, with which it achieves specific understanding.[16]

3. The third species is when one asks, Whose is a thing? As when one asks, Whose is the intellect? To which one must reply that it is man's, as a part belongs to the whole, and a horse to its master.

E. The fourth rule has two species, to wit, formal and final.

1. The formal aspect is when one asks, Why does a thing exist? As when one asks, Why does the intellect exist? To which one must reply that it is because of its specific matter and form, with which it has a specific understanding and with which it acts in accordance with its own species.

2. The second species is with respect to end, as when one asks, Why does the intellect exist? To which one must reply, So that objects may be intelligible, or, So that one may have knowledge of things.

F. The fifth rule asks about quantity, and has two species:

1. The first is what one inquires about continuous quantity, as when one says, How much intellect is there? To which one must reply that there is as much as there can be through spiritual quantity, and this quantity has nothing to do with points or lines.

2. The second species is when one inquires about discrete quantity, as when one says, How much intellect is there? To which one must reply that there is as much as the amount of its correlatives, by which it is diffused and sustained, that is to say, the intellective, intelligible, and understanding, with which it operates theoretically and practically, with respect to the general and the particular.

G. The sixth rule concerns quality, and it has two species:

1. The first is when one asks, What is the characteristic and primary quality of intellect? To which one must reply, The intelligibility with

which it is clothed. Extrinsic understanding is a secondary and more distant property, with which the intellect understands a man, a lion, etc. It is of this that the intrinsic and substantial understanding of the intellect is clothed, and similarly for what is extrinsically intelligible.

2.   The second species is when one inquires about appropriated quality, as when one asks, What is an appropriated quality of the intellect? To which one must reply, Believing, doubting, or supposing. For these acts are not those of the intellect proper, but of the understanding.

H. The seventh rule inquires about time, and it has fifteen species signified by the rules of C, D, K, as is pointed out in the *Ars magna*. But since this Art is brief, we must discuss this rule in few words, as when we ask, In what way does the intellect exist in time, if it is not made up of points and lines? To which one must reply that the intellect exists in time because it had a beginning and because it consists of temporal succession, by means of the motion of the body to which it is attached.[17]

I. The eighth rule inquires about place, and it has fifteen species signified by the rules of C, D, K, as is pointed out in the *Ars magna*. Thus when one asks, Where is the intellect, one can answer briefly that it is in the subject in which it is, like a part in the whole, not however confined but rather diffused in it, for the essence of intellect has nothing to do with point, line, or surface.

K contains two rules, namely of modality and instrumentality.

K-1. The modal rule has four species, as when one asks (1) How does the intellect exist? (2) How does one part exist in another? (3) How do the parts exist in the whole, and the whole in its parts? and (4) How does it transmit its likeness outside itself? To which one must reply that subjectively it exists in the manner already determined through the abovementioned species. Objectively, it understands by finding the middle term existing between subject and predicate designated by the figures, and by multiplying alien species abstracted from sense and imagination, which are characterized and understood in its own intellectual faculty.

K-2. The second rule of K has four species, as when one asks, (1) With what does the intellect exist? (2) With what does one part exist in another? (3) With what do the parts exist in the whole, and the whole in its parts? and (4) With what does it transmit its likeness outside itself?[18] To which one must reply that it exists with its correlatives, without which it can neither exist nor understand. And it understands with alien species, from which it fashions an instrument for understanding.

So much for the rules with which the intellect solves questions, which it does by reducing them by means of rules; by keeping in mind what a rule and its species mean subjectively; by reducing a question by means of principles and rules; by having the intellect discard whatever question is dubious as a result of applying the definitions of principles; by choosing and by understanding intelligibly the affirmative or negative side of the question; and this so that the intellect be removed from doubt.

Part V, Which Treats of the Table[19]

This table is the subject in which the intellect becomes universal, because by said table it understands and abstracts many particulars on all matters, with the principles surveying the particulars objectively, and the rules subjectively. And this it does by applying to each question twenty arguments to explain said question, one argument being extracted from each compartment of a given column.

The table, as one can see, has 7 columns, in which the 84 columns of the *Ars magna* are implicit. In this table T means that the letters which come before it belong to the First Figure, and those after it to the Second Figure.[20]

By means of this table the intellect is ascendant and descendant. It is ascendant when it ascends to things that are prior and more general, and descendant when it descends to things that are posterior and particular. And in addition it is connective, since it can connect columns, as, for instance, the column of B C D with that of C D E, and so on.

Part VI, Which Treats of the Evacuation of the Third Figure

The intellect evacuates the compartments of the Third Figure by extracting from them as much as it can, taking from each compartment those things that the letters signify, so as to apply the things signified to

The Table

B C D	C D E	D E F	E F G	F G H	G H I	H I K
B C T B	C D T C	D E T D	E F T E	F G T F	G H T G	H I T H
B C T C	C D T D	D E T E	E F T F	F G T G	G H T H	H I T I
B C T D	C D T E	D E T F	E F T G	F G T H	G H T I	H I T K
B D T B	C E T C	D F T D	E G T E	F H T F	G I T G	H K T H
B D T C	C E T D	D F T E	E G T F	F H T G	G I T H	H K T I
B D T D	C E T E	D F T F	E G T G	F H T H	G I T I	H K T K
B T B C	C T C D	D T D E	E T E F	F T F G	G T G H	H T H I
B T B D	C T C E	D T D F	E T E G	F T F H	G T G I	H T H K
B T C D	C T D E	D T E F	E T F G	F T G H	G T H I	H T I K
C D T B	D E T C	E F T D	F G T E	G H T F	H I T G	I K T H
C D T C	D E T D	E F T E	F G T F	G H T G	H I T H	I K T I
C D T D	D E T E	E F T F	F G T G	G H T H	H I T I	I K T K
C T B C	D T C D	E T D E	F T E F	G T F G	H T G H	I T H I
C T B D	D T C E	E T D F	F T E G	G T F H	H T G I	I T H K
C T C D	D T D E	E T E F	F T F G	G T G H	H T H I	I T I K
D T B C	E T C D	F T D E	G T E F	H T F G	I T G H	K T H I
D T B D	E T C E	F T D F	G T E G	H T F H	I T G I	K T H K
D T C D	E T D E	F T E F	G T F G	H T G H	I T H I	K T I K
T B C D	T C D E	T D E F	T E F G	T F G H	T G H I	T H I K

the proposition, and it thus becomes applicative, investigative, and inventive. We will give an example of this in one compartment, and the others are to be dealt with in similar fashion.

From the compartment of B C the intellect draws forth 12 propositions by saying:

goodness is great
goodness is different
goodness is concordant
greatness is good
greatness is different
greatness is concordant

difference is good
difference is great
difference is concordant
concordance is good
concordance is great
concordance is different[21]

And having formed these 12 propositions by changing subject into predicate and conversely, the compartment is evacuated of these propositions.

Then it is evacuated of 12 middle terms. And they are called middle terms because they are placed between subject and predicate, with which they accord in genus or species. And with these middle terms, the intellect can become disputative and determinative. Thus, for instance, one can say, Everything which is magnified by greatness is great; goodness is magnified by greatness; therefore goodness is great, and so on for the others.

After performing this evacuation, the intellect evacuates the same compartment by means of 24 questions, since two questions are implicit in each proposition. Thus one has:

goodness is great:
> Whether goodness is great.
> What is great goodness?

goodness is different:
> Whether goodness is different.
> What is different goodness?

goodness is concordant:
> Whether goodness is concordant.
> What is concordant goodness?

greatness is good:
> Whether greatness is good.
> What is good greatness?

greatness is different:
> Whether greatness is different.
> What is different greatness?

greatness is concordant:
> Whether greatness is concordant.
> What is concordant greatness?

difference is good:
> Whether difference is good.
> What is good difference?

difference is great:
> Whether difference is great.
> What is great difference?

difference is concordant:
> Whether difference is concordant.
> What is concordant difference?

concordance is good:
> Whether concordance is good.
> What is good concordance?

concordance is great:
> Whether concordance is great.
> What is great concordance?

concordance is different:
> Whether concordance is different.
> What is different concordance?

Once this evacuation of questions has been carried out, the intellect then evacuates the compartment with the definitions of goodness and greatness, and with the three species of difference and concordance that appear in the Second Figure. Then it evacuates the compartment with the three species of Rule B and with the four species of Rule C. Having carried out this evacuation, the intellect solves the aforementioned questions in said evacuation, by observing the conditions of the compartment, affirming, or denying. And thus the intellect banishes doubts from the compartment, remaining in it calmly and positively. Moreover it now knows itself to be completely general and artful, and clothed in great knowledge.[22]

Four

THE RENAISSANCE

The term "the Renaissance" suggests a unitary period, but the Renaissance developed very differently in areas as culturally distinct as Italy, Germany, the Netherlands, and Spain. The situation in Spain was so different, in fact, that some scholars have denied that there was a Spanish Renaissance. Some appeal to Jacob Burckhardt's view of the Italian Renaissance as paradigmatic; others adopt the German model whereby Renaissance and Reformation are inseparable. The Spanish Renaissance was admittedly shorter and less pervasive compared to other countries, and it was ultimately choked off by intolerance and the Inquisition. But Spain had its Renaissance.

The period produced exemplary humanists such as Antonio de Nebrija, Hernán Núñez, and Juan Luis Vives. Nebrija studied in Italy under the humanist Lorenzo Valla before returning to Spain to prepare a Spanish grammar (the first of a vernacular language), a Latin-Spanish dictionary, a history of the Catholic monarchs Fernando and Isabel (Ferdinand and Isabella), and other works. He was also one of the diverse group of scholars at the University of Alcalá de Henares who edited the Polyglot Bible, with parallel texts in Hebrew, Aramaic, Greek, and Latin, from 1502 to 1514. Núñez also collaborated on the Polyglot Bible, prepared critically acclaimed editions of Seneca, Pliny the Elder, and Pomponius Mela, and held chairs of rhetoric and Greek. Humanist even in his aversions, Núñez advised Juan Ginés de Sepúlveda to avoid reading theologians so as not to ruin his style. Vives, however, was the most international of Spain's humanists. A friend and collaborator of Erasmus and Thomas More, Vives was a luminary of the first rank; his works went through some five hundred editions.

In addition to humanist scholarship, Spain was caught up in the wave of religious reform sweeping across Europe. Cardinal Jiménez de Cisneros, who founded the University of Alcalá de Henares in 1499, reformed his own Franciscan order and stimulated comparable reforms in other orders by insisting that monks observe their vows of poverty. As archbishop of Toledo, Cisneros ordered that clergy give up their concubines and took the momentous step of naming Bartolomé de Las Casas Protector of the Indians. Dovetailing with these Cisnerian reforms, an Erasmian movement based on the reformist ideals of Erasmus' *Enchiridion militis Christiani* attracted learned adherents from all over Spain during more than four decades (c. 1516–1559).

Spain also showed Renaissance affinities in other ways. Its register of Renaissance writers is headed by Miguel de Cervantes, who lived in Italy and became an aficionado of Italian literature. Spain developed its own Renaissance architectural style: the plateresque. Like England and France, it moved decisively toward the formation of a nation state, unifying Aragon and Castile, annexing Navarre, and conquering Granada, the last Muslim province of the peninsula, in 1492. Finally and most conspicuously, it led the geographical explorations of the period with its conquests in the New World.

JUAN LUIS VIVES

Juan Luis Vives was born in Valencia in 1492, the year of both the fall of Granada and the expulsion of the Jews from Spain. After completing his primary studies in Valencia, Vives attended the University of Paris, where he formed an abiding dislike of its degenerate scholasticism and a penchant for Renaissance humanism. About 1514 he launched his teaching career in Bruges, where there was a colony of Valencians that included his future wife, Margarita Valdaura. In 1520 he began to collaborate with Erasmus on a new edition of Augustine's works, and in 1523, aided by Thomas More, he moved to England to teach at Oxford. There he became embroiled in Henry VIII's attempt to annul his marriage to his Spanish wife, Catalina (Catherine) of Aragon. When Vives sided with Catalina in 1527, Henry clapped him in jail for six weeks and the scholar prudently left England in 1528. The problem was where to go. Vives came from a family of converted Jews and had already turned down a chair at the University of Alcalá de Henares, perhaps the leading humanist institution in Spain, in 1522. His father had been burned alive as a relapsed Jew by the Inquisition in 1526, and his mother, who had died in 1508, was to be exhumed and burned in 1529. Thus he returned to Bruges, where in the remaining years of his life, despite poverty and illness, he produced some of his finest work. He died there in 1540.

Renaissance humanists of whatever stripe tended to reject Scholastic scholarship, which remained the dominant tradition in Spain. Separating the two camps were contrasting sets of beliefs and emotions, some of which stand out in high relief in a revealing anecdote from Vives' *Adversus pseudodialecticos* (Against the Pseudodialecticians). Upon observing a Scholastic writer composing a book of syllogisms "while drinking in the baths of St. Martin," Vives and two friends amused themselves by "diligently singing to surround the author with a great noise" and thereby spoil the work.[1] This visceral spurning of Scholasticism was characteristic of Renaissance humanists, who prided themselves on cultivating rhetoric rather than dialectic, literature rather than logic.

Precisely these commitments underlie the psychology Vives presents in *De anima et vita* (On the Soul and Life). To clarify the nature of the soul, Vives mines the rhetorical and literary classics, dredging up a great deal of traditional material. Nevertheless, his elegant Latin often succeeds in striking vivid, novel notes. In discussing the association of ideas, for example, he observes that every time he sees the house in Bruges owned by his friend Idiáquez, he thinks of his friend, but not the reverse; and that eating cherries makes him feel ill because years before, in Valencia, he ate cherries with a bad taste and suffered fever. Based on these experiences, he infers that the less important idea leads generally to the more important, but not the reverse.[2] This use of introspection is fresh, completely foreign to Aristotle's *De anima* or the psychological portions of Aquinas' *Summa theologiae*, for instance.[3]

This volume's selections from *De anima et vita* are taken from Book 3, which Ortega y Gasset called "the first modern theory of the passions."[4] The theory is modern in its appearance in 1538—some 111 years before Descartes' *The Passions of the Soul*. It is also modern in its motivation. Vives complains that ancient thinkers such as Aristotle, the Stoics, and Cicero failed to treat the passions with sufficient diligence and sets off on his own to rectify the matter. In addition, the theory is modern in the looser sense that anyone conversant with the contemporary debate on emotion can find an interlocutor here. Like contemporary cognitive theorists, Vives highlights the role of judgment in emotion. And though he relies on the still standard theory of humors handed down from Hippocrates and Galen,[5] his insistent explorations of the physiology of emotion should be congenial to contemporary physiological theorists.

The selected chapters from Book 3 illustrate the major heads of Vives' classification of emotions. Chapter 1 presents the classification that successive chapters develop. Carlos Noreña has pointed out, however, that this classification "was not very important to Vives," and that the treatise "subverts the initially promised order of classification."[6] That is, not all emotions in the classification are allotted chapters, and not all chapters deal with emotions from the classification. While these selections may serve as a convenient gateway to the theory, it should be borne in mind that they can mislead, making the theory seem tighter and tidier than it actually was.

On the Soul and Life

The Passions

BOOK THREE

Chapter 1. The Classification of Emotions

All the emotions of the soul are about some good or about some evil as far as evil is the opposite of good, movements toward the good or away from and against evil. The good and the evil can be something present, past, or possible. The absence of good counts as evil and the absence of evil is equivalent to the good. As soon as the good becomes known to us, it attracts us. This initial attraction, that is called "liking," can be compared to the first swell of a soft-blowing breeze. When confirmed, it turns into love. Movement of the soul about a present good which we possess is called joy; movement about a future good is called desire, which falls within the boundaries of love.[1] The first emotion against evil is irritation, the opposite of liking. When confirmed, it becomes hatred. The emotion about a present evil is sadness; fear, if it is about a future

---

From Juan Luis Vives, *The Passions of the Soul: The Third Book of De Anima et Vita*, introduction and translation by Carlos G. Noreña (Lewiston, NY: Edwin Mellen, 1990). Reprinted by kind permission of the Edwin Mellen Press.

one. The emotions against a present evil are anger, envy, and indignation. Against a future one, courage and daring. Under the heading of love we find favor, reverence, and compassion. Under joy, pleasure, under desire, hope, and under sadness, bereavement. Pride is a monster composed of many emotions, joy, desire, and confidence.

All these emotions can stretch into the past: we hate, love, and feel compassion for those who are already dead. Emotions can also project themselves toward possible objects and those that are similar to past objects, such as fables which we know not to be real, or into future objects we consider as present. Thus, for instance, we now can hate the Anti-Christ. We can also feel emotions about objects that can be considered as future, as when we love a great, courageous, and noble man that a story tells us is going to exist. We even feel emotions about past things as if they were to happen in the future. When we read history, hope grips our souls with suspense and we worry about the final outcome of events.

It should be emphasized that since emotions are actual or possible movements of the soul, such things as equanimity, peace of mind, meekness of character, or composure should not be counted among them. For these are not emotions nor effects of emotions or born from a judgment, as the Stoics mistakenly taught. They are natural and depend on individual disposition, such as crying when we are sad, dismaying when we fear, or gesturing with jubilation in times of intense joy.

Some emotions are naturally powerful, such as love and hatred; others are powerful because of external circumstances compounding the situation. All of them, however, derive special strength from the constitution of the body, as I have just indicated.[2] Some emotions thrive in the company of others, some are curbed and kept in check by others. Love causes envy, hatred, or anger when somebody hates or harms something dear to us. Anger gives rise to the desire of and the joy in revenge. Whoever loves something hopes that it will take place so he may enjoy it and fears it might never happen. If it happens, he rejoices; if what he expects does not happen, he becomes sad. Again, a great joy can be spoiled by sadness, jealousy is weakened by compassion or fear and grief is taken away by another grief.[3] Pain and sadness can be removed by fear. When a fight seems dangerously close, even the cripple can run under the enemy's pressure.

These disturbances of the soul are similar to waves and tides: some reinforce the preceding ones while others weaken and oppose them. In the same way as during a civil war nobody listens to the better but to the stronger party, so too in the conflict of our emotions no one obeys the just but rather the strongest ones, passions that make the whole soul a law unto itself, as vehement love usually does. Those who out of fear yield their fortunes, wives, or children to a victor or a thief do so because they love themselves more than they love others. But those who, contrariwise, prefer dying in the fight to suffering such infamy and who persecute and abuse their enemies out of hatred, anger or envy, risk grave peril by their actions because they passionately love themselves, because they are self-serving, self-indulgent, and enslaved to themselves. Those, however, who do not love themselves that dearly are less obstinate and rough in their behavior, and are not carried away with such vehemence in seeking the fulfillment of their desires.

Chapter 2. Love

Whatever is judged to be good, as soon as it is presented to the will, moves and attracts the will to it by some natural affinity similar to that between truth and the mind or between beauty and the eyes. This motion of the will—which we shall call liking or endearment—is a certain cheerfulness of the will, something like a facial expression or a smile, by which the will enjoys what is good and congenial to it. Speechless animals bear witness to love through external signs such as leaps, boisterous sounds, and submissive behavior. Human beings express love through a placid look, a relaxed countenance, a happy smile. At the first sight of the good, both men and beasts forsake any harsh feelings they might have and become gentle and subdued.

Love is confirmed liking and can be understood as an inclination or forward motion of the will toward the good, a going out of the will to embrace the approaching good, a going out that results in the craving to be united with it. This kind of love is called desire or concupiscence when its object is judged to be good for no other reason than its usefulness, because it is useful to the lover. There are two kinds of concupiscence: desire, when we wish a future good we do not possess, and appetite for conservation when we wish to retain what we actually possess. We love in this way whatever we consider useful and congenial to our soul, body, or personal well-being. Many people love God Himself in this manner, just because He is the Creator and Giver of great gifts. There are, however, occasions when something is loved for itself without any consideration of utility to us. This is true and authentic love, such as the love among friends, the best example of which is the love of parents for their children. Friendship is born out of love when the beloved loves and the love is mutual.

The good that love seeks is not limited to the present but extends also to the past, as our love for great historical figures whose virtue we greatly admire. Love tends also toward the future or toward fictional and fabulous objects on account of their verisimilitude, as I noted before. Goodness is inferred from actions. We think that people are good when they fulfill their duties toward God, country, parents, rulers, masters, friends, children, neighbors, allies, fellow citizens, and strangers. The range of human duties is extremely wide in scope, as Cicero rightly noticed: "There is no aspect of life, either private or public, lacking in obligations."[4]

Men accounted good are those who have helped, are helping, or will help others in the greatest possible number. And since we all are most dear to ourselves, we love those who have done a favor to us or to those we love, such as our own children and best friends. Love makes all into one. We therefore think that those who have helped us or those who are linked to us by love are performing their obligation and are good people loving what deserves to be loved. We all think of ourselves as worthy of love, otherwise nobody would desire his own preservation. Even those who hurt themselves do it out of self-love, to escape other pressing or threatening evils. From this love of ourselves proceeds the love for our children as parts of ourselves, for our relatives and our own deeds. We love the other as an *alter ego* because he is similar to ourselves. To some extent, similarity produces identity. That is why animals tend to associate with their like, why children hug and kiss mirrors where they see their own image and think other children like themselves are living. One can only guess how much love Adam experienced when he first saw Eve and in her he discovered himself under a totally new form.

Similarity of mind is much stronger than that of body in winning the love of others, even though the former is itself brought about by resemblance in bodily constitution and temperament, by intellectual pursuits and beliefs, by life style and manners. Habits and routines bring souls closer to one another. Hence the friendship among relatives and friends, fellow citizens and students, members of the same religion, colleagues and household inmates. Some people feel an amazing spiritual sympathy for each other, a sympathy that unites them in a natural and secret harmony and immediately ties their wills together. This is why we are capable of loving at first sight people we have never met before. By contrast, a certain incompatibility of the mind makes us sometimes dislike and hate total strangers, or prevents us from trusting and loving even those to whom we owe some favors. Sometimes the similarity in physical temperament is nothing but a mental compatibility that causes a harmony similar to the harmony of sounds in a melody or the harmony of humors in a healthy body. One seeks others not because they are similar but because they fit well with oneself and because such union results, as it were, in a harmonious and pleasant sound, the sound of liking and disliking the same things. Consequently, it often happens that people of radically different character in physical temperament strike up a most solid friendship. As Plutarch wrote about this type of love: "You will never know where it came from or how it came in."

As we judge inward goodness from outward deeds, so too we think that the face is an image of the soul and are naturally inclined to love beautiful people. "A beautiful face," wrote Mimus, "is a silent credential," unless we know from a past experience that we are dealing with a wicked soul, an ugly guest in a beautiful mansion.[5] The most enticing looks are not the pretty ones but the graceful, the pleasant, those enhanced by modesty and admiration. Such looks are evident proof of a properly formed mind.

But there are other reasons why beauty attracts love as amber attracts straw, reasons we shall take from Plato and his disciples. The love that created, ordered, beautified, and permeated the universe is attracted toward Beauty to conform to its source. Furthermore, we appreciate and admire Beauty as a great good because all things beautiful are nothing but a ray and trace of God's infinite Beauty, and as divine Beauty is the cause of true love, so too its image is the cause of the image of love. The beauty of the body, through the refined elegance and harmony of its proportions, expresses the beauty of the spirit. Inward perfection begets outward perfection; the former we call goodness, the latter beauty.

Goodness is the seed of beauty as much as beauty is the blossom of goodness, as the Greeks express in the word *kalokagathía*. Therefore our souls are attracted to beauty as to their likeness, because in it they discover, admire and love a corporeal expression of the spiritual gifts received from God. The soul embraces what is like itself and despises as strange and alien any form of ugliness. Nature, education, or custom have drawn within everybody the image of beauty and goodness, and the image of ugliness and malice. The external look of things evokes this internal image: if they agree with the form of goodness and beauty, we love them; if they fit the image of the ugly and the vicious, we reject them. Hence the variety and conflict of opinions regarding goodness and evil, beauty, and ugliness. One can understand this harmony of body and soul by considering the relation between a work of art and its image in the mind of the artist.

Moreover, the Author of everything was moved by His Own Goodness to create this immense universe. The Beauty that permeates everything is only a radiation of that Goodness. The more of that Beauty something has received, the more lovable it is, since goodness is the cause of love and Beauty and Love are the offspring of the same parents. This is also why there are several kinds of beauty. The first creative beam fell on the mind, embellishing it with a contemplative intelligence, the supreme form of beauty. The second fell on the active powers of the lower rank, impregnating them with seeds for the propagation of the species. The lowest and most impure fell on gross matter, shaping and coloring it with a variety of forms. Such are the characteristics of the different kinds of Beauty, gleams of God's infinite light. Our intelligence can climb and reach the first two degrees of love, but our imagination, mired in the lowest two, causes the love of the corporeal, the desire to procreate in and from the beautiful a likeness of itself, the object of our affections.

The final and supreme power of love is to transform the many into one, to convert plurality into identity. Therefore whoever loves or renders a service to the beloved, seems to do the same for the lover, particularly if he does it for the sake of or at the entreat of the lover. We love therefore those loved by those who are dear to us. By its own nature love ties together whatever it touches. Hatred separates and divides. We must nevertheless beware of loving that which we would like to enjoy by ourselves to the exclusion of anybody else, the source of rivalry and ill will. The love of concupiscence can still some times turn into true love. At first we love the doctor because of our health, but later, when the doctor has helped us to recover it, we truly and sincerely love him as a person. Love swells with the importance and frequence of gifts. Thus, the greatest and most ardent love is the love for God of those people who properly understand His bountiful nature. The love of gratitude becomes more intense the less we deserved the benefit and the less demanding the benefactor was, as parents are, and, above all, Christ is. As it is good to repel and prevent evil, so it is evil to be an obstacle to the good.

Love is not true and authentic until any appearance of utility has been excluded. As beneficent people are loved, so too benefactors love the people they help as if it were their obligation to love, as fathers love their children and teachers love their disciples. Furthermore, the love of the benefactor is usually more intense than that of the beneficiary, because the former loves out of his own goodness and the latter out of necessity. To the benefactor belong the honor and glory of being the greater and the more powerful. To the beneficiary, as to the inferior, a certain feeling (so to speak) of bashfulness. Therefore, the benefactor has a stronger and better source of love, his own will and goodness. Since the object of love is the good, love proceeds with more ease and power from the good toward the good than from necessity toward the good. The benefactor acts because he wants to act; the beneficiary, because he has to. As the proverb says: "Although love is like fire, it tends to descend, not to ascend." Parents love their children more than the children love them. Teachers love their disciples more than the reverse. The same happens with tutors and children entrusted to them. But the greatest love is God's love towards us. Therefore Saint John wisely called God not a lover but Love Itself, and so did Dionysius in his treatise *Sacred Names.*[6] We can properly say that God loves, performs, perfects, embraces and attracts everything toward Himself according to the greatness of His goodness.

Among the things that move us to love, nothing is stronger and more powerful than love, nothing provokes love as much as love. There is no love potion stronger or more reliable than love itself. Love is not a matter of words. As the author of the *Epigrams* said: "Marcus, if you want to be loved, love."[7] Love, however, has to be true and honest. Feigned or pretended love lacks nerve and strength. Painted fire does not cause any heat and the marble statue of a lion does not roar in rage. This mutual generation of love can be explained in two ways. According to some philosophers the seeds of love can be found in the secret and natural interconnection of all things. This connection is such that touching one thing causes the motion of all that are similar to it, as it happens with the strings of a lyre. According to others, the reason is that whenever we know we are loved, we are inclined to think that the person who loves us is good and that one properly performs a bounden duty when one loves what is lovable, and for this reason the lover is loved in return as good. Thus, many a lover goes unloved simply because the beloved is unaware of being loved.

The Platonists seek deeper explanations. Likeness, they say, is the great begetter of love because everyone is naturally most dear to himself and the essence we all share in common transforms the other into an *alter ego.* If you are like me, I have to be like you. The same likeness which leads you to love me, compels me to love you. Furthermore, lovers have engraved in their souls the face and picture of their beloved ones. Their souls become a mirror in which the form of the beloved is reflected. When the beloved recognizes himself in the soul of the lover, he is moved to love him in whom he recognizes himself as a guest, as infants kiss their own images in a mirror. Besides, the lover gives himself as a slave to the beloved knowing that the beloved loves and takes care of him as the beloved's own possession.

Were we able to contemplate the will itself, we would understand the nature of love. Only God, the searcher of hearts, is capable of doing that. But since our will is concealed under many different wrappings, neither the eyes of the body nor the eyes of the mind can pierce into it. We know the will through its actions, whether they are great or numerous, spontaneous or eager. And when somebody is incapable of acting but gives good and timely advice, he is letting us know that he is making an effort, either by tentative communication or by the clear expression of some emotion, to reveal his will.[8] We know that those we hate, hate us; that those we love, love us, and that those we are angry at, are angry at us because they either share our joy and our sadness or shed tears to give a clear demonstration of the way they feel.

We consider worthy of our love and friendship those who comply with our wishes, praise us and think well of us. "Praise," said the comedian, "makes friends and truth causes hatred."[9] We love those who provide us with pleasures and keep sorrows away from us.[10] We hate and avoid those who criticize, contradict, and humiliate us. The former seem to share our feelings while the latter seem to have contrary and repulsive ones. They (the latter) prefer showy to useful things, vain pleasures to solid and permanent gains. The young and adults given to pleasure prefer a pimp, a loafer, or a gambler to a wise and prudent man. Swine too like mud better than precious stones.

Qualities that are both unassuming and gentle—such as fairness, modesty, moderation, and frugality—gain the love of everyone, either because we find their excellence to be harmless or because we love what is humble and are intimidated by what is superior to us. This is done under a pretended sense of independence that has turned into arrogance in the rotten soil of our depraved nature. Moreover, we assume that those who are simple, modest, kind and meek think well of us and consider us worthy of respect and benevolence, unlike those who are constantly criticizing and chastising everybody. Sobriety and soft-spokenness are among the gentle virtues of which we are fond. We dislike the garrulous and untrustworthy, those who pry into the misfortunes of their friends, not to help them, as decent people do, but maliciously to satisfy their morbid curiosity and to have much to gossip about among their acquaintances. Horace wrote: "Keep away from the curious, he is always a prattler."[11] Prattlers are extremely concerned with finding the problems of other households but remain indifferent and aloof in times of prosperity. We like as friends those who easily forget or forgive the injuries they have received, and dislike those who constantly remember them. We like those who do not find fault in our services and we seek out eagerly the friendship of those whose loyalty toward friends can be counted upon. Thus Dionysius, the tyrant of Syracuse, desired to be a third party to the friendship between the Pythagorean philosophers Damon and Pythias, whose loyalty under the threat of death had been celebrated in literature.[12] We enjoy remembering past hardships but enjoy even more remembering those who under such circumstances did not abandon us but helped us as much as they could. As the saying goes: "True friends are only known in times of true need." And in the same spirit the Lord said to his disciples: "You are the ones who remained with me at the time of my tribulations."[13] We cannot love those we fear because we consider them powerful rather than good. Prudence without justice becomes suspect and appears as cunning and fraud.

Trust and love have the same roots, the judgment that something is good. Therefore love reinforces trust and trust strengthens newborn love. Love is a warm emotion that readily comes to birth in warm temperatures, characters, circumstances, places, times and occupations. But many warm people tend to quit loving for trivial reasons, sometimes because they are easily offended, sometimes because other emotions— such as envy, anger or pride—choke love like thorns. Their superficial and unreliable disposition makes them decide to love something else and forsake their former love. When the blood is thin and the spirits are scarce, the flame that had first arisen in light tinder is easily extinguished with a light motion. But when the burning stuff in a warm temperament is thick, solid, and resistant to change, love becomes the controlling power unless it is threatened by other equally heated emotions, such as rage, arrogance, and envy. Calm and sanguine people are also less irritable and more persevering and loyal in loving. Their love might be less ebullient, but it has more substance to it. The former can be compared to a flame, the latter to burning lumber. Those excel in vehemence, these in perseverance. Any one can see young friends who are willing to risk their lives for each other (something a father would find hard to do for his only son), as we know from a famous case of friendship.[14] But their love is only a flare quickly consumed by a passing flame, while the love of a father is solid and lasting. Cooler temperaments are slow and more constant. For in this case dense and dry material is ignited, and, like iron, it makes excellent and long-lasting fuel for fire.

Chapter 3. Love of Desire

Desire is the appetite of what appears to be good and useful, a good we seek to obtain when absent and preserve when present.[15] Goods contribute to our existence and well-being. To the former belong things that are naturally necessary to protect and propagate life, such as food, drinks, medicines, fire, living quarters and clothing. These are labeled appetites rather than desires. When the soul is stung by appetite as by a silent prick of nature, it ignores and bypasses judgment as in the case of thirst and hunger—which are therefore called poor advisers[16]—or in the case of the whimsical cravings pregnant women experience.[17]

To arrange for our well-being we secure conveniences such as well-prepared food, wine, beer, wool and linen fabrics, all the external comforts common to man and beast, even far-fetched pleasures and sensual delights. We humans have also invented many others, such as nobility, honor, reputation, riches, and glory. We increased them in such number and weight that our desires erupt like a swarm, endlessly and out of any proportion. Pliny the Younger rightly said: "No animal has a greater desire of all things than man; no animal has fewer needs."[18] We were given desire to seek what seems good to us and to preserve what we possess. Our desire stretches out to God, who is the true and permanent good of man. But since God is immense, the spread of our desire becomes immense as well and cannot be satisfied with anything but God in Whom it finally rests.

We seek with more intensity and preserve with more diligence what appears to us more conducive to our ends. But there is a great variety of opinion regarding this matter. To the young, pleasure seems the most important good; to the adult man, respectability; to the sick, health; to the old, comestibles; to the ruler, glory; and to each according to the disposition of body and soul, as I remarked before. Hot temperaments have sharp and vehement desires which they seek to satisfy quickly, but these desires are as peculiar as they are fickle, as I said in writing about love. Cold temperaments, on the other hand, have fewer and sluggish desires, but they are stubbornly directed toward the object of their choice or their excitement.

Confidence decreases desire, and fear increases it. Those who are sure that they will not lack what they need—the young, the courageous and the drunk whose pericardial blood is abundant and hot—are not anxious about acquiring or preserving it. To the same group belong those who have no experience of want or ignore how things are acquired and lost. Those who fear want are anxious to seek and protect what they need, such as the handicapped, the sick, women, the old, and in general those whose pericardial blood is scarce and lukewarm. These people are naturally anxious about not being able to meet their needs, not by the force of any reasoning or guessing about a future good, but because fear and apprehension oppress their hearts. This is why people who were splendid and lavish when young, become very stingy and mean when they get old and those who were generous when healthy become obsessed with the most trivial things when they are sick and even reject healthy food because it costs more than they are willing to pay. Similarly, those who were greedy when sober become prodigal when they get drunk.

People too who have acquired something with great effort tend to hold fast more tightly to it, because they fear having to work again or because things acquired with much pain become more dear, as if we had paid a great price for them. Such is the case with the money earned by a hard working businessman, or a son to his mother, or all of us to Christ, who redeemed us with his blood. On the contrary, what has been easily acquired is also neglected, as it frequently happens with inherited property.

Man was endowed with industriousness, readiness, and audacity to make him seek what he wants. He was given caution, fear, and the daring to face pressing threats to make him keep and protect it.

Desires are named after their particular objects. The desire of money is called avarice, the desire of honor ambition, the desire of tasty things gluttony, the desire of sex lust and numberless others that are peculiar to each folk and language, among which Greek is the richest. But the most important are those related to the conduct of life, to vice and virtue. Justice has to do with money, honor and rank. Temperance with the sense of taste and touch. Curiosity is related to knowledge. The desires of things indifferent—such as horses, hunting, shows and others—are innumerable, scientifically untractable, and not worth pursuing.

Chapter 8. Joy and Gladness

Joy is a motion of the soul caused by the judgment of a good that is present or clearly approaching. The avoidance of evil is equivalent to the good, except that joy always accompanies the good, but is not always present when evil is absent. When a disease that bothers us disappears, one does not feel any joy by the change, and if one does, it is only a lighter and mild kind of joy we call cheerfulness.

Genuine apprehension of a good befalling someone else, who yet is not so close to us as to make him one with us, occasions a pleasant feeling in our soul similar but not identical to joy, a feeling we call gladness. The same occurs when we think of future or past goods and even past evils; we experience this gladness also when we indulge in our own goods with moderation.

Joy is associated with a strong excitement, and almost always is about something we have desired intensely, or about something for which we have made great efforts and worked hard, or about something that happens suddenly and beyond any expectation of ours. This excitement expands our heart, so much that sometimes people die of joy, as it happened to some women in the second Punic War who died suddenly when they saw safe and sound the sons who had been reported as dead. People die faster of a great joy than of a grave pain.

The expansion of the heart and the failure of the breast to keep it under control causes laughter, exultation, gestures of joy, and in some cases, even madness. A moderate joy or cheerfulness as well as gladness itself cleanse the blood with their heat; make us more healthy, and give us a clean, pleasant, and bright color, as the Wise says: "A joyful heart is the health of the body; but a depressed spirit dries up the bones."[19] Those who have a soft heart are easily susceptible to joy and sadness, as wax accepts a seal; those who have a hard and warm heart, rejoice quickly and for a long time. On the contrary, those whose heart is cold and hard with black bile are inclined to be and remain sad. Sadness is an earthly, cold, and dry emotion; joy is warm and moist, and thrives therefore in children, the young, the healthy, and in people who have leisure and security. Fear makes joy impossible, particularly if the cause of our fear is more important than the cause of our joy. Joy thrives also in the spring, in temperate climates, in parties, celebrations, and banquets.

When joy approaches, most people tend to remove all the obstacles to it and react poorly to anything that might disturb them or interrupt the course of joyful events. At the beginning of a feast, a game or a meal, they simply refuse to listen to anything sad as it would be a conversation about death, restraint, poverty, politics, business, the severe demands of virtue and frugality. All this talk is offensive at that time. But when joy has been exhausted, they are willing to listen and are more easily moved than before, remembering how fleeting happiness is, how fast the pleasant seems to fly away. It is also possible that when their heart cools off, they become more open to serious thoughts. Joy increases by thinking about the good we have acquired, by considering how large, how new and how rare and unusual it is, by realizing that it happens to only the very few and mostly to extremely important and powerful persons. Joy decreases with thoughts contrary to those.

Chapter 11. Irritation

Thus far we have discussed man as such; henceforth we shall consider him as a dreadful and cruel beast. The emotions that proceed from an apparent evil brutalize and degrade the human spirit in an amazing way.

The first bite of evil is called irritation, our initial brush with it. Irritation is the pain we feel at our first contact with something discordant and harmful, a pain that causes other emotions: hatred, envy, anger. This pain of the soul is similar to the bodily pain we feel when we get plucked or stung: it proceeds from an evil that offends us, that is contrary and inconvenient to us, that opposes our interest, as when we see something ugly, or hear dissonant and harsh sounds. Things can be fitting to our body or to our soul. It befits the body to have the harmony of health. When such harmony is unfavorably altered, we dislike it, as when we stumble against something, are struck or pushed, wounded or repressed, extremely hot or cold, thirsty or hungry, and so on.

Spiritual harmony of the soul can be found first of all in the senses: each sense agrees with certain things but turns away and rejects their opposites. The eyes like certain colors and beautiful proportions, the ears like the concert of sounds, the sense of taste and the sense of smell have their preferences, the sense of touch likes the proportion of the main qualities. Another harmony is found in the internal senses, such as in the imagination, the cause of all the pleasures and fears we experience in dreams. This is also experienced by beasts; they too avoid or attack whatever is alien or contrary to their natures. There is finally a double harmony in our reason: one pertains to truth and speculative knowledge, the other to our actions. An action can be manual and then is called work; or deal with the proper conduct of life, and then it falls under the exercise of foresight.

We all find lies offensive if they are presented as truth; but we enjoy a fictitious accommodation of truth, such as a picture or a caricature. The knowledge, arts, and disciplines that do not go well with our own intellectual talent, offend us; not to the extent that we vengefully attack them, but we merely hold them in disfavor, unless wantonness or pride makes us reject as ugly anything that is not pleasing to us or is not something with which we ourselves are endowed.

What is fitting and proper in life springs from righteous, dutiful, and virtuous behavior. But there are practically no written formulas for such behavior; it all depends on individual judgment and assessment. It is almost incredible how different are the irritations people have; it is practically impossible to find two people who like the same thing. Everybody follows his own emotions and character rather than the right scrutiny of reason. Hence the differences in judgment. Human reason is either the same or at least not very diverse, but the characters and dispositions of people are infinitely dissimilar and incompatible. Furthermore, there is nothing at all more controversial and capable of different points of views and arguments than to decide what are the proper duties of life. No matter what opinion you hold in these matters, you will find as many reasons for as against it. Hence the mistakes and deceptions of those who fail to examine in depth each of these issues.

The fourth spiritual harmony is that of the will with that which has been judged good for each person here and now. The feeling of irritation proceeds from here: the will is strong and desires very much what we think to be good; while we deem evil, injurious, and fit to repel relentlessly whatever is its opposite. The deeper our irritations penetrate us, the more grievous they are. Everything has an essence, its true and intimate self; whatever touches it, touches and hurts the thing itself, causing a most intense irritation. Thus the most serious irritations have to do with our will, the less serious with our reason and senses, and the lightest with our bodily feeling. We are not offended when our body gets hurt but our will is untouched. What we can take from our closest friends would be intolerable to us if done by others; a lie we like because it pleases our will, would offend us very much if it was said to please somebody else.

Irritation presupposes sensation; what is not sensed, is not offensive. Man is annoyed by flies, but not the elephant who does not even notice them. Therefore, those who by nature, habit, or weakness have a delicate sensitivity, are easily irritated. I am not speaking only about the external senses, but about all the aspects of the reason and the will. Children and women are sensitive by nature; people who are spoiled—such as softly reared children including those raised by widowed mothers, rulers, the wealthy, people whom everybody pleases and flatters but nobody contradicts, and people who always succeed—are sensitive by habit; the sick and old, the tired, the hungry, the thirsty, those troubled by serious mental disturbances, such as people who cannot satisfy their intense sexual desires, are sensitive by weakness. Insomnia, anxiety, fear, terror, everything that makes our body dry and hot increases also our sensitivity. Irritation is an emotion of dry and hot people, and thrives in hot bodily temperaments, places, and seasons.

Lack of experience is also a source of much and frequent irritation. People who are novices and inexperienced in something, are often offended and confused by the most trivial causes, simply because they are not used to them. Those, for instance, who have never left home before and travel for the first time, condemn and detest as absurd, silly, and barbaric anything done differently from what they were used to in their parental home, although what they condemn is frequently better than what they were used to see there. People who are seasoned by experience, those who are used to suffering insults and abuses—as Socrates who learned at home the patience he displayed in his public life—and those who have often been the victims of fortune's assaults, are not that sensitive.

To list all the irritations that are peculiar to different individuals would be an endless task: some people cannot bear the shrill noise of a saw, the grunting of a pig, the tearing of a piece of cloth, the cracking of a burning coal with tongs. Others are offended by certain ways of gesturing, seating, walking, moving the hands, speaking, even by a wrinkle in other peoples' clothing. Who will be capable of explaining the peevishness of this difficult animal we call man? He is intolerable to others and finds others intolerable, each one of us is that way. No wonder one cannot find anything excellent, rich, and holy enough to please everybody in a crowd. There are people so used to despising everything that they contract the habit of getting irritated at anything whatsoever, beyond any reason and distinction. To them it is wise not to approve anything, no matter how perfectly done; to seek with amazing perversity of judgment what to condemn in everything. These people are pleased to be known as such, and get the reputation of a great intelligence among stupid spectators; they fail to see that it is much easier for everybody to condemn everything without distinction than to differentiate between the good and the evil, as sensible and intelligent people do.

Irritation is minimized by its contrary causes. Extreme irritation is called exasperation, while the weakest form of it is called aversion or annoyance, an irritation that disappears by mere distraction or by separation. Thus people who are in a good mood avoid those who are sad, or those who have a good sense of humor avoid those who are stern and serious, as the launderer avoids the coal heaver.

Exasperation shakes the entire body and inflames the heart. If it is repressed and cannot explode, it turns into masochistic rage or into sadistic behavior, even against the innocent. Rage turns against itself, exacerbates, and spreads.

Man was given the feeling of irritation to make him recoil immediately after the first taste of evil, to prevent him from proceeding further and perhaps even from getting used to it and liking it. Irritation's opposite is the feeling of fondness, and its absence is a deep-rooted equanimity by which one can easily endure what others find intolerable.[20]

Chapter 14. Hatred

Hatred is a deeply rooted irritation by which we wish to hurt seriously those we think have offended us. This kind of irritation is not limited to the past or the present, but covers also the future and the possible. We therefore hate those who have hurt, are hurting, will, or could hurt us. Suspicion has great influence here and is inspired by our distrustful character or by a conjecture derived from reflection or from the experience that such a person did hurt others, or that his parents and relatives have hurt us.

Some times we suspect people because they look like those who usually are harmful to others: such as those who are tough, bold, and mindless; and behave like hungry or excited beasts. Those who have been hurt by many people become less and less frequently irritated than others, but they are more fearful and suspicious, and consequently have more propensity to hate, unless they are calmed down by their natural goodness or by wise considerations, as in the case of Socrates. Even animals hate whatever resembles that which has hurt them.

Cowards have a propensity to hate because they fear threats from every corner and hate any kind of strength and power by which their bodies or fortunes could be hurt. Hence the great cruelty of those who are at the same time powerful and fearful, as we have learned from Caligula, Nero, and other cowardly princes. Those who have antagonized the powerful, hate them violently because they fear their punishment and would wish they could get rid of them to live in security. Hence the old proverb: "Offenders do not forgive."

The causes of violent hatred depend on individual values. The most serious offense to an ambitious person is to have something said, done, or thought against his reputation; to a greedy one, something against his interest; to a religious person, something that offends his pious feelings; to a good citizen, something against his country and the public welfare.

Hatred prevails more easily if it replaces love, as when we realize that something is not what we thought it to be. Hatred becomes even more violent when we realize that such a person is exactly the opposite: that the person we love for his kindness, is really greedy; or that the person we love as energetic is lazy. This happens also when love is opposed by an aggravating cause of hatred, as when we are cheated by somebody whom we have observed being generous to others.

Hatred proceeds from the cold and the dry and thrives therefore in such people, locations, and climates, as among melancholics, in winter, during sickness, when one is needy, hungry, or has a bad name. In all these cases hatred casts deep roots, but remains weak and inactive; with heat, however, it becomes violent and aggressive. The proud, the envious, those who are naturally malicious or have become so by habitually rejoicing at the suffering of others, have a tendency to hate. Those who are madly in love with themselves hate others for the slightest reason, complain constantly that they are being hurt, and interpret everything as an insult.

Hatred is reinforced by frequent spells of anger; hence the saying that "hatred is nothing but inveterate anger." Envy reinforces hatred and makes it hatred of the most violent and cruel kind. It is much easier to quell some hatred caused by a serious injury or insult, than a hatred caused by envy. Hatred springing from fear interferes with thinking since we hate to consider what terrifies us. But hatred mixed with anger and envy compels us to think constantly. In times of prosperity we want our enemies to suffer, as Terence in one of his comedies makes Parmeno answer to the sycophant Gnatus: "Do you see something you do not like?"[21]

In hard times we fear that our enemies might rejoice, as Nestor says in Homer: "Our strife will make Priam happy."[22] Consequently we try as hard as possible not to look sad and depressed to our enemies, unless we use our industry to evade the hatred that springs from envy, as Dionysius at Corinth.[23] We rejoice when those we hate, suffer; and more so if their suffering affects that through which they offended us, as when the defiant is deprived of strength, the arrogant man loses authority, or the wealthy one loses the fortune he had abused.

Love is born from the happy feeling of what is good; hatred, from the bitter feeling of what is bad. Because of our weakness the good is never pure and enduring, but makes only a weak impression on us. The bad, on the other hand, finds in us a place to entrench itself, leaves a more permanent mark, and is therefore more lasting and burdensome. Hatred, then, overcomes us faster than love, strikes deeper roots in us, and has a stronger fiber; it just finds in us a most congenial soil. Cicero said: "The one who hurts, remembers; the one who feels good, forgets."[24]

From hatred proceeds slander, and when it becomes more intense, violence and cruelty. Love invites us to behave well; hatred prevents us from it and provokes us to hurt others. Hatred plants the seeds of discord and cunningly attempts to endanger the person we hate, for example, by making him run into the anger of somebody who could hurt him badly. The hater always wishes evil to the hated person, in any possible way, through himself or through others, in secret or in public.

Hatred is dulled by things warm and wet, by cheerful and exceptionally prosperous events, by causes that are contrary to it and give birth to love. Such causes are sometimes stronger than, equal to, or even weaker than the causes of hatred, depending on the mood of the individual at the time. Hatred is eradicated by mercy, removed by hope or by the firm desire of getting something useful or pleasant from our enemy, something from which we might come to think that he is worthy of our love. Hatred is weakened by an even stronger hatred, or by our concern and anxiety about other important matters.

When the causes of hatred disappear, hatred vanishes too, as when somebody completely changes, especially if we find another reason for loving him: if he is a relative, a neighbor, a very educated person, somebody who is very useful to the country, or a person who has significantly improved his way of life. The contempt for earthly things and the lifting of our minds to things heavenly and eternal, can also avert any hatred and hostility. How can any person exclusively interested in his heavenly destination be at all concerned with the little problems of this earthly pilgrimage? Hatred is weakened if one gets into the habit of giving a good interpretation to what others say and do. Such a way of thinking removes the very source of the offense and thus the cause of hatred itself.

Chapter 19. Sadness

Sadness, an emotion totally opposed to joy, is a dejection of the mind by an evil that is or is held to be present. Cicero calls this "affliction" (*aegritudo*).[25] I could easily quote his description of the components of this emotion according to the Stoics. And I would have done it had I thought, as I do not, that the Stoics' teaching was correct or that Cicero had accurately observed and considered this matter. I would not mind if somebody wants to read the text, which is easily available in the fourth book of the *Tusculan Disputations.*

Sadness is sometimes caused by the mere absence of something good, as the sadness of a mother when her only son leaves home. Many people become sad after having enjoyed pleasures, banquets, joyful holidays. The desire of what has been lost makes us nostalgic; our mind is always restless seeking something. A mare too feels the same way when her offspring is taken away. Sadness causes black bile, and is intensified by black bile or by any thought of evil. One sees melancholic people who are sad although nothing bad has happened to them and they themselves cannot give any reason for their feelings.

The effect of this black humor is to darken our minds; our souls become lifeless and our faces betray the obfuscation of the spirit. As Cicero said: "I was bewildered by sadness."[26] Niobe reportedly was turned into a stone from sadness.[27] When the brain cools off, one becomes drowsy, as the Psalmist says: "My soul has become drowsy out of sadness."[28] Sadness makes us hate other men, light itself, and everything human; sadness invites more sadness and rejects anything cheerful or relaxing. This is what happened to Octavia when her son Marcellus died in his youth.[29] Sadness tends to swell and never thinks to have grieved enough. According to Lucanus this is what Cornelia, Pompey's wife, said in the paroxysm of her pain: "It is a shame not to be able to die of pain alone after your departure."[30]

The sadness of the fearful constantly grows: they suspect even the most remote dangers and cast a wide web of imagined evils from which more and more evils are born. Finally, they fall into self-hatred, despair, and rage, as we read about Hecuba, who was transformed into a dog for this reason.[31]

Sadness dries up the body and contracts the heart to such an extent that in people who died of sadness the heart was not much bigger than a membrane. The heart emaciates the face, its own image, and ends destroying our health. The consequences of sadness are weeping, wailing, and groaning. This emotion is cold and dry. It therefore thrives in cold climates and places, mostly among people with a melancholic disposition, in the fall and winter, in cloudy days, and at night. It finds more victims in the north than in Spain or in Italy. On the other hand, light and fair weather cheer up the soul, and, as Pliny said, "The sun shatters the sad darkness of sky and soul."[32]

Like joy, sadness too is increased when shared with others. When we are full of joy, we rejoice with the joy of those who are dear to us; when we are sad, we realize that besides our own problem there are people who love us and are equally afflicted, since love tends to make all into one. It is not the same with those who do not love one another in this way: their joy is not increased when shared with others, as when they share profits, victory in war, games, or civil suits. But their sadness is alleviated because they find some consolation in the fact that they are not the only miserable ones, and that others feel sorry for their misery, implying that their sufferings are undeserved.[33] And if somebody suffers because we suffer, but his pain does not bounce back on us, we feel as if part of our burden had been shouldered by others. This is why the joy of others exacerbates our sadness. In festivities and public entertainments our sadness is repressed inside and grows by contrast with its opposite, as the winter makes our bodies warmer. When we think that others are not at all affected by our grief, we become indignant, and feel sorry for ourselves. Sadness then is renewed with another evil.

Sadness is mitigated when the evil is gone, the lost good is recovered, or there is a rush of cheerful events that are greater and more valuable to us than those whose absence we deplored. Sadness is also weakened by things that warm up the black bile, such as warm and moist food, and especially by wine, as the Scripture says: "Give wine to the sad."[34] Beautiful sights and sounds, open skies and fields, green pastures, and music also help, although there is a kind of music that makes the sad even sadder.

People who are accustomed to suffering become callous and are less affected by sadness; great evils seem to make us insensitive to the minor ones. Sadness is also dispelled by the distraction of occupations, pleasant stories, and by common sense. It helps to consider that the cause of our grief is not as great as it seems, that it is not in proportion to our suffering, that we lose more by feeling sad than by losing the things whose loss we deplore, such as business, opportunities of profit, personal dignity, reputation, fame, glory, and similar sources of personal satisfaction. It helps to think that it is not as bad as it seems, not to the person to whom it happens, not to us, not to our dearest friends; to think that something better is about to happen or has already happened to us; to think that our problem is the fate of everybody, that it comes from the One whose will and judgment one must yield to; to think that sadness is no remedy at all.

Finally, as with other diseases of the soul, it is possible to drive out a nail with another nail by showing that one should ignore the danger of an imminent evil and consider only the one that is already present. It would be foolish to regret the loss of money when we are in danger of becoming captives, dying, or losing our children. It helps also to remind ourselves that we can still hope for the greatest goods, fame, the immortality of our name, the dignity and favor of our prince, and, above all, eternal happiness.

Chapter 21. Fear

Aristotle defines fear as the imagination of an approaching evil.[35] We fear dangerous situations that are harbingers of upcoming evils, such as storms and bad weather that are followed by flood, hunger, and pestilence. We also fear the anger and irritation of those who are able and willing to hurt us, for they are a clear sign that something bad is about to happen. We fear the cunning and the temperamental more than the simple and the open-minded. Those who are feared by others are themselves fearful, as Laberius said: "Those whom many fear have many to fear."[36] Those who cause others to fear, unless they are insane, realize they are threatened by all those who would like to get rid of their fear, as the old saying goes: "They hate whom they fear." The only exception to this rule will be when we fear those who are totally incapable of hurting anybody, because they lack the will or the power to do so. This, however, is seldom the case because no one is so weak that, given the opportunity, it could not hurt someone. Distant evils, such as an uncertain death, which even the elderly hope is still far off, disturb us less.

Aristotle defines fear in another way as a disturbance of the soul caused by the thought of a future evil, something that could trouble or even destroy us. He says that we do not fear everything; we do not fear that a particular person might become criminal or ignorant, but only what can cause trouble to our souls or damage our bodies.[37] This is normally true in our life as citizens, the life he has in mind in his rhetorical precepts. Most people do not count ignorance or vice among evils, but only what hurts their body or their feelings. But more intelligent people fear ignorance of the good and vice no less than others fear sickness and death. Consequently, a better definition of fear would be as follows: a dejection caused by what looks to an individual as an imminent evil. Since fear is caused by the thought of what is dangerous, those who are more reflective—such as the prudent, the sober, and the experienced—fear more.

Close dangerous situations, even if they have nothing to do with us, instill fear in us because they mean that evil is not far away. "Close" can mean a small distance, as in the saying: "When you see the house of your neighbor in flames, and so on."[38] It can also be close in the sense of being similar: when the thief sees another thief being hanged, he fears; a pregnant woman fears when she sees another woman dying in childbirth. One is even more agitated and perplexed when the resemblance is closer: when a bandit who robbed and assaulted his victim is being punished, he who has confessed both crimes is terrified. But if there is any difference, if the latter robbed but did not hurt his victim, the fear is less; if one was alone and the other had accomplices; if one was caught because he was spending the night in a public inn and the other in a cave. When somebody dies of high fever caused by excessive drinking, the moderate drinker will be less fearful if he suffers the same fever.

The first effect of fear is to contract and to weaken the heart. Nature tries to help by sending down the heat of the upper body, and if this is not enough, the heat of the lower extremities; hence the pale face and the cold body. When the heart becomes shaky, the entire body shakes following the motion of the heart; hence the trembling and the stammering of the tongue. The same can be observed in other emotional states that cause a very fast heart beat, as in anger, joy, or in exercise. But when we fear, our voice becomes weak because heat descends from the heart and the upper body; when we are angry, the voice is deeper because the same heat goes up. Fear also makes one's hair stand on end: coldness narrows the passages and hair becomes rigid. Those who have a small amount of warm pericardial blood are cowards by temperament. Therefore those animals whose heart is too large in proportion to the amount of blood, are naturally fearful, such as the hare, the dove, and the deer. They just lack the bile that can warm up the blood. Those animals whose yellow bile swells up, have a great amount of warm pericardial blood, and become naturally strong and active. Animals whose pericardial blood is thick, abundant, and warm, are self-confident and daring; they are rich in heat, and this is most important to the feeling of confidence. They also have a compact and firm matter that sustains the heat for a long time. When the heat is small and kept inside the breast, the heart becomes weaker and shakier; then the face blushes with fear, a clear sign of pusillanimity. Those who become pale are more courageous: nature strengthens their heart by reinforcing it with heat and blood. But if this heat descends further and abandons the heart, then fear increases and the bowels become loose. Homer had a natural reason when he said that the heart dropped to the coward's feet. Any form of heart oppression caused by grief, fear, irritation, or inhibited desire, is called anxiety. One can also be anxious without feeling any emotion, when a thick humor weighs upon the heart.

These are the bodily consequences of fear. The spiritual ones are as follows: fear disturbs and confuses our thinking. Somebody put it rightly: "How can anyone who is constantly burdened by the fear of poverty, slavery, or death, be able to inquire into the nature of the heavens and the elements?" Or the other saying: "Fear drives away any wisdom from my soul."[39] To remain calm in times of danger, to be able to think and to have at one's disposal a realistic plan, as Livy wrote about Hannibal and Sallust about Jugurtha, is characteristic of men who are not only strong and calm in dangerous situations, but also of men who are sharp and extremely intelligent.[40] These people have become so after prolonged and varied experience, or were formed and taught by nature itself. Their blood around the heart is abundant, warm, fluid, and capable of sending to the brain subtle and temperate spirits. Pliny said: "No animal is more confused by fear than man." Let his own writings give evidence for this.[41]

Naturally fearful people scarcely find reasons persuasive enough to regain control and self-confidence. Nature weighs heavily through this original disposition, unless one often and seriously thinks about how despicable the dangers really are and how important it is to face evils with a firm attitude. The purpose of this thinking is to convince ourselves that the evils we fear are not that harmful, that greater benefits would follow from overcoming them, and that greater evils would also follow from not doing so. Sallust puts in Catilina's mouth these wise words: "I know well, soldiers, that a speech of your leader is not enough to instill courage, that words do not transform cowards into heroes nor weaklings into strong men. The courage that is usually shown in war is the courage each one has by nature or by habit. It is useless to exhort those who are not excited by glory and the challenge of danger. Fear blocks the ears of the spirit."[42] If you try to persuade a coward that fear itself is more harmful and aggravates our problems, he will fear even more, as it happens with contagious diseases: our imagination hurts more and causes a double fear, the fear of the disease and the fear of fear itself.

The consequences of fear are as follows: depression, self-incrimination, flattery, adulation, suspicions. Strong people are cautious in finding remedies to the problems at hand; weak people are worried, agitated, dejected. They become lazy, desperate, and depressed; they feel that everything threatens and weighs them down. No misery of the soul can be compared to fear, no slavery of any kind is uglier than fear. The hatred of those who cause others to fear is sharpened by that fear like a knife is sharpened by a grindstone, as the hatred toward a tyrant when the spirit seeks to assert its own freedom. In these and similar circumstances, the cold blood begins to warm up; one regains his strength, and as a reaction, one seeks revenge with passion. Sometimes this makes heroes out of the fearful, and despotic rulers out of those who were accustomed to obey. They simply shake off their former oppressors with tremendous force.

Fear, like almost every emotion, makes us suspicious. Fearful people distrust and exaggerate everything. There is no danger in reality as big as what they imagine. It is therefore comforting to those who have fears about something dear to them to get involved or at least to have a clear knowledge of the danger at hand. Ovid expressed this feeling very well in Penelope's words: "It would be better if the walls of Troy were still standing," and the lines that follow. The poem is well known.[43]

Fear increases when its causes increase. It gets worse when those who are familiar with a danger and know well the terrible consequences it could have, also become frightened; passengers are terrified when the pilot is scared by a storm. And when those who are normally fearless become panicky, our fear increases, as when a raw recruit sees a veteran shaking with fear. Dangers terrify us more when our protection weakens: the masses are deeply disturbed when they see the fear of their magistrates or of those who used to look after them in times of danger, as the chicks tremble when the mother hen is all agitated. Also, when we have had bad experiences, later we are more fearful; gladiators who have been critically wounded in their first encounter, are more afraid of combat. We feel safe when by reflection, or through ignorance, we believe there is no danger. Reflection makes us feel safe after we survive a danger and reach the conclusion that it is all over, or, in general, when we look down on future events and believe nothing will hurt us.[44] Those who do not care any more about a threatened good—wealth, reputation, or life—also feel safe; there is nothing left to care or fear about.

Ignorant people are those who do not think: those who are sleeping, children, drunkards, the inexperienced. People whose thought is totally removed from danger by other considerations and concerns are also ignorant; the same applies to those who are shaken by a violent passion, such as anger, envy, or desire.

We also feel safe when, as I said, we think there is no danger. But we feel confident when in the midst of dangers we get tough and face the evils at hand. Confidence is caused by an increase in our body's heat, by drinking wine for instance, or by anything that strengthens our heart. It can also be caused by some intense emotion, such as anger, love, or desire; or by the fear of a greater evil. All these replace courage in our soul, even among the very cowardly. Confidence can also be instilled by some types of music, as it is written about the musician Timothy who was able to provoke Alexander of Macedon to a fight with the songs of his lyre, and soon thereafter to calm him by changing the rhythm.

Courage is the lifting and bracing up of our souls to reject what is bad and to reach what might be difficult but good. Since courage is inseparable from a warming up of the blood, it is attributed to the irascible part of our nature, a topic I already touched when I discussed anger.

The appraisal of danger depends on the circumstances of space, time, and the energy of the people involved, ourselves and our enemies. These considerations can aggravate our opinion of the danger at hand, or they can also mitigate it by thinking that here and now we cannot be hurt by those who do not want to hurt us, or love us, or are too good to hurt us, as it is the case when we have confidence in God. Those who are not able to hurt us, or lack the power to do so, will not dare to hurt us because they ignore or do not understand their power, as it happens with horses, bulls and many people. With respect to ourselves we have to take into consideration our possessions, our relatives, and our friends. We must also consider and compare the strength and resources we have to protect what is under threat, with the resources of the threatening agent. When we talk about intelligence we must consider wit, erudition, eloquence; when we talk about health, we must consider the constitution and strength of the body, food, medicines. With respect to social position, we must consider wealth. In relation to personal dignity, we must take into consideration our authority and the favorable attitude of others. All these circumstances are very complex, but this is not the place to discuss them.

Those who have faced the same danger many times and escaped unscarred or with only minimal damage, become more confident in the future, as veteran soldiers in war. New, sudden and unexpected dangers strike with consternation even the strongest souls. What we saw coming, what we have familiarized ourselves with through frequent consideration, does not disturb us as much. Thinking takes the place of the experience of suffering; it hardens our soul. The examples of others make us stronger: if he or the other was able to do it, why not I? am I smaller? We become even stronger if we think we have more energy and resources than those who bravely faced and overcame other dangerous situations; if we think we possess what it takes to bear and avoid such dangers: eloquence, prudence, beauty, strength, the help of friends, circumstances of space and time, the favor of the prince or God.

When we think that the imminent evil is neither too great nor too harmful, our souls feel stronger. This happens, for instance, when we know that some thing is prepared for us that is better and would amply compensate for any possible loss: wealth, knowledge, glory, eternal life. The horror and dismay that are caused by fear can also stretch back into the past, as Virgil says: "It is frightening to remember."[45] There is a story about a Jew in France who returned home from the fields at night while sleeping on top of his donkey. On their way they crossed a broken bridge that had only one narrow board left. When on the following day he thought about the terrible danger he had been in, he fainted. The imagination makes things present, as I said before. Fears can also extend toward the possible. A married couple, seated next to the fireplace, felt miserable and began to cry when they began talking about the possibility of losing their only son, who was whole and hearty. The tyranny of the imagination applies to all emotions.

Fear was given to man to enable him to avoid, before it happens, whatever could hurt him.

Five

THE AGE OF DISCOVERY

The belief that the earth is spherical appears to be at least as old as Pythagoras; by the end of the Middle Ages, no educated person demurred. The size of the earth was still a matter of controversy, however. Aristotle had asserted that the earth was a sphere of no great size, adding that the belief in a continuous ocean from the pillars of Heracles to India is not incredible (*On the Heavens* 298a9–13). Pierre d'Ailly's *Imago mundi*, which Columbus studied and carefully annotated, contended that the East Indies were relatively close to Europe and thus could be reached by sailing west. Perhaps reinforced by contact with Paolo Toscanelli, Columbus believed that the East Indies were only some three thousand miles west of Europe. Had he known that the correct figure is closer to twelve thousand miles, he would probably never have undertaken his journey.

Thanks to this false but fortuitous belief, the defining event of the Age of Discovery is Columbus' first voyage in 1492, funded by the Catholic monarchs Fernando and Isabel (Ferdinand and Isabella). It created an upheaval without precedent. Among its sequels were a number of pressing moral problems, chiefly the legitimacy of the Spanish claim to the newly discovered lands and the justice of war against the natives. These problems were addressed professionally by religious and academic authorities. Alonso de la Vera Cruz, an Augustinian monk whose treatise on logic was the first philosophical work of the New World, investigated the morality of the Spanish conquest in his *Relectio de dominio infidelium et justo bello* (On Dominion over Unbelievers and Just War). But the most conspicuous of those who attempted to brake the great wheel of conquest were Dominican monks. As early as 1510, Dominicans newly arrived in the New World were preaching against abuse of the Indians. Francisco de Vitoria, an eminent Dominican theologian, wrote on the legitimacy of the conquest and the theory of just war. Bartolomé de Las Casas, who eventually became a Dominican, devoted fifty years of his life to an impassioned defense of the Indians. To illustrate the reflections of Spanish Dominicans on the moral problems of the conquest, Vitoria's *De Indis relectio posterior, sive de iure belli* and excerpts from Las Casas' *En defensa de los indios* are included here.

The Spanish Renaissance and the Age of Discovery clearly overlap chronologically to a great degree. They overlap very little in scholarly aims and methods, however. During the period from about 1455, the year of the Renaissance publication of the Gutenberg Bible, to about 1559, the year of the Counter-Reformation's first Roman *Index librorum prohibitorum*, Spanish philosophy divides into two streams: the dominant Scholastic tradition, represented in this anthology by Vitoria and Las Casas, and the minority humanist position, represented by Vives. The Scholastic reliance on dialectical argumentation contrasts sharply with the humanist pursuit of rhetorical eloquence.

FRANCISCO DE VITORIA

Francisco de Vitoria was probably born in 1492 (the same year as Vives) to a family of Basques in Burgos.[1] Unlike worldly thinkers such as Seneca and Llull, Vitoria led a retired life circumscribed by two encompassing institutions: the university and the Church. Having entered the Dominican order at the monastery of San Pablo in Burgos around 1506, he was sent to the University of Paris in 1509 to study arts and then theology. In 1516 he began to teach theology at Paris, and there received his theological licentiate and doctorate in 1522. His Parisian period was brought to a close the following year by his appointment as professor of theology and director of studies at the College of San Gregorio in Valladolid, then the capital of Spain. In 1526, however, Vitoria was elected to the principal chair of theology at the University of Salamanca, a position he occupied for the rest of his life. At Salamanca he earned a reputation as a consummate professor, introducing major innovations in the classroom. Rather than lecture on the *Sentences* (*Libri IV sententiarum*) of Peter Lombard, the canonical theological textbook since the twelfth century, Vitoria followed the practice of Peter Crockaert, one of his professors at the University of Paris, and used the *Summa theologiae* of Thomas Aquinas instead. In addition, Vitoria brought the practice of *dictatum*, or slow dictation of lectures, from Paris, which permitted his auditors to take notes verbatim. The use of *dictatum* had the unintended effect of securing Vitoria's reputation for posterity, since he published nothing except some prefaces to edited works during his lifetime. Only the notes of his students preserved his thought and permit him to be represented in volumes such as this one. By the time Vitoria died in 1546, his influence reverberated throughout Spain. Twenty-four of his former students held chairs of arts or theology at the University of Salamanca and at least two at the University of Alcalá de Henares. The University of Salamanca maintains a classroom in his honor.

The texts published under Vitoria's name are of two types: lectures and relections. The lectures are on Aquinas' *Summa theologiae* and Peter Lombard's *Sentences*. The relections, or rereadings, are public lectures on some point covered by the course he taught that academic year. Though Vitoria's relections are works of academic theology, they range over current events to a surprising degree. They treat Henry VIII's divorce, the wars between France and Spain, and the Spanish conquest of the New World. Vitoria's relections on the conquest were to become the apparent motive of Samuel Johnson's outburst to Boswell: "I love the University of Salamanca; for when the Spaniards were in doubt as to the lawfulness of their conquering America, the University of Salamanca gave it as their opinion that it was not lawful."[2]

The conquest is explored in two relections, the first of which is *De Indis* (On the American Indians). This was written for the academic year 1537–1538 but not delivered until January 1539.[3] It defends three main theses: (1) The natives of the New World had legitimate claim to their lands before the arrival of the Spaniards. (2) Some reasons used to justify the conquest are illegitimate (for example, that discovery gives the Spanish title, that the natives are sinners). (3) Some reasons used to justify the conquest are legitimate (for instance, defense of the innocent against native tyrants, mental incapacity of the natives). This third thesis has been variously interpreted. In 1550, Juan Ginés de Sepúlveda and Bartolomé de Las Casas clashed over it in their celebrated debate at Valladolid. Sepúlveda appealed to these reasons to justify the conquest. Las Casas retorted that they are purely hypothetical: *if* the natives were mentally incapable, for example, then Spanish rule would be justified; but since they are not, not.[4] That Las Casas was closer to Vitoria's intention than Sepúlveda seems probable.[5]

The other relection touching the conquest of the New World is *De Indis relectio posterior, sive de iure belli* (On the Law of War), which is included in its entirety here. Delivered in June 1539 as a sequel to *De Indis*, the relection is an abstract discussion of the concept of a just war, whose primary intended application is the Americas. In question 1, Vitoria proposes necessary conditions for a just war that build on the work of his fellow Dominican, Thomas Aquinas.[6] Finer points such as conscientious objection, noncombatant immunity, and treatment of prisoners of war are developed in questions 2 and 3. The square brackets in the text set off the translators' conjectures and emendations.

The fact that both of Vitoria's New World relections rely on the law of nations, a body of law originating in ancient Rome and continually developed down to his day,[7] has excited scholarly polemic. Some commentators interpret Vitoria's extension of the law of nations to the New World as the founding of international law, while others maintain that international law does not originate until Hugo Grotius' *De jure belli ac pacis* (On the Law of War and Peace) of 1625.[8] It seems only fair, however, to acknowledge Vitoria's originality in extending the law of nations to the Americas.

On the Law of War

Can War Ever Be Just?

RELECTION OF THE LEARNED MASTER FRIAR
FRANCISCO DE VITORIA *ON THE LAW OF WAR*
DELIVERED BY HIM AT SALAMANCA, A. D. 1539

[Introduction]

Since it emerges finally, after the lengthy discussion in my first relection on the just and unjust titles of the Spanish claim to the barbarian lands of the so-called Indians, that possession and occupation of these lands is most defensible in terms of the laws of war, I have decided to round off the previous relection with a brief discussion of these laws. Since I shall be prevented by the strict time limit from dealing with every topic which might be discussed under this head,[1] I have not given my pen the freedom to rove as broadly and profoundly as the subject requires, but only so far as the short time at our disposal allows. I shall merely note here

From Francisco de Vitoria, *Political Writings*, edited and translated by Anthony Pagden and Jeremy Lawrance. © Cambridge University Press 1991. Reprinted with the permission of Cambridge University Press.

the most salient propositions on the topic, confining myself to the briefest proofs and ignoring many of the doubts which might arise in the course of a thorough discussion. I shall thus consider four problems:

1. Whether it is lawful for Christians to wage war at all
2. On whose authority war may be declared or waged
3. What may and ought to be the causes of the just war
4. What Christians may lawfully do against enemies, and to what extent.

These, then, will be the problems to be discussed in the first question.

[Question 1, Article 1: Whether it is lawful for Christians to wage war]

PROCEEDING TO THE FIRST, it seems that *wars are altogether prohibited for Christians*:

1. Christians are prohibited from defending themselves, according to the passage in Romans which says: "Dearly beloved, defend not yourselves, but rather give place unto wrath" (Rom. 12:19).[2] And the Lord said in the Gospels, "whosoever shall smite thee on thy right cheek, turn to him the other also"; and in the same passage, "I say unto you, That ye resist not evil" (Matt. 5:39). Elsewhere He says: "they that take the sword shall perish with the sword" (Matt. 26:52).[3] It is not enough to reply that these words are not precepts, but advice. The objection against warfare would stand, even if wars undertaken by Christians were merely "against the Lord's advice."

BUT ON THE OTHER HAND the opinion of all the doctors and the accepted custom of the Church are against this conclusion, for they all show that wars are in many cases lawful. Of course, despite the agreement of all Catholics on this point, we find if we investigate the question that Martin Luther, who has left no nook untainted with his heresies, denies that Christians may lawfully take up arms, even against the Turks. He bases his view on the passages quoted above, and on the argument that if the Turks invade Christendom, this must be (as he puts it) "the will of

God," which it is not lawful to resist.[4] But in this matter Luther has not been as successful in hoodwinking his fellow Germans—a nation suckled from infancy on war—as he has been with his other dogmatic opinions. On the other hand, even Tertullian does not seem to reject the argument against warfare out of hand; indeed, in his book *De corona* 11 he discusses whether soldiering is a fit occupation for a Christian, and finally seems to waver towards the opinion that fighting is unlawful for Christians, "who," he says, "should not even fight cases in the courts."

I REPLY, disregarding these peculiar aberrations, with a single proposition:

1. *A Christian may lawfully fight and wage war.* This conclusion is proved by Augustine in several places; he eloquently sets out the arguments in its favor in his *Contra Faustum* 22.74–5, *Quaestiones in Heptateuchum* 6.10 (on Josh. 8:2), *De ciuitate dei* XIX.12, *Contra Faustum* 22.70, *Ep.* 138.15 to Marcellinus, and *Ep.* 189.6 to Boniface.[5] According to Augustine the proof is furnished by the words of John the Baptist to the soldiers: "Do violence to no man, neither accuse any falsely" (Luke 3:14). Augustine comments (*Ep.* 138.15 = *Decretum* C.23.1.2):

> If Christian discipline were to condemn war altogether, surely the advice given in the Gospel to the men seeking salvation would have been to throw away their arms and avoid military service altogether. Yet what was said to them was: "Do violence to no man, and be content with your wages."

A second proof, this time by reason, is provided by Aquinas (*ST* II-II.40.1). According to the passage in Romans, "for he beareth not the sword in vain; for he is the minister of God, a revenger to execute wrath upon him that doeth evil" (Rom. 13:4), it is lawful to draw the sword and use weapons against malefactors and seditious subjects within the commonwealth; therefore it must be lawful to use the sword and take up arms against foreign enemies too. So princes are told in the psalm: "Deliver the poor and needy: rid them out of the hand of the wicked" (Ps. 82:4).

Third, war was permitted under the natural law, as shown by Abraham, who fought against the four kings (Gen. 14:14–16); it was also permitted in Mosaic law, as the cases of David and the Maccabees show. But the law of the Gospels does not prohibit anything which is permitted by natural law, which is why it is called the "law of liberty" (Jas. 1:25; 2:12), as Aquinas elegantly shows (*ST* I-II.108.1 ad 2; cf. *On Civil Power* 1.5 ad 6). Therefore anything which is permitted in natural and Mosaic law is by that token permitted in evangelical law. And there can be no doubt about the rights of defensive war, since "it is lawful to resist force with force" (*Vim ui repellere licet, Digest* I.1.3, and X.5.12.18).

Fourth, the same proof holds true also for offensive war; that is to say, not only war in which property is defended or reclaimed, but also war in which vengeance for an injury is sought. This is proved by the authority of Augustine contained in the canon *Dominus Deus noster (Decretum* C.23.2.2): "The usual definition of just wars is that they are those which avenge injustices (*iniurias*) in cases where a nation or city is to be scourged for having failed to punish the wrongdoings of its own citizens, or restore property which has been unjustly stolen" (*Quaest. in Heptateuch.* 6.10).[6]

Fifth, a further proof concerning offensive war is that even defensive war could not conveniently be waged unless there were also vengeance inflicted on the enemy for the injury they have done, or tried to do. Otherwise, without the fear of punishment to deter them from injustice, the enemy would simply grow more bold about invading a second time.

The sixth proof is that the purpose of war is the peace and security of the commonwealth [as Augustine says in *De ciuitate dei* XIX.12, and in his *Ep.* 189.6 to Boniface. But there can be no security for the commonwealth] unless its enemies are prevented from injustice by fear of war. It would be altogether unfair if war could only be waged by a commonwealth to repel unjust invaders from its borders, and never to carry the conflict into the enemies' camp.

A seventh proof is based on the purpose and good of the whole world. Surely it would be impossible for the world to be happy—indeed, it would be the worst of all possible worlds—if tyrants and thieves and robbers were able to injure and oppress the good and the innocent without punishment, whereas the innocent were not allowed to teach the guilty a lesson in return.

The last proof is the authority and example of saints and good men, always the strongest argument in any moral question. Many of them have not only protected their homes and property with defensive war, but also punished the injuries committed or even planned against them by their enemies with offensive war. Take, for example, the case of Jonathan and Simon, who avenged the murder of their brother John on the children of Jambri (1 Macc. 9:32–42). In the Christian Church the same is true of Constantine the Great, Theodosius the Great, and many other distinguished Christian emperors who waged countless wars of both kinds, though they had saintly and learned bishops as their advisers.

The conclusion, then, is beyond doubt.

Question 1, Article 2: On whose authority may war be declared or waged?

PROCEEDING TO THE SECOND, we may answer with these propositions:

1. *Any person, even a private citizen, may declare and wage defensive war.* This is clear from the principle "force may be resisted by force" quoted above from the *Digest*. From this we may gather that any person may wage war without any other person's authority, not only for self-defense but also for the defense of their property and goods.

But this proposition raises a first doubt: whether one may retaliate against an attack by a robber or enemy when it is possible to evade the attack by running away?[7] St. Antonino of Florence replies that one may not, since this would no longer be a defensive action of the necessary "irreproachable moderation."[8] A man is required to defend himself with the minimum possible harm to his attacker; therefore, if by resisting he will be forced either to kill or gravely wound his attacker, it seems that he is required to take any possible opportunity of escape by running away. But Nicolaus de Tudeschis, in his commentary on the decretal *Olim causam quae* (X.2.13.12 §17), makes a distinction: if the victim of the attack would incur great dishonor by flight, he is not required to run away and may repel the attack by retaliating in kind; but if he stands to lose none of his fame or honor (as is the case with a monk or peasant attacked by a powerful nobleman, for example), then he had better run away. Bartolus of Sassoferrato, on the other hand, holds that one may lawfully defend oneself in any circumstances without running away, since "to run away is itself an injury" (in *Digest* XLVIII.8.9 and 19.1; XLVII.10.15). Yet, if it is lawful to make armed resistance for the defense of property, as admitted in the decretal *Olim causam quae* (X.2.13.12) adduced by Nicolaus de Tudeschis above, and also in *Dilecto* (*Sext* 5.11.6), then it must be all the more justifiable in the defense of the person, since "personal injury is worse than loss of property" (*Digest* XLVIII.19.10). This opinion seems convincing and safe enough, especially as it is supported by civil law (as in *Digest* XLVIII.8.9); no one can sin by following the authority of the law, for laws justify in the forum of conscience. Hence, even if natural law did not permit us to kill in defense of our property, civil law appears to have made it permissible. And this, I may say, holds true not only for the laity, but also for the clergy and the religious, so long as there is no hint of provocation.

2. SECOND, *any commonwealth has the authority to declare and wage war.* For the proof of this proposition, it is to be noted that the difference in this respect between a private person and the commonwealth is that the private person has, as I have said, the right to defend himself and his property, but does not have the right to avenge injury, nor even, indeed, to seize back property which has been taken from him in the past. Self-defense must be a response to immediate danger, made in the heat of the moment or *incontinenti* as the lawyers say.[9] Once the immediate necessity of defense has passed, there is no longer any license for war. In my opinion, however, a man who has been unjustly struck may strike back immediately, even if the attack would probably have gone no further. For example, to avoid disgrace and humiliation a man who has been struck in the face with the fist may immediately retaliate with his sword, not to avenge himself but (as explained above) to escape dishonor and loss of face. The commonwealth, on the other hand, has the authority not only to defend itself, but also to avenge and punish injuries done to itself and its members. This is proved by Aristotle's dictum that "the commonwealth should be self-sufficient" (*sibi sufficiens*) (*Politics* 1280b33–35); the commonwealth cannot sufficiently guard the public good and its own stability unless it is able to avenge injuries and teach its enemies a lesson, since wrongdoers become bolder and readier to attack when they can do so without fear of punishment.[10] So it is necessary for the proper administration of human affairs that this authority should be granted to the commonwealth.

3. THIRD, *in this matter the prince has the same authority as the common-wealth.* This proposition is expressly expressed in Augustine's dictum: "The natural order, being concerned with peace, requires that the authority and decision to undertake war be in the hands of princes" (*Contra Faustum* 22.75). And it is proved by the following argument: the prince must be chosen by the commonwealth, therefore he is the authorized representative of the commonwealth. Indeed, where the commonwealth has a legitimate prince, all authority rests in his hands, and no public action can be taken, whether in peace or in war, without him.

But the nub of the problem is to define the commonwealth, and say who is properly its prince. The short answer is that the commonwealth is, properly speaking, a perfect community (*perfecta communitas*); but this too needs clarification. What is a "perfect" community? Let us begin by noting that a "perfect" thing is one in which nothing is lacking, just as an "imperfect" thing is one in which something is lacking: "perfect" means, then, "complete in itself" (*quod totum est, perfectum quid*). A perfect community or commonwealth is therefore one which is complete in itself; that is, one which is not part of another commonwealth, but has its own laws, its own independent policy, and its own magistrates. Such commonwealths are the kingdom of Castile and Aragon, and others of the same kind.[11] It does not matter if various independent kingdoms and commonwealths are subject to a single prince; such commonwealths, or their princes, have the authority to declare war.

But it may fairly be asked whether, if several such commonwealths or princes share a single prince, they can of themselves wage war without the authority of their supreme sovereign? I reply that they undoubtedly can. Thus kings who are subject to the emperor can wage war on each other without waiting for the emperor's leave, since (as I said above) a commonwealth must be self-sufficient, which it cannot be without this ability.

But it clearly follows from the preceding argument that princelings who are not sovereigns of independent commonwealths, but simply rulers of parts of a greater commonwealth, cannot declare or wage war. For example, the lands of the Duke of Alba or the Count of Benavente are parts of the kingdom of Castile, not independent commonwealths.

Despite all this, however, it must be admitted that for the most part these matters are done according to the law of nations or human law;

and therefore, custom may establish the right and authority to wage war. If any city or prince has obtained the customary right to wage war on their own account, then this right may not be contested, even if in other respects the commonwealth is not independent.[12]

Furthermore, this license and authority to wage war may be conferred by necessity. If, for example, one city attacks another in the same kingdom, or if a duke attacks another duke, and if the king fails, through negligence or timidity, to avenge the damage done,[13] then the injured party, city or duke, may not only defend itself, but may also carry the war into its attacker's territory and teach its enemies a lesson, even killing the wrongdoers. Otherwise the injured party would have no adequate self-defense; enemies would not abstain from harming others, if their victims were content only to defend themselves. By the same argument, even a private individual may attack his enemy if there is no other way open to him of defending himself from harm.

This will suffice for the discussion of this article.

Question 1, Article 3: What are the permissible reasons and causes of just war?

PROCEEDING TO THE THIRD, which brings us closer to the subject of our barbarians, we may reply with the following propositions:

1. FIRST, *difference of religion cannot be a cause of just war.* This proposition was amply proved in the previous relection, where I refuted the fourth title offered to justify the enslavement of the barbarians, namely "that they refuse to receive the Christian faith" (*On the American Indians* 2.4). This is the opinion of St. Thomas (*ST* II-II.66.8 ad 2) and of all the other doctors; I know of no one who thinks the contrary.

2. SECOND, *enlargement of empire cannot be a cause of just war.* This proposition is too well known to require further proof. If it were not so, both parties in a war would have equally just cause to fight, and both would be innocent; from this it would follow that it was unlawful for either side to kill the other; and this would be self-contradictory, for it would mean that the war was just, but the killing was unjust.

3. THIRD, *the personal glory or convenience of the prince is not a cause of just war.* This proposition is also well established. The prince must order

war and peace for the common good of the commonwealth; he may not appropriate public revenues for his own aggrandizement or convenience, still less expose his subjects to danger. This is the difference between a legitimate king and a tyrant: the tyrant orders the government for his own profit and convenience, whereas the king orders it for the common good, as Aristotle demonstrates (*Politics* 1295a19–21). The prince has his authority from the commonwealth, and must therefore exercise it for the good of the commonwealth; and laws must not be framed for the convenience of any private individual, but for the common utility of the members of the commonwealth, as stated in the canon *Erit autem lex* (*Decretum* D.4.2), citing St. Isidore (*Etymologies* V.1.21). Therefore the laws of war ought to be for the common utility, not for the utility of the prince. This is the difference between free men and slaves, as Aristotle shows in *Politics* 1253b15–1255b40. Masters use their slaves for their own convenience, without consideration of the slaves' convenience; free men, on the other hand, do not live for the convenience of others, but for themselves. For a prince to abuse his position by forcing his subjects into military service and by imposing taxes on them for the conduct of wars waged for his convenience rather than the public good, is therefore to make his subjects slaves.

4. FOURTH, *the sole and only just cause for waging war is when harm has been inflicted.* This is first proved by the authority of Augustine: "The usual definition of just wars, etc." (*Quaest. in Heptateuch.* 6.10). It is also the conclusion of St. Thomas (*ST* II-II.40.1) and all the doctors. Similarly, offensive war is for the avenging of injuries and the admonishment of enemies, as we have seen; but there can be no vengeance where there has not first been a culpable offense; *ergo*, etc. Likewise, a prince cannot have greater authority over foreigners than he has over his own subjects; but he may not draw the sword against his own subjects unless they have done some wrong; therefore he cannot do so against foreigners except in the same circumstances. The confirmation of this is the passage about the prince in the epistle of Paul to the Romans, cited above: "For he beareth not the sword in vain; for he is the minister of God, a revenger to execute wrath upon him that doeth evil" (Rom. 13:4). It follows from this that we may not use the sword against those who have not harmed us; to kill the innocent is prohibited by natural law. For the moment I postpone the question of whether God made any

other special teachings in this matter; He is the lord of life and death, and may dispose differently if He sees fit.

5. FIFTH, *not every or any injury gives sufficient grounds for waging war.* The proof of this proposition is that it is not lawful to inflict cruel punishments such as death, exile, or confiscation of goods for all crimes indiscriminately, even on our own common people and native subjects of the realm. Therefore, since all the effects of war are cruel and horrible—slaughter, fire, devastation—it is not lawful to persecute those responsible for trivial offenses by waging war upon them. The wicked man "shall be beaten according to his fault, by a certain number" (Deut. 25:2).

Therefore it is not lawful to start war for every reason or injury. And this is sufficient for this article.

Question 1, Article 4: what, and how much, may be done in the just war?

PROCEEDING TO THE FOURTH, let us make the following propositions:

1. FIRST, *in the just war one may do everything necessary for the defense of the public good.* This is obvious, since the defense and preservation of the commonwealth is the purpose of war. We have proved that this is lawful in the case of a private individual in his own defense, and therefore it must be all the more so in the case of a commonwealth or its prince.

2. SECOND, *in the just war it is also lawful to reclaim all losses, or their precise value.* This is too well known to need proof. This is the reason for undertaking war in the first place.

3. THIRD, *it is lawful to seize the goods of the enemy as indemnity for the costs of war, and for all losses unjustly caused by the enemy.* This is clear, since enemies who have caused injury are bound to make such restitution, and princes may accept and sue for all such things in war. If there was a legitimate arbiter to judge between the two parties to a war, he would have to condemn the unjust aggressor and perpetrator of the damage not only to the restitution of all goods stolen, but also to making good the costs and losses incurred by the war. But a prince who wages a just war acts the part of the judge in the contention which is the

cause of war, as I shall shortly show, and therefore he too may demand all these things from his enemy. As I said before, if a private individual when he has no other redress is permitted to seize what he is owed from his debtor, then a prince may do so too.

4. FOURTH, *a prince may do everything in a just war which is necessary to secure peace and security from attack,* for instance pulling down fortresses and all other such actions of this kind. The proof of this is that, as I have said above, the purpose of war is peace, and therefore those who wage just war may do everything necessary for security and peace. Tranquility and peace are counted among the good things which men strive for; without security, all the other good things together cannot make for happiness. When enemies upset the tranquility of the commonwealth, therefore, it is lawful to take vengeance upon them.

5. FIFTH, this is not all that is allowed in the just war, but even after the victory has been won and property restored to its rightful owners, and peace and security are established, *it is lawful to avenge the injury done by the enemy, and to teach the enemy a lesson by punishing them for the damage they have done.* For the proof of this point it should be noted that the prince has the authority not only over his own people but also over foreigners to force them to abstain from harming others; this is his right by the law of nations and the authority of the whole world. Indeed, it seems he has this right by natural law: the world could not exist unless some men had the power and authority to deter the wicked by force from doing harm to the good and the innocent. Yet those things which are necessary for the governance and conservation of the world belong to natural law. What other argument than this can we use to prove that the commonwealth has the authority in natural law to punish those of its own members who are intent on harming it with execution or other penalties? If the commonwealth has these powers against its own members, there can be no doubt that the whole world has the same powers against any harmful and evil men. And these powers can only exist if exercised through the princes of commonwealths. Therefore it is certain that princes have the power to punish enemies who have done harm to the commonwealth; and even after the war has been duly and justly carried to its conclusion, these enemies remain as hateful to the prince as they would be to a proper judge. This is proved and confirmed by the authority of the best men. As demonstrated above in the case of the Mac-

cabees (1.1, proof 6), those who wage war do not do so only to recover their losses but also to avenge injury; and this has also been the practice of most Christian kings. The simple rout of the enemy is not enough to cancel out the shame and dishonor incurred by the commonwealth; this must be done by the imposition of severe penalties and punishments. Amongst other things, a prince is required to defend and preserve the honor and authority of the commonwealth.[14]

[Question 2: Doubts concerning the justice
and conduct of war]

NOW FROM EVERYTHING THAT HAS BEEN SAID ABOVE there arise a number of doubts.[15] The first concerns the article on "the reasons and causes of just war" (1.3):

[Question 2,] Article 1: Whether it is enough for the just war that the prince should believe that his cause is just

PROCEEDING TO THE FIRST, let us make the following propositions:

1. FIRST, *this is not always enough.* The first proof is that in lesser cases it is not enough, either for the prince or for private subjects, to believe that they are acting justly, as is well known. It is possible that they act in vincible error, or under the influence of some passion. Any man's opinion is not sufficient to make an action good; it must be an opinion formed according to the judgment of a wise man, as is clear from Aristotle's *Nicomachean Ethics* (1106b36–1107a2; cf. *On the American Indians* 1.1). Furthermore, it would otherwise follow that most wars would be just on both sides. It does not usually happen that princes wage war in bad faith; for the most part they believe that their cause is just. In these circumstances, then, all the belligerents would be innocent, and consequently it would not be lawful for either side to kill anyone on the other. Even the wars of Turks and Saracens against Christians would be justified, since these peoples believe that they are serving God by waging them.

2. SECOND, *for the just war it is necessary to examine the justice and causes of war with great care, and also to listen to the arguments of the*

opponents, if they are prepared to negotiate genuinely and fairly. As Terence says, "in every endeavor the seemly course for the wise man is to try persuasion before turning to force" (*Eunuchus* 789). One must consult reliable and wise men who can speak with freedom and without anger or hate or greed. This is obvious.

[Question 2, Article 2: Whether subjects are required to examine the causes of war]

THE SECOND DOUBT is this: *whether subjects are required to examine the cause of war,* or whether they may go to war without any inquiry on this matter, as officers of the law may carry out the commands of a judge without questioning his orders.

IN REPLY let us make the following propositions:

1. FIRST, *if the war seems patently unjust to the subject, he must not fight, even if he is ordered to do so by the prince.* This is obvious, since one may not lawfully kill an innocent man on any authority, and in the case we are speaking of the enemy must be innocent. Therefore it is unlawful to kill them. In this case the prince commits a sin in declaring war; but "they which commit such things [as] are worthy of death, not only do the same, but have pleasure in them that do them" (Rom. 1:32). So even soldiers, if they fight in bad faith, are not excused. Furthermore, one may not kill innocent members of the commonwealth at the prince's behest, and therefore one may not kill foreigners either.

And from this flows the corollary that if their conscience tells subjects that the war is unjust, *they must not go to war even if their conscience is wrong,* for "whatsoever is not of faith is sin" (Rom. 14:23).

2. SECOND, all senators and territorial magnates, and in general *all those who are admitted or called or of their own accord attend the public or royal council are in duty bound to examine the cause of just war.* This is obvious, because any person who has the power to prevent his neighbors' danger or loss is obliged to do so, especially when it is a question of danger of death and greater evils, as it is in war. If such men can by examining the causes of hostility with their advice and authority avert a war

which is perhaps unjust, then they are obliged to do so. If an unjust war is started because they neglect to do this, then they are taken to have given their consent to it; if a man can prevent something which he ought to prevent, but fails to do so, then the blame rests with him. Besides, the king is not capable of examining the causes of war on his own, and it is likely that he may make mistakes, or rather that he *will* make mistakes, to the detriment and ruin of the many. So war should not be declared on the sole dictates of the prince, nor even on the opinion of the few, but on the opinion of the many, and of the wise and reliable.

3. THIRD, *lesser subjects who are not invited to be heard in the councils of the prince nor in public council are not required to examine the causes of war, but may lawfully go to war trusting the judgment of their superiors.* This is proved, in the first place, because it would be impossible, and inexpedient, to put the arguments about difficult public business before every member of the common people. Second, men of lower condition and class cannot prevent war even if they consider it to be unjust, since their opinion would not be heard; it would therefore be a waste of time for them to examine the causes of war.

4. FOURTH, *there may nevertheless be arguments and proofs of the injustice of war so powerful, that even citizens and subjects of the lower class may not use ignorance as an excuse for serving as soldiers.* It is clear, for example, that such ignorance may be willful and wicked, deliberately fostered out of hostility. Besides, if it were not so even the infidels would be justified in following their princes to war, and it would not be lawful for Christians to make reprisals against them, for it is certain that they believe they have just cause in their wars. Furthermore, the soldiers who crucified Christ could have used this excuse of ignorance since they were following the orders of Pilate; and so might the Jews, who followed their leaders in shouting "Away with him, away with him, crucify him" (John 19:15). None of these excuses can be accepted; *ergo,* etc.

[Question 2, Article 3: What is to be done when the justice of war is undecided?]

THE THIRD DOUBT is *what is to be done when the justice of a war is debatable,* when both parties seem to have convincing reasons on their side?

IN REPLY let us make the following propositions, beginning with the arguments which concern princes:

1. FIRST, *if one has a legitimate possession, even though some particular doubt remains over his title, another prince may not seek to take it away by force of arms.* For example, if the king of France is in legitimate possession of Burgundy, even though his right to it may be doubtful it does not seem that our Emperor may seize Burgundy by force; on the other hand, the king of France ought not to try to seize it. This is proved by the legal maxim that in cases of doubt possession is nine parts of the law. It is not lawful to rob a man of his property simply on the grounds that one disputes his right to possess it. If the case were to be tried before a duly constituted judge, he would never dispossess the man of his property while the case remained unresolved; therefore, since the prince who seeks justice is himself the judge in the case, he cannot lawfully plunder the possessor as long as some doubt about the title remains. Another argument is that, if it is never lawful to dispossess the legal owner in an unresolved civil or private case, then it cannot be lawful in the disputes of princes, since the laws are the prince's laws. If according to human laws it is not permissible to dispossess a legitimate owner in an unresolved case, then such action may justly be objected to in the case of princes. Besides, if this principle were not observed, both sides in a war would be just and the war could never be settled.

2. SECOND, *if a city or province of doubtful title has no legitimate owner* (for instance, if it is left unclaimed by the death of the legitimate owner, and it cannot be established whether the heir is the king of Spain or the king of France), *in law it is apparent that if one of the two claimants is willing to negotiate a division of the territory or compensation for part of it, then the other prince must accept the negotiation, even when he is stronger and has the power to take the whole territory by force of arms.* He would not in this case have just cause for war, as is proved by the fact that the other prince could not be said to be doing him any unjust harm by asking for an equal share in a case where he has an equal claim. In private cases, even disputed ones, it is not lawful for one of the parties to preempt the whole of the disputed property; therefore it cannot be lawful in the disputes of princes either. Finally, in this case too, the war would be just on both sides; the just judge would not give the whole territory to one or the other side, but would divide it between them.

3. THIRD, even when a prince enjoys peaceful possession, *if he is in doubt about his rightful title he must carefully examine the case and listen peacefully to the reasons of the other side, to see if a clear decision can be reached in favor of himself or the other party.* The proof of this proposition is that if, despite his doubts, he neglected to find out the truth, he would no longer possess the territory in good faith. In matrimonial cases, even a man who has legitimate conjugal rights must unquestionably take steps to verify the matter if he begins to suspect that his wife is married to another man; therefore the same reason must hold true of other cases. Princes are the only judges in their own affairs, since they have no superiors; but it is clear that if anyone raises an objection to another's just title to his property, the judge is bound to examine the case, and therefore princes are similarly bound to examine their own title in cases of doubt.

4. FOURTH, *once the case has been examined as long as is reasonable, if the doubt remains unresolved, the legitimate owner is not required to relinquish his territory, but may henceforth own it lawfully.* This is obvious, first of all because a judge is not required in these circumstances to dispossess him of his property, so he himself cannot be required to relinquish it, either wholly or in part. In the matrimonial case above, for example, the husband is not required to give up his conjugal rights if the doubt remains unresolved after due examination, as stated in the decretals *Inquisitioni tuae respondentes* (X.5.39.44) and *Dominus* (X.4.21.2). The same must therefore hold in other cases. Pope Hadrian VI expressly states in his *Quodlibets* 2 that one may lawfully retain possession when in doubt.

So much, then, for the propositions concerning princes in an unresolved dispute. But what of their subjects, when in doubt about the justice of war? Hadrian himself in the same passage (*Quodlibets* 2 ad 1) says that a subject who is in doubt about the justice of war may not lawfully go to war at the command of his superior. He proves this assertion by arguing that the subject who does go to war in these circumstances is not acting in good faith, and therefore runs the danger of incurring mortal sin. The same opinion is formulated by Silvestro Mazzolini da Priero in his *Summa Syluestrina, s.v.* bellum 1 §9.

BUT AGAINST THIS let us make the following proposition:

5. FIFTH, *in the first place, there is no doubt that in defensive wars subjects are not merely permitted to follow their prince into battle even where the justice of the case is in doubt, but are indeed bound to do so; and in the second place, that the same is true also of offensive wars.* The first proof of this is that, as has been said already, a prince neither can nor ought always to explain the reasons for war to his subjects; if subjects were unable to fight until they understood the justice of the war, the safety of the commonwealth would be gravely endangered. Second, in cases of doubt the safer course should be followed; but if subjects fail to obey their prince in war from scruples of doubt, they run the risk of betraying the commonwealth into the hands of the enemy, which is much worse than fighting the enemy, doubts notwithstanding; therefore they had better fight. Another clear proof is that an officer of the law must carry out the sentence of a judge even if he doubts" its justice; to argue the contrary would be extremely dangerous. Augustine says bluntly in his *Contra Faustum* 22.75: "If ordered to do so, a just man may righteously go to war, even under a sacrilegious king, so long as he is either certain the order is not against God's precept, or uncertain whether it is" (*Decretum* C.23.1.4). There you have it: Augustine said plainly that when it is uncertain (that is, unresolved) whether the war is against God's precept, the subject may lawfully fight. Even Hadrian could not get round this quotation from Augustine; twist and turn as he may, my conclusion is undoubtedly Augustine's. It is no reply to say that such a man is required to rid himself of his doubts and persuade himself in conscience of the justice of the war, since it is clear, morally speaking, that he cannot do so, as in other cases of doubt.

Hadrian's mistake seems to lie in his assumption that, if I am in doubt whether the prince's war is just or whether the cause of a particular war is just, it follows immediately that I must doubt whether or not I may lawfully fight. I admit that it is never lawful to act against a conscientious doubt, so that if I am in doubt whether I should act or not it is a sin to act. But it is incorrect to deduce that if I am in doubt as to whether the cause of war is just, I must therefore doubt whether I may lawfully make war, or fight in that war. In fact, we must deduce just the opposite: if I am in doubt about the justice of war, it follows that it is lawful for me to go to war at the command of my prince. In the same way, if an officer of the law is in doubt whether the judge's sentence is just, it is quite invalid to conclude that he must doubt whether he may lawfully carry out that sentence; on the contrary, indeed, he knows very well that he is required to carry out the sentence of his superior. It is equally invalid to argue that if I doubt whether a woman is my wife, I am not bound to perform my duty as a husband.

[Question 2, Article 4: War cannot be just on both sides]

THE FOURTH DOUBT is this: *whether war can be just on both sides.*

IN REPLY let us make the following propositions:

1. FIRST, except in ignorance it is clear *that this cannot happen.* If it is agreed that both parties have right and justice on their side, they cannot lawfully fight each other, either offensively or defensively.

2. SECOND, where there is provable ignorance either of fact or of law, *the war may be just in itself for the side which has true justice on its side, and also just for the other side, because they wage war in good faith and are hence excused from sin.* Invincible error is a valid excuse in every case. This is often the position of subjects: even if the prince who wages war knows that his cause is unjust, his subjects may nevertheless obey him in good faith, as explained in the previous article. In such situations, the subjects on both sides are justified in fighting, as is well known.

[Question 2, Article 5: If a belligerent discovers that his cause is unjust, must he make restitution?]

THE FIFTH DOUBT follows from the preceding one: *if a prince or a subject who has started to fight an unjust war in ignorance subsequently realizes the injustice of his cause, is he required to make restitution?*

IN REPLY let us make the following proposition:

1. FIRST, if he was in the first place led to believe in the justice of his cause by probable reasons, *once he realizes its injustice he must restore anything he has taken which he has not already spent;* that is, everything he has gained as net profit, but not his expenses. It is a rule of law that a man who is not guilty must not suffer loss. Thus a man who in good faith

attends a sumptuous dinner in a thief's house, where of course stolen goods are consumed, is not required to make restitution (except perhaps of the amount he would have spent at home on his everyday meal).

Again, if a man was unsure of the justice of the war, but obeyed the command of his prince, Silvestro Mazzolini da Priero opines that he would have to make a complete restitution, because he fought in bad faith (*Summa Syluestrina, s.v.* bellum 1 §9). Against this, then, let us make a second proposition:

2. SECOND, the man in this position *is no more required to repay what he has spent than the previous one,* since, as I have already said, such a man in fact fights lawfully and in good faith. But if he was truly in doubt as to whether he could lawfully go to war, Silvestro Mazzolini da Priero's point might then be true, on the grounds that the man acted against his conscience.

To CONCLUDE, the salient point to be considered is that war in itself is just; it is unjust and unlawful only in its accidents. But it is clear that one may have a right to reclaim a city or province, and yet find that right nullified by the danger of provoking greater conflict. As I have said, wars should only be waged for the common good (1.3 §12); if the recovery of one city is bound to involve the commonwealth in greater damage, for instance the devastation of several cities, heavy casualties, or rivalry between princes and the occasion of further wars, there can be no doubt that the prince should cede his right and abstain from war.

Question 3: What may be done in a just war

ABOUT THE OTHER QUESTION there also arise a number of doubts; I mean the fourth article (1.4), which was "what, and how much, may be done in the just war?" The first doubt—and a strong one too—is this:

Question 3, Article 1: Whether one may kill innocent people in a just war

PROCEEDING TO THE FIRST, it seems that one may:

1. We read in Josh. 6:21 that the children of Israel killed the children in Jericho, and Saul slew the children and young women of Amalek

(1 Sam. 15:3, 8), both on the authority and command of the Lord. "Whatsoever things were written aforetime were written for our learning" (Rom. 15:4); therefore it must still be true today that it is lawful to kill the innocent if the war is just.

BUT ON THE OTHER HAND let us make the following propositions:

1. FIRST, *it is never lawful in itself intentionally to kill innocent persons.* This is proved, in the first place, by Exod. 23:7, where it says "the innocent and righteous slay thou not." Second, the foundation of the just war is the injury inflicted upon one by the enemy, as shown above (1.3 §13); but an innocent person has done you no harm. *Ergo,* etc. Third, within the commonwealth it is not permissible to punish the innocent for the crimes of the evil, and therefore it is not permissible to kill innocent members of the enemy population for the injury done by the wicked among them. Fourth, the war would otherwise become just on both sides, since it is clear that the innocent would also have the right to defend themselves. All this is confirmed by Deut. 20:10–20, where the children of Israel are commanded, when they have captured a city, to smite every male thereof with the edge of the sword, but to spare the women and the little ones.

It follows that even in wars against the Turks we may not kill children, who are obviously innocent, nor women, who are to be presumed innocent at least as far as the war is concerned (unless, that is, it can be proved of a particular woman that she was implicated in guilt). It follows also that one may not lawfully kill travelers or visitors who happen to be in the enemy's territory, who are presumed innocent.[16] And the same is true of clergy and monks, unless there is evidence to the contrary or they are found actually fighting in the war. I think there can be no doubt about this.

2. SECOND, *it is occasionally lawful to kill the innocent not by mistake, but with full knowledge of what one is doing, if this is an accidental effect:* for example, during the justified storming of a fortress or city, where one knows there are many innocent people, but where it is impossible to fire artillery and other projectiles or set fire to buildings without crushing or burning the innocent along with the combatants. This is proven, since it would otherwise be impossible to wage war against the guilty, thereby preventing the just side from fighting. Nevertheless, we must remember the point made a moment ago (2.5, conclusion; and cf. *On*

Civil Power 1.10): that care must be taken to ensure that the evil effects of the war do not outweigh the possible benefits sought by waging it. If the storming of a fortress or town garrisoned by the enemy but full of innocent inhabitants is not of great importance for eventual victory in the war, it does not seem to me permissible to kill a large number of innocent people by indiscriminate bombardment in order to defeat a small number of enemy combatants. Finally, it is never lawful to kill innocent people, even accidentally and unintentionally, except when it advances a just war which cannot be won in any other way. In the words of the parable: "Let the tares grow until the harvest, lest while ye gather up the tares, ye root up also the wheat with them" (Matt. 13:24–30).

Against this, one may ask whether it is lawful to kill people who are innocent, but may yet pose a threat in the future. For example, the sons of Saracens are harmless, but it is reasonable to fear that when they reach manhood they will fight against Christendom. And according to the previous argument adult enemy civilians are also presumed innocent, but they too could later take up arms and fight. The question is whether it is lawful to kill such people; and the answer would seem to be yes, since one is permitted to kill other innocent people too, as an accidental effect. When, in Deut. 20:10–20, the children of Israel are commanded, when they have captured a city, to smite every adult male thereof with the edge of the sword, it is not to be supposed that every one of them is a combatant.

In reply, however, I say this: it is perhaps possible to make a defense of this kind for killing innocent people in such cases, but I nevertheless believe that it is utterly wrong. It is never right to commit evil, even to avoid greater evils. It is quite unacceptable that a person should be killed for a sin he has yet to commit. In the first place, there are many other measures for preventing future harm from such people, such as captivity, exile, etc. It is not lawful to execute one of our fellow members of the commonwealth for future sins, and therefore it cannot be lawful with foreign subjects either; I have no doubts on this score. It follows that, either after the battle has been won or even in the midst of hostilities, if a man's innocence is proved and the soldiers are able to set him free, they must do so. As for the authorities adduced to prove the contrary, we may reply that the passages in question refer to a special command of God, who was angry with the peoples in question and wished to destroy them utterly, just as he rained fire on Sodom and Gomorrah which devoured both guilty and innocent together. But he is the Lord of all, and did not intend this to be a general rule. The same reply holds true for the passage from Deut. 20: though what is said there is intended as a general law of war for all time, what the Lord seems to have meant was that in reality all the adult men in an enemy city are to be thought of as enemies, since the innocent cannot be distinguished from the guilty, and therefore they may all be killed.

[Question 3, Article 2: Whether one may plunder innocent people in a just war]

ANOTHER VALID DOUBT is *whether one may nevertheless plunder the innocent in the just war.*

IN ANSWER TO THIS let us make the following propositions:

1. FIRST, it is certain *that we may plunder them of the goods and property which have been used against us by the enemy.* This is clear, because otherwise we cannot gain victory against them. Indeed, we may take the money of the innocent, or burn and ravage their crops or kill their livestock; all these things are necessary to weaken the enemies' resources. There can be no argument about this.

From this there flows the corollary that if the state of war is permanent, it is lawful to plunder the enemy indiscriminately, both innocent and guilty, since the enemy rely upon the resources of its people to sustain an unjust war, and their strength is therefore weakened if their subjects are plundered.

2. SECOND, if the war can be satisfactorily waged without plundering farmers or other noncombatants, *it is not lawful to plunder them.* This is the opinion of Silvestro Mazzolini da Priero in his *Summa Syluestrina, s.v.* bellum 1 §10: since war is justified on the grounds of injury received, it cannot be lawful in the law of war to kill or plunder the innocent if the injury can be compensated in any other way. Indeed, Mazzolini adds that even if there is just cause to plunder the innocent, once the war is over the victor is required to restore whatever is left of the property he

has taken from them. But I do not think this latter condition is necessary, since, as I shall show below, if they have acted in accordance with the laws of war, all gains are at the disposal of those who have waged the just war. Hence it is my opinion that the victors are not required to restore those things which they have rightfully captured. Nevertheless, Mazzolini's opinion is merciful, and not unreasonable. More, it is quite unlawful to plunder travelers or visitors unless their guilt is proven, since they are not of the enemy but are presumed to be innocent.

3. THIRD, if the enemy refuse to restore the property they have unjustly seized, and the injured party is unable to recover his property in any other way, then *he may seek redress in any way he chooses, from the innocent or the guilty*. For example, if French bandits plunder Spanish territory and the king of France refuses to compel them to make restitution, though able to do so, then the Spaniards may, with their prince's permission, plunder French merchants or farmers, however innocent they may be; though the French commonwealth or king may not initially have been to blame, by their refusal to punish the injustice done by their own subjects they put themselves in the wrong, as Augustine says (*Quaest. in Heptateuch.* 6.10), and the injured prince can therefore seek satisfaction from any or all the members of the offending commonwealth. Hence the letters-of-marque or *reprisals* granted by princes in these cases are not in themselves altogether unjust;[17] because of the negligence and injustice of another prince, the prince gives to one of his subjects the right to recover his property even from innocent victims. Such grants are nevertheless dangerous, as they give an excuse for mere piracy.

[Question 3, Article 3: Whether one may enslave the innocent in a just war]

A THIRD DOUBT, given that one may not lawfully kill children and innocent noncombatants, is *whether one may nevertheless enslave them*.

IN ANSWER TO THIS let us make the following proposition:

1. THAT *one may lawfully enslave the innocent under just the same conditions as one may plunder them*. Freedom and slavery are counted as goods of fortune; therefore, when the war is such that it is lawful to

plunder all the enemy population indiscriminately and seize all their goods, it must also be lawful to enslave them all, guilty and innocent alike. Hence, since our war against the pagans is of this kind, being permanent because they can never sufficiently pay for the injuries and losses inflicted, it is not to be doubted that we may lawfully enslave the women and children of the Saracens. But since it seems to be accepted in the law of nations that Christians cannot enslave one another, it is not lawful to enslave fellow-Christians, at any rate during the course of the war. If necessary, when the war is over one may take prisoners, even innocent women and children, but not to enslave them, only to hold them to ransom; and this must not be allowed to go beyond the limits which the necessities of warfare demand, and the legitimate customs of war permit.

[Question 3, Article 4: Whether one may execute hostages]

A FOURTH DOUBT is *whether one may execute enemy hostages, either received during a truce or taken in war, if the enemy break their promises?*

IN ANSWER TO THIS let us make the following single proposition:

1. THAT *if the hostages would otherwise be combatants,* for instance if they have already borne arms against us, *they may be executed;* but *if they are noncombatants,* it is clear from what has been said that *they may not.* There is no arguing against this.

[Question 3, Article 5: Whether one may execute all the enemy combatants]

THE FIFTH DOUBT is *whether one may execute all the enemy combatants in a just war?*

IN ANSWERING THIS let us remember the following points: that war is waged, in the first place, for our own defense and the defense of our property; then, for the recovery of property that has been seized; third, in revenge for an injury received; and lastly, to establish peace and security. With these premises in mind, let us make the following proposition:

1. In the actual conflict of battle, or during the storming or defense of a city, in short so long as matters hang dangerously in the balance, *it is lawful to kill indiscriminately all those who fight against us.* It is clear that the combatants cannot very well wage war without eliminating their opponents. But the whole point of this doubt is, rather, *whether we may lawfully kill all the enemy combatants after victory has been gained,* when there is no longer any danger from them. And the answer to this would seem to be that we may, according to the passage in Deuteronomy quoted above, where the Lord included amongst his precepts the particular command to put to death all the inhabitants of a captured city, with these words:

> When thou comest nigh unto a city to fight against it, then proclaim peace unto it. And if it make thee answer of peace, and open unto thee, then it shall be that all the people that is found therein shall be tributaries unto thee, and they shall serve thee. And if it will make no peace with thee, but will make war against thee, then thou shalt besiege it; and when the Lord thy God hath delivered it into thine hands, thou shalt smite every male thereof with the edge of the sword, but the women and the little ones. (Deut. 20:10–14)

BUT ON THE OTHER HAND let us make the following further propositions:

2. *After victory has been gained and the matter is beyond danger, we may lawfully kill all the enemy combatants.* The proof of this is that war is not only ordained for the recovery of lost possessions, but also for the avenging of injury, and therefore one may lawfully execute those responsible for the injury inflicted. Furthermore, we have the same right against our fellow members of the commonwealth when they commit crimes, and therefore we must have this right against foreigners, since (as discussed above) by the laws of war the prince has the same authority over the enemy as a judge or legitimate prince. And last, although there may be no present danger from the enemy, there can be no future guarantee of our security from their attack.

3. However, *it is not always lawful to execute all the combatants for the sole purpose of avenging injury.* The proof of this is that, when dealing with our fellow members of the commonwealth, if the crime is the re-

sponsibility of an entire city or province, it is not lawful to kill all the delinquents; in a popular rebellion, it would not be permissible to execute and destroy the entire populace. It was for just such an act that Theodosius was excommunicated by Ambrose.[18] Such action would be against the public good, which is the purpose of war and peace. And if this is so, then it cannot be lawful to kill all enemy combatants either. We must take account of the scale of the injury inflicted by the enemy, of our losses, and of their other crimes, and base the scale of our revenge on this calculation, without cruelty or inhumanity. In this connection, Cicero remarks that we should punish wrongdoers only so far as justice and humanity permit (*De officiis* II.5.18). Sallust also says that "our ancestors, the most God-fearing and righteous of men, never took anything from the vanquished except the license to do harm" (*Coniuratio Catilinae* 12.3–4).

4. *It is sometimes lawful and expedient to kill all the enemy combatants.* The proof runs as follows: war is waged to produce peace, but sometimes security cannot be obtained without the wholesale destruction of the enemy. This is particularly the case in wars against the infidel, from whom peace can never be hoped for on any terms; therefore the only remedy is to eliminate all of them who are capable of bearing arms against us, given that they are already guilty. This is how the precept given in Deut. 20 should be understood. In other cases, however, in wars against fellow-Christians I do not believe that it is permissible. The necessary result would be to provoke further offenses and wars between princes (Matt. 18:7): therefore, if the victor were always to put to death all his adversaries, great harm would result for humankind. It is better that the punishment be fitted to the crime, and the wicked man beaten according to his fault, by a certain number of stripes (Deut. 25:2–3). And in this connection it must be taken into consideration that subjects neither must nor ought to examine the causes of war, but may follow their prince into war, content with the authority of their prince and public council; so that in general, even though the war may be unjust on one side or the other, the soldiers on each side who come to fight in battle or to defend a city are all equally innocent. Once they are defeated and pose no further threat, it is my opinion that not so much as a single one of them should be killed, so long as the presumption is that they fought in good faith.

[Question 3, Article 6: Whether one may execute those
who have surrendered or been taken prisoner]

THE SIXTH DOUBT is *whether one may execute those who have surrendered
or been taken prisoner, supposing that they too were enemy combatants?*

I REPLY that, in itself, there is no reason why prisoners taken in a just
war or those who have surrendered, if they were combatants, should
not be killed, so long as common equity is observed. But as many practices in war are based on the law of nations, it appears to be established
by custom that prisoners taken after a victory, when the danger is past,
should not be killed unless they turn out to be deserters and fugitives.
This law of nations should be respected, as it is by all good men. As for
those who surrender, however, I have neither read nor heard of such a
custom of leniency.

[Question 3, Article 7: Whether all the booty taken
in war belongs to the captors]

THE SEVENTH DOUBT is *whether all the booty taken in war belongs to those
who capture it?*

IN ANSWER TO THIS let us make the following proposition:
   1. There is no doubt that *all booty taken in a just war up to a value sufficient to recompense the property unjustly seized by the enemy, and also including reparation of the costs of the war, become the property of the captors.
No proof of this conclusion is needed, since this is the very purpose of war.*
   But setting aside considerations of restitution and reparation and insisting solely on the laws of war, we must make a distinction between
booty which consists of movable goods such as money, clothes, or gold,
and real or immovable property such as land, towns, and forts. In this
connection let us make the following additional proposition:
   2. At least in the law of nations (*ius gentium*) all movable goods become the property of the captors, even if their value exceeds that of
compensation of losses. This is clear from the words of the laws *Si quid
bello* and *Hostes* (*Digest* XLIX.15.28 and 24), from the canon *Ius gentium* (*Decretum* D.1.9), and more expressly still from the law *Item ea*

quae ab hostibus (*Institutions* II.1.17), where it is stated that "by the law of nations (*ius gentium*) all booty taken from the enemy immediately becomes ours, to the extent that even free men may be taken into slavery by us." Ambrose tells us in his *De Abraham* I.3 that when Abraham slew the four kings the booty belonged to him as victor, even though he refused to accept it (Gen. 14:14–24); this passage is cited in *Decretum* C.23.5.25, and is supported by the authority of the Lord's words in Deut. 20:14, where it is said of the capture of a city that "all that is in the city, even all the spoil thereof, shalt thou take unto thyself; and thou shalt eat the spoil of thine enemies, which the Lord thy God hath given thee."

This is the opinion held by Hadrian in his *Quaestiones* on the fourth book of Lombard's *Sentences,* in the question devoted to restitution, in particular in the just war; and by Silvestro Mazzolini da Priero, in his *Summa Syluestrina, s.v.* bellum 1 §1 and §10, where he says that "when the cause is just, one is not required to restore property captured as booty, as stated in the canon *Si de rebus* (*Decretum* C.23.7.2); whence we infer that goods taken in a just war are not to be counted towards the satisfaction of the principal injury, as Guido de Baysio holds in his *Rosarium* on the canon *Dominus Deus noster iubet* (C.23.2.2)." The same view is held by Bartolus of Sassoferrato on the law *Si quid in bello* mentioned above (in *Digest* XLIX.15.28). And this is to be understood as true, even if the enemy is prepared to make satisfaction for the losses and injury caused. Nevertheless, Silvestro Mazzolini da Priero sets a limit to this right, and correctly so, proposing that it should extend only so far as is consonant with an equitable satisfaction of the damage and injury sustained. We are not to suppose that if the French lay waste a single village or some paltry town in Spain, the Spaniards thereby have the right to plunder the whole of France, even if they are able to do so. They must do so only in proportion to the extent of their own losses.

But this conclusion leads to a further doubt: whether it is lawful to allow our soldiers to sack a city? Let us therefore make a further proposition:

3. THIRD, *this is not of itself unlawful if it is necessary to the conduct of the war,* whether to strike terror into the enemy or to inflame the passions of the soldiers. So says Silvestro Mazzolini da Priero, *Summa Syluestrina, s.v.* bellum 1 §11). It is likewise permissible to set fire to a city when there are reasonable grounds for doing so. But this sort of

argument licenses the barbarians among the soldiery to commit every kind of inhuman savagery and cruelty, murdering and torturing the innocent, deflowering young girls, raping women, and pillaging churches. In these circumstances, it is undoubtedly unjust to destroy a Christian city except in the most pressing necessity and with the gravest of causes; but if necessity decrees, it is not unlawful, even if the probability is that the soldiery will commit crimes of this kind. Their officers, however, have a duty to give orders against it.

4. FOURTH, notwithstanding all this, *soldiers may not plunder or burn without the authority of their prince or commander*. The soldiers are not the judges, but simply the executors; if they behave otherwise, they must make restitution.

But the question of immovable property is more difficult. In this connection, let us state these further propositions:

5. FIFTH, there is no doubt that *it is lawful to occupy and keep land and forts*, to the extent necessary for compensation of losses. There is certainly no reason in divine or natural law why this dispensation should be more applicable to movable goods than to immovables.

6. SIXTH, to protect life and safety where there is danger from the enemy, *it is lawful to occupy and hold any enemy fort or city which is necessary for our defense*.

7. SEVENTH, for an injury received *it is also lawful to deprive the enemy of part of his land in the name of punishment*, that is, in revenge and according to the scale of the injury. By this token, it is sometimes lawful to occupy a fort or town, but the governing factor in this case must be moderation, not armed might. If necessity and the requirements of war demand that the greater part of enemy territory or a large number of cities be occupied in this way, they ought to be returned once the war is over and peace has been made, only keeping so much as may be considered fair in equity and humanity for the reparation of losses and expenses and the punishment of injustice. Punishment should fit the crime; it would be intolerable if we were allowed to occupy the whole kingdom of France because they had plundered a few cattle or burnt a single village. But the fact that we may occupy a part of enemy territory or an enemy city on these grounds is quite clear from the passage already cited from Deut. 20 where the Lord gives permission to occupy a city

which has refused to surrender peacefully in war. Likewise, we are allowed to punish our own domestic malefactors by depriving them of a fortress or house, according to their crime, and therefore we must have the same right against our external enemies. Similarly, a legitimate judge of a higher court may fine the perpetrator of a crime by confiscating a city or fort belonging to him; so a prince who has been offended may do the same, since the law of war effectively makes him judge.

It was in this way and on these grounds that the Roman Empire was built up and extended, using the law of war as their title to occupy the cities and lands of enemies who had done them injury; and yet the justice and legitimacy of the Roman Empire is defended by Augustine, Jerome, Ambrose, Aquinas, and other holy doctors. Indeed, our Lord and Savior Jesus Christ seems to have signaled his approval of the empire in those words of His, "Render therefore unto Caesar the things which are Caesar's" (Matt. 22:21); and Paul too, when he appealed to Caesar's judgment seat (Acts 25:10–11), and when he admonished his brothers to be subject unto the higher powers and to pay tribute to their princes (Rom. 13:1–6), since at that time all princes had their authority under the Roman Empire.[19]

[Question 3, Article 8: Whether one may impose tribute
on a defeated enemy]

THE EIGHTH DOUBT is *whether one may impose tribute on a defeated enemy?*

I REPLY that *it is certainly lawful to do so,* not only for the compensation of losses, but also as punishment and revenge. I have already said enough above to prove this point, and the passage cited from Deut. 20 leaves no room for doubt.

[Question 3, Article 9: Whether one may depose the
enemy's princes and set up new ones]

THE NINTH DOUBT is *whether we may depose the enemy's princes and set up new ones in their place, or take over the government ourselves?*

IN ANSWER TO THIS let us make the following propositions:

1. *It is not lawful to do this in every case, or for any cause of just war.* This is clear from what has been said: punishment should not exceed the crime. On the contrary, punishments should be diminished in favor of mercy. This is a rule not only of human law, but also of natural and divine law.[20] Therefore, although the harm done by the enemy may be a sufficient cause of war, it will not always be sufficient to justify the extermination of the enemy's kingdom and deposition of its legitimate native princes; this would be altogether too savage and inhuman.

2. However, it cannot be denied that there may sometimes be legitimate reasons for supplanting princes, or for taking over the government. This may be because of the number or atrocity of the injuries and harm done by the enemy, and especially when security and peace cannot otherwise be ensured, when failure to do so would cause a dangerous threat to the commonwealth. This is clear enough; if it is lawful to occupy a city for this reason, as explained above, then it must be lawful to remove its princes.

But it is to be noted, with reference to articles 6, 7, 8, and 9, that sometimes, and indeed often, not only the princes themselves but also their subjects, though in fact they have no just cause, nevertheless wage war in good faith—and in such good faith, I emphasize, that they are to be excused from any guilt. Take, for example, the case of a war waged, after careful examination, on the advice of judgment of the wisest men: in this event, no person who is not directly responsible should be punished, and though the victor may lawfully recover the property which was seized from him, and perhaps even his war expenses, he may not kill anyone after victory has been won, nor exact just retribution, nor demand satisfaction from the temporal property of the vanquished, since all these things can only be done in the name of punishment; manifestly, punishment should not fall upon the innocent.

[Conclusion: Three rules of war]

FROM ALL THIS we may deduce a few rules and canons of warfare:

1. FIRST CANON: since princes have the authority to wage war, *they should strive above all to avoid all provocations and causes of war.* If it be

possible, the prince should seek as much as lieth in him to live peaceably with all men, according to Paul's words in Rom. 12:18. He should remember that other men are his neighbors, whom we are all enjoined to love as ourselves (Matt. 22:39); and that we all have a single Lord, before whose tribunal we must each render account for our actions on the day of judgment. It is a mark of utter monstrousness to seek out and rejoice in causes which lead to nothing but death and persecution of our fellowmen, whom God created, and for whom Christ suffered death. The prince should only accede to the necessity of war when he is dragged reluctantly but inevitably into it.

2. SECOND CANON: once war has been declared for just causes, the prince should press his campaign not for the destruction of his opponents, but *for the pursuit of the justice for which he fights and the defense of his homeland,* so that by fighting he may eventually establish peace and security.

3. THIRD CANON: once the war has been fought and victory won, he must use his victory with moderation and Christian humility. The victor must think of himself as a judge sitting in judgment between two commonwealths, one the injured party and the other the offender; he must not pass sentence as the prosecutor, but as a judge. He must give satisfaction to the injured, but as far as possible without causing the utter ruination of the guilty commonwealth. Let him remember above all that for the most part, and especially in wars between Christian commonwealths, it is the princes themselves who are completely to blame; for subjects usually fight in good faith for their princes.

And so I end this whole disputation about the Indians, which I have undertaken for the glory of God and the utility of my fellow-men.

Here ends the second relection On the Indies *of the very reverend Father and most erudite Master Friar Francisco de Vitoria, which he delivered at Salamanca in the year of Our Lord 1539, on the 19th day of June, to the glory of almighty God and the Blessed Virgin Mary His mother, and for the teaching of our fellow-men.*

Friar Juan de Heredia

BARTOLOMÉ DE LAS CASAS

During the forty years from his birth in Seville in 1474 up to 1514, Bartolomé de Las Casas was swept along by events occasioned by the conquest of the New World. At age eighteen he witnessed Columbus' jubilant passage through the streets of Seville at the end of his first voyage. Las Casas' father sailed on Columbus' second voyage and returned with a Taino Indian servant for his son. In 1502 Las Casas himself made the crossing, accompanying his father in a group of some 2,500 colonists led by Nicolás de Ovando to the island of Hispaniola. His help in quashing a native revolt there secured him an *encomienda* (land and the labor of its native population) as a reward; in 1513, after participating in the conquest of Cuba, he received another.[1] Las Casas treated his workers humanely, and he was unmoved by four Dominicans who came to Hispaniola in 1510 and preached against the exploitation of the natives. The *encomendero* Las Casas became a priest in 1512 or 1513, perhaps the first to be ordained in the New World. Nevertheless, he began to be disturbed by Spanish abuses. At the massacre of natives at Caonao, Cuba, he saw a stream of Indian blood running "as if many cows had been killed."[2] In 1514, while preparing his sermon for Pentecost, he came across the scriptural passage "Tainted his gifts who offers in sacrifice ill-gotten goods!"[3] Obsessed with these words, Las Casas agonized over his status as an *encomendero*. Were his own goods ill-gotten, his gifts tainted? He decided, at length, that they were.

With this conviction, in 1514 Las Casas freed his Indians, returned to Spain, and resolved to take up the fight against Spanish oppression of the native peoples. Appointed Protector of the Indians by the archbishop of Toledo, Cardinal Jiménez de Cisneros, in 1516, Las Casas devised a scheme to replace the *encomienda* system.[4] The Indians were to have their own villages, work under the supervision of carefully selected Spaniards, and share in the profits from their work. To implement these ideas, Las Casas finagled a land grant on the Venezuelan coast. Everything conspired against him, however. Spanish slavers preyed on the region's natives; the natives counterattacked, killing monks and torching monasteries; and his colonists made off to Florida with Ponce de León. Deeply shaken, Las Casas retired to a Dominican monastery on Hispaniola and in 1523 became a Dominican monk. For the next eleven years he studied theology and law and initiated his *Historia de las Indias;* in his own words, "he appeared to sleep."[5]

The final period of Las Casas' life commenced in 1534 when his ship, becalmed almost two months in transit from Hispaniola to Peru, was forced to land in Nicaragua. The Spanish governor of Nicaragua was planning to launch an expedition of conquest and slavery, but Las Casas attacked the plan from the pulpit and managed to persuade the empress of Spain to postpone the expedition for two years. In 1537, when Pope Paul III's bull *Sublimis Deus* proclaimed the rationality of the Indians and their capacity to receive the faith, Las Casas made it the theoretical basis of his missionary work. He wrote *De unico vocationis modo* (The Only Method of Attracting All People to the True Faith), which urged peaceful persuasion rather than armed conquest as a method of conversion. Returning to Spain in 1540, Las Casas drafted the *Brevísima relación de la destrucción de las Indias* (Very Brief Account of the Destruction of the Indies) to publicize the abuses of the conquest.[6] He also pushed hard for legislative reforms, obtained when Carlos (Charles) V's New Laws of 1542 prohibited further Indian slavery and ordered the dismantling of the *encomienda* system. To help enforce these laws, Las Casas accepted the bishopric of Chiapas, Mexico, in 1544. In his first pastoral letter he announced that slaveholders and *encomenderos* who had not made restitution for their gains would be denied absolution. The ensuing revolt of the landowners was practically universal; Las Casas was shot at, threatened, ridiculed, defied, and reviled. The

New Laws were deemed unenforceable, and in 1545 the Emperor repealed the law for phasing out *encomiendas*. Returning to Spain in 1547, Las Casas was soon involved in a running dispute with Juan Ginés de Sepúlveda, a Renaissance humanist, imperial chronicler, and apologist for the conquest. The argument came to a head when Carlos V, distressed by Las Casas' unrelenting criticism, halted all further expeditions of conquest in the New World and convened a panel of jurists and theologians at Valladolid in 1550 to hear both men present their views. Who won the debate is unclear, although there is some evidence that Las Casas persuaded most of the panel's theologians and Sepúlveda most of the jurists.[7] During the final years of his life, Las Casas hounded the Spanish court, crying out for justice and sometimes even obtaining it. He died in Madrid in 1566.

Las Casas' part in the debate at Valladolid was published as *En defensa de los indios*, a selection from which is included below. Sepúlveda had argued that war against the peoples of the New World is just for four reasons: (1) the natives are barbarians; (2) to punish them for crimes against natural law; (3) to prevent them from oppressing and killing innocent people; and (4) to prepare the way for preaching the faith. Since both human sacrifice and cannibalism were known practices in some parts of the New World, the third argument was probably Sepúlveda's strongest; Las Casas responds to it in the following passages. Bracketed passages in the text are the translator's.

In Defense of the Indians

On Human Sacrifice and Cannibalism

Chapter Twenty-Eight *[bis]*

Therefore when unbelievers are discovered to be committing a crime of this kind (that is, killing infants for sacrifice or cannibalism), they are not always to be attacked by war, although it may be the business of the Church to try to prevent it. But there must be lengthy consideration beforehand, so that in trying to prevent the death of a few innocent persons we should not move against an immense multitude of persons, including the innocent, and destroy whole kingdoms, and implant a hatred for the Christian religion in their souls, so that they will never want to hear the name or teaching of Christ for all eternity. All this is surely contrary to the purpose intended by God and our mother the Church. Instead, war must be avoided and that evil tolerated at least for a while—indeed, in some cases permanently—as will be explained. One must, rather, think out some prudent and Christian argument by which they will cleanse everything by the word of God, or they will refrain from

From Bartolomé de Las Casas, *In Defense of the Indians*, translated, edited, and annotated by Stafford Poole, C.M. (DeKalb: Northern Illinois University Press, 1974). Material used courtesy of Northern Illinois University Press.

that inhumanity because of warnings, entreaties, or exhortations. For that practice is not that common among all the Indian peoples. And if it is, no great number of persons are killed. Otherwise all would have been totally destroyed before this. And yet we find that all the regions are densely populated.

Now the fact that one must refrain from war, and even tolerate the death of a few innocent persons, is proved by arguments and many authorities.

The first argument is this: According to the rule of right reason when we are confronted by two choices that are evil both as to moral guilt and punishment and we cannot avoid both of them, we ought to choose the lesser evil. For in comparison with the greater evil, the choice of the lesser evil has the quality of a good. This is what the Philosopher teaches.[1] Now the death of a small number of innocent persons is a lesser evil than the eternal damnation of countless numbers of persons killed in the fury of war.

Again, the death of the innocent is better or less evil than the complete destruction of entire kingdoms, cities, and strongholds. For not all of them eat the flesh of the innocent but only the rulers or priests, who do the sacrificing, whereas war brings the destruction of countless innocent persons who do not deserve any such thing. Therefore if those evils cannot be removed in any other way than by waging war, one must refrain from it and evils of this kind must be tolerated.

Furthermore, it is incomparably less disastrous that a few innocent persons die than that Christ's holy name be blasphemed by unbelievers and that the Christian religion be brought into ill repute and be hated by those peoples and by others to whom word of this flies, when they hear how many women, children, and aged people of their nation have been killed by the Christians without cause, as will unavoidably happen, and indeed has happened, in the fury of war. What, I ask, will be the result, if not a perpetual barrier to their salvation, so that there will be no further hope for their conversion? Therefore when there is a question of war over a cause of this kind it is better to let a few innocent persons be oppressed or suffer an unjust death. In fact it would be a very great sin, and against the natural law, to wage war on these unbelievers for this reason. This is proved in the following way.

According to right reason, and therefore the natural law, it is evident that in every case and in every matter that concerns two evils, especially those involving moral guilt, one must choose that which is less harmful or is thought to be less harmful. Therefore to seek to free innocent persons in the case proposed, within their territories, as has been proposed, would be against the natural law and a sin, which, although not mortal, is very serious indeed. This is evident because the greater the damage sin inflicts, the more serious it is, according to Saint Thomas.[2] And this is true even if that damage is not intended or foreseen, since everything that necessarily follows upon a sin belongs in some way to the very species of the sin. From such a war a countless number of innocent persons of both sexes and all ages will unavoidably perish, and the other evils that have been mentioned will necessarily follow upon that war. Therefore anyone who would try to free those who suffer evils of this type by means of war would commit a very serious mortal sin.

This argument is strengthened by the rules the doctor-jurists give concerning the well-known permission, which happens when evils and even serious sins are permitted so that more serious evils in the state may be avoided or so that the good by which the condition of the state is strengthened should not be obstructed. This is evident in the permission for prostitutes in the cities and for Jewish rites. For this reason, in the case proposed, the ruler or governor of each state ought by right to tolerate an evil from which it is hoped there will arise some advantage to the state or some impending evil will be prevented. If he should fail to do this, he would surely commit a mortal sin.[3]

The second outstanding proof of the conclusion mentioned above is this: We have a negative commandment, that is, "You shall not kill," which must be observed in every case, nor is it lawful to violate it in any place or circumstance. This is found in the twentieth chapter of Exodus.[4] Again, in the twenty-third chapter of this book is another, stricter commandment. God says "See that the man who is innocent and just is not done to death and do not acquit the guilty."[5] The same thing is also in the thirteenth chapter of Daniel.[6] And so Saint Thomas says "To hand an innocent man over to suffering and death against his will is wicked and cruel."[7] For God added threats against the transgressors of laws he wished to have observed inviolably and strictly. This is a strong sign that the Lord wants them to be scrupulously observed, according to the words of Exodus in the passage cited above: "You must not be harsh with the widow or with the orphan; if you are harsh with them, they will surely cry out to me, and be sure I shall hear their cry; my anger will flare and I shall kill you with the sword, your own wives will be widows, your own children orphans, etc."[8] Another negative commandment, which we have in God's name, is in the twenty-fourth chapter of Deuteronomy: "Fathers may not be put to death for their sons, nor sons for fathers. Each is to be put to death for his own sin."[9] Now if, for this reason, wars are waged against the Indians, an enormous multitude of blameless and innocent persons who are completely free of those crimes will perish; and the son will bear the iniquity of his father, the father the iniquity of the son. Therefore such a war is wicked, and God will pursue with a mortal hatred those who wage the war, along with those who command it and those who give advice or help to them.

To make clearer what we said (a short while back) about another, stricter commandment, that is, "See that the man who is innocent and just is not done to death,"[10] we must note that there are four kinds of human acts.[11] Some are good in the absolute sense, so that they cannot be evil in any way, for example, to adore, worship, and love God and one's neighbor for the sake of God. Some are evil and foul in the absolute and full sense, so that they cannot be good in any way but are inseparable from their depravity and wickedness, according to the Philosopher throughout the second book of *Ethics.* For this reason they can never be lawful. Adultery, ingratitude, theft, and even lying (which, being evil in itself, must be avoided, as he says in the fourth book of the same work) are of this class. Others, when considered in themselves, connote some depravity and seem to be foul, but once some quality or circumstance is added, they are lawful. Of this type is killing or striking a man, both of which, considered in themselves, display disorder and depravity. However, if you add [the circumstance] that a judge hangs a thief, he acts well and brings the grace of Christ to himself. To be sure, certain human acts are indifferent; that is, they are neither evil nor good, for example, going to the marketplace.

The killing of innocent persons, then, belongs to the second type. This can never be lawful by reason of any accidental circumstance, according to Saint Thomas,[12] who concludes that it is not lawful to kill an innocent person under any circumstance, and he says that human law cannot permit that a good man be killed without cause.[13] Moreover, Abulensis, in his commentary on Genesis, says that killing an innocent person is always evil and in no way can it become good.[14] From this it is clear that this commandment is most strict and that by no argument or circumstance can it ever be lawful by human law or by the command of a ruler to kill innocent and harmless persons in order that other innocent persons might be freed from death, especially when the latter, who are killed unjustly, are few, as is true in our case, and those to be killed in order to free these few are many.

Chapter Thirty-Three

. . . Let us put the case that the Spaniards discover that the Indians or other pagans sacrifice human victims or eat them. Let us say, further, that the Spaniards are so upright and good-living that nothing motivates them except the rescue of the innocent and the correction of the guilty. Will it be just for them to invade and punish them without any warning? You will say "No, rather, they shall send messengers to warn them to stop these crimes." Now I ask you, dear reader, what language will the messengers speak so as to be understood by the Indians? Latin, Greek, Spanish, Arabic? The Indians know none of these languages. Perhaps we imagine that the soldiers are so holy that Christ will grant them the gift of tongues so that they will be understood by the Indians? Then what deadline will they be given to come to their senses and give up their crimes? They will need a long time to understand what is said to them, and also the authority and the reasons why they should stop sacrificing human beings, so that it will be clear that evils of this type are contrary to the natural law.

Further, within the deadline set for them, no matter what its length, they will certainly not be bound by the warning given them, nor should they be punished for stubbornness, since a warning does not bind until the deadline has run out. Likewise, no law, constitution, or precept is binding on anyone unless the words of the language in which it is proposed are clearly understood, as the learned jurists say. It is enough to cite Felinus, who makes a number of points on this subject,[15] and Gómez, who considers the subject at great length in his commentary on rules for the chancery.[16]

Now, I ask, what will the soldiers do during the time allowed the Indians to come to their senses? Perhaps, like the forty monks Saint

Gregory sent to convert the English, they will spend their time in fasting and prayer, so that the Lord will be pleased to open the eyes of the Indians to receive the truth and give up such crimes. Or, rather, will not the soldiers hope with all their hearts that the Indians will become so blind that they will neither see nor hear? And then the soldiers will have the excuse they want for robbing them and taking them captive. Anyone who would foolishly and very unrealistically expect soldiers to follow the first course knows nothing about the military mind. They would hope with all their hearts that the Indians would either misunderstand or reject the warning out of hand. Then the army might realize its wishes and proceed against them with fire and sword and all the misfortunes of total war, so that, after shedding the blood of innumerable persons, the soldiers will seize their goods and make slaves of the survivors in violation of the Lord's command and the rule of charity, by which they were bound to give up property and life for the salvation of their neighbor. Even the presence of the Emperor would not restrain them from thievery and bloodshed for more than two days, especially if the enterprise was of a type to encourage greed. I know for sure of occasions when many of our soldiers inflicted sword wounds on Indians who were approaching the Spanish camps weighed down with chickens, fruit, and all sorts of food to offer the Spaniards in deference. Returning to camp, they said that the approaching Indians were armed. To have their story accepted, they told of the Indians' treacherously shooting arrows at them. Thus, under this pretext, the soldiers attacked and either killed or made slaves of people who were quite innocent and had not thought of such a thing.

Further, let us suppose that such a thing does not happen to the Indians and, after more or less time, they may come to understand the warnings of the Spaniards. What if they say that they do not kill the innocent for sacrifice or cannibalism but only those condemned to death for their crimes, or those captured in a just war, or those who have died a natural death? Therefore they do no harm to innocent people but only to themselves in eating the flesh of humans like wild beasts. In this case, will not the reason for freeing innocent people from an unjust death cease to be valid? Therefore there is nothing with which the Christians can reproach them, for there can be cases in which it is lawful to eat human flesh, for example, necessity and extreme hunger. Without committing a sin, one may eat someone who starved to death or who was condemned to death. The eating of human flesh, which is called a wild and bestial act by Aristotle,[17] is against the natural law for two reasons: (1) if innocent people are killed so that their flesh may be eaten and (2) because eating human flesh is so savage that even beasts that eat the carcasses of their own kind are rare indeed. When, however, human flesh is eaten out of necessity and innocent people are not killed, but the corpses are of people already dead or of criminals, then surely it is not against the natural law, and no sin is committed. Saint Augustine cites a case of this sort: "Both ancient history and current unhappy experience provide instances of people, famished and overcome by hunger, using human flesh as food."[18] Here he cites the story from 4 Book of Kings [2 Kings] of the two women of a Samaritan city who ate the son of one of the women when the city was besieged by the Assyrian army. They sinned because they killed an innocent person. If their own children had died naturally and the women were suffering extreme hunger, they would not have committed sin in eating the flesh of the dead boy.

There is a story of some Spaniards who once ate the liver of a dead companion. Returning to the island of Cuba from the recently discovered Yucatán, they left their ships and, without any food, went toward the mountains. One of them, named Biver, whom I knew very well, died of hunger, and his companions, hoping to avoid the same fate, ate his liver. The same thing happened in the famous Spanish city of Numancia. Its citizens, oppressed by extreme hunger during a siege by Scipio, ate human corpses. This event was reported by the Bishop of Gerona in these words: "Besieged and driven in the end by hunger to eat human flesh, the people of Numancia offered to surrender to Scipio if he would give them humane treatment."[19]

Suppose, then, the unbelievers were to maintain that they eat only people of this kind, that is, those who have died or who have been legally condemned to death, but do not kill the innocent, when the matter can be fully known, especially if the ruler, whose word is in law presumed to be true, [should say so]. Would it not be unjust to wage war on them before the matter is certainly and fully understood?

Let us suppose, further, that it is true and that it is known that, of their own free will and out of a bestial inclination, they eat the bodies of those who have died naturally or who have been executed for their crimes, or even those who were prisoners of war (and undoubtedly this is a crime and a bestial vice), I ask can war be waged against them—justly—simply for this reason? Certainly we cannot wage war against them for any crime they may commit, including idolatry, as we have proved already by ten reasons. Other than their own rulers, judges, or kings, there is no ruler or judge in the world who can punish crimes of this sort.

Chapter Thirty-Four

We have to come to the same conclusion about the crime of human sacrifice, which is said to be one of their practices. It would not be right to make war on them for this reason because, as has been said, it is difficult for them to absorb in a short time the truth proclaimed to them through messengers and also because the Indians are under no obligation to believe the Spaniards, even if they force the truth on them a thousand times. Why will they believe such a proud, greedy, cruel, and rapacious nation? Why will they give up the religion of their ancestors, unanimously approved for so many centuries and supported by the authority of their teachers, on the basis of a warning from a people at whose words there are no miracles to confirm the faith or to lessen vice?

Even though the Indians cannot be excused in the sight of God for worshiping idols, they can be completely excused in the sight of men, for two reasons. First they are following a "probable" error, for, as the Philosopher notes, that is said to be probable which is approved by all men, either by the majority of wise men or by those whose wisdom has the greatest following.[20] Further, he says: "That must necessarily be judged to be good or better which is so judged by all, or the majority of persons of good judgment, or by those who are thought to be the more prudent, even if only one person is forming the judgment."[21] Judgments of this type, approved by the opinions of such men, are called "morally certain," according to the same Philosopher, whom all philosophers and theologians follow.[22]

Convictions about the gods, the duty of offering sacrifice to them, and the manner and things to be sacrificed are fully agreed on by all the known Indian nations, and these gods are worshiped by those who are reputed to be sacred and holy men (that is, their priests) and their idolatry is established by the decrees of their laws, the sanction of their rulers, and the penalties leveled against transgressors. Finally, since their idols are not worshiped secretly but publicly and religiously in their temples—and this from the earliest centuries—it is clear that the error of these people is probable. Nor should we be surprised if they do not immediately respond to our first preaching.

Also, they are surely in probable error about their practice of human sacrifice, since the ancient history of pagans and Catholics alike testifies that almost all peoples used to do the same thing. This is what Eusebius says:

> It was common for all men, on the day customarily set for human sacrifice, to sprinkle the altar with human blood. This was the practice in ancient times when calamity or danger threatened. The ruler of the city or nation would offer to the avenging demon his favorite child as a ransom for the redemption of the whole people and the one chosen would be slain in a mystic rite.[23]

He goes on:

> Human sacrifice is demanded by the demons who from time to time afflict many cities and nations with plagues and sudden calamities and ceaselessly harass the people in frightful ways until appeased by the blood of the victims offered them.

Again, Clement says that some of the peoples of western India, who may have been very much like those we are dealing with, used to sacrifice foreigners to their gods and then eat them.[24] Eusebius writes the same thing in the work we have already cited.

In addition, Lactantius says:

> Among the people of Taurus, an inhuman and savage nation, there was a law that a stranger should be sacrificed to Diana and sacrifice was offered for a long time. The Gauls placated Hesus and Teutates with human blood. Even the Latins were not free of such barbarism. Indeed, even now the Latin Jupiter is worshiped with human blood. However, we should not be astonished at the barbarians whose religion matches their morals. Are not our own people who boast of their meekness and

gentleness often more inhuman than those who practice such sacrilegious rites?[25]

Further on he notes: "It is now evident that this practice of human sacrifice is very ancient, for in honor of Saturn people used to be thrown into the Tiber from the Milvian Bridge."

And in regard to innocent children, he says:

I find no words to tell of the children who were sacrificed to the same Saturn because of a hatred for Jupiter. Men were so barbarous and so inhuman that they labeled as sacrifice that foul and detestable crime against the human race which is parricide, when, without any sign of family love, they blotted out tender and innocent lives at an age which is especially dear to parents, etc.

And again:

The Carthaginians had the custom of offering human victims to Saturn and when they had been conquered by Aglothocles, the King of Sicily, they thought their god was angry with them and so that they might more diligently blot out their crime, they sacrificed two hundred noble children.

Plutarch writes that the Romans failed to punish some barbarians who were sacrificing men to the gods, because they knew that it was done from custom and law.[26] Plutarch also says that the Romans themselves did the same thing at times. Here are his words:

When the Romans discovered that certain barbarians had sacrificed a man to their immortal gods, the magistrates thought that they should be summoned and punished. Later they released them when they learned that the barbarians did this because of a certain law and custom and so they forbade them to do it again. This was because a few years before they themselves had struck down two men and two women in the cattle-market at Rome. It does not seem right that they should do this and yet find fault with the savages who did the same. Were they persuaded that to offer a man to the immortal gods was evil, but to offer him to the demons was a necessity? Did they think that those who did this sort of thing from custom and law committed sin, while they believed that by following the command of the Sibylline Books, they were not guilty of the same crime?

The Greek historian Herodotus tells us that the Scythians had a custom of sacrificing to their gods one out of every hundred prisoners of war.[27] He also says that the Scytho-Tauran peoples in Germany sacrifice everyone who is shipwrecked on their shores, as well as strangers, to Iphigenia, daughter of Agamemnon. The same thing is recorded by Solinus[28] and Pomponius Mela.[29] Diodorus Siculus writes that the Galatians sacrificed to their gods captives or those condemned for their crimes. Strabo reminds us that our own Spanish people, who reproach the poor Indian peoples for human sacrifice, used to sacrifice captives and their horses.[30] He says that they forced some to live next to the Duero River in a Spartan manner. He continues:

> Those who are given to sacrifice also practice divination with entrails, especially those of their captives. They cut off the right hands of their victims and offer them to the gods. They eat a goat which they sacrifice to Mars, as they do with prisoners and horses.

Moreover, similar practices of other peoples are narrated in other works of Strabo.[31] Polydor Vergil also has recorded many similar and significant details.[32] Because, then, human sacrifice to the gods has been customary among so many different peoples, surely the Indians, in sacrificing men for many centuries, are in probable error.

We know that famous philosophers have lived in many parts of the world. According to Augustine, even though they knew the stories about the gods to be mere fables and judged them to be undeserving of divine honors (this group included Cicero and Seneca), they did not wish to turn the people from an ancient custom that had been accepted for so many centuries.[33] Why, then, should it be thought that at the words of Christian soldiers, [who exceed the barbarous peoples in their wicked deeds, and are a nation not yet known and frightful in appearance, that does not eat human flesh but surpasses them in all wicked deeds], the Indians ought to turn from a religion that has been accepted for many centuries, sanctioned by the laws of many rulers, and strengthened by the example of so many of their prudent men? As Chrysostom says, in matters that are sacred and of great importance and very difficult to give up they would be fickle and worthy of reproach and punishment if they put aside the many and great testimonies of such great authority and believe these soldiers in this matter, without being convinced by more probable reasons (which cannot be done in a short time) that the Christian religion is more worthy of belief.[34]

They should be ashamed who think to spread the gospel by the mailed fist. Men want to be taught, not forced. There is no way, however, for our religion to be taught in a short time to those who are as ignorant of our language as we are of their language and their religion, until those who prudently hold fast [to these beliefs] are convinced by reason. For, as we have said, there is no greater or more difficult step than for a man to abandon the religion he has once embraced.

Chapter Thirty-Five

The second major proof why the Indians should not immediately believe that human sacrifice to their gods is evil is that evidence cannot be presented to them in a few, or even many, words [to show] that human sacrifice to the true God or the presumed god (if he is worshiped as the true God) is forbidden by natural reason. Rather, by the same natural reason they can show not only that men should be sacrificed to God but that it would not be enough to sacrifice angels (if it were possible to sacrifice angels).

We argue this point by first offering four principles.

The first principle is that no nation is so barbarous that it does not have at least some confused knowledge about God. Now all persons understand God as that than which there is nothing better or greater. This is the teaching of [John] Damascene.[35] He says: "God does not leave us totally engulfed in ignorance of himself. Rather, the knowledge that God exists has been naturally engrafted and implanted by him in all persons."[36] Again, Cicero says: "No man is so inhuman that an opinion about the divinity has not filled his mind."[37] And, "No nation is so wild or fierce that it does not know that a god must be had," even if it does not know what sort.[38] Aristotle says that all men are agreed that this glorious first body, that is, heaven, is the dwelling place of the supreme being, that is, God, [the expression "all men" referring] to the Greeks and others of the early nations who knew God exists and is divine.[39] Boethius teaches both points in these words: "The common reasoning of human minds proves that the true God, the ruler or source of all things, is good. For since nothing can be imagined better than God, who doubts the goodness of him who has no better?"[40]

The second principle is that, by a natural inclination, men are led to worship God according to their capacities and in their own ways. The reason for this is that they naturally conclude and believe that they belong to him and that their lives and whatever they have come from him. And so Saint Thomas writes: "Now since men believe that all things are given by and proceed from him, the intellect judges that everything is owed to God."[41] Moreover, the Philosopher writes: "Even natural reason itself dictates that the very highest and best things must be offered to God because of his excellence."[42] Again, he says: "Man's friendship for the gods is the same as toward those who excel others in goodness. And in friendships, the greater the excellence of the friend, the more he deserves."[43] Again, he says: "No one can ever give to the gods in accordance to their dignity, but each must do the most he can."[44] Saint Thomas has the same teaching:

> Man is in debt to God for two reasons. (1) Because of the benefits received from him; (2) because of the sins committed against him. . . . Man can never completely satisfy these two obligations to God, since, even according to the Philosopher, in honors due to parents and to God, it is impossible for man to repay in any adequate way. However, it is enough that man repay proportionately what he can.[45]

From these statements it is obvious that, by natural law, men are obliged to honor God by the best means available and to offer the best things in sacrifice. The conclusion that follows from this is that neither a particular man nor a whole community, taken as a unit, nor a whole kingdom can repay God for the benefits it received, even if they were to give their property and endure labors, vigils, and finally life and death itself for God's glory, no matter how unwilling God may be to reward such deeds in the other life, because God, who by his indescribable generosity has given us so many and so admirable benefits, owes us nothing. For this reason the Psalmist says: "What return can I make to the Lord for all his goodness to me?"[46] As if he were saying: "I have nothing and can do nothing to repay God for these things for which I recognize that I am indebted to him." The reason for this is that a man in no way injures his property even if he makes use of it without rewarding it because there is no political or civil right between a man and his property, according to the Philosopher.[47] But all creatures, including us, are the property of God. Therefore it is absolutely impossible that God would do us harm if he were not to reward the services we might perform for his honor, because there cannot be a political right—or right in the strict sense—between God and us. For although God gives eternal happiness to those who have charity, he is not obliged to do so from justice, insofar as this implies a strict right that denotes complete equality between the two parties. As the Apostle says, "What we suffer in this life can never be compared to the glory as yet unrevealed, which is waiting for us."[48]

Yet there is said to be between God and man a certain right of condescension; that is, the Lord, drawing on the riches of his mercy, is pleased to set up a certain kind of proportional equality between himself and men. In other words, he wills to be obligated to men, and men to him. Thus he is bound to give eternal life to those who persevere in faith and charity until death, not because our merits demand it but from the disposition established by him by which he wishes a kind of justice of condescension and, as it were, a kind of agreement between him and us, so that, in the works of charity, God may be bound to give us eternal life. And this is called justice, not in the strict sense but after a manner of speaking. Moreover, in this sense God would be said to do an injustice if he did not give eternal life to those who die in charity. And this is the meaning of the Apostle's words "All there is to come now is the crown of righteousness reserved for me,"[49] that is, of justice by reason of this agreement or pact. God, then, owes us nothing except by right of condescension. But we must offer him whatever we have and are: our wealth, energies, life, and our very soul for his service. We are bound to this by a greater bond since he has given his life for us.

The third principle is that there is no better way to worship God than by sacrifice, which is the principal act of *latria,* which is owed to God alone. Nor is there any better way for men to show in their external acts that they are grateful and subject to God. For sacrifice is the sign that he to whom it is offered is God, and it is most certain that there has never been a nation so barbarous, brutal, and foolish as to offer sacrifice to anyone other than the one who was thought to be God. As Saint Augustine says:

> For who has ever thought that sacrifice should be offered, except to the one whom he knew or thought or imagined to be God? . . . That the worship of God by means of sacrifice is ancient is sufficiently indicated by those two famous brothers, Cain and Abel. God found fault with the sacrifice of the older and looked favorably on that of the younger.[50]

Saint Thomas teaches the same thing: "Now no one has ever thought that sacrifice should be offered to anyone for any other reason than that he believed or thought he believed that he was God."[51]

The fourth principle is that offering sacrifice to the true God or to the one who is thought to be God comes from the natural law, whereas the things to be offered to God are a matter of human law and positive legislation. For this reason this matter is either left to the whole community or to those who represent it, such as the ruler, or, lacking this, it is entrusted to each private individual to decide what he will use for his sacrifice.

The first statement is evident from the three preceding principles. By nature, all nations know that God surpasses anything that can be imagined and that they have life and every possession from him. And by nature they understand that they owe God the greatest reverence and worship because of his incomparable excellence and majesty, and all agree that the principal act of *latria,* which is owed to God alone, is sacrifice. It follows, then, that they are obliged by the natural law to offer sacrifice, by which men show, more than by any other external act, that they are grateful and subject to God. And so there has never been a nation so barbarous as not to judge by a natural impulse that sacrifice is owed to the true God or to him whom they mistakenly thought is the true God.

The second proof of the first statement is what Saint Thomas says: "At all times and among all nations there has always been some offering of sacrifices." And the reason for this is that

> natural reason tells man that he is subject to a higher being, on account of the defects which he perceives in himself, and in which he needs help and direction from someone above him, and whatever this superior being may be, it is known to all under the name of God, and consequently the offering of sacrifice is a matter of the natural law.[52]

The same statement is proved, in the third place, from the lawyers who teach that religion belongs to the law of nations.[53] They call the natural law the law of nations only because men use it.[54] Men put the law of nations into practice as soon as they began to grow in numbers, since the peoples who lived during the first centuries taught many things by natural instinct. From this, then, arose the practice of sacrifice as produced by natural instinct. Offering sacrifices, therefore, is a very old practice, introduced by the natural law.

The second statement—that offering this or that thing as a sacrifice is a matter of human law, whereas the law of nature does not prescribe anything definite—is also proved by the fact that even if something may generally be of the natural law, the disposition and arrangement of when and how it should be done is positive; that is, a certain determination of the natural law is laid down by the ruler or the state. For example, men are obliged to give some time to divine matters and to worship God by some external acts, which the theologians call acts of *latria*. This is dictated by natural reason. But the fact that the seventh day should be dedicated to divine worship is a human statute that is laid down by the Church, to which Christ gave the right to establish laws concerning divine worship, even though the seventh day (Sunday) has taken the place of the Sabbath, which God commanded by positive law to be dedicated to divine things. So, too, the law of nature teaches that the guilty must be punished, but human law teaches what the penalty should be. In the same way, although nature itself teaches and leads man to offer sacrifice to God, it is not the law of nature but men themselves who, by means of human laws, teach what should be offered as sacrifice, that is, cattle or sheep or the like. This is clear in the sacrifices of the various nations cited above. Likewise, some sacrificed swine to Ceres, horses to Phoe-bus, geese to Diana, asses to Priapus, and other such things.[55]

The second statement is also proved by what the Philosopher says in the Fifth Book of the *Ethics,* where, speaking about the natural law and positive law, he writes that all men have the same opinion about natural truths but differ in laws and practices. For when he speaks about sacri-fices, he says:

> One law is natural, the other legitimate, that is, the legal or positive law. Now the natural is that which has the same force everywhere, for ex-ample, fire burns both here and in Persia, not because it seems so or does not seem so. But the legitimate, that is, the legal, is that which does not differ one way or another at its source but differs when it is established, as, for example, that the ransoming of captives be done at a certain price or that a goat be offered in sacrifice instead of two sheep, and whatever is provided for by individual laws, such as performing sacred rites to Brasis, etc.

Notice that he teaches that the law of nature does not change because one person wishes to fulfill it while another does not. For what is good cannot be made evil by the will of men. For example, the law of nature teaches us to redeem a captive who is suffering injury and to offer sacri-fice to God. And, willingly or unwillingly, all men are obliged to do so, but how large the amount to be paid for captives and what should be sacrificed are taught by human laws. Once these are passed, they should be observed, and it is unlawful to violate them. For example, we read that the Athenians and the Spartans, during a war with each other, made an agreement that the freedom of prisoners could be bought for a cer-tain price. Likewise, if it were established that not one but two sheep should be offered as a sacrifice or that sacrifices should be made and feasts celebrated by some well-deserving person in the state—as the Amphipolitans decreed that sacrifices should be offered by Brasis (who some think was a Spartan king, others a Spartan queen) because of the favors granted to his nation—it is in no way lawful to violate these sac-rifices and the form as sanctioned by law. If, however, the law provides no sanction, each private individual could sacrifice whatever he wishes and could redeem a prisoner at any price he wishes. For the natural law does not teach these matters, and in morally indifferent matters each person can follow his own judgment and lay down rules for his wife and children as he wishes, according to the Philosopher.[56] Speaking about families in his city, he says: "Every household is ruled by its oldest member, and so are the descendants who branch out from it, because of the blood relationship. And this is what Homer means, 'And each one must give laws to sons and to wives,' for people used to live scattered about in this way in ancient times."[57]

Now Genesis (chapter 4) proves that unless a certain form or definite victim for sacrifice were defined by law, each person could lawfully sacrifice what he willed. In this chapter, Cain is said to have offered ears of wheat and the fruits of the earth, while Abel, who was a shepherd, sacrificed the firstborn of his flock to the Lord. However, after he made a covenant with Abraham and his descendants, the Lord, through Moses, regulated the sacrifices that were to be offered to him, that is, cattle and sheep from among the four-footed animals and turtledoves and pigeons from among the birds.[58]

Chapter Thirty-Six

On the basis of these principles one can arrive at what we taught previously: within the limits of the natural light of reason (in other words, at the point at which divine or human positive law ceases and, one may add, where grace and doctrine are lacking), men should sacrifice human victims to the true God or the reputed god, if the latter is taken for the true God. We draw this conclusion: Just as men naturally know that God exists and think that there is nothing better or greater than he, since whatever we own, are, or are capable of is given to us by his boundless goodness, we do not adequately repay him even if we offer him all that is ours, even our life.

The greatest way to worship God is to offer him sacrifice. This is the unique act by which we show him to whom we offer the sacrifice that we are subject to him and grateful to him. Furthermore, nature teaches that it is just to offer God, whose debtors we admit we are for so many reasons, those things that are precious and excellent because of the surpassing excellence of his majesty. But, according to human judgment and truth, nothing in nature is greater or more valuable than the life of man or man himself. Therefore nature itself dictates and teaches those who do not have faith, grace, or doctrine, who live within the limitations of the light of nature, that, in spite of every contrary positive law, they ought to sacrifice human victims to the true God or to the false god who is thought to be true, so that by offering a supremely precious thing they might be more grateful for the many favors they have received. For the natural law teaches gratitude in such a way that we not only do good to our benefactor but also try to repay him in an abundant manner for the benefits we have received, giving due consideration to the benefits, the benefactor, and the motive for which he confers the benefits on us.[59]

The kindness by which the Lord created us, endowed us with so many gifts, and enriched us with so many good things comes from his immense charity and boundless goodness and gives birth in us to innumerable good things, and even life itself, and, finally, whatever we are. However, since we cannot give adequate thanks for so many favors, we are obliged to present what seems to us to be the greatest and most valuable good, that is, human life, and especially when the offering is made for the welfare of the state. For the pagans thought that through sacrifices of this type they could divert evils from their state and gain good will and prosperity for their kingdoms. Therefore whoever sacrifices men to God can be drawn to this action by natural reason, especially if he lacks Christian faith and instruction. All of this is corroborated by what Dionysius of Halicarnassus writes:

> When the peoples of Italy tried to appease the gods by offering various first-fruits after they had been afflicted with many evils, a certain old man told them that they were deceiving themselves if they thought that there was no reason why they were being tried by the gods. For, as he said, they rightly and justly gave the first-fruits of other things but, in the judgment of the gods, they still owed the first-fruits of what was most valuable to the gods, that is, their offspring. If, then, the gods would accept one of these or the part still due, their petition would be complete. When they had heard this advice, some thought that he spoke correctly, while others thought that his reasoning was deceptive. When someone suggested that they seek the opinion of the god as to whether he would be willing to receive men as tithes, they sent soothsayers and the god answered that they should do so. . . .[60]

Chapter Thirty-Eight

To sum up this . . . argument, we shall recapitulate everything that has thus far been established by the reasons and citations given earlier, but especially after chapter 30, which has tried to show that unless a war can prevent the evils of which the innocent are victims, the war should be brought to an end and one should pay no attention to those who commit these wrongs. This is our position, for it is well known that evidence, or even probability, that human sacrifice is at least contrary to reason cannot be easily imparted to unbelievers of this type, [who] believe that they and all their possessions are owed to God and that the idols they worship are the true God, a belief that is supported by a great many witnesses of the highest authority and superior to all others, such as kings, princes, high priests, theologians, prophets, or soothsayers. These latter are held in greatest reverence because the people think these men have frequent communication with the gods, from whom they receive secrets and the knowledge by which they predict future events. For these things they have approved custom, positive law, precept, and common error, and so they have a basis for a plausible argument in favor of human sacrifice.

Again, by reason of their corrupt morals they can eat human flesh so long as they do not kill anyone for this purpose. Although this is a bestial vice, except under pressure of necessity, it is in no way punishable by a foreign nation, nor can war be waged against them on this account, especially as they can offer some pretext in excuse for eating human flesh, as we have said. Nor can those who are so concerned to free the innocent easily convince them of the contrary.

Also, since they rejoice in holding that blasphemous notion that in worshiping their idols they worship the true God, or that these are God, and despite the supposition that they have an erroneous conscience, even if the true God is being preached to them by better and more credible as well as more convincing arguments, together with the good example of Christians, they are bound, without doubt, to defend the worship of their gods and their religion by going forth with their armies against all who attempt to take those things from them or injure them or prevent their sacrifices—to fight, kill, capture, and exercise all the rights consequent on a just war according to the law of nations. Furthermore, it is certain that among those who have been defiled by these detestable rites are kings and great lords, whom a large number of persons must follow: subject peoples, relatives by blood and marriage, allies (friendly or otherwise), and also persons imbued with the greatest zeal for their gods and religion. For this is a common cause for all of them who, in what appears to be a just cause that they hold to be in their favor, rouse their communal spirit to fight courageously, and who prefer death rather than failure in avenging their own injuries and those of their gods and in driving such aggressors from their country.

Equally clear is the kind and number of evils that will follow from this: many massacres, many burnings, many murders, the butchery of infants, children, women, the old, the doddering, the weak, the sick, and other harmless persons as well as the devastation of provinces, the destruction of cities, towns and peoples, many kings and lords stripped and pillaged of their dignities, dominions and honors, the loss of freedom and property, and the many foul and disgraceful crimes that will be committed by the licentiousness of the soldiers—what debauchery, rape, incest, and adultery!

With what hatred, surely, will those who suffer such evils pursue the Christian people and the God of the Christians, the true God who should be adored? How many thousand souls will meanwhile plunge into the deep pit and perish forever? And all this, indeed, that we might rescue a few innocent persons. Will these, our sacrifices, be pleasing in the sight of the divine goodness? In truth they will be as acceptable as the offering of a person "slaughtering a son before his father's very eyes."[61] Who but a man that is wicked or foolish admits a cure that is worse than the disease? Who, to prevent a few from being sacrificed to idols, would want the eternal death of countless souls who do not deserve such a fate? These things are foreign to the teaching of Christ and the example of the Apostles, nor are they pleasing to anyone but cruel and inhuman plunderers or certain ignorant enemies of Christ's glory, who in their own way make Sodom look just.

Six

THE COUNTER-
REFORMATION

"Counter-Reform" is an ambiguous term with distinct, though related, religious and political senses. Less apt in its religious sense, the
term connotes a temporal and causal sequence: Protestant Reform provokes Catholic Counter-Reform. But this obscures the genesis of the
Counter-Reformation in earlier Catholic reform, much of which preceded the Lutheran revolution. Institutional efforts at reform like the
Fifth Lateran Council (1512–1517) complemented the work of individual reformers such as Jiménez de Cisneros, John Colet, and Erasmus. Hence the Council of Trent (1545–1563), the central event of the
Counter-Reformation, was one part maturation of Catholic reform and
one part response to Protestant reform. The period produced a bevy of
reforming leaders, some later named saints—in Spain, Ignatius of Loy-
ola, founder of the Society of Jesus, and Teresa of Avila and John of the
Cross, reformers of the Carmelites. One gauge of the depth of Catholic
reform is the radical change in the papacy. The Renaissance pope Julius II (1503–1513) was a warrior and patron of artists such as Bramante,

Raphael, and Michelangelo. Half a century later, the Counter-Reformation pope Pius V (1566–1572) was in comparison a puritan; he deemed pagan images unfit for his residence, passed a bewildering variety of sumptuary laws, and forbade Roman homeowners to visit taverns.

"Counter-Reform" also has the political sense of converting Protestant states into Catholic ones. The Wars of Religion, in which religious motives mixed with political, economic, and social interests, were waged across Europe between about 1560 and 1648. From 1562, when France declined into civil war and ceased to support the Lutheran states, to 1629, when the Holy Roman Emperor's Edict of Restitution aimed to restore ecclesiastical lands seized by Protestants since 1552, there was a genuine possibility of large-scale Protestant reverses. The most serious attempts were spearheaded by the Spanish king Felipe (Philip) II, the most powerful Catholic ruler of the era. Had he managed to suppress the revolt in the Netherlands, beginning in 1566, or had his Armada prevailed against England in 1588, the political configuration of Europe could have been fundamentally altered.

The Counter-Reformation, however defined, encompasses some of the highest and lowest points in Spanish history. Within a century—from the merger of Castile and Aragon in 1479 to the inheritance of Portugal in 1580—Spain had become the dominant power in Europe and the Americas. But a century later—from the death of Felipe II in 1598 to that of Carlos (Charles) II in 1700—it had fallen to second rank. The seeds of Spain's relatively precipitous decline in power, however, had been planted long before Felipe's death. As early as 1412, laws of *limpieza de sangre* (purity of blood) were discriminating against new Christians (those descended from Jewish or Muslim converts to Christianity) in favor of old Christians; by 1547 these laws extended all over Spain. The Spanish Inquisition, created by the Catholic monarchs in 1478 to be independent of the papacy, played a dual political and religious role in the newly united nation. The Jews, who had been driven out of England in 1290 and France in 1306, were expelled from Spain in 1492; the remaining Muslims followed in 1502. By the beginning of the sixteenth century, then, Spain was united by a peculiar form of national Catholicism. The fusion of this national religion with the political efforts of the Counter-Reformation produced an expansive and explosive

Catholic military crusade. As the Wars of Religion wore on into the seventeenth century, however, Spain suffered serious military reverses, especially in the Thirty Years' War and the Eighty Years' War with the Dutch, which resulted in Spain's loss of the Netherlands. The economic consequences of continual warfare would have been debilitating in any case, but they were multiplied by the structure of Spanish society. Because the population was composed primarily of impoverished lower classes, large landowners, nobility contemptuous of work, and a disproportionate number of clergy, there was no middle class of consequence. Hence the Spanish economy overspent and underproduced. Beginning in the reign of Felipe II, the monarchy suffered bankruptcy approximately every twenty years.

The cultural situation during the Counter-Reformation is equally chiaroscuro. The early Counter-Reformation was characterized by an eruption of Scholastic creativity—in the jurisprudence of Domingo de Soto, the theological methodology of Melchor Cano, the moral probabilism of Bartolomé de Medina, the controversy over free will between Domingo Báñez and Luis de Molina, the political theory of Juan de Mariana, and the metaphysics of Francisco Suárez. The latter part of the Counter-Reformation, on the other hand, was dominated by a decadent Scholasticism, which choked the universities and religious orders like a weed. Convoluted though the period is, Suárez stands out clearly as its greatest abstract thinker.

FRANCISCO SUÁREZ

Francisco Suárez was born in Granada in 1548. Although his father was a lawyer, Francisco and his siblings showed a marked vocational affinity for the Church; five of the seven children who survived to adulthood pursued ecclesiastical careers, and Francisco was tonsured at the age of ten in preparation for his. At age thirteen he entered the University of Salamanca, where he studied under Juan Mancio, Francisco de Vitoria's pupil and successor to the principal chair of theology. At age sixteen Suárez failed the examination for admittance to the Society of Jesus. He was the only one of fifty candidates to be rejected, and a second attempt only confirmed the initial result. Nevertheless, the examiners were over-ruled by the Jesuit provincial, who was impressed by the young man's eagerness, and Suárez was admitted to the Society with the unpromising rank of Indifferent. Returning to Salamanca to continue his studies, he met with adversity; everyone seemed to progress in the classroom except him. Discouraged, he petitioned the rector to give up his studies, but the rector urged him to stay the course. Suárez floundered on but suddenly righted himself intellectually, developing a particular flair for philosophy. Thereafter he lived the externally uneventful life of an academic and churchman. He was ordained in 1572; taught philosophy at Salamanca (1570) and Segovia (1571–1574); and served as professor of theology at Avila (1575), Valladolid (1576–1580), Rome (1580–1585), Alcalá (1585–1593), Salamanca (1593–1597), and Coimbra (1597–1615).

His career bore the stamp of the most extraordinary dedication and discipline. He once observed that

> my one ambition, which I have endeavored to realize without flinching
> in the face of any labor or effort, has always been to know and to make
> known the truth and nothing but the truth. A partisan spirit has never in-
> spired, and never will inspire, any of my opinions. I have never sought
> anything more than the truth, and I desire that those who read my books
> should seek it in their turn.[1]

He died in Lisbon in 1617.

Although Suárez did not begin publishing until he was forty-two, he wrote unceasingly from then on. His literary output has been conservatively estimated as the equivalent of two hundred and eighty works of seventy-five thousand words each.[2] His writings share many affinities with those of his fellow Scholastics Vitoria and Las Casas, as one might expect. But there are at least two striking differences. The works of Vitoria and Las Casas are deeply engaged with events in the New World, but Suárez's entire corpus seems to contain only one clear reference to the Native Americans and the Spanish conquest.[3] Second, the principles discussed by Vitoria and Las Casas are usually within shouting distance of concrete cases, while Suárez's work is informed by an exceptional drive to abstraction.

The prime example of this abstraction is Suárez's *Disputationes metaphysicae*, the fullest if not the final flower of Scholastic metaphysics. Within a few years of its publication in 1597, it went through twenty editions; it was used as a textbook in Protestant as well as Catholic universities and dominated the field for two centuries. Descartes is said to have packed his copy wherever he traveled.

Almost as influential, however, was Suárez's *De legibus* (On Laws), which appeared in 1612. The selection from this work that appears here should be viewed against the backdrop of the long-running clash between England and Spain. The quarrel unfolded along many fronts. It was at first a domestic and political affair: the nasty divorce of Henry VIII and his Spanish wife, Catalina (Catherine). But it soon turned religious when Henry, who had earned the title "Defender of the Faith" for combating Luther's ideas, recast himself as the father of English Protestantism—in Spanish eyes, a heretic. By the time Henry died in 1547, the quarrel had become dynastic: Henry and Catalina's daughter Mary was queen of England from 1553 to 1558, and when she married the soon-to-be Felipe II in 1554, he became the unpopular king consort of England until her death. The conflict eventually turned military. English sea dogs raided Spanish shipping to support the revolt against Felipe in the Netherlands, and war between Spain and England broke out in 1585. Finally, it was ideological: although both countries were monarchies, they employed very different considerations in defense of the monarch's power. James I, who became the first Stuart king of England in 1603, wrote *The True Law of Free Monarchy* to defend the concept of a monarchy free from control by Parliament, church, and customs of the past. The monarch ruled by divine right, he claimed, and hence was responsible to God alone.[4] In opposition to this view, Suárez extrapolated a form of populism based on previous political theory.[5] Its general outlines are visible in the following selection from Book 3 of *De legibus,* which treats positive human law. The text includes the translators' bracketed emendations.

On Laws

Power and the People

BOOK III

Chapter I
Does Man Possess the Power to Make Laws?

1. We are speaking . . . of man's nature and of his legislative power viewed in itself; for we are not considering, at present, the question of whether anything has been added to or taken from that power through divine law, a matter which will be taken up later.

The question under consideration, then, is as follows: is it possible— speaking solely with reference to the nature of the case[1]—for men to command other men, binding the latter by [man's] own laws?

A reason for doubting that they can do so, may lie in the fact that man is by his nature free and subject to no one, save only to the Creator, so

---

Reprinted by permission of the publisher, the Carnegie Endowment for International Peace, from vol. 2 of *Selections from Three Works of Francisco Suárez, S.J.*, translated by Gwladys L. Williams, Ammi Brown, and John Waldron, revised by Henry Davis, S.J., Carnegie Classics of International Law Series no. 20 (Oxford: Clarendon Press, 1944). www.carnegieendowment.org.

that human sovereignty is contrary to the order of nature and involves tyranny....

2. .... [W]e shall make first the following statement: a civil magistracy accompanied by temporal power for human government is just and in complete harmony with human nature. . . .

3. The basic reason for this assertion is to be sought in Aristotle's *Politics* (Bk. I [, chap. v = p. 1254 B]). This reason is expounded by St. Thomas (*Opuscula,* XX: *De Regimine Principum,* Bk. I, chap. i), and also, very neatly, by St. Chrysostom (*On First Corinthians,* Homily XXXIV [, no. 5]). It is founded, moreover, upon two principles.

The first principle is as follows: man is a social animal, and cherishes a natural and right desire to live in a community. In this connection, we should recollect the principle already laid down, that human society is twofold: imperfect, or domestic; and perfect, or political. Of these divisions, the former is in the highest degree natural and (so to speak) fundamental, because it arises from the fellowship of man and wife, without which the human race could not be propagated nor preserved; wherefore it has been written, "It is not good for man to be alone." From this union there follows as a direct consequence the fellowship of children and parents; for the earlier form of union is ordained for the rearing of the children, and they require union and fellowship with their parents (in early life, at least, and throughout a long period of time) since otherwise they could not live, nor be fittingly reared, nor receive the proper instruction. Furthermore, to these forms of domestic society there is presently added a connection based on slavery or servitude and lordship, since, practically speaking, men require the aid and service of other men.

Now, from these three forms of connection there arises the first human community, which is said to be imperfect from a political standpoint. The family is perfect in itself, however, for purposes of domestic or economic government.

But this community—as I have already indicated, above—is not self-sufficing; and therefore, from the very nature of the case, there is a further necessity among human beings for a political community, consisting at least of a city state (*ciuitas*), and formed by the coalition of a number of families. For no family can contain within itself all the offices and arts necessary for human life, and much less can it suffice for attaining knowledge of all things needing [to be known].

Furthermore, if the individual families were divided one from another, peace could scarcely be preserved among men, nor could wrongs be duly averted or avenged; so that Cicero has said (*De Amicitia*):[2] "Nothing in human affairs is more pleasing to God our Sovereign, than that men should have among themselves an ordered and perfect society, which (continues Cicero) is called a city state (*ciuitas*)." Moreover, this community may be still further augmented, becoming a kingdom or principality by means of the association of many city states; a form of community which is also very appropriate for mankind—appropriate, at least, for its greater welfare—owing to the above-stated reasons, applied in due proportion, although the element of necessity is not entirely equal in the two cases.

4. The second principle is as follows: in a perfect community, there must necessarily exist a power to which the government of that community pertains. This principle, indeed, would seem by its very terms to be a self-evident truth. For as the Wise Man says (Proverbs, chap. xi [, v. 14]): "Where there is no governor, the people shall fall"; but nature is never wanting in essentials; and therefore, just as a perfect community is agreeable to reason and natural law, so also is the power to govern such a community, without which power there would be the greatest confusion therein. . . .

5. There is, in fine, an *a priori* reason in support of this view, a reason touched upon by St. Thomas in the *Opuscula* [XX: *De Regimine Principum*, Bk. I, chap. i] above cited, namely: that no body can be preserved unless there exists some principle whose function it is to provide for and seek after the common good thereof, such a principle as clearly exists in the natural body, and likewise (so experience teaches) in the political. The reason for this fact, in turn, is also clear. For each individual member has a care for its individual advantages, and these are often opposed to the common good, while furthermore, it occasionally happens that many things are needful to the common good, which are not thus pertinent in the case of individuals and which, even though they may at times be pertinent, are provided for, not as common, but as private needs; and therefore, in a perfect community, there necessarily exists some public power whose official duty it is to seek after and provide for the common good.

The righteousness of and necessity for civil magistracy are clearly to be deduced from the foregoing, since the term "civil magistracy" signifies nothing more nor less than a man or number of men in whom resides the above-mentioned power of governing a perfect community. For it is manifest that such power must dwell in men, inasmuch as they are not naturally governed in a polity by the angels, nor directly by God Himself, Who acts, by the ordinary law, through appropriate secondary causes; so that, consequently, it is necessary and natural that they should be governed by men. . . .

Chapter II
In What Men Does This Power to Make Human Laws Reside Directly, by the Very Nature of Things?

1. The reason for doubt on this point is the fact that the power in question dwells either in individual men; or in all men, that is to say, in the whole body of mankind collectively regarded.

The first alternative cannot be upheld. For it is not true that every individual man is the superior of the rest;[3] nor do certain persons, [simply] by the nature of things, possess the said power in a greater degree than other persons [, on some ground apart from general superiority], since there is no reason for thus favoring some persons as compared with others.

The second alternative would also seem[4] to be untenable. For in the first place, if it were correct, all the laws derived from such power would be common to all men. And secondly, [so the argument runs] no source can be found, from which the whole multitude of mankind could have derived this power; since men themselves cannot be that source—inasmuch as they are unable to give that which they do not possess—and since the power cannot be derived from God, because if it were so derived, it could not change but would necessarily remain in the whole community in a process of perpetual succession, like the spiritual power which God conferred upon Peter and which for that reason necessarily endures in him or in his successors, and cannot be altered by men.

2. It is customary to refer, in connection with this question, to the opinion of certain canonists who assert that by the very nature of the

case this [legislative] power resides in some supreme prince upon whom it has been divinely conferred, and that it must always, through a process of succession, continue to reside in a specific individual. The Gloss (on *Decretum*, Pt. II, causa vii, qu. i, can. ix) is cited [by way of confirmation]; but the passage cited contains simply the statement that the son of a king is lawfully king, which is a very different matter, nor does it assert that this mode of succession was perpetual among men. Another Gloss (on *Decretum*, Pt. I, dist. x, can. viii) is also cited, because it declares that the Emperor receives his power from God alone. But that Gloss, in its use of the exclusive word "alone," is intended to indicate simply that the Emperor does not receive his power from the Pope; it is not intended to deny that he receives it from men. For, in this very passage, it is said that the Emperor is set up by the army in accordance with the ancient custom mentioned in the *Decretum* (Pt. I, dist. xciii, can. xxiv). The said opinion, then, is supported neither by authority nor by a [rational] basis, as will become more evident from what follows.

3. Therefore, we must say that this power, viewed solely according to the nature of things, resides not in any individual man but rather in the whole body of mankind. This conclusion is commonly accepted and certainly true. It is to be deduced from the words of St. Thomas ([I-II,] qu. 90, art. 3, ad 2 and qu. 97, art. 3, ad 3) in so far as he holds that the prince has the power to make laws, and that this power was transferred to him by the community. The civil laws (*Digest*, I.iv.i and I.ii.2, §11) set forth and accept the same conclusion. And it is upheld at length by Castro (*De Potestate Legis Poenalis*, Bk. I, chap. i, § *Postquam*), as well as by Soto (*De Iustitia et Iure*, Bk. I, qu. i, art. 3). One may also consult Soto (ibid., Bk. IV, qu. ii, arts. 1 and 2), Ledesma ([*Theologiae Moralis*,] II, Pt. IV, qu. xviii, art. 3, doubt 10), Covarruvias (*Practicae Quaestiones*, chap. i, [no. 2,] first concl.), and Navarrus (on *Decretals*, Bk. II, tit. i, chap. xiii, notab. 3, no. 119).

The basic reason in support of the first part of the conclusion is evident, and was touched upon at the beginning of our discussion, namely, the fact that in the nature of things all men are born free; so that, consequently, no person has political jurisdiction over another person, even as no person has dominion over another; nor is there any reason why such power should, [simply] in the nature of things, be attributed to certain persons over certain other persons, rather than *vice versa*. One might make this assertion only: that at the beginning of creation Adam possessed, in the very nature of things, a primacy and consequently a sovereignty over all men, so that [the power in question] might have been derived from him, whether through the natural origin of primogeniture, or in accordance with the will of Adam himself. For it is so that Chrysostom (*On First Corinthians,* Homily XXXIV [, no. 5]) has declared all men to be formed and procreated from Adam alone, a subordination to one sole prince being thus indicated. However, by virtue of his creation only and his natural origin, one may infer simply that Adam possessed domestic—not political—power. For he had power over his wife, and later he possessed the *patria potestas* over his children until they were emancipated. In the course of time, he may also have had servants and a complete household with full power over the same, the power called "domestic." But after families began to multiply, and the individual heads of individual families began to separate, those heads possessed the same power over their respective households. Political power, however, did not make its appearance until many families began to congregate into one perfect community. Accordingly, since this community had its beginning, not in the creation of Adam nor solely by his will, but rather by the will of all who were assembled therein, we are unable to make any well-founded statement to the effect that Adam, in the [very] nature of things, held a political primacy in the said community. For such an inference cannot be drawn from natural principles, since it is not the progenitor's due, by the sole force of natural law, that he shall also be king over his posterity.

But, granted that this inference does not follow upon natural principles, neither have we sufficient foundation for the assertion that God has bestowed such power upon that [progenitor], through a special donation or act of providence, since we have had no revelation to this effect, nor does Holy Scripture so testify to us. To this argument may be added the point made by Augustine and noted in our preceding chapter [chap. i, sect. i], namely, that God did not say: "Let us make man that he may have dominion over men," but rather did He say: [Let us make man that he may have dominion] over other living creatures.[5]

Therefore, the power of political dominion or rule over men has not been granted, directly by God, to any particular human individual.

4. From the foregoing, it is easy to deduce the second part of the assertion [at beginning of Section 3], namely, that the power in question resides, by the sole force of natural law, in the whole body of mankind [collectively regarded].

The proof is as follows: this power does exist in men, and it does not exist in each individual, nor in any specific individual, as has also been shown; therefore, it exists in mankind viewed collectively, for our foregoing division [into the two alternatives] sufficiently covers the case.

However, in order that our argument may be better understood, it must be noted that the multitude of mankind is regarded in two different ways.

First, it may be regarded simply as a kind of aggregation, without any order, or any physical or moral union. So viewed, [men] do not constitute a unified whole, whether physical or moral, so that they are not strictly speaking one political body, and therefore do not need one prince, or head. Consequently, if one regards them from this standpoint, one does not as yet conceive of the power in question as existing properly and formally; on the contrary, it is understood to dwell in them at most as a fundamental potentiality,[6] so to speak.

The multitude of mankind should, then, be viewed from another standpoint, that is, with regard to the special volition, or common consent, by which they are gathered together into one political body through one bond of fellowship and for the purpose of aiding one another in the attainment of a single political end. Thus viewed, they form a single mystical body which, morally speaking, may be termed essentially a unity; and that body accordingly needs a single head. Therefore, in a community of this kind, viewed as such, there exists in the very nature of things the power of which we are speaking, so that men may not, when forming such a group, set up obstacles to that power; and consequently, if we conceive of men as desiring both alternatives—that is to say, as desirous of so congregating, but on the condition (as it were) that they shall not be subject to the said power—the situation would be self-contradictory, and such men would accordingly fail to achieve any [valid end]. For it is impossible to conceive of a unified political body without political government or disposition thereto; since, in the first place, this unity arises, in a large measure, from subjection to one and the same rule and to some common superior power; while furthermore, if there were no such government, this body could not be directed towards one [common] end and the general welfare. It is, then, repugnant to natural reason to assume the existence of a group of human beings united in the form of a single political body, without postulating the existence of some common power which the individual members of the community are bound to obey; and therefore, if this power does not reside in any specific individual, it must necessarily exist in the community as a whole.

5. To what has been said above, we should add the statement that the power in question does not reside in the multitude of mankind by the very nature of things in such wise that it is necessarily one sole power with respect to the entire species, or entire aggregate, of men existing throughout the whole world; inasmuch as it is not necessary to the preservation or welfare of nature, that all men should thus congregate in a single political community. On the contrary, that would hardly be possible, and much less would it be expedient. For Aristotle (*Politics*, Bk. VII, chap. iv [, §7]) has rightly said that it is difficult to govern aright a city whose inhabitants are too numerous; accordingly, this difficulty would be still greater in the case of a kingdom excessively large, and therefore, it would be greater by far (we are referring to civil government) if the whole world were concerned.

Consequently, it seems to me probable that the power of which we speak never existed in this fashion in the whole assemblage of mankind, or that it so existed for an exceedingly brief period; and that, on the contrary, soon after the creation of the world, mankind began to be divided into various states in each one of which this power existed in a distinct form. Thus it is that Augustine (*On the City of God*, Bk. XV, chap. viii) concludes from the fourth chapter of Genesis, that Cain, before the Flood, was the first to establish an individual kingdom and commonwealth. Moreover, in another passage of the same work (Bk. XVI, chap. iv), Augustine adds that, according to the tenth chapter of Genesis, after the Flood, Nemrod was [the first to do so]. For Cain first brought about a division of the perfect community, separating himself from his father's family; and Nemrod did likewise, at a later period, with respect to Noe.

6. Finally, it may be concluded from the foregoing that this power to make human laws of an individual and special nature, laws which

we call civil, as if to indicate that they are ordained for one perfect community—it may be concluded, I say—that this power never existed in one and the same form throughout the whole world of men, being rather divided among various communities, according to the establishment and division of these communities themselves. Thus we also conclude that—before the coming of Christ, at least—this civil power did not reside in any one specific man with respect to the whole world. For at no time did all men agree to confer that power upon a particular ruler of the entire world, neither have we any knowledge of its bestowal upon some particular individual by God; inasmuch as such an idea might most easily be entertained with regard to Adam, and we have already shown it to be inapplicable to him [*supra*, section 3 of this chapter]. Finally, as is evident in the light of history, no one has ever acquired such power through war or any other similar means.

As to what should be said, however, with respect to the situation after the advent of Christ, that is a matter which I shall take up in the following Book.[7]

But these statements are not incompatible with what we have already said regarding the *ius gentium*. On the contrary, they serve to confirm those earlier assertions. For even though the whole of mankind may not have been gathered into a single political body, but may rather have been divided into various communities, nevertheless, in order that these communities might be able to aid one another and to remain in a state of mutual justice and peace (which is essential to the universal welfare), it was fitting that they should observe certain common laws, as if in accordance with a common pact and mutual agreement. These are the laws called *iura gentium;* and they were introduced by tradition and custom, as we have remarked, rather than by any written constitution. Moreover, they comprise that twofold body of law—special and common[8]—which Gaius distinguished in the *Digest* (I.i.9). . . .

Chapter IV
Corollaries From The Doctrine Set Forth Above

1. From our discussion in the preceding chapter, we may draw certain inferences which will throw a great deal of light on all that we have to say.

The first inference is this: although the power in question is in an absolute sense an effect of the natural law, its specific application as a certain form of power and government is dependent upon human choice. This inference may be explained as follows: political government, according to the doctrine set forth by Plato in the Dialogue on *The Statesman*, or *On Kingship*[9] [chap. xxxi = p. 291 D], and in the *Republic* [Bk. I, chap. xii; Bk. IV, *passim*, especially at end = p. 445 D E], as well as by Aristotle in the *Politics* (Bk. III, chap. v), and in the *Ethics* (Bk. VIII, chap. x), takes three simple forms. These forms are: monarchy, or government by one head; aristocracy, or government by the few and the best; and democracy, or government by the many and the common people. From these, it is possible to make up various mixed forms of government, that is to say, forms compounded of these simple ones by drawing either from all three or from two of them. Bellarmine (*De Potestate Summi Pontificis*, Bk. I, from the beginning and through several chapters) may be consulted, for he has treated of the matter at length and very satisfactorily. Thus men are not obliged, [simply] from the standpoint of natural law, to choose any given one of these forms of government.

We grant, indeed, that monarchy is the best among the three; as Aristotle demonstrates very fully and as one may infer from the government and providential plan of the universe in its entirety, the government and plan which ought to be the most excellent, so that Aristotle concludes (*Metaphysics*, Bk. XII, at end [= p. 1076 A]): "Therefore, let there be one prince." This conclusion is also supported by the example of Christ the Lord in the institution and government of His Church. And, finally, the prevailing usage among all nations is an argument in favor of the same view. Although—as I was saying—we grant this to be true, nevertheless, other forms of government are not [necessarily] evil, but may, on the contrary, be good and useful; so that, consequently, men are not compelled by the sheer force of the natural law to place this power either in one individual, or in several, or in the entire number of mankind; and therefore, this determination [as to the seat of the power] must of necessity be made by human choice.

Moreover, experience similarly reveals a great deal of variety in connection with this [most excellent type of government]. For monarchies may be found in this place or in that, and rarely in their simple form; since—given the frailty, ignorance and wickedness of mankind—it is as a rule expedient to add some element of common government which is executed by a number of persons, this common element being greater or smaller according to the varying customs and judgment of men. Accordingly, this whole matter turns upon human counsel and human choice.

We infer, then, that by the nature of things, men as individuals possess to a partial extent (so to speak) the faculty for establishing, or creating, a perfect community; and, by virtue of the very fact that they establish it, the power in question does come to exist in this community as a whole. Nevertheless, natural law does not require either that the power should be exercised directly by the agency of the whole community, or that it should always continue to reside therein. On the contrary, it would be most difficult, from a practical point of view, to satisfy such requirements, for infinite confusion and trouble would result if laws were established by the vote of every person; and therefore, men straightway determine the said power by vesting it in one of the abovementioned forms of government, since no other form can be conceived, as is easily evident to one who gives the matter consideration.

2. The second inference [to be drawn from the preceding chapter] is as follows: civil power, whenever it resides—in the right and ordinary course of law—in the person of one individual, or prince, has flowed from the people as a community, either directly or indirectly; nor could it otherwise be justly held.

This is the common opinion of the jurists, as indicated by their comments on certain laws of the *Digest* (I.iv.1 and I.ii.2). Moreover, the same conclusion is upheld in these laws themselves; by Panormitanus and other canonists (on *Decretals,* Bk. IV, tit. xvii, chap. xiii); by St. Thomas (I-II, qu. 90, art. 3 and qu. 97 [, art. 3]); by Cajetan (in the above-cited work, *De Potestate Papae,* Pt. II, chaps. ii and x [chap. ix]); by Vitoria (in his *Relectio* on this very subject [*De Potestate Civili*]); and by other authorities to whom reference has been made.

A reason for this view, supplied by what we have said above, is the fact that such power, in the nature of things, resides immediately in the community; and therefore, in order that it may justly come to reside in a given individual, as in a sovereign prince, it must necessarily be bestowed upon him by the consent of the community.

Again, the same view may be explained by means of a comprehensive enumeration of the various aspects of the matter.[10]

For [in the first place,] the power in question may be considered as having been bestowed upon kings immediately by God Himself. Yet such a bestowal, although it has sometimes occurred—as it did in the case of Saul and in that of David—has nevertheless been extraordinary and supernatural in so far as concerned the mode [of imparting power]. In the common and ordinary course of providence, however, such cases do not come to pass, since—in the natural order—men are governed in civil affairs not by revelations, but by natural reason. Neither may a valid objection be based upon the assertions in certain Scriptural passages, as in the fourth chapter of Daniel, that God gives kingdoms and changes them at His will; or as in the forty-fifth chapter of Isaias, which declares that God made Cyrus a king; wherefore Christ said [to Pilate] (John, chap. xix [, v. 11]): "Thou shouldst not have any power against me, unless it were given thee from above." For the meaning of these passages is simply that all of the events mentioned come to pass only through the special providence of God, Who either ordains or permits them, as Augustine has said (*On the Gospel of John,* Tract. VI [, chap. i, §25] and *Against Faustus,* Bk. XXII, chap. lxxiv); but this fact does not prevent such [bestowals and transferences of power] from being executed by human agency; just as all the other effects wrought through secondary causes are attributed primarily to the providence of God.

3. A second possibility is that this power may reside in a king through hereditary succession. Some jurists, indeed, are of the opinion that such was the case from the very beginning; but others rightly point out that succession necessarily presupposes the existence of dominion or power in the person succeeded, so that we must of necessity trace it to some one who was not the successor of another, since the succession cannot reach back *ad infinitum.* Therefore, with respect to that first possessor, we ask whence he has derived the kingdom and power, since he does not possess it inherently and by natural law. Title by succession, then, cannot be the primary source of this power as it resides in the sovereign. Therefore, the first possessor must have derived the supreme power directly from the commonwealth, while his successors must derive it from that same source indirectly, [yet] fundamentally. Moreover, since any possession passes into the hands of a successor with its accompanying obligations, the conditions attaching to the kingly power when it was transmitted by the commonwealth to the first king, pass to his successors, so that they possess that power together with the original obligations.

4. A third title of royal power is wont to arise on the basis of war, which must be just war in order to confer a valid title and dominion. Consequently, many persons believe that kingdoms were originally introduced through tyranny rather than true power. This belief is attested by Alvaro Paez (*De Planctu Ecclesiae*, Bk. I, chap. xli), by Driedo (*De Libertate Christiana*, Bk. I, chap. xv), and by Petrus Bertrandi (in his treatise *De Origine et Usu Iurisdictionis*, Qu. i). Accordingly, when the kingly power is held solely through unjust force, there is no true legislative power vested in the king; yet it is possible that, in the course of time, the people may give their consent to and acquiesce in such sovereignty, in which case the power in question is [once more] traced back to an act of transmission and donation on the part of the people. It may sometimes happen, however, that a state not previously subject to a king is subjected through a just war. But such an event is always an incidental circumstance (as it were) of the punishment of some wrongdoing; so that the state in question is bound to obedience and to acquiescence in such subjection; and therefore, this mode [of acquiring kingly power] also includes, in a sense, the consent—whether expressed or [implicitly] due—of the state.

However, we are now treating of this power chiefly in so far as it is inherently capable of being introduced and bestowed upon one man. And finally, if we give the matter sufficient consideration, we shall find that when such subjection to one king is imposed by means of a just war, it is presupposed that he possesses the royal power by virtue of which he is able to declare that war; and this power is simply a just extension (so to speak) of the power of his kingdom; so that such kingly power is always to be traced back to some individual who attained it, not through war, but through just election or the consent of the people.

We rightly conclude, then, after this comprehensive enumeration [of the various titles to royal power], that the said power has been derived [in every case] by the prince from the state.

5. It may, indeed, be objected that from our conclusion it follows that this royal power pertains exclusively to human law, a deduction which would seem to be contrary to the language of the Scriptures: "By me, kings reign [. . .]" (Proverbs, chap. viii [, v. 15]); and again, "For he is God's minister," etc. (Romans, chap. xiii [, v. 4]).

Another deduction from the same conclusion is that the kingdom must be superior to the king, since it has given the king his power; whence a further inference is drawn, namely, that the kingdom may, if it shall so choose, depose or change its king, a deduction which is altogether false.

Consequently, Vitoria (above cited [*De Potestate Civili*]) held that the royal power should be described absolutely as derived from divine law and as having been given by God, with the intervention of human choice. On the other hand, Bertrandi, Driedo (above cited) and Castro (*De Potestate Legis Poenalis* [Bk. I, chap. i]) uphold the opposite doctrine, which is doubtless the true doctrine, if one is speaking in a formal sense of the royal power as such and in so far as it exists in one man. For this governing power, regarded from a political viewpoint and in its essence, is undoubtedly derived from God, as I have said; yet the fact that it resides in a particular individual results—as has been demonstrated—from a grant on the part of the state itself; and therefore, in this sense, the said power pertains to human law. Moreover, the monarchical nature of the government of such a state or province is brought about by human disposition, as has already been shown; therefore, the principate itself is derived from men. Another proof of this derivation is the fact that the power of the king is greater or less, according to the pact or agreement between him and the kingdom; therefore, absolutely speaking, that power is drawn from men.

6. The passages cited from Holy Scripture, however, are to be interpreted as having two meanings. One is as follows: the power in question, viewed in itself, is derived from God; and it is just and in conformity with the divine will. The other meaning is this: assuming that the said power has been transferred to the king, he is now the vicar of God, and natural law makes it obligatory that he be obeyed. The case is similar to that of a private individual who surrenders himself by sale to be the slave of another; so that the resulting power of *dominium* has, in an absolute sense, a human derivation, yet the slave is [also] bound by divine and natural law—once we assume that the contract has been made—to render obedience to his master.

Thus the reply to the confirmation [of the opposing view] consists clearly in a general denial of the [second] deduction [and its corollary].[11] For, once the power has been transferred to the king, he is through that power rendered superior even to the kingdom which bestowed it; since by this bestowal the kingdom has subjected itself and has deprived itself of its former liberty, just as is, in due proportion, clearly true in the case of the slave, which we have mentioned by way of illustration. Moreover, in accordance with the same reasoning, the king cannot be deprived of this power, since he has acquired a true ownership of it; unless perchance he lapses into tyranny, on which ground the kingdom may wage a just war against him, a point which we consider elsewhere.[12]

7. A third inference to be drawn from our preceding chapter[13] is as follows: in view of the nature of things—that is to say, according to the natural and ordinary course of human events—there are no civil laws established universally for the whole world and binding upon all men.

This fact is evident, indeed, from the term itself, since we are speaking of human laws as strictly distinguished from the *ius gentium,* and therefore called civil, for the reason that they are peculiar to one city state or one nation, as the *Digest* (I.i.9) declares. We are furthermore speaking of laws which can be established by natural power, omitting for the present the consideration of supernatural power. Accordingly, such laws demand, as by an intrinsic condition, that they should not be of a universal nature.

The reason [in support of our third inference] is the fact that *a priori* there is in existence no legislative power with jurisdiction over the whole world, that is, over all mankind; and therefore, no civil law can be thus universal. The consequent is clearly true, since no law extends its force beyond the limits of the legislator's jurisdiction. "For we know," says Paulus [*Digest,* II.i.20], "that every law is addressed to those who are under the jurisdiction of that law"; since "he who pronounces judgment outside the territory [of his jurisdiction] may be disobeyed with impunity," as the laws declare; and therefore, much less are we bound to obey, outside his own territory, the person who decrees law, or legal precepts [for that territory]. The antecedent, moreover, is manifestly true in the light of what has already been said. For the power in question does not reside in the whole community of mankind, since the whole of mankind does not constitute one single commonwealth or kingdom. Nor does that power reside in any one individual, since such an individual would have to receive it from the hands of men, and this is inconceivable, inasmuch as men have never agreed to confer it [thus], nor to establish one sole head over themselves. Furthermore, not even by title of war, whether justly or unjustly, has there at any time been a prince who made himself temporal sovereign over the whole world. This assertion is clearly borne out by history. And therefore, the ordinary course of human nature points to the conclusion that a human legislative power of universal character and world-wide extent does not exist and has never existed, nor is it morally possible that it should have done so.

However, an objection with respect to the emperor would straightway present itself [to those who support the view above set forth]. I shall deal with this objection in the following Book.[14]

Thus the whole world—even though it be governed and bound by civil laws, as is morally certain in the case of all nations enjoying any form of civil government and not entirely barbarous—is nevertheless not ruled throughout by the same laws; on the contrary, each commonwealth or kingdom is governed, in accordance with an appropriate distribution, by means of its own particular laws.

And as to how the power in question finds a place within the Church of Christ, or whether it has been specifically instituted therein, these are questions which we shall discuss later.

8. By way of a fourth inference, we may briefly deduce from the discussion [in the preceding chapter], the ways in which this power to make human laws may be imparted.

For it should be pointed out that, originally, the said power can be received directly from God; since there is no other possible origin for it—as we have shown in that previous chapter—and since God, as the Author of all good things, is therefore the Author of all powers and especially of this power. For the latter most particularly rests upon divine providence, being necessary to good moral conduct, and to the proper preservation and government of mankind. Consequently, the said power must have been transferred to some possessor immediately by God; for if it resides mediately in any being, it necessarily resides immediately in some other being, since it cannot be traced back *ad infinitum.*

There are two ways, however, in which this power may be derived from God; that is to say, it may be derived naturally, as from the Author of nature, or supernaturally, as from the Author of grace. We shall treat of the latter mode in Book Five,[15] but the first has been sufficiently expounded in our previous discussion.

Accordingly, it is furthermore clear that the power in question may [also] be received immediately from men, and mediately from God. Indeed, such is usually the case with regard to natural power. For though it resides immediately in the community, it is conferred through the latter upon kings or princes or senators, since it is rarely or never retained in the community as a whole in such a way as to be administered immediately thereby. Nevertheless, after that power has been transferred to a given individual, and even though it may pass as the result of various successions and elections into the possession of a number of individuals, the community is always regarded as its immediate possessor, because, by virtue of the original act of investiture, it is the community that transfers the power to the other possessors. The case is similar to that of the papal power which, in spite of the fact that it is transferred to various persons in turn, as the result of various elections, comes always to every one of these persons from God, its immediate source. . . .

Seven

THE ENLIGHTENMENT

Spain in the eighteenth century experienced a period of recovery, compared to its seventeenth-century decline. A convenient date from which to track the upward turn is 1714, a year that offers a revealing window on political, economic, and ideological change. The War of the Spanish Succession, fought between supporters of the Austrian Hapsburgs and the French Bourbons for the vacant Spanish throne, ended with treaties in 1713 and 1714. These confirmed Philip of Anjou, Louis XIV's grandson, as Felipe V, the first Bourbon ruler of Spain. The initial years of Felipe's reign were marked by the struggle between what were later termed *las dos Españas:* traditional Spain, rooted in local custom and privilege, and modern Spain, bent on enlightened reform. Throughout the century, in fits and starts, Bourbon rulers tended to centralize power in an attempt to reform the country from above. This tendency culminated in the enlightened despotism of Carlos (Charles) III (1759–1788), whose ministers attacked the prerogatives of guilds, monopolies, and the Church. In addition to these political developments, the Spanish economy in 1714 was well along in a gradual process of recovery that began toward the end of the seventeenth century and accelerated in the second half of the eighteenth. Finally, the term "*novatores*" (innovators) first appeared in 1714, in Francisco Palanco's *Dialogus physico-theologicus contra philosophiae novatores*. It referred to Spanish natural philosophers who, beginning in the late seventeenth century, rebelled against the Aristotelian and Scholastic approach to natural philosophy and wished to replace the traditional theological worldview with a scientific one. By 1714 these philosophers were sufficiently prominent to merit their own label and Francisco Palanco's ire. The views of the *novatores* were typically disseminated at court, in *tertulias* (regular, informal social gatherings), and through the proceedings of newly founded medical and scientific societies—rarely in the universities and religious orders, which remained redoubts of decadent Scholasticism.

As the century progressed, the views of the *novatores* mixed with other currents in the stream of the European Enlightenment. The result in Spain was an eclectic group of enlightened thinkers, including the skeptical physician Martín Martínez, who described Scholastic philosophy as "contentious clamoring"; the essayist Benito Jerónimo Feijóo, who defended Martínez in his first published work; the literary scholar Gregorio Mayans y Siscar, the first biographer of Cervantes and editor of Vives' collected works; the Count of Aranda, who prepared Carlos III's decree expelling the Jesuits in 1767; the Count of Campomanes, an economist, historian, and minister to Carlos III; and Gaspar Melchor de Jovellanos, a judge, minister, reformer, and writer. The outlook of this diverse group can be sampled in the selection by Feijóo.

BENITO JERÓNIMO FEIJÓO

Benito Jerónimo Feijóo y Montenegro was born in 1676 in Casdemiro, a Spanish village near the Portuguese border in the northwestern region of Galicia. As the oldest of ten children of a family of hidalgos, Feijóo was entitled to inherit the family estate, but he chose a monastic career instead. At age fourteen he took the Benedictine habit at the monastery of San Julián de Samos in Galicia. He studied theology in various schools prior to earning bachelor's and doctoral degrees in theology at the University of San Vicente in Oviedo. The monastery of San Vicente in this Asturian city was Feijóo's home for the rest of his life. He advanced steadily through the academic and monastic ranks, occupying three chairs of theology in succession and twice serving as abbot of the monastery. Ill health forced him to retire from academic life in 1739, but he read and wrote assiduously until shortly before his death in 1764.

A surviving account by one of Feijóo's contemporaries describes his imposing physical presence and lively, penetrating eyes.[1] He was a prodigious reader, typically seated with a book in his hands,[2] and slept scarcely four hours a night.[3] Surprisingly, perhaps, for one so dedicated to his work, Feijóo bloomed late in print. His first publication, a letter defending the skeptical medicine of Martín Martínez, did not appear until 1725, his fiftieth year. But Feijóo's reputation rests primarily on two later works. The nine volumes of *Teatro crítico universal* (Universal Theater of Criticism) were published from 1726 to 1740 and the five volumes of *Cartas eruditas y curiosas* (Learned and Inquisitive Letters) from 1742 to 1760. The spirit of both works can be roughly approximated by an anecdote from Feijóo's boyhood:

> When told that it was dangerous to eat immediately after drinking chocolate, or to fall asleep immediately after taking a purgative, he risked the consequences of eating and sleeping under these dangerous conditions to see what really would happen to him. And having survived his experiments and having found that fact failed to fit theory, he thereafter became predisposed to distrust any assertion about the natural world which had not been or could not be checked.[4]

Feijóo grew up to be a great debunker, a harbinger of enlightenment who campaigned tirelessly against superstition and trumpeted the good news of scientific discovery. He wrote on an encyclopedic range of topics: philosophical skepticism, agriculture, freemasonry, the causes of love, historiography, demonic possession, Boyle's Law, dueling, church music, the medical practice of bloodletting, phonetic spelling, the microscope, and much else.

Feijóo's two principal works caught the spirit of the age. A steady stream of visitors, letters, and books from Europe and the Americas washed through his cell in Oviedo. Some four to five hundred thousand volumes of his work are estimated to have been sold during his lifetime,[5] and translations appeared in French, English, Italian, German, and Portuguese. But along with fame came controversy. Between 1728 and 1788, 115 works on Feijóo are known to have been published— some to attack, others to defend him.[6] Inevitably, Feijóo was drawn into polemics. The war of words was escalating when, in 1750, Fernando VI decreed that no further attacks on Feijóo's work would be permitted.

Why the controversy? Feijóo dealt bluntly with prejudice and superstition, writing in a tone that was "calculatedly offensive."[7] He took on the medical establishment, calling Hippocrates "that famous murderer." He criticized the abuse of arguments from authority. He exposed false miracles. In addition, he refused to trade intellectual detachment for adherence to a philosophical system. He was a critic of Scholasticism, though educated in it; a defender of Descartes, though opposed to animal mechanism; and an exponent of Bacon's philosophy of experience, though committed to reason as well as the senses.

One of Feijóo's contrarian essays is "Defensa de las mujeres" (A Defense of Women), which is Discourse 16 of the first volume of *Teatro crítico universal*. The essay confronts misogyny in the forms best known at the time. Feijóo's defense develops along several fronts, but he is principally concerned to vindicate women's intellectual capacities. To appreciate his audacity, we have only to compare his defense with later dicta by some of the luminaries of the French Enlightenment. Voltaire's *Philosophical Dictionary* includes this observation on the sexes: "Among a hundred men, there is scarcely one that possesses genius; and among women, scarcely one among five hundred." Rousseau's *Émile* contrasts female with male education: "The search for abstract and speculative truths, principles, and scientific axioms, whatever tends to generalize ideas, does not fall within the compass of women; all their studies ought to have reference to the practical. . . . Woman has more spirit and man more genius; woman observes and man reasons." Diderot's essay "On Women" follows the same line: "We have more intellect than women; women more instinct than we."

The fact that a work as contemporary in spirit as the "Defensa" seems not to have been translated into English since the eighteenth century would be a worthy topic for another essay by Feijóo.[8] A contemporary translation of the first ten of twenty-four sections of the essay is included here.[9]

A Defense of Women

Equality despite Difference

1.

I face an uphill battle. I contend not only with the ignorant herd, for to defend all women amounts to offending almost all men. Rarely do we take an interest in the priority of our own sex without disparaging the other. Common opinion has become so contemptuous of women that it scarcely admits any good in them. It fills them with moral defects and physical imperfections. But, above all, it limits their intellects. That is why, after briefly defending women on other counts, I will devote more attention to their aptitude for all types of science and higher knowledge. . . .

The worst of the herd very frequently represent the female sex as a sewer of vice, as if men were the only repositories of virtue. True, a great deal of invective in innumerable books encourages them to the point that they will hardly admit that a single woman is good. They attempt to join a modest face to a lascivious soul in even the most promising women:

Translated for this volume by John R. Welch.

Aspera si visa est, rigidasque imitata Sabinas,
Velle, sed ex alto dissimulare puta.[1]

[If she seems harsh and imitates the severe Sabine women, she thinks you should prefer her, but she dissembles from the start.]

Against such insolent slander, contempt and loathing are the best defense. Not a few of those who most frequently and luridly paint the defects of women are the most solicitous to win their favor. Euripides slandered women terribly in his tragedies, yet, according to Athenaeus and Strabo, he was very much their lover in private. He execrated them in the theater and idolized them in the bedroom. Boccaccio, who was excessively lewd, wrote the violent satire titled *Labyrinth of Love* against women.[2] How can this be? Perhaps they attempt to conceal their inclinations behind the fiction of being judgmental. Perhaps the brutish satiety of appetite breeds a restless tedium that sees nothing but indignities in the other sex. Or perhaps this abuse is revenge for favors denied; some men are wicked enough to say that a woman is not good precisely because she does not want to be bad. This unjust complaint is sometimes vented in atrocious revenges, as the unhappy case of Madame Douglas, a very beautiful Irishwoman, illustrates. Guillaume Leout, enraged because she would not yield to his desires, accused her of the crime of lèse majesté. He managed to prove this calumny by bribing witnesses, and she was put to death. Leout later confessed this, as La Mothe le Vayer relates.[3]

I do not deny that many women have vices. But, really, if we look into the genealogy of their disorders, we will surely find their origins in the persistent impulses of individuals of our own sex. Whoever wants to make women good should convert the men. For in women shame is a natural barrier against the batteries of appetite, and rarely is this wall breached from the interior of the plaza.

The animadversions against women in some of the Scriptures should be understood as directed only at perverse women, who undoubtedly exist. And even those passages that concern the female sex in general prove nothing. The doctors of the soul warn against women just as the doctors of the body warn against fruit. Fruit is good, useful, and beautiful in itself, though harmful if abused. Besides, we understand the scope of these passages concerning risk in light of their intention to ward off danger.

And tell me, those who suppose that the female sex has more vices than our own, how can this be squared with the Church's practice of favoring women especially with the epithet "devout"? And with the claims by learned doctors that more women than men will be saved, even taking into account the proportion of the greater number of women?[4] This can only be based on the observation that women have a greater inclination to piety.

I am aware of an objection made with much fanfare and no truth: that women are the cause of all evils. In an attempt to prove this, even the humblest people repeat insistently that Florinda brought about the loss of Spain[5] and Eve that of the whole world.

But the first example is absolutely false. Count Julian was the one who brought the Moors to Spain. His daughter did not persuade him to do so; she only communicated her outrage to her father. Poor women! If they are attacked by some insolent male, are they to be deprived of unburdening themselves with father or spouse? That is just what their aggressors would like. If an unjust revenge should ever be carried out, the fault would lie with him who wielded the sword and him who offered the insult—not with the innocent insulted woman. These faults would be due to men.

If the second example proves that women in general are worse than men, it also proves that angels in general are worse than women. For just as Adam sinned because of a woman, the woman sinned because of an angel. Actually, whether Adam or Eve sinned more gravely is not really clear; the authorities are divided. Cajetan excuses Eve on the grounds that she was deceived by a creature of superior shrewdness and intelligence, whereas this was not the case with Adam. This would make her offense considerably less serious than his.

2.

Let us pass from the moral to the physical, which is more to the point. The preference for the robust over the delicate sex is so taken for granted that many do not hesitate to consider the female defective and even monstrous. They affirm that nature intends to generate the male and only through error or defect, whether of matter or capacity, does it produce the female.

Admirable physicists! From this we would infer that nature intends its own ruin, for the species cannot survive without both sexes. We would also infer that human nature has more errors than successes if the common opinion that it produces more women than men is true.[6] And how could the formation of females be attributed to weakness or defective matter when they are repeatedly born from robust, well-constituted parents in the prime of life? Even if humanity were to conserve its original innocence, which would preclude such defects, would not some women have to be born? Would there not be a need to propagate the species?

I well know that there was an author who swallowed this absurdity out of declared spite against the female sex. This was Almeric of Bene, a twelfth-century Parisian doctor. Among other errors, he declared that if the age of innocence had lasted, all individuals of our species would be male and that God would have to create each one himself, just as he had created Adam.

Almeric was a blind follower of Aristotle. Hence all, or almost all, his errors were consequences extracted from Aristotle's doctrines. Seeing that Aristotle claims in more than one place that females are defective animals and their generation accidental, unintended by nature, Almeric inferred that there would be no women in a state of innocence. Thus a heretical theology often follows an errant physics.

But the great loyalty Almeric professed for Aristotle went badly for both Almeric and Aristotle. The Council of Paris condemned Almeric's errors in 1209, and the same Council prohibited Aristotle's books, a prohibition later confirmed by Pope Gregory IX. Since Almeric had been dead for a year when his dogmas were condemned, his remains were unearthed and cast into a foul place.

Hence we should not let ourselves be influenced by Aristotle's followers, however learned and even innocent of Almeric's error, who proclaim that the female sex is defective only because Aristotle said so. It is true that Aristotle treated women badly. He was excessive not only in declaring their physical defects but, with even greater vehemence, their moral failings (which will be treated elsewhere). Who would not think that he was temperamentally averse to the female sex? But this is not true at all. He loved two women dearly. His love for the first, Pythias, who was the daughter or niece of Hermeias, tyrant of Atarneus, led him to the delirium of offering incense to her as to a god. There are also tales of an insane affair with a servant, although Plutarch does not lend them credence. But Plutarch lived long after Aristotle, and Theocritus of Chios, who as Aristotle's contemporary is more credible, satirized him for obscenity in a vivid epigram. This is another example of how mordacity against women is quite often accompanied by an intemperate inclination for them, as we noted above.

From the same physical error that condemns women as imperfect animals springs another theological error: that these imperfect creatures will be perfected at the resurrection by being transformed into males, as if grace must finish what nature has left undone. This error was impugned by Saint Augustine in *De civitate Dei* (Book 22, chapter 17).

The error is very similar to that of vain alchemists. Believing that nature attempts to produce gold but through incapacity produces an imperfect metal instead, they urge art to perfect the work of nature by transforming iron into gold. But the alchemical error turns out to be more tolerable. It does not touch matters of faith. And regardless of nature's intent and the imaginary capacity of art, gold is in fact the noblest metal; the others are quite inferior to it. With the theological error, by contrast, all is false: that nature always intends the male; that its operations degenerate in the female; and, worst of all, that these mistakes must be corrected at the resurrection.

3.

Yet I do not approve the rashness of Zacuto Lusitano in the introduction to *De morbis mulierum*. He employs frivolous arguments in favor of women, alleging their physical superiority to men. With better arguments one might undertake to show this, but my aim is to establish equality, not superiority.

Setting aside the question of intellect for treatment later on, we must recognize the difficulty of the equality thesis. For there are three qualities in which men appear to have a decided advantage over women:

robustness, constancy, and *prudence.* But even if women concede these advantages, they can still claim a tie by noting their superiority in three other qualities: *beauty, docility,* and *simplicity.*

Robustness, which is a physical quality, can be counterbalanced by beauty, which is also physical. In fact, many would give greater weight to beauty. They would be correct if the value of qualities were determined precisely by their tendency to flatter the eye. But since public utility should count more in a sound judgment, I think robustness should be preferred to beauty. The robustness of men provides essential support to the three columns that sustain any republic: war, agriculture, and mechanics. Except by accident, I do not know what important fruit the beauty of women yields. Some would argue that, far from being advantageous, it brings grave harm in the excessive passions it inspires, the rivalries it provokes, and the care, anxiety, and suspicion it occasions in those responsible for its custody.

This accusation is unfounded, though; it stems from lack of observation. If all women were ugly, the less deformed would be thought just as attractive as the beauties of today. They would therefore wreak the same havoc. The least ugly in Greece would be the conflagration of Troy, like Helen; and the least ugly in King Roderic's palace would be the ruin of Spain, like Florinda.[7] Countries where the women are less graceful have no fewer excesses than countries where they are more charming and proportioned. Even in Russia, which has more beautiful women than any other country in Europe, there is not as much abandon as in other nations, and conjugal fidelity is much more strictly observed.

Beauty in itself, then, is not to blame for the evils attributed to it. But in this case I vote for robustness, which I judge to be much more estimable than beauty. And so, in this respect, men have the advantage. However, women can avail themselves of the maxim of many of the learned, honored in many illustrious schools, that the will is a nobler faculty than the intellect. This favors their cause. For if robustness wins out in the intellect because it is more estimable, beauty holds sway over the will since it is more lovable.

The quality of constancy, which ennobles men, can be offset by that of docility, which sparkles in women. Here we are not speaking of these qualities formally as virtues, for this would not permit us to consider them physically. Rather, we view them as rooted and outlined in the temperament, whose unformed embryo is indifferent to good and bad usage. Instead of speaking of constancy or docility, then, it would be better to speak of flexible or inflexible natures.

To the objection that women's docility often declines into superficiality, I respond that men's constancy often degenerates into stubbornness. I confess that firmness in a good cause is the author of great good, but it cannot be denied that obstinacy in evil is the root of great harm. If someone objects that invincible adherence to good or evil is a characteristic of angels, I answer that this is not so certain that great theologians do not deny it. In addition, many properties that stem from the excellence of superior natures issue from the imperfection of inferior ones. According to St. Thomas, the more perfect angels understand through fewer notions; for human beings, though, to have fewer notions is a defect. Learning would be a blemish on the intellect of an angel, but it enlightens that of a human being.

The prudence of men is balanced by the simplicity of women. We could state the case more strongly, for simplicity would be much better for the human race than prudence for each of its members. Everyone thinks that the Golden Age was characterized by innocence, not prudence.

If someone counters that much of what passes for innocence in women is indiscretion, I answer that much of what is called prudence in men is duplicity, backstabbing, and treachery, which are worse. Even the indiscrete forthrightness of women, who sometimes bare their souls against the rules of reason, is a good sign. Since none of us are ignorant of our own vices, those who find nontrivial vices within take care to bar the door to curiosity's spies. Those who commit crimes at home will not hold permanent open house. Malice is always accompanied by caution. So whoever easily bares one's soul knows it cannot be very dirty. Viewed in this light, women's innocence is always estimable: when corrected by sound judgment, it is an excellence; when not, it is a good sign.

4.

In addition to the good qualities already mentioned, women possess the most beautiful and transcendent of all, which is shame. This is so characteristic of women that even corpses retain it, if what Pliny says is true. He claims that drowned men float face up and drowned women face down: *Veluti pudori defunctarum parcente natura* [As if nature respected the modesty of dead women].[8]

When asked what color most becomes a woman's face, a philosopher answered with truth and wit: the color of shame. In my opinion, this is women's greatest advantage over men. Shame is a barricade that nature has erected between virtue and vice. It is the shadow of beautiful souls and the visible character of virtue, according to a discerning French-man. At greater length, St. Bernard illustrated it with epithets: precious stone of customs, torch of modest souls, sister of continence, safeguard of repute, honor of life, seat of virtue, tribute of nature, and emblem of all decency.[9] Rightly and subtly, Diogenes called it virtue's dye. It is in fact a bulwark, great and strong, that confronts vice and protects the en-tire fortress of the soul. Once it is breached, as St. Gregory of Nazianzus observes, no evil will meet resistance: *Protinus extincto subeunt mala cuncta pudore* [As soon as modesty is extinguished, all evils slip in].

Some will object that shame is a notable protector of exterior action but not of internal consent; hence vice has an open invitation to triumph through invisible assaults that the wall of shame cannot impede. Even if this were so, shame would provide priceless protection, for at least it would prevent an innumerable number of scandals and their disastrous consequences. On further reflection, though, we see that it defends— usually, if not always—against silent escalades in hidden recesses of the soul. For very rarely is internal consent not accompanied by action, and action fixes criminal feelings in the soul, increasing and strengthening vicious tendencies. It is true that moral clumsiness does sometimes infil-trate the spirit without being acted on. But it does not lodge there as a servant and much less as an owner. It simply wanders in and out.

The passions remain weak and act timidly without the food that nourishes them. This is mainly true of persons who blush quite easily. For them, spirit and visage communicate so directly that they suspect whatever is being plotted in the retired precinct of the spirit could emerge in the open plaza of the face. In fact, the most hidden feelings are painted on their cheeks at each step; the color of shame is the only one that can form images of invisible objects. Thus the fear that what is imprinted in the spirit could be read on one's face can serve to rein in women's outbreaks of desire.

In addition, many women reach the point of being ashamed all by themselves. This heroic delicacy of shame, which the ingenious Father Vieyra treated in one of his sermons, is not purely ideal, as some coarse spirits think. It is practical and real in individuals of the noblest kind. Demetrius of Phaleron understood this. He instructed the youth of Athens that at home they should feel shame before their parents; when not at home, before all who see them; and when alone, before their own selves.

5.

I think I have indicated enough advantages on the part of women to balance and perhaps even surpass those of men. Who will pronounce judgment in this case? If I had the authority, I might resolve the issue by saying that the qualities in which women excel tend to make them better in themselves, while those in which men excel make them more useful to the public. But since my role here is not that of a judge but a lawyer, the case will have to remain undecided for now.

Even if I had the requisite authority, it would be necessary to postpone judgment, for someone could argue in favor of men that the good qualities attributed to women are common to both sexes. This is true. But it is just as true that both sexes have the good qualities attributed to men. To be clear, it is necessary to point out the excellences found much more frequently in members of each sex and much less so in those of the other. I admit, then, that there are docile, innocent, and blushing men.

Blushing is a good sign in women, but it is even better in men. It indicates a generous nature and sharp wits. John Barclay, whose subtle wits entitle him to a vote of special note, remarks this more than once in his *Satyricon*. Although not an infallible sign, I have observed this so often that I never expect good from a lad with a bold face.

I claim, then, that various individuals of our sex have the fine qualities that ennoble the opposite sex. But this in no way inclines the balance in our favor, for equal weight must be given to the many women who have the excellences of which men boast.

6.

A thousand able princesses have exhibited political prudence. No age can overlook the first woman that history retrieves from myth: Semiramis, queen of the Assyrians.[10] Educated in infancy by doves, she later rose above eagles, for she knew not only how to exact blind obedience from the subjects her husband bequeathed her but made subjects of neighboring nations and neighbors of distant ones, extending her conquests from Ethiopia to India. Artemisia, queen of Caria, was revered by her subjects throughout her long widowhood. Caria was attacked by the Rhodians, but with two singular stratagems, in just two strokes, she destroyed the invading army. Then, passing rapidly from defense to offense, she conquered the island of Rhodes. The two Aspasias successfully administered their respective states. Pericles, the husband of one, and Cyrus, son of Darius Nothus, the suitor of the other, had complete confidence in their ability to govern. The prudent Phila, daughter of Antipater, advised her father on the affairs of Macedonia as a girl and later managed to extricate her husband, the rash and shallow Demetrius, from many difficulties. The wily Livia appears to have been more astute than Augustus was insightful, for he would never have given her such power over him had he known. The shrewd Agrippina, whose arts were disastrous for herself and the world, employed them to promote her son Nero to the throne. The wise Amalasuntha, though less given to understand the languages of peoples subject to the Roman Empire, governed with great skill during the minority of her son Athalaric.

Skipping over many and nearing our own epoch, we cannot forget Elizabeth of England, a woman formed equally by the three Graces and the three Furies. Her sovereign conduct would be the admiration of Europe forever if her vices had not been so entwined with her principles that they became indispensable. Posterity will always view her political image colored—or, better, stained—with the blood of innocent Mary Stuart, queen of Scots. Catherine de Médicis, queen of France, negotiated shrewdly to keep the hostile parties of Catholics and Calvinists in balance and prevent the ruin of the crown. She showed the skill of an acrobat on a high and delicate cord who skillfully manipulates two opposed weights, delighting the bystanders by flaunting risk and avoiding a fall. Our Isabel of Castile would not have been inferior to any of these in the administration of government had she actually ruled in addition to being queen.[11] Nevertheless, her actions showed consummate prudence on many occasions. Even Laurentius Beyerlink says in his eulogy that there was no great undertaking of her time in which she did not play a part or the whole: *Quid magni in regno, sine illa, imo nisi per illam fere gestum est?* [How great is the kingdom without her when, indeed, almost nothing was done except through her?]. At least the discovery of the New World, the most glorious event in Spain in many centuries, would not have been achieved had Isabel's magnanimity not overcome Fernando's fear and laziness.

Though I am not very sure of the numbers, most queens who had long reigns as absolute monarchs seem to be celebrated in the histories as excellent rulers. But women are so unfortunate that the many illustrious examples are eclipsed by a Brunhild, a Fredegund, the two Juanas of Naples, and a few others. Granted, the first two had more than enough malice, but they did not lack shrewdness.

The view that a crown does not sit well on a woman's head is not as universal as is commonly thought. According to Pliny, women reigned for many centuries on Meroë, an island formed by the Nile—or a peninsula, as moderns prefer—in Ethiopia. The Queen of Sheba was one of them. Based on the fact that Christ our Savior referred to her as "the Queen of the South,"[12] a title that suggests a vast domain in that part of the world, Father Cornelius a Lapide thinks that her empire extended far beyond Meroë and may have included all of Ethiopia. Even if this domain extended no further than Meroë, it would have been considerable, for writers such as Thomas Corneille affirm that the island, or peninsula, of Meroë is larger than Great Britain. Aristotle says that women, in accordance with the laws of Lycurgus, played a large part in the political affairs of the Lacedaemonians.[13]

Women also reign on the large island of Borneo in the Indian Ocean, according to Mandelslo's account in the second volume published by Olearius. Their husbands enjoy no other prerogative than that of being their most qualified vassals. On the island of Formosa in the South China Sea, the prudent conduct of idolatrous women is so satisfactory that they alone are entrusted with the priesthood and all that pertains to matters of religion. In politics, as interpreters of the will of their gods, they enjoy more power than senators in some respects.

However, the common practice of nations is more in line with reason, which corresponds to the divine decree in paradise that announced the subjection of our first mother, and all her daughters in her name, to men.[14] It is only necessary to correct people's impatience with laws that require obedience to women rulers; likewise, the exaggerated esteem for our own sex that sometimes prefers an incompetent boy to a mature woman. The ancient Persians carried this to a ridiculous extreme. When the widow of one of their kings was found to be pregnant and their magi foresaw the birth of a male, they crowned the queen's womb and proclaimed the fetus their king, giving him the name Shapur before birth.[15]

7.

We have been discussing political prudence, limiting ourselves to just a few examples and omitting many. To talk of economic prudence would be pointless, for everywhere we observe houses well managed by women and others mismanaged by men.

Let us turn instead to strength, a quality that men consider inseparable from their own sex. I would agree that heaven has favored men greatly in this respect, but not that it is their birthright or theirs exclusively, unshared with the opposite sex.

Not a century has passed without being ennobled by courageous women. I omit the heroines of Scripture and the holy martyrs, for feats performed with supernatural aid are credits to divine power, not women's natural capacity. But there have been so many women of vigorous hand and heroic courage that they throng together in the theater of memory.

Beside the Semiramises, the Artemisas, the Tomiris, and the Zenobias appears Aretaphila, spouse of Nicocrates, the king of Cyrene in Libya. In her incomparably generous person, the tenderest love of country, the greatest bravery of spirit, and the subtlest command of language competed mutually. To liberate her country from the violent tyranny of her husband and to avenge the death he had inflicted on her first husband in order to possess her, she led a conspiracy against him and despoiled him of kingdom and life. When Leander, Nicocrates' brother in dominion and in cruelty, succeeded him, Aretaphila had the courage and craft to fling this second tyrant from the world. She crowned her illustrious actions by removing the crown that the Cyrenians, grateful for so many benefits, had placed on her head.

Drypetina, daughter of the great Mithradates and his inseparable companion in so many hazardous projects, unfailingly demonstrated the strength of soul and body promised in infancy by the singular fact of having been born with two rows of teeth. After her father had been undone by the great Pompey, she found herself in an indefensible castle besieged by Manlio Prisco. Rather than suffer the ignominy of slavery, she took her own life.

The Roman girl Cloelia, imprisoned by Lars Porsena, king of the Etruscans, overcame a thousand difficulties, escaped from prison, and bested the waves of the Tiber on a horse—or, according to some, with her own arms—to successfully reach Rome.

Arria, wife of Caecina Paetus, who was condemned to death for participating in the conspiracy of Camillus against the emperor Claudius, resolved not to survive her spouse. After she tried in vain to shatter her skull against a wall, she was put in Caecina's cell. There she exhorted him to anticipate the executioner's stroke with his own hand and led the way by plunging a dagger into her breast.

Epponina, whose husband Julius Sabinus had arrogated the title of Caesar to himself in Gaul, endured unspeakable trials with rare constancy. Finally, when Vespasian condemned her to death, she told him nobly that she would die content, for she would not live to see such a bad emperor on the throne.

Recent centuries have produced vigorous women comparable to those of antiquity. Joan of Arc was the pillar who sustained a vacillating monarchy in its hour of need. Like English and French arms, English and French views of her clash. The English attributed her feats to a pact with the devil; the French, to divine favor. The English may have been motivated by hatred; the French, by politics. In that great swoon of peoples and soldiers, the flagging spirits of the French soared on the conviction that a heavenly ally had provided an instrument of miraculous aid: a magnanimous and watchful maid.

Margaret of Denmark conquered the kingdom of Sweden in the fourteenth century, taking King Albert prisoner, and led writers of her time to refer to her as the second Semiramis.

Marulla of the Greek island of Lemnos saw her father die in the Turkish siege of the fortress of Cochin. Snatching his sword and buckler, she summoned the entire garrison and led them against the enemy with such ardor that they not only repulsed the attack but obliged the pasha Süleyman to lift the siege. General Loredan of Venice, who controlled the area, rewarded this feat by allowing her to choose any husband she pleased from the most illustrious condottieres of his army and offering her a suitable dowry in the name of the Venetian republic.

Blanca di Rossi, the wife of the Paduan condottiere Battista Porta, bravely defended the town of Bassano in the march of Trevigiano from her post on the walls. When the town was taken through treason and her husband imprisoned and killed by the tyrant Ezzelino, she was unable to resist the brutal advances of the tyrant, enamored by her beauty, except by throwing herself from a window. After recovering from her injuries—perhaps against her will—and suffering the opprobrium of the barbarian's force in bitter pain and constant fidelity, she opened her husband's sepulcher and there took her own life.[16]

Bona, a humble country girl of the Valtellina, was discovered tending sheep by Pietro Brunoro, a famous Parmesan condottiere, on one of his marches.[17] Taken by her bold vivacity, he carried her off to be an accomplice of his incontinence. But she also came to share in his glory. After exchanging their irregular life for holy matrimony, she not only fought ferociously as a private soldier at every opportunity but became so skilled in the art of war that she was entrusted with several campaigns. She commanded the conquest of the castle of Pavorio from the Venetians for Francesco Sforza, duke of Milan, and perished in the front ranks of the assault.

María Pita was a Galician heroine in the siege of La Coruña by the English in 1589. The enemy was already in the breach and the garrison ready to surrender when she, with ardent but vulgar eloquence, rebuked the Galicians' cowardice, seized a sword and buckler from a soldier, and cried out for anyone with honor to follow her. Inflamed with rage, she fell upon the breach, her martial spirit throwing off sparks that caught fire in the honor of soldiers and citizens. They closed ranks with such force that they inflicted 1,500 enemy deaths (among them a brother of the general, Henry Norris) and forced an end to the siege. Felipe II rewarded her courage by granting her the rank and salary of second lieutenant for the rest of her life, and Felipe III extended the rank and salary of honorary second lieutenant to her descendants.

María de Estrada, consort of Pedro Sánchez Farfan, a soldier of Hernán Cortés, well deserves to be remembered for the many strange feats related by Friar Juan de Torquemada in the first volume of his *Monarquía indiana*. Describing Cortés' mournful exit from Mexico after the death of Montezuma, he speaks of her as follows:

> María de Estrada showed herself to be very courageous in this difficulty and conflict. With a sword and buckler in her hands, she did marvelous things. She attacked the enemy with great courage and spirit, forgetting that she was a woman and fighting as if she were one of the most valiant men in the world. Exhibiting the courage that men of courage and honor tend to have in such situations, she performed so many marvelous feats that all who observed her were struck with fear and amazement.

Referring to the battle between Spaniards and Mexicans in the valley of Otumpa (or Otumba, as don Antonio de Solís calls it), Torquemada returns to the memory of this illustrious woman in these words:

> In this battle, according to Diego Muñoz Camargo in his *Memoria de Tlaxcala*, María de Estrada fought on horseback armed with a lance, as virilely as if she were one of the most valiant men of the army, and surpassing many.

The author does not say where this heroine was from, but the last name suggests she was from Asturias.

Ana de Baux, a dashing Flemish woman from a village near Lille, concealed her sex in the clothes of a man to preserve her honor from military insult in the wars of the last century. She went to war, serving for a long time and on many occasions with great courage, and rose to the rank of company lieutenant. After she was taken prisoner by the French, her sex was discovered. Marshal Seneterre offered her a company in the service of France, but she refused rather than make war against her prince. Returning to her country, she became a nun.

I have not mentioned the Amazons previously in order to discuss them separately. Some authors deny their existence, but many more affirm it. We can concede that the history of the Amazons is intermixed with much myth: that they killed all their sons and lived completely separated from men, seeking them out just once a year to be impregnated. The encounters with Hercules and Theseus, the aid of the ferocious Penthesilea to afflicted Troy, and perhaps the visit of their queen Thalestris to Alexander are cut from the same cloth. But we cannot deny with impunity, in the face of so much ancient testimony, that there was a formidable body of warlike women in Asia who were called Amazons.

Suppose even this is denied. Then to make up for the Amazons taken away from us in Asia, Amazons would appear to the glory of women in the other three parts of the world: America, Africa, and Europe. In America the Spanish discovered them armed along the banks of the largest river in the world, the Marañón, which is why the river was given the name it has today: the Amazon. In Africa they are to be found in a province of the empire of Mwene Matapa. They are said to be the best soldiers in that entire country, although some geographers consider that these women warriors inhabit a separate state.

In no European country have women chosen the military as their profession, but we could call women who band together to defeat their country's enemies Amazons. This was the situation of the French women of Bellovacis or Beauvais when that city was besieged by the Burgundians in 1472. They fought under the leadership of Jeanne Hachette, who had thrown the first enemy standard-bearer off the walls. The day of the assault they vigorously repulsed the enemy. In memory of this feat, the city still celebrates an annual festival in which the women enjoy the singular privilege of marching in procession before the men. The women of the Echinades (or, in Latin, Cursolares), the islands in whose waters the battle of Lepanto was won, acted comparably. The year before this celebrated battle, the Turks attacked the principal island. The Venetian governor Antonio Balbo and the inhabitants were so terrified that they fled during the night. But the women, having been persuaded by a priest named Antonio Rosoneo, stayed behind to defend the town. That is in fact what they did, to the great honor of their sex and the shame of our own.

8.

This record of magnanimous women would be incomplete without saying something about a charge that men often make against women, claiming that it reveals their weakness or inconstancy. Women, they claim, cannot keep a secret. Cato the Censor admitted no exceptions whatever in affirming that to confide a secret to any woman is one of the greatest errors a man can make. But Cato was refuted by his own great-great-granddaughter Portia, the daughter of Cato the Younger and wife of Marcus Brutus. She obliged her husband to tell her the great secret of the plot against Caesar by an extraordinary proof of courage and constancy: the great wound she cut deliberately in her thigh with a knife.

Pliny speaks for magicians when he says that applying the heart of a certain bird to a sleeping woman's bosom makes her reveal her secrets. Elsewhere he says the same thing about the tongues of certain vermin. To get women to yield confidences must not be so easy if magicians have to rummage around in nature's hideaways for keys to open their hearts. But we can laugh at these inventions with Pliny himself and concede that there are very few women who can keep a secret. But, on the other hand, the most expert politicians confess that very few men can be trusted with important secrets either. If gems of this sort were not so rare, rulers would not value them so highly; they scarcely have anything more valuable among their richest possessions.

We do not lack examples of women who have been unfailingly constant in keeping secrets. When Pythagoras was near death, he entrusted all his writings, which included the most recondite mysteries of his philosophy, to his wise daughter Damo. He ordered her never to publish them, and she obeyed to the letter even when reduced to extreme poverty. Although she could have sold those books for a great sum of money, she chose to be faithful to her father's trust rather than to escape the anguish of poverty.

The magnanimous Aretaphila, who was mentioned above, attempted to take her husband Nicocrates' life with a venomous potion before resorting to an armed plot. Her plan was discovered, and she was tortured to make her disclose the remaining details. But the force of pain could not loosen her grip on her spirits and her speech. Despite the rigors of torment, she not only refused to disclose her intent, but she was clever enough to persuade the tyrant that the liquid she had prepared was a love potion meant to inflame his passion. This ingenious fiction turned out to work like a love potion, in fact; Nicocrates loved her much more, satisfied that anyone who would go to this extreme to solicit his ardor must necessarily yearn for him greatly.

In the plot contrived by Aristogiton against Hippias, tyrant of Athens, which began with the death of Hippias' brother Hipparchus, a courtesan who knew the identities of the conspirators was tortured. To quickly disabuse the tyrant of the illusion that he could extort her secret, in his presence she cut off her tongue with her teeth.

Once evidence of the conspiracy of Piso against Nero began to emerge, the most illustrious men of Rome yielded to the force of torment. Lucan exposed his own mother as an accomplice; others betrayed their most intimate friends. Only Epicharis, an ordinary woman who knew about it all, endured lash and fire and other horrors without surrendering the slightest detail.

I knew a woman who was put on the rack because of an atrocious crime her masters had committed. She withstood the trials of that rigorous test not to save herself but only to save her masters. For she had such a small part of the blame—due to ignorance of the gravity of the matter or because she acted on orders or for other reasons—that she could not have been penalized in any way that even approached the rigors of torture.

But force has failed to wring out the hearts of any number of women. I heard someone who had attended these sessions say that many would confess at the point of being stripped for execution but very rarely after this martyrdom of modesty had occurred. What womanly excellence! Their own modesty obliges them more than all the executioner's force.

Some will no doubt regard the parallels I have drawn between women and men as flattery. But I would remind any who do that Seneca, who spared no one his stoicism and whose severity puts him beyond any suspicion of fawning, spoke of women no less favorably. He acknowledges their absolute equality to men in all worthy natural dispositions or capacities. These are his words: *Quis autem dicat naturam maligne cum mulieribus ingeniis egisse, et virtutes illarum in arctum retraxisse? Par illis, mihi crede, vigor, par ad honesta (libeat) facultas est. Laborem doloremque ex aequo si consuevere patiuntur* [But who can say that nature has been grudging with women's innate qualities and has narrowly restricted their virtues? Believe me, they have the same vigor and the same capacity for honor, if they wish. They have the same endurance in work and pain, if they are accustomed].[18]

9.

We come now to the major bone of contention: the question of intellect. I confess that if reason does not avail me here, I can hardly appeal to authority. For with very few exceptions, the writers who treat this matter find the opinion of the vulgar so congenial that they speak almost uniformly of women's intellect with contempt.

The authority of most of these books can be effectively undermined by a defense that the Sicilian Carducci employs for other purposes in his dialogues on painting. A man and a lion walking down a road began to argue about which are braver: humans or lions. Each favored his own species. They passed by a well-made fountain, and the man noticed that it was capped by a marble statue of a man tearing a lion to pieces. Turning to his opponent, he said in the triumphant voice of one with a conclusive argument: "Now you can stop deceiving yourself that lions are braver than humans. There you see a lion whimpering and surrendering its life to a man." "A fine argument that is," replied the lion, smiling. "A human being made that statue, so it counts for little that the sculptor portrayed humans favorably. I promise you that if a lion had made the statue, it would have turned the tables and put the lion on top of the man, making mincemeat out of him for dinner."

The moral: men wrote these books that impugn women's intellect, but if women had written them, we men would find ourselves scorned. Some women have done just this. Among the works of Lucrezia Marinella, a Venetian scholar, is *The Nobility and Excellence of Women, and The Defects and Vices of Men,* which argues for the superiority of her sex to our own. The learned Jesuit Juan de Cartagena says that he saw and read this book with great pleasure in Rome, and I have seen it in the Royal Library in Madrid. The truth of the matter is that neither they nor we can serve as judges in this case because we are interested parties. Since angels have no sex, they are unbiased; they would be the ones to pronounce judgment here.

Most importantly, those who rate women's intellect so low that it is almost at the level of pure instinct do not deserve to be admitted to the discussion. Take those who claim that the most a woman can do is govern a henhouse, for instance. And the prelate cited by Francisco Manuel in his *Letter and Guide for the Married*, who said that the woman who knows most knows how to organize a linen chest. People like these may be respectable for other reasons, but not for these maxims. The most benign interpretation they admit is that of amusing hyperbole. In fact, it is common knowledge that there are women who have known how to govern and organize religious communities and even those who have known how to govern and organize entire republics.

This talk against women comes from superficial men. They see that women ordinarily know only the domestic crafts to which they have been assigned, and they infer—without even knowing that they infer, for they do not reflect on the process—that women are incapable of anything else. The dullest logician knows that deficiency of act does not imply deficiency of potency. Hence the fact that women do not know other things does not imply that they cannot know other things.

We know no more than we study. But it does not follow that our capacity extends no further than its present application. If people dedicated themselves to agriculture (as the distinguished Thomas More proposed in his *Utopia*) in such a way that they knew nothing else, would this ground the inference that they could know nothing else? Among the Druze of Palestine, women are the only repositories of letters. Almost all of them know how to read and write, and whatever literature the Druze possess is stored in the minds of the women and hidden from the men, who engage only in agriculture, war, and negotiation. If the whole world were to adopt the same custom, women would doubtless consider men unfit for letters, just as men take women to be unfit today. As this hypothetical judgment would be clearly mistaken, so is the one that is actually made today. They spring from the same source.

10.

This source may also ground some of Father Malebranche's views in *The Search after Truth*, though he is much gentler with women. He concedes women a known advantage over men in the discernment of sensible things, but he considers them much less competent with abstract ideas. The reason for this, he indicates, is the softness of their brains. But we know that everyone seeks these physical causes and identifies them in their own way after experience has confirmed, or is thought to have confirmed, the effects. This is how Malebranche contracted the very intellectual ailment he wished to remedy in the human race: error occasioned by common prejudices and ill-considered principles. Doubtless he arrived at this judgment by letting himself be dragged along by common opinion or by noticing that women reputed to be clever reason more easily and accurately than men about sensible things and much less so—if they are not completely silent—about abstract matters. But this is not the result of unequal talent; it comes from different application and use. Women occupy themselves much more with the seasoning of a delicacy, the adornment of a dress, and other such things than men, and so they reason and speak about them with greater accuracy and ease. By contrast, rarely do women think about theoretical questions or abstract ideas, so they are easily found to be clumsy when they do treat these matters. To get a clearer idea of their capacities, observe those alert and flirtatious women who occasionally enjoy thinking about the delicacies of Platonic love. When they happen to reason about them, they outstrip the most sensible man who has not explored these bagatelles of fantasy.

However great our ability, we generally seem coarse and thickheaded in those matters that we do not treat or use. A farm laborer whom God has given very sharp wits, as sometimes happens, will seem quite inferior to a simple-minded politician in discussing reasons of state if the laborer never thinks about anything but farming. And the shrewdest politician, if a pure politician, will just rave if he meddles in matters like organizing squadrons and doing battle. An intelligent military man who overhears such talk would consider the politician fatuous, as Hannibal deemed a great Asian orator who plunged into a discussion of war in his and King Antioch's presence.

The same thing happens with women and men. Consider a highly intelligent woman at home, her thoughts occupied with domestic matters all day long. She does not hear—or half hears, if someone does speak in front of her—of other spheres. Her husband, though not nearly as gifted, deals frequently with religious authorities and able politicians outside the home and in this way acquires varied news, familiarity with public affairs, and weighty advice. If he should speak of these matters in which he has acquired a little understanding in front of his wife and she should happen to remark on them, regardless of her intelligence she will necessarily be at a disadvantage, for she has no instruction whatever. Her husband and anyone else who happens to hear her will think her a fool. And the husband will think himself wise as an owl.

This is the story of untold women. Though much more able than the ambient males, they are considered incompetent to think about certain matters. Given these conditions, to think badly or not at all does not depend on lack of talent; it depends on lack of information. Without information even an angelic intellect would stall. Yet the men triumph, even if they are less able. They appear superior because they are equipped with information.

In addition to the advantage of information, there is another of great importance. Men are quite accustomed to meditate, speak, and reason about matters in their sphere of application, while women rarely think of them. When the occasion arises, then, men can speak with forethought, whereas women must speak without it.

Because men communicate reciprocally about these matters, some shine with the light of others. In reasoning about such topics, then, they employ not only their own ideas but those of others as well. The mouth of a single man can give voice to not just one intellect but many. Yet since women confer not about these abstract topics but about their labors and other domestic matters instead, one woman does not enlighten another. So if it happens that they do have to talk about abstract matters, in addition to having to reason without information and forethought, each woman must rely on her own solitary light.

These advantages may permit a man of very limited understanding to speak more and better about abstract matters than a highly perspicacious woman. The advantages are so great that, if not kept in mind, the interaction between a perspicacious woman and a coarse man may give the impression that he is sensible and she foolish.

In fact, ignoring these advantages has led many men, including some who were otherwise sensible and wise, to profess great contempt for women's intellect. Indeed, they have brayed so much about the dullness of women's wits that many women—perhaps the majority—have actually been convinced of it.

Eight

THE GENERATION OF '98

The Spanish colonies in the Americas, one by one, gained their independence between 1814 and 1833; the only exceptions were Cuba and Puerto Rico. The Cuban struggle for independence was sporadic, beginning with the Ten Years' War from 1868 to 1878, flaring up again in 1879–1880, and entering its final phase in 1895. Meanwhile, rebels in the Philippines—named after Felipe (Philip) II, who had sent the Spanish expedition that founded the first permanent Spanish settlement in the archipelago in 1565—were rising up in arms against their colonial masters. By 1898, Spain was facing united populaces in open rebellion in both the Pacific east and Atlantic west. When the United States' battleship *Maine* was mysteriously blown up in Havana harbor on February 15, 1898, large segments of the American populace, already sympathetic to the Cuban revolutionaries, clamored for intervention. War was declared by both Spain and the United States in April and concluded in December. By the terms of the Treaty of Paris, Spain lost its last American colonies—Cuba and Puerto Rico—and its last Asian ones—the Philippines and Guam.

Hence it took three hundred years, from the death of Felipe II to the Spanish-American War, for Spain's overseas empire to trickle away. The war, referred to in Spain as "the disaster," became the catalyst for a prolonged period of national soul-searching. Leading roles in this process were played by members of what came to be known as the Generation of '98. Some of these are inevitably regarded as more central than others. But the trajectory of the Generation as a whole can be indicated by a few instances of early unity and later dispersion among key members.

An instance of early unity was the formation of the so-called Group of Three, consisting of Pío Baroja, Ramiro de Maeztu, and Azorín (the later pen name of José Martínez Ruiz) in 1901. In December of that year, with the support of Miguel de Unamuno, the group published a manifesto urging the application of social science to relieve rural poverty, hunger, alcoholism, and prostitution and the establishment of obligatory education, rural credit unions, and legalized divorce.

This manifesto grew out of earlier attempts at reform by Krausists, Krauso-positivists, and regenerationists. Krausism was a philosophical movement based on the ideas of the German Romantic Karl Krause, who advocated the moral ideal of a cosmopolitan League of Humanity and "panentheism" as a middle way between pantheism and theism. Krausism took hold in Spain through the efforts of Julián Sanz del Río, whose *Ideal de la humanidad para la vida* (Ideal of Humanity for Life), published in 1860, sparked a movement of cultural renewal. Krausism reinforced the liberalism that led to the overthrow of Spain's constitutional monarchy in 1868 and the short-lived Republic of 1873. It also produced the Institución Libre de Enseñanza (Free Institute of Instruction), founded in 1876 by Francisco Giner de los Ríos and other Krausists and intended to be free of influence by church and state. From about 1875 on, Krausism took a positivist turn under the sway of Comtean, Darwinian, and Spencerian ideas. Out of this Krauso-positivist soil grew the principal figure of the regenerationist movement, Joaquín Costa, who taught for several years at the Institución Libre de Enseñanza. Costa's 1901 work, *Oligarquía y caciquismo como la forma actual de gobierno en España: Urgencia y modo de cambiarla* (Oligarchy and Caciquism as the Present Form of Government in Spain: The Urgency and Mode of Changing It), famously denounced the corrupt parliamentary system associated with the restored constitutional monarchy as the principal obstacle to the regeneration of Spain. Regenerationist thought left deep impressions on the members of the Group of Three and on Unamuno during their early development. Hence the group's manifesto was not a superficial reaction to the Spanish-American War; it sprang from an older and deeper ideological crisis.

Despite the initial unity among these three members of the Generation of '98, they soon went their separate ways. Baroja, the leading novelist of the period, was liberal, anticommunist, and politically skeptical. Azorín, an outstanding literary critic, essayist, and novelist, was to serve several times as a conservative legislator. Maeztu, a journalist and social theorist, evolved from outspoken liberalism to support for the dictatorship of Primo de Rivera and the conservative movement Acción Española. But the quintessential figure of the period is the multifaceted Unamuno—essayist, novelist, poet, dramatist, and philosopher.

MIGUEL DE UNAMUNO

Miguel de Unamuno y Jugo was a Basque, born in Bilbao in 1864. His father died when he was six years old, and Unamuno was raised primarily by his mother and grandmother, both devout Catholics. In 1880 he moved to Madrid to begin his university studies in philosophy and letters, earning his doctorate in 1884. After a number of unsuccessful attempts to obtain a university position, he was appointed professor of Greek at the University of Salamanca in 1891. By then, Unamuno had moved from his childhood faith to atheistic humanism, soaked up Herbert Spencer and Karl Marx, and joined the PSOE (Partido Socialista Obrero Español), the socialist workers' party founded in 1879 by Pablo Iglesias. But 1897 brought a crisis. On March 21 or 22, during a night of insomnia, Unamuno was seized by the conviction that his heart was failing and he was about to die. The next morning he went to a Dominican monastery and spent three days there in prayer. Looking back at this episode, Unamuno compared it to the conversion of St. Paul. He began to abandon his previous positions, finding them overly intellectual, and to function as a kind of loyal opposition to Christianity—a posture he maintained for the rest of his life. One of his later biographers has dubbed him "the lone heretic."[1]

Unamuno's opposition was not confined to Christianity. Temperamentally, he seems to have been "born *anti*," a veritable "challenge on legs."[2] He was named rector of the University of Salamanca in 1900, at the age of thirty-six, but the government stripped him of his rectorship in 1914 in a row over a Colombian student's degree. He began to attack King Alfonso XIII in print, leading to legal charges of which Unamuno was convicted in 1920, and his criticism of the dictatorship of Primo de Rivera provoked his exile in 1924. In 1931 he was made a deputy of the Second Republic and restored to the rectorship at Salamanca, presumably for life. But when the Spanish Civil War broke out in 1936, Unamuno supported the Nationalist rising, thereby losing his rectorship a second time. He quickly repudiated the Nationalists, however. On October 12, 1936, he confronted General Millán Astray, the founder of the Foreign Legion and an influential adviser to Franco, in a venomous public dispute.[3] That was Unamuno's last address. The Nationalists placed him under house arrest, and he died in Salamanca on the last day of that year.

Unamuno as adversary: Why? The answer seems to lie somewhere between Socrates and Erostratus. Just as Socrates cast himself as the gadfly to Athens, stinging its citizens in order to wake them up and spur them on in the pursuit of virtue and knowledge, Unamuno wrote to awaken minds, to combat spiritual laziness, and to assuage pain by inflicting higher pain.[4] And like Erostratus, the shepherd who burned the temple of Artemis at Ephesus simply to be remembered by future generations, Unamuno was ravenous for fame:

> The man of letters who tells you that he despises glory lies like a rogue. . . .
>
> When doubts invade and cloud our faith in the immortality of the soul, the longing to perpetuate our name and fame picks up painful drive and verve. And hence that tremendous struggle to individualize ourselves, to survive somehow in the memory of others and posterity, that struggle a thousand times more terrible than the struggle for life, that gives tone, color, and character to our society in which the medieval faith in the immortal soul is disappearing. We each seek to affirm ourselves, if only in appearance.
>
> . . . There are those who yearn even for the gallows to gain fame, even an infamous fame: *avidus malae famae*, as Tacitus said.
>
> And this Erostratism, what is it finally but the longing for immortality—if not the real thing at least its name and shadow?[5]

Unamuno got his fame; he also became the leading figure of the Generation of '98. Enormously prolific, he published novels, essays, plays, and poetry in addition to philosophy. His principal philosophical work, *Del sentimiento trágico de la vida en los hombres y en los pueblos* (On the Tragic Sense of Life in People and Peoples), appeared in 1913.[6] One of the last romantic works written in Spain, it celebrates life over thought, desire over reason, and the concrete individual over abstract generalization. The tragic sense of life, it argues, is experienced acutely but not exclusively by certain individuals, such as Unamuno, and by certain peoples, such as the Spanish. This tragic sense originates in conflict: the conflict between the desire to be immortal and the reasoned belief in mortality. Rather than trying to resolve the conflict by softening or negating one of its terms, Unamuno embraces it and promotes it as the foundation of an ethics, an esthetics, a religion, and even a logic.[7]

The following selection from this work outlines an ethics steeped in the tragic sense of life. Although the ethics is literally quixotic, inspired by Cervantes' famous character and hence nourished by the Catholicism of Spain's Golden Age, Unamuno amplifies it along lines marked out by two Protestant thinkers: Martin Luther and Søren Kierkegaard.[8] Yet another Protestant—Immanuel Kant—serves Unamuno as a foil for his own ideas. Kantian ethics and Unamunian ethics are cousins, in fact, for both thinkers expounded ethics in which the actor's intention determines the rightness of actions. But for reasons that emerge in the following selection, Unamuno rejects the Kantian approach as one-sided and pedantic.

The Tragic Sense of Life

A Quixotic Ethics

Chapter XI. The Practical Problem

L'homme est périssable. —Il se peut; mais périssons en résistant, et,
si le néant nous est réservé, ne faisons pas que ce soit une justice.
—Sénancour, Obermann, lettre XC

Several times in the wandering course of these observations I have been
bold enough to define, in spite of my horror of definitions, my own position vis-à-vis the problem I have been examining. But I know there is
bound to be some dissatisfied reader, indoctrinated in some dogmatism
or other, who will say: "This man cannot make up his mind; he vacil-
lates; first he seems to assert one proposition, then he maintains the opposite; he is full of contradictions; it is impossible to place him. What is
he?" There you have me: a man who affirms opposites, a man of contradiction and quarrel, as Jeremiah said of himself; a man who says one

---

From *Selected Works of Miguel de Unamuno,* vol. 4, *The Tragic Sense of Life in Men
and Nations,* edited by Anthony Kerrigan and Martin Nozick, translated by Anthony Kerrigan, Bollingen Series 85 (Princeton: Princeton University Press, 1972).
Reprinted by permission of Princeton University Press.

thing with his heart and the opposite with his head, and for whom this strife is the stuff of life. It is a clear-cut case, as clear as the water which flows from the melted snow upon the mountain tops.

I shall be told that mine is an untenable position, that a foundation is needed upon which to build our actions and our works, that it is impossible to live by contradictions, that unity and clarity are essential conditions for life and thought, and that it is imperative to unify the latter. And so we are back where we started from. For it is precisely this inner contradiction which unifies my life and gives it a practical purpose.

Or, rather, it is the conflict itself, this selfsame passionate uncertainty which unifies my action and causes me to live and work.

We think in order that we may live, I have said, but perhaps it would be more correct to say that we think because we live, and that the form of our thought corresponds to the form of our life. Once more I must point out that our ethical and philosophical doctrines in general are no more than *a posteriori* justifications of our conduct, of our actions. Our doctrines are usually the means by which we seek to explain and justify to others and to ourselves our own mode of action—to ourselves, be it noted, as well as to others. The man who does not really know why he acts as he does, and not otherwise, feels the need to explain to himself his reason for so acting, and so he manufactures a motive. What we believe to be the motives for our conduct are usually mere pretexts. The reason which impels one man carefully to preserve his life is the same reason given by another man for shooting himself in the head.

Nevertheless it cannot be denied that reasons, ideas, exert an influence on human actions, and sometimes even determine them by a process analogous to that of suggestion in the case of a hypnotized person, and this is due to the tendency of all ideas to resolve themselves in action—for an idea in itself is but an inchoate or aborted act. It was this tendency which suggested to Fouillée his theory of idea forces.[1] But ordinarily ideas are forces which we reconcile with other deeper and much less conscious forces.

But leaving all this to one side for a moment, I should like to establish the fact that uncertainty, doubt, the perpetual wrestling with the mystery of our final destiny, the consequent mental despair, and the lack of any solid or stable dogmatic foundation, may all serve as basis for an ethic.

Whoever bases or thinks he bases his conduct—his inner or outward conduct, his feeling or his action—on a dogma or theoretical principle which he deems incontrovertible, runs the risk of becoming a fanatic; moreover, the moment this dogma shows any fissure or even any weakness, he finds the morality based on it giving way. If the ground he thought firm begins to rock, he himself trembles in the earthquake, for we are not all like the ideal Stoic who remains undaunted among the ruins of a world shattered to pieces. Luckily, the matter which underlies his ideas will tend to save him. For if a man should tell you that he does not defraud or cuckold his best friend because he fears hellfire, you may depend upon it that he would not do so even if he stopped believing in hell, but would instead invent some other excuse for not transgressing. And this truth is to the honor of the human race.

But whoever is convinced that he is sailing, perhaps without a set course, on an unstable or sinkable craft, will not be daunted if he finds the deck giving way beneath his feet and threatening to sink. For this type of man acts as he does, not because he believes his theory of action to be true, but because he believes that by acting thus he will make it true, prove it true, and that by thus acting he will create his spiritual world.

My conduct must be the best proof, the moral proof, of my supreme desire; and if I do not finally convince myself, within the limits of the ultimate and irremediable uncertainty, of the truth of what I hope for, it is because my conduct is not sufficiently pure. Virtue, therefore, is not based upon dogma, but dogma upon virtue, and it is not faith which creates martyrs but rather martyrs who create faith. There is no security or repose—so far as security and repose are attainable in this life which is essentially insecure and lacking in repose—save in passionately good conduct.

Conduct, which is practice, is the proof of doctrine, which is theory. "If any man will do his will," the will of Him who sent Jesus, "he shall know of the doctrine, whether it be of God, or whether I speak of myself," said Jesus (John 7:17). And there is a well-known saying of Pascal: "Begin by taking holy water and you will end by becoming a believer." And pursuing a similar line of thought, Johann Jakob Moser, the pietist, concluded that no atheist or naturalist has the right to regard the Christian religion as devoid of truth so long as he has never tried keeping its precepts and commandments.[2]

What is the anti-rational truth of our heart? It is the immortality of the human soul, the truth of the persistence of our consciousness without any termination whatever, the human finality of the Universe. And what is its moral proof? We may formulate it thus: Act so that in your own judgment and in the judgment of others you may deserve eternity, act so that you may be irreplaceable, act so that you do not deserve death. Or perhaps thus: Act as if you were to die tomorrow, but only in order to survive and become eternal. The end-purpose of morality is to give personal, human finality to the Universe; to discover the finality it possesses—if it does in fact possess any—and discover it by acting.

More than a century ago, in 1804, the deepest and most intense of the spiritual sons of the patriarch Rousseau, most tragic of French men of feeling (not excluding Pascal), Sénancour, in Letter XC of that series which constitutes the immense monody of his *Obermann,* wrote the words which I have placed as epigraph to this chapter: "Man is perishable. . . . That may be; but let us perish resisting, and if annihilation must be our portion, let us not make it a just one."[3] If you change this sentence from a negative to a positive form—"And if annihilation must be our portion, let us make it an unjust reward"—you get the firmest basis for action by the man who cannot or will not be a dogmatist.

The pessimism which Goethe puts into the mouth of Mephistopheles when he makes him say "Whatever has achieved existence deserves to be destroyed" ("denn alles was entsteht / Ist wert, dass es zugrunde geht"), is a pessimism which is irreligious and demoniacal, which incapacitates us for action and leaves us without any ideal defense against our own penchant for evil. It is this pessimism which we know as evil, rather than the pessimism which consists in deploring and fighting the fear that everything is doomed to annihilation in the end. Mephistopheles asserts that whatever has achieved existence deserves to be destroyed, annihilated, but not that it will be destroyed or annihilated: and we assert that whatever exists deserves to be exalted and made eternal, even if no such destiny is achieved. The moral attitude is altogether different.

Yes, everything deserves to be eternalized, absolutely everything, even evil itself, for what we call evil would lose its malignancy in being made eternal and thereby losing its temporal nature. For the essence of evil consists in its temporal nature, in the fact that it is not directed toward any ultimate and permanent end.

And it might not be superfluous here to say something about the difference between what is called pessimism and what is called optimism—one of the most confusing of differences, not less than the confusion between individualism and socialism. In all truth, it is scarcely possible to say what pessimism really is.

Just today I read in *The Nation* an article entitled "A Dramatic Inferno," which deals with a translation into English of the works of Strindberg, and it begins with the following judicious observation:

> If there were in the world a sincere and total pessimism, it would of necessity be silent. The despair which finds a voice is a social mood, it is the cry of misery which brother utters to brother when both are stumbling through a valley of shadows which is peopled with comrades. In its anguish it bears witness to something that is good in life, for it presupposes sympathy. . . . The real gloom, the sincere despair, is dumb and blind; it writes no books, and feels no impulse to burden an intolerable universe with a monument more lasting than brass.[4]

This judgment doubtless conceals some sophistry, for a man really in pain cries out, even if he is alone and there is no one to hear him, thus alleviating his pain, though his reaction may be conditioned by social custom. Does not the lion, alone in the desert, roar if he has an aching tooth? But apart from this qualification, there is no denying the substance of truth underlying the quoted observation. Pessimism which protests and defends itself cannot truly be said to be pessimism. And, strictly speaking, it is not pessimism at all to hold that nothing ought to perish, while it is pessimism to affirm that, though nothing may perish, everything ought to.

Pessimism, moreover, may possess different values. Eudaemonistic or economic pessimism denies happiness; ethical pessimism denies the triumph of moral good; religious pessimism despairs of the human finality of the Universe and of the eternal salvation of the individual soul.

All men deserve to be saved, but, as I have said in the previous chapter, whoever desires immortality with a passion and even against all reason deserves it most of all. The writer H. G. Wells, who has given himself over to prophecy (not an uncommon phenomenon in his country), tells us in his *Anticipations* that "Active and capable men of all forms of religious profession today tend in practice to disregard the question of immortality altogether." And this is so because the religious professions of these active and capable men of whom Wells speaks are usually no more than a lie, and their lives are a lie, too, if they pretend to base them upon religion. But perhaps what Wells tells us is not basically as true as he and others like him imagine. Those active and capable men live in the midst of a society imbued with Christian principles, surrounded by institutions and social reactions produced by Christianity, so that a belief in the immortality of the soul runs deep in their own souls like a subterranean river, neither seen nor heard, but watering the roots of their deeds and their motives.

In all truth it must be admitted that there exists no more solid foundation for morality than the foundation provided by the Catholic ethic. Man's end-purpose is eternal happiness, which consists in the vision and enjoyment of God *in saecula saeculorum.* Where that ethic errs, however, is in the choice of means conducive to this end; for to make the attainment of eternal happiness dependent upon believing or not believing that the Holy Ghost proceeds from the Father and the Son and not from the Father alone, or in the divinity of Jesus, or in the theory of the hypostatic union, or even in the existence of God is nothing less than monstrous, as a moment's reflection will show. A human God—and we can conceive of no other—would never reject whoever could not believe in Him with his head; it is not in his head but in his heart that the wicked man says there is no God, that is: he does not *want* God to exist. If any belief could be linked with the attainment of eternal happiness it would be the belief in this happiness itself and in the possibility of attaining it.

And what shall we say of that other notion of the emperor of pedants, to the effect that we have not come into the world to be happy but to fulfill our duty ("Wir sind nicht auf der Welt, um glücklich zu sein, sondern um unsere Schuldigkeit zu tun")?[5] If we are in this world *for something* (*um etwas*), whence can this *for* be derived but from the very essence of our own will, which asks for happiness and not duty as ultimate end? And if we were to attempt to attribute some other value to this *for*, an "objective value," as some Sadducean pedant might say, then we would have to recognize that this objective reality—the reality which would remain though humanity should disappear—is as indifferent to our duty as to our happiness, as little concerned with our morality as with our felicity. I am not aware that Jupiter, Uranus, or Sirius would allow their courses to be affected because we do or do not fulfill our duty any more than because we are or are not happy.

These reflections must appear ridiculously vulgar and superficial, the reflections of a dilettante. (The intellectual world is divided into two classes: dilettanti on the one hand, pedants on the other.) What can we do about it? Modern man resigns himself to the truth, and to not knowing the complex of culture: witness Windelband's testimony on this head in his study of Hölderlin's fate.[6] Yes, the cultured are resigned, leaving a few poor savages like ourselves for whom resignation is impossible. We do not resign ourselves to the idea of having to disappear some day, and the great pedant's critique does not console us.

The epitome of everything sensible was expressed by Galileo Galilei: "Some perhaps will say that the bitterest pain is the loss of life, but I say that there are others more bitter; for whoever relinquishes life loses at the same time the power to lament this loss or any other." Whether Galileo was conscious or not of the humor in this sentence I do not know, but in any case the humor is tragic.

But, to turn back, I repeat that if any belief could be linked with the attainment of eternal happiness, it would be the belief in the possibility of its realization. And yet, strictly speaking, not even this will do. The reasonable man says in his head "There is no other life after this one"; but only the wicked man says it in his heart. Yet, since the wicked man himself may be no more than a man in despair, a desperado, can a human God condemn him because of his despair? Despair alone is misfortune enough.

In any event, let us adopt the formula of Calderón in *Life is a Dream:*

> I am dreaming and would
> do and act well, for not even
> in dreams are good works lost.

But are good works not really lost? Did Calderón really know? He went on to add:

Let us attend on eternity
which is truly living fame
wherein good fortune never wanes
nor glory ever quiet stay.

Is that really true? Did Calderón know?

Calderón had faith, a robust Catholic faith; but for whoever cannot have faith, for whoever cannot believe what Don Pedro Calderón de la Barca believed, there always remains the attitude of *Obermann.*

If annihilation must be our portion, let us act in such a way that we make it an unjust portion; let us fight against destiny, even without hope of victory; let us fight quixotically.

We fight against death not only by longing for the irrational, but also by acting in such wise that we become irreplaceable, impressing our seal upon others, working upon our fellow men and dominating them, giving ourselves to them and making ourselves eternal through them insofar as possible.

Our greatest effort must be the endeavor to make ourselves irreplaceable, to make a practical truth of the theoretical fact (if the term "theoretical fact" does not involve a contradiction in terms) that each one of us is unique and irreplaceable, and that no one else can fill the gap left by our death.

In all truth every man is unique and irreplaceable: another I is inconceivable; each one of us—our soul, not our life—is worth the whole Universe. I say our soul and not our life deliberately, for I am thinking of those who assign a ridiculously excessive value to life: they do not really believe in the spirit, that is, in their own personal immortality, and so they inveigh against war and the death penalty, for example, precisely because they do not really believe in the spirit, in whose service life should be, and thus they overvalue life. But life is of use only insofar as it serves its lord and master, spirit, and if the master perishes along with the servant, then neither the one nor the other is of any great value.

And to act in such a way as to make our annihilation unjustified, in such a way as to make our brothers and sisters, our children and their children, and the children of these children, all feel that we ought not to have died is something within the reach of all men.

The doctrine of the Christian redemption is based on the fact that the unique man, Man, the Son of Man, that is, the Son of God, suffered passion and death, when He, given His sinless condition, did not deserve to die; and that this propitiatory and divine victim died in order to rise again and to raise us from the dead, thus delivering us from death by virtue of applying His merits to us and by showing us the way of life. And the Christ who gave Himself entirely to His brothers in humanity with total self-abnegation is the model for our action.

All of us, each one of us, can and ought to resolve to give as much of himself as he can, and even more than he can, exceeding himself, going beyond himself, making himself irreplaceable, giving himself to all others so that they may give him back himself in them. And each one of us starts from his civil calling or office as point of departure: the word office, *officium*, means obligation, debt, in a concrete sense, and that is what it always ought to mean in practice. We ought not so much try to seek the particular vocation or calling we think most suitable for ourselves as to make a vocation of the employment in which luck or Providence or our own will has placed us.

Perhaps Luther rendered no greater service to Christian civilization than that of establishing the religious value of the civil professions as such, thus revoking the monastic and medieval idea of the religious vocation, an idea which was enveloped in the mist of extravagant and imaginative passions and which gave rise to terrible human tragedies. If we could only enter a cloister and scrutinize the religious vocation of the poor men whom the selfishness of their parents forced as children into a novice's cell and who suddenly awake, if they ever do awake at all, to the worldly life! Or if we could examine the careers of those whom their own autosuggestion had deceived! Luther, who saw the life of the cloister at close quarters and endured it himself, was able to understand and sense the religious value of the civil professions, to which no man is bound by perpetual vows.

Everything the Apostle said in the fourth chapter of his Epistle to the Ephesians with regard to the Christian vocation should be applied to civil life, inasmuch as today among ourselves the Christian—whether he know it or not, whether he like it or not—is the citizen. And just as the Apostle exclaimed, "I am a Roman citizen!" each one of us, even the atheist, may exclaim, "I am a Christian!" And this sentiment implies the *civilizing* of Christianity—in the sense of making it civil, or dis-ecclesiasticizing it. And that was Luther's task, though he himself later founded a Church.

"The right man in the right place" is an English expression. And in Spain, we, too, use the phrase "Cobbler, stick to thy last!" Who knows what position suits him best and for which he is most fitted? Does a man himself know it better than others, or do they know it better than he? Who can measure capacities and aptitudes? The religious attitude, un-doubtedly, is to make whatever occupation we happen to pursue the right one, and only as a last resort to change it for another.

This question of a proper vocation is possibly the gravest and most deep-seated of social problems, the basis of all other questions. The quintessential so-called "social question" is perhaps not so much a prob-lem of the distribution of wealth, that is, of the products of labor, as a problem of the distribution of vocations, that is, of the modes of produc-tion. It is not a question of aptitude—something impossible to ascertain without first putting aptitude to the test, and not clearly indicated in any man, since a man is not born, but made, for the majority of vocations— it is not a question of any special aptitude, but of social, political, and customary considerations which determine a man's occupation. At cer-tain times and in certain countries it is a matter of caste and heredity; at other times and in other places, it is the guild or corporation; in later times, the machine; in almost all cases it is a matter of necessity, almost never of free choice. The tragedy of it all culminates in those meretri-cious occupations in which a living is earned by selling one's soul, where the workman works in the knowledge that his work is not only super-fluous but also a perversion of social values, for he may be producing a venom designed to annihilate him, an artifact which will perhaps be used to murder his children. Herein lies the fundamental problem, and it is not a matter of wages.

I shall never forget a scene to which I was witness on the banks of the estuary of Bilbao, my native city. A workman in a shipyard was ham-mering away at something or other, quite obviously in a listless fashion, going through the motions of earning his wage without any energy, when suddenly a woman's cry rent the air calling "Help!" A child had fallen into the water. The listless worker was instantly transformed and, in an access of energy, speed, and cold-blooded decision, threw off his clothes and plunged into the water to rescue the drowning child.

Possibly the reason why there is comparatively less ferocity behind the socialist agrarian movement is that though the field worker does not earn more or live better than the industrial worker or the miner, he does have a clearer notion of the social value of his work. Sowing grain is a different matter from extracting diamonds from the earth.

Perhaps the greatest social progress consists in a certain undifferentiation of labor, in the facility for leaving one form of work to take up another, not necessarily a more lucrative form but simply a nobler form of work—for there are definite degrees of nobility in labor. But unhappily it is only too seldom that a man who keeps to one occupation without changing it does so from any attempt to make a "religious" endeavor of it, or that the man who changes his occupation for another does so from any religiosity of motive.

And of course we all know of cases where a man evades the strict performance of his duty, justifying his attitude on the ground that the professional entity of which he forms part is poorly organized and does not function as it should, and that he therefore is fulfilling a higher duty by not serving. Such people call the literal carrying-out of duties routine disciplinarianism; and they speak of bureaucracy and the Pharisaism of public functionaries. All this is as if an intelligent and perspicacious military officer, realizing the deficiencies in his country's military organization, were to denounce them to his superiors and perhaps even to the public—thus doing his "higher duty"—and then, in the field, were to refuse to carry out an operation assigned to him, because he believed its success was a minimal possibility, or even that defeat was certain while those deficiencies went uncorrected. He would of course deserve to be shot. And as regards the question of Pharisaism . . . .

And there is always a way of obeying an order while yet retaining command, a way of carrying out an order one deems to be absurd, while remedying its absurdity, even if it be by one's own death. When in the course of my own official bureaucratic capacity I have chanced upon some legislative measure which, by reason of its manifest absurdity, has fallen into disuse, I have nevertheless always endeavored to apply it. There is nothing worse than a loaded pistol left lying idle in some corner: a child comes along, gets to playing with it, and shoots his father. Laws fallen into desuetude are the most terrible of laws, especially when the cause of the desuetude is that the law is a bad one.

And these are not vague suppositions, least of all in our country. For while certain people go about on some mission or other, fulfilling some ideal duties or responsibilities—that is to say fictitious ones—they themselves do not put their whole souls into the immediate and concrete endeavors upon which they live, and the rest—the vast majority—perform their functions merely to "do their duty" as the vulgar and terribly immoral phrase puts it, in order to get out of a fix, going through the motions, getting the job done, paying lip-service rather than doing it justice, for the sake of the emolument, whether it be money or something else.

Here behold one type of shoemaker, living off making shoes, but doing it with the minimum workmanship needed to keep his clientele. Then you have this other shoemaker, living on a rather different spiritual plane, for he is possessed by the instinct of workmanship, and out of pride of self or as a point of honor works to earn the reputation as best shoemaker in town, or in Christendom, even if this renown will not earn him any more money or more clientele, but only more renown and prestige. But there is a still higher degree of moral perfection as concerns the office of shoemaker, and that is for the shoemaker to work in order to become for his fellow townsmen the one and only shoemaker, the one who makes their footwear so well that they will miss him when he "dies on them," and not merely "dies,"[7] and they will all feel that he ought not to have died at all; and this will come about because he made their footwear in the thought of sparing them from thinking of their feet when they could be thinking of higher things, of the highest truths; in short, he made their footwear with love in his heart for them and for God in them—he made their footwear religiously.

This pedestrian example I have chosen deliberately, for the ethical sense, let alone the religious one, is very low in our cobblers' shops. . . .

Because of the stricture which says that "in the sweat of thy face shalt thou eat bread," many people regard work as a punishment and do not show any regard for civil employment beyond its economico-political, or, at best, its aesthetic value. For such people—chief among them the Jesuits—there are two distinct enterprises: the inferior, ephemeral one of earning a living, of earning our bread, for ourselves and our children, in an honorable manner (though the elasticity of honor is well known), and the grand enterprise of our salvation, of winning eternal glory. The inferior or worldly enterprise is to be undertaken not only insofar as it allows us, without deceit and without detriment to our fellows, to live decently and in accord with our social position, but also in a manner to afford us the greatest possible amount of time to attend to the other, grander, enterprise. And there are those who, rising a bit above this concept, a concept more economic than ethical, of our civil employment, attain to an aesthetic concept and aesthetic sense of it, and they set themselves the task of acquiring distinction and renown in their occupation, even to the point of making out of it an art for art's sake, an art for beauty's sake. But it is imperative to rise still higher than this, to attain to an ethical sense of our civil employment, a sense deriving from our religious feeling, from our hunger for eternity. To work, each one of us, at our own civil occupation, with our eyes fixed on God, to work for the love of God—which is equivalent to saying for the love of our eternalization—is to make of this work a religious one. . . .[8]

I am well aware that those who say ethics is a science will say that all this commentary of mine on this head is nothing but rhetoric. Each of us has his own language and his own passion: at least the passionate man does, and if a man does not have passion, science is of little avail to him.

The passion which finds its expression in this rhetoric is called egotism by the "ethical scientists." But this *egotism* is the only true cure for *egoism* or spiritual avarice, the vice of keeping and saving oneself for oneself rather than striving to make oneself eternal by giving oneself.

"Be nought, and thou shalt be more than aught that is," said Fray Juan de los Angeles in one of his *Dialogues*.[9] But what does it mean to "Be nought!"? May it not paradoxically mean, as sometimes happens with the mystics, the opposite of what it seems literally to mean? Is not the entire ethic of submission and quietism an immense paradox, or rather, a great tragic contradiction? Is not the monastic ethic, the purely monastic ethic, an absurdity? And I mean here, when I speak of the monastic ethic, the ethic of the solitary Carthusian, that of the hermit, who flees the world—perhaps taking it with him nonetheless—so that he may live alone, by himself in the company of a God who is as alone and solitary as himself. I do not mean the ethic of the Dominican inquisitor who scoured Provence in search of Albigensian hearts to burn.

"Let God do it all," some reader may exclaim. But if a man folds his arms, God will go to sleep.

It is this Carthusian ethic, and the scientific ethic which derived from ethical science, which may well be a matter of egoism and coldness of heart. O ethics as science! Rational and rationalistic ethics! Pedantry of pedantries, all is pedantry! . . .

And here we might pose the question which, according to Plato, was posed by Socrates, and that is whether or not virtue is knowledge, a question which is equivalent to asking whether or not virtue is rational.

The ethicists—those who maintain that ethics is a science, those whom the reading of these digressions will provoke to exclaim "Rhetoric, rhetoric, rhetoric!"—they will believe, I suppose, that virtue is attained through science, through rational study, and even that mathematics help us be better men. I do not know if they are right, but it seems to me that virtue, like religion, like the longing never to die—and all three are fundamentally the same—are the fruit of passion.

"But what then is passion?" I shall be asked. I do not know; or rather, I know full well, because I feel it, and since I feel it there is no need for me to define it to myself. Nay, more: I fear that if I were to arrive at a definition of it, I should cease to feel and to possess it. Passion is like suffering, and like suffering it creates its object. It is easier to find fuel for the fire than to find fire for the fuel.

And this, I know well enough, may seem like so much empty sophistry. And I shall also be told that there is a knowledge of passion and a passion of knowledge, and that in the moral sphere reason and life unite.

I do not know, I do not know, I do not know. . . . And perhaps what I am saying, though I say it somewhat more obscurely, is essentially the same as what my imaginary adversaries, whom I imagine in order to have someone to oppose, say in their turn, only they say it more clearly, more definitely, and more rationally. I do not know, I do not know. . . . But only, the things they say leave me cold and strike me as being emotionally empty.

But returning to our former question: is virtue a matter of knowledge? Is knowledge virtue? Here we have two separate questions in reality. Virtue may be knowledge, the knowledge of how to conduct oneself well, without all other aspects of knowledge being a matter of virtue. Machiavelli's virtue is knowledge, but it cannot be said that his *virtù*, his artistic excellence, is always a moral virtue. It is well known, moreover, that the most intelligent or the most learned men are not necessarily the best men.

No, no, no! Physiology does not teach us how to digest, nor logic how to reflect, nor aesthetics how to feel beauty or express it, nor ethics how to be good. And we are lucky if these sciences do not teach us to be hypocrites, for pedantry, whether the pedantry of logic, or of aesthetics, or of ethics, is essentially nothing but hypocrisy.

Reason may perhaps teach us certain bourgeois virtues, but it does not produce either saints or heroes. For the saint is one who does good not for the sake of the good, but for the sake of God, for the sake of becoming eternal.

Perhaps, on the other hand, culture, that is, Culture—O Culture!—the work, primarily, of philosophers and men of science, was not made by either heroes or saints! For saints have concerned themselves very little with the progress of human culture; they have concerned themselves rather with the salvation of individual souls, the souls of those individuals among whom they lived. Compared to Descartes, of what account is St. John of the Cross, that incandescent little friar, as he has been culturally—but perhaps not in a cultured manner—described?[10]

What have all the saints, burning with religious charity toward their fellows, hungering to have themselves and their neighbors made eternal, longing to set fire to the hearts of others, what have they done to advance the progress of science or of ethics? Did any one of them perchance invent the categorical imperative, as did the old bachelor of Königsberg, who if he was not a saint deserved to be one?

One day, the son of a grand professor of ethics, a professor who scarcely ever allowed that imperative to leave his lips, complained to me that his life was a barren sterility of spirit and that he lived in an inner vacuum. And I was forced to tell him:

"The fact is, my friend, that your father could count on an underground river, a ready current of ancient belief from his childhood and of hopes in the beyond. And while he thought he was nourishing his soul on that imperative or on something of a like nature, he was in reality drinking the waters of his beginnings. And he has perhaps given you the flower of his spirit, that is, his rational doctrines regarding ethics, but he has not given you the root, not the subterranean source, not the irrational substratum."

Why did Krausism happen to take root here in Spain, rather than the doctrines of Hegel or Kant, which are rationally and philosophically much more profound than Krausism?[11] Because Krausism was brought here with its roots intact. The philosophical thought of a nation or of an epoch is, so to say, its flower, the part which is external and above ground. But this flower, or if you wish, this fruit, draws its juice from the roots of the plant, and these roots, which are in and under the earth, are its religious sense. Kant's philosophical thought, the ultimate flower of the mental evolution of the Germanic people, has its roots in Luther's religious sense, and it is not possible for Kantianism, especially the practical part of it, to take root and bring forth flower and fruit in nations which have not experienced the Reformation and which perhaps were not capable of undergoing the experience. Kantianism is Protestant, and we Spanish are fundamentally Catholic. And if Krause put down some roots here—more than is commonly supposed and less ephemeral than is imagined—it is because Krause had his roots in pietism. And pietism, as Ritschl demonstrated in his history of that tendency, *Geschichte des Pietismus,* possesses specifically Catholic roots and signifies the permeation, or rather the persistence, of Catholic mysticism within the heart of Protestant rationalism. And this explains why not a few Catholic thinkers in Spain were touched by Krausist doctrine.

And since the Spanish are Catholics, whether we know it or not, or whether we like it or not, and although some of us may presume to be rationalists or atheists, it may be that the greatest service we can render to the cause of culture, and of religiosity, which is of more worth than culture—unless indeed culture and religiosity are the same thing—is in endeavoring to realize and clarify this subconscious, social, or popular Catholicism. And that has been the work in hand in this study.

What I have called the tragic sense of life in men and in nations is at any rate the Spanish tragic sense of life, that of Spanish people and of the Spanish nation, as it is reflected in my consciousness, which is a Spanish consciousness, made in Spain. And this tragic sense of life is essentially the Catholic sense of it, for Catholicism, above all popular Catholicism, is tragic. The people abominate comedy. When Pilate, the epitome of the refined gentleman, the superior person, the aesthete—the rationalist if you like—proposes to give the people comedy and mockingly presents Christ to them, saying "Behold the man!," the people go mad and cry out "Crucify him! Crucify him!" They do not want comedy, but tragedy. And the work which Dante, that great Catholic, called the *Divine Comedy* is the most tragic work ever written.

In these essays I have endeavored to reveal the soul of a Spaniard, and therewith the Spanish soul as such, and in the course of so doing I have advisedly curtailed the number of quotations from Spanish sources and, perhaps excessively, scattered citations from non-Spanish sources. For the fact is that all human souls are brother souls.

There is one figure, a comically tragic figure, a figure in which is revealed all that is profoundly tragic in the human comedy, the figure of Our Lord Don Quixote, the Spanish Christ, in whom is resumed and enclosed the immortal soul of my people. Perhaps the passion and death of the Knight of the Sorrowful Countenance is the passion and death of the Spanish people, its death and resurrection. And there exists a Quixotic philosophy and even a Quixotic metaphysics, and also a Quixotic logic and a Quixotic sense of religion. This philosophy, this logic, this ethics, this religious sense is what I have tried to outline, to suggest rather than to develop, in the present work; not to develop rationally, of course, for Quixotic madness does not admit of scientific logic.

Nine

THE SCHOOL OF MADRID

The Spanish Republic of 1873 was dissolved in December 1874 and the constitutional monarchy restored in 1875. Despite opposition from republicans, syndicalists, intellectuals, sectors of the army, and Catalan and Basque nationalists, the monarchy and parliamentary system condemned by regenerationists survived relatively unscathed until about 1917. But the system began to unravel when socialist and anarchist unions cooperated in a twenty-four-hour general strike, army officers set up juntas to protest low pay and favoritism, and republicans and regional separatists stepped up their opposition. As successive short-lived governments demonstrated their impotence, events began to spiral out of control. The highly successful general strike organized by anarchists in Barcelona in 1919 was followed by escalating violence between employers and anarcho-syndicalists. The effort to pacify the Spanish protectorate in Morocco, established in 1912, met disaster at the massacre of Annual in 1921. With over half of the population of Spain alienated from the political system and many receptive to the regenerationist Joaquín Costa's call for an "iron surgeon," General Primo de Rivera announced in 1923 that he was taking over the government. In the absence of serious opposition, his *pronunciamiento* simply became a fact.

The dictatorship of Primo de Rivera was faced with two outstanding problems: a revolutionary labor movement and war in the Moroccan protectorate. It dealt with the labor issue by cooperating with the socialist union and suppressing its anarchist rival. In collaboration with France, it achieved military success in the Moroccan protectorate by 1927. Nevertheless, support for the dictatorship had eroded almost entirely by 1929. The economic situation, which had been favorable during the first years of the general's rule, was deteriorating rapidly. And the regime had managed to estrange almost every major collective in Spain, including the army and the monarchy. Once the disaffection of military leaders became clear, King Alfonso XIII dismissed the ailing dictator on January 28, 1930.

On November 15, 1930, the philosopher José Ortega y Gasset published a famous article that concluded with the words, "Spaniards, your state is no more! Reconstitute it! *Delenda est Monarchia.*" There was little delay in heeding his advice. In the municipal elections of April 12, 1931, the cities voted overwhelmingly for republican candidates even though a majority nationwide cast their ballots for monarchists. Alfonso XIII took the electoral hint and abdicated rather than risk civil war. On April 14 the Spanish state was reconstituted as the Second Republic.

The latter part of the Second Republic, roughly from 1933 to 1936, is the temporal setting for the School of Madrid in the strict sense of the term. But the School's antecedents reach back to 1910, when Ortega y Gasset became professor of metaphysics at the University of Madrid. Over the following years, the other principal members of the School occupied chairs at the same institution. Manuel García Morente was appointed professor of ethics in 1912; Xavier Zubiri, professor of the history of philosophy in 1926; and José Gaos, professor of introductory philosophy in 1933. The reform of higher education carried out by the Second Republic turned this group of colleagues into the nucleus of a school. When the Faculty of Philosophy and Letters was granted the autonomy to organize its own program of studies, García Morente became its dean in 1932 and Gaos the director of the common course of introductory studies in 1934. But Ortega was always its central figure. Excerpts from his *Historia como sistema,* which dates from the apogee of the School of Madrid, are included here.

The School was broken up by the Spanish Civil War (1936–1939), and its members went into exile. Gaos found political asylum in Mexico, Zubiri taught and studied in Paris during the Civil War, and Ortega and García Morente lived in various places in Europe and Argentina for a decade. Although the latter three eventually returned to Spain, Gaos remained in Mexico—an event with far-reaching cultural consequences. He viewed himself as *transterrado* rather than *desterrado,* as rerooted in new soil rather than uprooted from the old. As part of the diaspora of Spaniards from all walks of life who lived most or all of their postwar years in exile, Gaos exercised a formative influence on philosophy in his adopted country, which radiated outward to all of Latin America.[1]

JOSÉ ORTEGA Y GASSET

José Ortega y Gasset, the most prominent Spanish philosopher of the twentieth century, was born in Madrid in 1883. After acquiring a traditional education, he earned an undergraduate degree from the University of Madrid in 1902 and a doctorate from the same institution in 1904. By the time he was twenty, however, Ortega saw that the Francophile Spain of his era could learn no more from France. "Spain needed Germany," he decided, so off he went like a "young hawk," ravenous "to bring German culture to . . . the ruin [of the hawk's 'Spanish castle'] and devour it there."[1] Between 1905 and 1911 he made four extended forays, above all to Marburg, where he fed on the Neo-Kantianism of Hermann Cohen and Paul Natorp. Although Ortega steeped himself in German thought, he quickly attained critical distance, propagating an attitude of independent appreciation as professor of metaphysics at the University of Madrid from 1910 to 1936. During these years the philosophy faculty at Madrid reached one of its highest levels ever, forming what was later described as the School of Madrid. When the Spanish Civil War broke out in 1936, Ortega emigrated, first to France, then to Holland, Argentina, and Portugal. From 1945 on he returned to Spain for protracted stays, founding the Institute of Humanities in Madrid with Julian Marías in 1948. He died in Madrid in 1955.

To understand Ortega's unrivaled influence in Spain, one must realize that he was not merely an academic. He once described himself as "university professor, journalist, man of letters, politician, café companion, bullfighter, 'man of the world,' something of a parish priest, and I don't know what all else."[2] Coming from a family of eminent journalists and politicians, he pursued these ancestral avocations, as well as philosophy, throughout the greater part of his career. He labored incessantly as a journalist, contributing regularly to periodicals and founding the authoritative *Revista de occidente* in 1923. His political activity included vocal opposition to the Spanish monarchy and the dictatorship of Primo de Rivera, and when the Second Republic was proclaimed in 1931, he was elected to its constituent assembly. Yet he denounced the extreme regionalism and anticlericalism of the Republic in a celebrated discourse of December 6, 1931, and by 1932 he had largely withdrawn from politics. But the central fact about Ortega is the dedication of his immense literary talent to the problems of Spain. The years in Germany precipitated his decision "to accept completely and unreservedly my Spanish destiny" and the sense that "[m]y individual destiny appeared to me and continues to appear to me inseparable from the destiny of my people."[3]

The quickest route into Ortega's thought is via his critique of the German philosophy on which he cut his teeth. He regarded the post-Kantian idealisms of Hegel, Fichte, and Schelling and the Neo-Kantian idealisms of Cohen and Natorp as paradigmatic philosophical systems, but he believed that the idealists carried system-building to such an extreme that system became an end rather than a means; they opted for architecture over truth. As a result, even though the idealists understood the role of consciousness in constituting reality, they were unable to grasp the true nature of consciousness. Idealism, Ortega concluded, is bankrupt. But Husserlian phenomenology falls into the same trap, by substituting an abstraction of consciousness for consciousness itself. Against all these philosophers, Ortega insisted that the self is an abstraction—but so is the thing. What is real is an *event*, the charged encounter of self and thing. "I am I plus my circumstance," Ortega liked to say.[4] Reality is relational.

The selections from Ortega's writings here are from five chapters of *Historia como sistema* (History as a System), published originally in English in 1935. Ortega presents a precocious diagnosis of the sciences in crisis. Concurring with Husserl's 1929 observation that the great Enlightenment faith in science has been lost, Ortega identifies "the terrorism of the laboratory" as one of the causes.[5] This peculiar terrorism, an Ortegian target as early as 1921, is epitomized by the Loeb anecdote in chapter 4 of the selection. Reason as employed in the laboratories, the reason of physics and mathematics, is ideally suited for divining the natures of things. But people do not have natures, Ortega claims. Human beings are constitutively unstable, "perforce free," and thus forced to compose the drama of their own lives.[6] Physico-mathematical reason is therefore inappropriate for human self-understanding. A grasp of the improvisational character of human life requires a different form of reason. Drawing on the ideas of Wilhelm Dilthey, Ortega looks forward to a new age informed by a new faith: the faith in historical reason.

Historia como sistema can be interpreted in part as a prophecy of postmodernism. To abandon idealism and the fixation on consciousness, Ortega wrote, is to abandon the modern age.[7] But even though Ortega's critique of scientific arrogance is congenial to postmodernism, he does not fall into the cognitive relativism associated with many forms of it. History is a system, the system of human experiences, and thus a system attuned to human reason.

History as a System

A Plea for Historical Reason

Human life is a strange reality concerning which the first thing to be said is that it is the basic reality, in the sense that to it we must refer all others, since all others, effective or presumptive, must in one way or another appear within it.

The most trivial and at the same time the most important note in human life is that man has no choice but to be always doing something to keep himself in existence. Life is given to us; we do not give it to ourselves, rather we find ourselves in it, suddenly and without knowing how. But the life which is given us is not given us ready-made; we must make it for ourselves, each one his own. Life is a task. And the weightiest aspect of these tasks in which life consists is not the necessity of performing them but, in a sense, the opposite: I mean that we find ourselves always under compulsion to do something but never, strictly speaking,

under compulsion to do something in particular, that there is not imposed on us this or that task as there is imposed on the star its course or
on the stone its gravitation. Each individual before doing anything must
decide for himself and at his own risk what he is going to do. But this
decision is impossible unless one possesses certain convictions concerning the nature of things around one, the nature of other men, of oneself.
Only in the light of such convictions can one prefer one act to another,
can one, in short, live.

It follows that man must ever be grounded on some belief, and that
the structure of his life will depend primordially on the beliefs on which
he is grounded; and further that the most decisive changes in humanity
are changes of belief, the intensifying or weakening of beliefs. The diagnosis of any human existence, whether of an individual, a people,
or an age, must begin by establishing the repertory of its convictions.
For always in living one sets out from certain convictions. They are the
ground beneath our feet, and it is for this reason we say that man is
grounded on them. It is man's beliefs that truly constitute his state. I
have spoken of them as a "repertory" to indicate that the plurality of
beliefs on which an individual, a people, or an age is grounded never
possesses a completely logical articulation, that is to say, does not form
a system of ideas such as, for example, a philosophy constitutes or aims
at constituting. The beliefs that coexist in any human life, sustaining,
impelling, and directing it, are on occasion incongruous, contradictory,
at the least confused. Be it noted that all these qualifications attach to
beliefs in so far as they partake of ideas. But it is erroneous to define
belief as an idea. Once an idea has been thought it has exhausted its
role and its consistency. The individual, moreover, may think whatever
the whim suggests to him, and even many things against his whim.
Thoughts arise in the mind spontaneously, without will or deliberation
on our part and without producing any effect whatever on our behavior.
A belief is not merely an idea that is thought, it is an idea in which one
also believes. And believing is not an operation of the intellectual mechanism, but a function of the living being as such, the function of guiding
his conduct, his performance of his task.

This observation once made, I can now withdraw my previous expression and say that beliefs, a mere incoherent repertory in so far as
they are merely ideas, always constitute a system in so far as they are

effective beliefs; in other words, that while lacking articulation from the logical or strictly intellectual point of view, they do nonetheless possess a vital articulation, they *function* as beliefs resting one on another, combining with one another to form a whole: in short, that they always present themselves as members of an organism, of a structure. This causes them among other things always to possess their own architecture and to function as a hierarchy. In every human life there are beliefs that are basic, fundamental, radical, and there are others derived from these, upheld by them, and secondary to them. If this observation is supremely trivial, the fault is not mine that with all its triviality it remains of the greatest importance. For should the beliefs by which one lives lack structure, since their number in each individual life is legion there must result a mere pullulation hostile to all idea of order and incomprehensible in consequence.

The fact that we should see them, on the contrary, as endowed with a structure and a hierarchy allows us to penetrate their hidden order and consequently to understand our own life and the life of others, that of today and that of other days.

Thus we may now say that the diagnosing of any human existence, whether of an individual, a people, or an age, must begin by an ordered inventory of its system of convictions, and to this end it must establish before all else which belief is fundamental, decisive, sustaining and breathing life into all the others.

Now in order to determine the state of one's beliefs at a given moment the only method we possess is that of comparing this moment with one or more other moments. The more numerous the terms of comparison the more exact will be the result—another banal observation whose far-reaching consequences will emerge suddenly at the end of this meditation.

II

A comparison of the state of beliefs in which the European finds himself today with that obtaining a mere thirty years ago makes it clear that this has changed profoundly, because the fundamental conviction has changed.

The generation that flourished about the year 1900 was the last of a very long cycle, a cycle which began towards the end of the sixteenth century and was characterized by the fact that men lived on their faith in reason. In what does this faith consist?

If we open the *Discours de la Méthode,* the classical program of the new age, we find that it culminates in the following sentences:

> Those long chains of simple and easy conclusions used by the geometricians for obtaining their most difficult proofs made me think that everything within the ken of man is interlaced in this same manner and that, if only we refrain from accepting as true what may be not true and from upsetting the order required for deducing one thing from the other, there can be nothing so remote that it will not finally be reached nor so hidden that it will not be discovered.[1]

These words are the cockcrow of rationalism, the moving reveille that ushers in a whole new age, our so-called modern age, that modern age whose death agony, whose swan song, as it seems to many, we are today witnessing.

There is at least no denying that between the Cartesian attitude of mind and our own no slight difference exists. What joy, what a tone of vigorous challenge to the universe, what an early-morning presumptuousness these magnificent words of Descartes reveal! The reader has observed: apart from the divine mysteries which his courtesy bids him leave on one side, to this man there is no problem that cannot be solved. He assures us that in the universe there are no arcana, no unconquerable secrets before which humanity must halt in defenseless terror. The world that surrounds man all about, existence within which constitutes his life, is to become transparent, even to its farthest recesses, to the human mind. At last man is to know the truth about everything. It suffices that he should not lose heart at the complexity of the problems, and that he should allow no passion to cloud his mind. If with serene self-mastery he uses the apparatus of his intellect, if in particular he uses it in orderly fashion, he will find that his faculty of thought is *ratio,* reason, and that in reason he possesses the almost magic power of reducing everything to clarity, of turning what is most opaque to crystal, penetrating it by analysis until it is become self-evident. According to this, the world of reality and the world of thought are each a cosmos corresponding one to the other, each compact and continuous, wherein nothing is abrupt, isolated, or inaccessible, but rather such that from any point in it we may without intermission and without leaping pass to all other points and contemplate the whole. Man with his reason may thus plunge tranquilly into the abysmal depths of the universe, certain of extracting from the remotest problem, from the closest enigma, the essence of its truth, even as the Coromandel diver plunges into the deeps of ocean to reappear straightway bearing between his teeth the pearl of great price.

In the closing years of the sixteenth century and these early years of the seventeenth in which Descartes is meditating, Western man believes, then, that the world possesses a rational structure, that is to say, that reality possesses an organization coincident with the organization of the human intellect, taking this, of course, in its purest form, that of mathematical reason. Here accordingly is a marvelous key giving man a power over things around him that is theoretically illimitable. Such a discovery was a pretty stroke of fortune. For suppose that Europe had not then come by this belief. In the fifteenth century it had lost its faith in God, in revelation, either because man had completely lost that faith or because it had ceased to be in him a living faith. Theologians make a very shrewd distinction, one capable of throwing light on not a few things of today, between a live and a sluggish faith. Generalizing this, I should formulate it thus: we believe in something with a live faith when that belief is sufficient for us to live by, and we believe in something with a dead, a sluggish faith when, without having abandoned it, being still grounded on it, it no longer acts efficaciously on our lives. It is become a drag, a dead weight; still part of us, yet useless as lumber in the attic of the soul. We no longer rest our existence on that something believed in; the stimuli, the pointers we live by no longer spring spontaneously from that faith. The proof is that we are constantly forgetting we still believe in it, whereas a living faith is the constant and most active presence of the entity we believe in. (Hence the perfectly natural phenomenon that the mystic calls "the presence of God." For a living love is likewise distinguished from a lifeless, dragging love in this, that the object loved is present to us without need of trance or fear of eclipse. We do not need to go in search of it with our attention; on the contrary, we have difficulty in removing it from before our inner eye. And this is not to say that we are always nor even frequently *thinking* about it, but simply that we constantly "count on it.") An illustration of this difference in the present situation of the European I shall shortly adduce.[2]

Throughout the Middle Ages the European had lived on revelation. Lacking it, limited to his own naked strength, he would have felt incapable of dealing with the mysterious surroundings that made up his world, with the misfortunes and trials of existence. But he believed with a living faith that an all-powerful, all-knowing being would unfold to him gratuitously all that was essential to his life. We may follow the vicissitudes of this faith and witness, almost generation by generation, its progressive decay. It is a melancholy story. Gradually the living faith ceases to take nutriment, loses its color, becomes paralyzed, until, from whatever motives —these lie outside my present inquiry—towards the middle of the fifteenth century that living faith is clearly seen to have changed to a tired, ineffective faith, if indeed the individual soul has not uprooted it entirely. The man of that age begins to perceive that revelation does not suffice to illumine his relations to the world; once more he is conscious of being lost in the trackless forest of the universe, face to face with which he lacks alike a guide and a mediator. The fifteenth and the sixteenth centuries are, therefore, two centuries of tremendous restlessness, of fierce disquiet, two centuries, as we should say today, of crisis. From this crisis Western man is saved by a new faith, a new belief: faith in reason, in the *nuove scienze*. Man, having again fallen, is born again. The Renaissance is the parturient disquiet of a new confidence based on physico-mathematical science, the new mediator between man and the world.

IV

Science is in danger. In saying this I do not think I exaggerate. For this is not to say that Europe collectively has made a radical end of its belief in science, but only that its faith, once living, is in our day become sluggish. This is sufficient to cause science to be in danger and to make it impossible for the scientist to go on living as he has lived till now, sleepwalking at his work, believing that the society around him still supports, sustains, and venerates him. What has happened to bring about such a situation? Science today knows with incredible precision much of what is happening on remote stars and galaxies. Science is rightly proud of the fact, and because of it, although with less right, it spreads its peacock feathers at academic gatherings. But meanwhile it has come about that this same science, once a living social faith, is now almost looked down upon by society in general. And although this has not happened on Sirius but only on our own planet, it is not, I conceive, bereft of importance. Science cannot be merely science about Sirius; it claims also to be science about man. What then has science, reason, got to say today, with reasonable precision, concerning this so urgent fact that so intimately concerns it? Just nothing. Science has no clear knowledge on the matter. One perceives the enormity of the position, the shame of it. The upshot is that, where great human changes are concerned, science, strictly so called, has got nothing exact to say. The thing is so enormous that it straightway reveals to us the reason. For it causes us to note that the science, the reason, in which modern man placed his social faith is, speaking strictly, merely physico-mathematical science together with biological science, the latter based directly on the former and benefiting, in its weakness, from the other's prestige—in short, summing both up together, what is called natural science or reason.

The present position of physical science or reason is in consequence somewhat paradoxical. If there is anything in the repertory of human activities and pursuits that has not proved a failure, it is precisely this science, when one considers it circumscribed within its genuine territory, nature. Within this order and ambit, far from having failed, it has transcended all our hopes. For the first time in history the powers of realization, of achievement, have outstripped those of mere fantasy. Science has achieved things that irresponsible imaginings had never so much as dreamed of. This is so unquestionable that one has difficulty in understanding straightway why man is not today on his knees before science as before some magic power. The fact remains that he is not on his knees; on the contrary, he is beginning to turn his back. He does not deny, he is not unaware of, its marvelous power, its triumph over nature, but he realizes at the same time that nature is only one dimension of human life and that a resounding success with regard to nature does not preclude failure with regard to the totality of our existence. Life at any instant is an inexorable balance, in which "physical reason" (*la razón física*) for all its partial splendor does not rule out the possibility of a heavy deficit. Even more, the lack of equilibrium between the perfection of its partial efficiency and its failure from the comprehensive point of view, which is final, is such in my opinion that it has contributed to the aggravation of our universal disquiet.

Man thus finds himself, when confronted with physical reason, in a state of mind comparable to that of Christina of Sweden, as described by Leibnitz, when, after her abdication, she caused a coin to be struck bearing the effigy of a crown and had these words inscribed in the exergue: *Non mi bisogna e non mi basta* [Neither necessary nor sufficient for me].

In the upshot the paradox resolves itself into a supremely simple observation. What has not collapsed in physics is physics. What has collapsed in it is the rhetoric, the trimmings of childish presumption, of irrational and arbitrary additions it gave rise to, what, many years ago, I styled "the terrorism of the laboratory." This is why ever since I began to write I have combated what I called scientific *Utopianism*. Open, for example, *El tema de nuestro tiempo* at the chapter entitled "The historic sense of Einstein's theory," written about 1921. There the following passage will be found:

It is incomprehensible that science, whose only pleasure lies in attaining to a true image of things, should nourish itself on illusions. I recall a detail whose influence on my thought was decisive. Many years ago I was reading a lecture of the physiologist Loeb on tropism. The tropism is a concept which has been invoked to describe and throw light on the law governing the elemental movements of the infusoria. The concept serves, indifferently well and with corrections and additions, to help us understand some of these phenomena. But at the close of this lecture Loeb adds: "The day will come when what we now call moral acts in man will be explained simply as tropisms." Such temerity perturbed me exceedingly, for it opened my eyes to many other judgments of modern science that are guilty, if less ostentatiously, of the same error. So then, I thought, a concept like the tropism, which is scarce capable of plumbing the secret of phenomena so simple as the antics of the infusoria, may at some vague future date suffice to explain phenomena as mysterious and complex as man's ethical acts! What sense is there here? Science has to solve its problems in the present, not transport us to the Greek kalends. If its present methods are insufficient to master now the enigmas of the universe, discretion would suggest that they be replaced by other and more effective ones. But the science *à la mode* is full of problems which are left intact because they are incompatible with its methods. As if it was the former that were under obligation to subordinate themselves to the latter, and not the other way round! Science is full of achronisms, of Greek kalends.[3]

When we emerge from a science so devoutly simple, bowing in idolatrous worship before pre-established methods, and approach the thought of Einstein there comes upon us as it were a fresh morning breeze. Einstein's attitude is radically different from that of tradition. With the dash of a young athlete we see him make straight for his problems and take them by the horns, using the method that lies nearest to his hand. Out of the apparent defects and limitations of science he draws virtue and tactical efficiency.

From this idea of the Greek kalends all my philosophic thought has emanated. There in germ is my whole conception of life as the basic reality and of knowledge as an internal—and not an independent or Utopian—function of life. Just as Einstein was then telling us that in physics it is necessary to elaborate concepts such as will make absolute motion impossible (absolute motion is immeasurable and before what cannot be measured physics is impotent), I considered it essential to elaborate a philosophy that should take its point of departure, its formal principle, from the exclusion of the Greek kalends. Because life is the opposite of these kalends. Life is haste and has urgent need to know what it is up against, and it is out of this urgency that truth must derive its method. The idea of progress, placing truth in a vague tomorrow, has proved a dulling opiate to humanity. Truth is what is true now and not what remains to be discovered in an undetermined future. Mr. Loeb—and his whole generation is with him—gives up his claim to a present truth of morality on the strength of the future attaining to a physics of morality: a curious way of existing at the expense of posterity while leaving one's own life shorn of foundations, of roots, of any profound implications in the scheme of things. The viciousness of this attitude is so radical that it appears already in the "provisional morality" of

Descartes. And so it happens that the first blow directed against the superficial framework of our civilization, our economics, our morals, our politics, finds man possessed of no truths of his own, of no clear, firm position on anything of importance.

The only thing he believed in was physical science, and when this received the urgent call to propound its truth on the most human problems, it did not know what to say. And suddenly Western man has received the impression of losing his footing, of finding himself without support, and has known a panic terror and believed himself to be sinking, making shipwreck in the void.

And yet, a measure of serenity is all that is needed for our feet once more to experience the delicious sensation of touching hard, solid mother earth, an element capable of sustaining man. As always, it is essential—and sufficient—instead of giving way to panic and losing one's head, to convert into a source of support the very factor that had engendered the impression of an abyss. Physical science can throw no clear light on the human element. Very well. This means simply that we must shake ourselves free, radically free, from the physical, the natural, approach to the human element. Let us instead accept this in all its spontaneity, just as we see it and come upon it. In other words, the collapse of physical reason leaves the way clear for vital, historical reason.[4]

VII

Physico-mathematical reason, whether in its crude form of naturalism or in its beatific form of spiritualism, was in no state to confront human problems. By its very constitution it could do no other than search for man's nature. And, naturally, it did not find it. For man has no nature. Man is not his body, which is a thing, nor his soul, psyche, conscience, or spirit, which is also a thing. Man is no thing, but a drama—his life, a pure and universal happening which happens to each one of us and in which each one in his turn is nothing but happening. All things, be they what they may, are now mere interpretations which he exercises himself in giving to whatever he comes upon. Things he does not come upon: he poses or supposes them. What he comes upon are pure difficulties and pure facilities for existing. Existence itself is not presented to him ready-made, as it is to the stone; rather, shall we say, looping the loop begun in the opening words of this article, on coming up against the fact of his existence, on existence happening to him, all he comes up against, all that happens to him is the realization that he has no choice but to do something in order not to cease existing. This shows that the mode of being of life, even as simple existing, is not a *being already*, since the only thing that is given us and that *is* when there is human life is the having to make it, each one for himself.[5] Life is a gerundive, not a participle: a *faciendum*, not a *factum*. Life is a task. . . .

At every moment of my life there open before me divers possibilities: I can do this or that. If I do this, I shall be A the moment after; if I do that, I shall be B. At the present moment the reader may stop reading me or may go on. And, however slight the importance of this article, according as he does the one or the other the reader will be A or will be B, will have made of himself an A or a B. Man is the entity that makes itself, an entity which traditional ontology only stumbled upon precisely as its course was drawing to a close, and which it in consequence gave up the attempt to understand: the *causa sui*. With this difference, that the *causa sui* had only to "exert itself" in being the *cause* of itself and not in determining what *self* it was going to cause. It had, to begin with, a *self* previously determined and invariable, consistent, for example, to infinity. . . .

Concerning these possibilities of being the following remarks fall to be made:

1. That they likewise are not presented to me. I must find them for myself, either on my own or through the medium of those of my fellows with whom my life brings me in contact. I invent projects of being and of doing in the light of circumstance. This alone I come upon, this alone is given me: circumstance.[6] It is too often forgotten that man is impossible without imagination, without the capacity to invent for himself a conception of life, to "ideate" the character he is going to be. Whether he be original or a plagiarist, man is the novelist of himself.[7]

2. That among these possibilities I must choose. Hence, I am free. But, be it well understood, I am free *by compulsion*, whether I wish to be or not. Freedom is not an activity pursued by an entity that, apart from and previous to such pursuit, is already possessed of a fixed being. To be free means to be lacking in constitutive identity, not to have subscribed

to a determined being, to be able to be other than what one was, to be unable to install oneself once and for all in any given being. The only attribute of the fixed, stable being in the free being is this constitutive instability. . . .

VIII

Yesterday I made the acquaintance of Hermione. She is a fascinating woman. Towards me she was deferential, insinuating. I think of making love to her, and of attempting to win her love in return. But can my authentic being, what I call *I,* consist in "being Hermione's lover"? Scarcely have I conjured up my love for Hermione in the mind's eye with a measure of precision when I emphatically turn down such a project of being. Why? I can find no objection to raise against Hermione, only the fact is . . . that I am fifty, and at fifty, although the body may have retained all the elasticity of thirty and the psychic impulses have lost none of their vigor, I cannot now "be Hermione's lover." But why? The point is this, that being a man of years I have already had time to be the lover of Cidalisa and the lover of Arsinoe and the lover of Glykeia, and I know now what "being a lover" is. I know its excellences, I know also its limitations. In short, I have experienced to the full that form of life that is called "loving a woman," and, frankly, I have had enough. And so it happens that the "cause" of my not being a lover tomorrow is precisely the fact that I have been one. If I had not been a lover, if I had not already experienced love to the full, I should be Hermione's lover.

Here, then, is a new dimension in this strange reality of life. Before us lie the diverse possibilities of being, but behind us lies what we have been. And what we have been acts negatively on what we can be. When I was a child I was a Christian; now I am one no longer. Does this mean, strictly speaking, that I do not go on being a Christian? The Christian I was, is he dead, annihilated? Of course not; of course I am still a Christian, but in the form of having been a Christian. Had I not known the experience of being a Christian, did I not have it behind me and go on being a Christian in this form of having been one, it is possible that, faced with the difficulties of life today, I might now resolve to be a

Christian. And what has happened to me in this matter is happening to many Europeans, who *were* Christians either on their own account or vicariously, from the recollection of their forefathers. Who knows, if one got to the bottom of things, whether it might not be said that it is happening to everybody, including those who believe in all good faith that they still are Christians? That it is possible to be a Christian today, just like that, in the fullness of the term and without reservations, is not so very certain. And the same might be said about being "a democrat," being "a liberal," being "*ancien régime,*" being "feudal."

If I do not make love to Hermione, if I do not turn Christian, accordingly, if the reality of my life at the moment is what it is, what it is going to be depends on what is commonly called "experience of life." This is a knowledge of what we have been that memory has preserved for us and that lies always to hand, accumulated in our today, in our actuality or reality. And it happens that this knowledge determines my life negatively in its "real" aspect, in its being. And from this it follows that constitutively my life is experience of life. My fifty years signify an absolute reality, not because the body may be growing weak or the psyche losing its grip, things that do not always happen, but because at that age one has accumulated a longer living past, one has been more things, and one "has more experience." The conclusion to be drawn from which is that man's being is irreversible, he is compelled ontologically always to advance on himself, and this not because a given instant of time cannot recur: on the contrary, time does not recur because man cannot go back to being what he has been.

But experience of life is not made up solely of my past, of the experiences that I personally have had. It is built up also of the past of my forebears, handed down to me by the society I live in. Society consists primarily in a repertory of usages, intellectual, moral, political, technical, of play and pleasure. Now, in order that a form of life—an opinion, a line of conduct—may become a usage, a thing of social validity, it is necessary, first, that time should elapse, and second, that the form in question should cease to be a spontaneous form of personal life. Usage is tardy in taking shape. Every usage is old. Expressed differently, society is, primarily, the past and, relatively to man, tardigrade. For the rest, the establishing of a new usage—a new "public opinion" or "collective belief," a new morality, a new form of government—the determination of *what* at each moment society *is going to be,* depends on what it has been, just as in the individual life. Western societies are finding in the present political crisis that they cannot, without more ado, be "liberal," "democratic," "monarchical," "feudal" or . . . "Pharaonic," precisely because they have already been these things, either in themselves or from experience of how others have been them. In the "political public opinion" of today, in the usage at present in force, an enormous amount of the past continues active; that opinion, that usage, is accordingly this past in the form of having been it. . . .[8]

In order to understand my conduct with regard to Hermione and to Christianity, or the reader's with regard to public problems, in order to discover the reason of our being or, what comes to the same thing, *why* we are as we are, what have we done? What was it that made us understand, *conceive,* our being? Simply the telling, the narrating that *formerly* I was the lover of this and that woman, that *formerly* I was a Christian, that the reader in himself or through others he has heard of was an absolutist, a Caesarist, a democrat, etc. In short, the reasoning, the *reason,* that throws light here consists in a narration. Alongside pure physico-mathematical reason there is, then, a narrative reason. To comprehend anything human, be it personal or collective, one must tell its history. This man, this nation does such a thing and is in such a manner, *because* formerly he or it did that other thing and was in such another manner. Life only takes on a measure of transparency in the light of *historical reason.* . . .

Man, in a word, has no nature; what he has is . . . *history.* Expressed differently: what nature is to things, history, *res gestae,* is to man. Once again we become aware of the possible application of theological concepts to human reality. *Deus, cui hoc est natura quod fecerit* . . . [God is like the nature he made], says St. Augustine.[9] Man, likewise, finds that he has no nature other than what he has himself done. . . .

There is no cause, therefore, for weeping overmuch concerning the mutability of everything human. This is precisely our ontological privilege. Progress is only possible to one who is not linked today to what he was yesterday, who is not caught for ever in that being which is already, but can migrate from it into another. But this is not enough: it is not sufficient that man should be able to free himself from what he is already and take on a new form, as the serpent sloughs its skin and is left with another. Progress demands that this new form should rise above the old and to this end should preserve it and turn it to account, that it should take off from the old, climbing on its shoulders as a high temperature mounts on lower ones. To progress is to accumulate being, to store up reality. This increase of being, it is true, when referred only to the individual, might be interpreted naturalistically as the mere development or *enodatio* of an initial disposition. With the evolutionary thesis still unproved, whatever its probability, it can be said that the tiger of today is neither more nor less a tiger than was that of a thousand years ago: it is being a tiger for the first time, it is always a first tiger. But the human individual is not putting on humanity for the first time. To begin with, he finds around him, in his "circumstance," other men and the society they give rise to. Hence his humanity, that which begins to develop in him, takes its point of departure from another, already developed, that has reached its culmination: in short, to his humanity he adds other humanities. He finds at birth a form of humanity, a mode of being a man, already forged, that he need not invent but may simply take over and set out from for his individual development. This does not begin for him—as for the tiger, which must always start again—at zero but at a positive quantity to which he adds his own growth. Man is not a first man, an eternal Adam: he is formally a second man, a third man, etc.

Mutable condition has thus its ontological virtue and grace, and invites one to recall Galileo's words: *I detrattori della corruttibilità meriterebber d'esser cangiati in statue* [The detractors of corruptibility deserve to be changed into statues].

Let the reader reflect closely on his life, studying it against the light as one looks at a glass of water to study its infusoria. If he asks himself why his life is thus and not otherwise, it will appear to him that not a few details had their origin in inscrutable chance. But he will find the broad lines of its reality perfectly comprehensible once he sees that he is thus because, in the last resort, the society—"collective man"—in which he lives is thus. And in its turn the mode of being of society will stand revealed, once there is discovered within it what that society was—what it believed, felt, preferred—at an earlier stage. That is to say that in his individual and fleeting today man will see, foreshortened, the whole of man's past still active and alive. For we can only throw light on yesterday by invoking the day before yesterday; and so with all yesterdays.

History is a system, the system of human experiences linked in a single, inexorable chain. Hence nothing can be truly clear in history until everything is clear. We cannot properly understand what this "rationalist" European is unless we know exactly what it was to be a Christian, nor what it was to be a Christian unless we know what it was to be a Stoic: and so the process goes on. And this systematism of *res gestae* becomes reoperative and potent in history as *cognitio rerum gestarum*. Every historic term whatsoever, to have exactness, must be determined as a function of all history, neither more nor less than each concept in Hegel's *Logic* has value only in respect of the niche left for it by the others.[10]

History is the systematic science of that radical reality, my life. It is therefore a science of the present in the most rigorous and actual sense of the word. Were it not a science of the present, where should we find that past that is commonly assigned to it as theme? The opposite—and customary—interpretation is equivalent to making of the past an abstract, unreal something lying lifeless just where it happened in time, whereas the past is in truth the live, active force that sustains our today. There is no *actio in distans*. The past is not yonder, at the date when it happened, but here, in me. The past is I—by which I mean my life.

Notes

Preface

1. Letter to Magda von Hattingberg, February 1, 1914, excerpted in *The Selected Poetry of Rainer Maria Rilke*, ed. and trans. Stephen Mitchell (New York: Vintage International, 1989), p. 334. Emphasis in original. This experience also figures in the tenth Duino elegy.

2. A. Robert Caponigri, *Contemporary Spanish Philosophy* (Notre Dame: University of Notre Dame Press, 1967), pp. vii–viii.

3. For more recent developments, English readers may consult the Caponigri volume cited in the previous note. For still more recent Spanish philosophy, see Javier Muguerza, *Ethics and Perplexity: Toward a Critique of Dialogical Reason* (Amsterdam and New York: Rodopi, 2004) and Reyes Mate, *Memory of the West* (Amsterdam and New York: Rodopi, 2004).

4. Neil McInnes, "Spanish Philosophy," in *The Encyclopedia of Philosophy*, ed. Paul Edwards (New York: Macmillan and The Free Press; London: Collier Macmillan, 1967), vol. 7, pp. 511–516; José Luis Abellán, "Spain, philosophy in," in *Routledge Encyclopedia of Philosophy*, ed. Edward Craig (London and New York: Routledge, 1998), vol. 9, pp. 70–77; and Walter B. Redmond, "Latin America, colonial thought in," in *Routledge Encyclopedia of Philosophy*, vol. 5, pp. 421–426.

SENECA

1. Although later writers have sometimes accused Seneca of hypocrisy, he appears to have died in full accordance with his principles. Tacitus' account of his suicide and his wife Paulina's suicide attempt is in *Annals* 15.62–64.

2. Bacon makes the point in the dedication of his *Essays*. Quoting Bacon, Robin Campbell asserts that "Seneca if anyone is the founder of the Essay." Campbell, "Introduction," in Seneca, *Letters from a Stoic* (Harmondsworth: Penguin, 1969), p. 20.

3. For instance, by Folly in Erasmus' *Praise of Folly*, ch. 30.

4. The description of theoretical topics as "less deserving" is from Letter 65, not included here.

Moral Letters (translator's notes)

1. A festival lasting several days, commencing on the 17th of December.
2. Epicureans. As the next sentence indicates, rich men sometimes had a room fitted out for the purpose.
3. Virgil, *Aeneid* VIII.364–365.
4. Virgil, *Aeneid* VIII.352.
5. Many ex-slaves had risen to high positions under Claudius and Nero.
6. Homer, *Iliad* XIX.228f., XXIV.601f.
7. Virgil, *Aeneid* VI.274–275.
8. St. Augustine quotes this fragment of Cleanthes as Seneca's (*De civitate Dei* V.8).

QUINTILIAN

1. *Institutio oratoria*, Book 6, preface, 2–13.
2. Walter J. Ong, *Orality and Literacy: The Technologizing of the Word* (1982; rpt. London and New York: Routledge, 1988), p. 109.
3. *Gorgias* 463b.
4. *Phaedrus* 257c and following.
5. *Rhetoric* 1.1, 1355a5–10. Plato's influence on Aristotle is especially noticeable in Book 2.
6. Cicero, *De oratore* 1.47; 3.57, 60–61, 71–72, 129.
7. "Das Zeitalter der Sophisten—unsere Zeit." Friedrich Nietzsche, *Die Unschuld des Werdens* (Stuttgart: A. Kröner, 1956), vol. 1, p. 32.

Institutio oratoria (translator's notes)

1. *De oratore* iii.15.
2. *Aeneid* iii.193.
3. Cf. Book I, Preface 9.
4. For the distribution of the Campanian lands.
5. I.e. φιλόσοφος, a term of which he was reputed the inventor.
6. *Brutus* xci.316; *Orator ad M. Brutum* xxx.107.
7. Quintilian's reverence for Cicero is such that he feels hampered in maintaining his thesis.

8. In a lost letter: cf. *Institutio oratoria* X.i.24 and Plutarch's "Life of Cicero" 24.

9. *Aeneid* i.151 and following.

10. "Color" is a technical term for "the particular aspect given to a case by skilful manipulation of the facts—the 'gloss' or 'varnish' put on them by the accused or accuser." William Peterson on *Institutio oratoria* X.i.116, in *Quintilian: Institutionis Oratoriae Liber X* (1891; rpt. Mundelein, IL: Bolchazy-Carducci Publishers, 2005), p. 76.

11. The date is uncertain, but the reference must be either to the Samnite war of 290 or the war with Pyrrhus.

12. Chs. xx, xxvii, and xxxi.

13. See *Institutio oratoria* III.vi.45.

14. Ibid.

15. Ibid.

16. See III.vi.23.

17. See III.vi.15.

18. Probably an allusion to contradictory laws. See VII.vii.

19. See VII.ix.

20. See III.vi.31.

21. I.e. natural philosophy in the widest sense.

22. See the previous paragraph.

23. *Orator ad M. Brutum* iii.12.

24. See II.i.9, III.v.5 and 10.

ISIDORE OF SEVILLE

1. "Introducción General," in San Isidoro de Sevilla, *Etimologías,* 2nd ed., trans. and notes by José Oroz Reta and Manuel-A. Marcos Casquero, intro. by Manuel C. Díaz y Díaz (Madrid: Biblioteca de Autores Cristianos, 1993), vol. 1, pp. 76–77. The Latin text of this bilingual Spanish and Latin edition is based on the respected text of Wallace M. Lindsay.

2. A complete English translation of the *Etymologiae* is *The Etymologies of Isidore of Seville,* trans. Stephen A. Barney, W. J. Lewis, J. A. Beach, and Oliver Berghof (Cambridge: Cambridge University Press, 2006). An older commentary with translations of many extracts is Ernest Brehaut, *An Encyclopedist of the Dark Ages: Isidore of Seville* (New York: Columbia University Press, 1912). More recently, Book 2 has been translated as *Etymologies, Book II,* ed. and trans. Peter K. Marshall (Paris: Société d'Édition "Les Belles Lettres," 1983). The passages translated for this volume are based on the Latin text of Oroz Reta and Marcos Casquero cited in note 1.

3. "Introducción General," in San Isidoro de Sevilla, *Etimologías,* vol. 1, pp. 169–170, 177–180.

4. The scholar was A. E. Anspach. The results of his research are compiled in J. M. Fernández Catón, *Las Etimologías en la tradición manuscrita medieval estudiada por el Prof. Dr. Anspach* (León: Centro de Estudios e Investigación "San Isidro," 1966). The total of 1,098 manuscripts is reported on p. 290.

5. "Introducción General," in San Isidoro de Sevilla, *Etimologías,* vol. 1, p. 200.

6. *Etymologiae,* Book 1, ch. 29.

7. For Plato, see *Cratylus* 422d, 423e; and R. M. van den Berg, *Proclus' Commentary on the Cratylus in Context: Ancient Theories of Language and Naming* (Leiden and Boston: Brill, 2008), ch. 1; for Isidore, see *Etymologiae,* Book 12, ch. 1, 1–2, and Book 1, ch. 29, 3.

8. Rhetorical syllogisms are discussed in Book 2, ch. 9; dialectical syllogisms in Book 2, ch. 28.

Etymologies (translator's notes)

1. Cf. Quintilian, *Institutio oratoria,* Book 12, ch. 1, included in this volume.

2. These are the five traditional parts of rhetoric. Cf. Cicero, *De inventione* 1.9.

3. Cf. Plato, *Phaedrus* 269d; Quintilian, *Institutio oratoria,* Book 1, preface, last paragraph, and Book 12, ch. 1, first paragraph, both included in this volume.

4. Porphyry's *Isagōgē* was the standard introduction to what was known of Aristotle's logic. Isidore discusses it in Book 2, ch. 25, and Aristotle's *Categories* and *On Interpretation* in the following two chapters. (These chapters are not included here.)

5. Isidore's reference to logic in this passage raises two significant problems. (1) What did Isidore actually say? The Oroz Reta–Marcos Casquero text cited in note 1 of this volume's introduction to Isidore of Seville reads *aut de Logica, pro qua nostri Theoreticam sibi vindicant, ut in* Cantico canticorum, *et* Evangeliis (*Etimologías,* vol. 1, p. 396). But Peter Marshall identifies St. Jerome as Isidore's source and gives the relevant passage as *aut de logica, pro qua nostri* θεολογικήν [theologikēn] *sibi uindicant, ut in* Cantico canticorum *et* euangeliis (*Etymologies, Book II,* p. 104 n. 230, citing Jerome's Epistola 30, 1). In other words, the Oroz Reta–Marcos Casquero text has Isidore talking of vindicating theory, whereas Marshall's version of the Hieronymian source speaks of vindicating theology. To complicate matters

further, *Patrologia Latina,* ed. J. P. Migne, presents the passage as *aut de Logica, pro qua nostri Theoricen sibi vindicant, ut in* Cantico canticorum, *et in* Evangeliis, and has harsh words for those who insist on *Theologiam* (*Patrologia Latina,* vol. 22, pp. 146–147, including note e). Nevertheless, Marshall remarks, "The manuscript evidence that Isidore read *theologiam* (not *theoricam* with Arevalo, or *theoreticam* with Lindsay) is overwhelming" (*Etymologies, Book II,* p. 105 n. 230). I have accepted this judgment here. (2) Like the English "for," the Latin *pro* is ambiguous. Among other senses, it may mean "instead of," "on behalf of," or "in virtue of." Some translators interpret Isidore's *pro* in the passage under discussion in the first sense: "or logic, instead of which our [philosophers] assert the claim of theology" (*An Encyclopedist of the Dark Ages,* p. 118); similarly, "or logic, in place of which our Christian writers appropriate theology, as in the *Song of Songs* and the *Gospels*" (*Etymologies, Book II,* p. 104). But others rely on the "in virtue of " sense: "or logic—by virtue of which our (Christian) writers lay claim to the theory of interpretation (*theoretica*) for themselves, as in the Song of Songs and the Gospels" (*The Etymologies of Isidore of Seville,* p. 80; cf. *Etimologías,* vol. 1, p. 397). Since Isidore is upholding the compatibility of logic and theology (or theory), I have preferred the "in virtue of " sense.

6. Elsewhere Isidore contrasts custom (*mos*), which is unwritten, and law (*lex*), which is written. Custom, he says, is approved by traditional usage and accepted in place of law in law's absence (Book 5, ch. 3, not included here).

7. Isidore seems to presuppose that divine law validates the natural law principle of communal possession of all things (see Book 5, ch. 4, immediately following). This principle conflicts with human laws that protect private property. To cross private property would therefore be right because it is authorized by divine law, but illegal because it is inconsistent with such human laws. An alternative but dubious gloss with references to further commentary can be found in Suárez's *De legibus,* Book 1, ch. 2. The passage is translated in *Selections from Three Works of Francisco Suárez, S.J.,* ed. James Brown Scott (Oxford: Clarendon Press and London: Humphrey Milford, 1944), vol. 2, pp. 35–36.

IBN RUSHD (AVERROËS)

1. For Aristotle's inferences, see for instance *Physics* 8.5–6, 10; *Metaphysics* 12.6–7.

2. *The Incoherence of the Philosophers,* trans. Michael E. Marmura (Provo, UT: Brigham Young University Press, 1997).

3. Oliver Leaman, *Averroes and His Philosophy*, rev. ed. (Richmond: Curzon, 1998), pp. 90–96.

MOSES MAIMONIDES

1. Maimonides, *The Guide of the Perplexed* (Indianapolis and Cambridge: Hackett, 1995), p. 41.
2. Ibid., p. 42.
3. Ibid., p. 45.
4. See Alfred L. Ivry, "Maimonides, *The Guide of the Perplexed* (ca. 1190): The Perplexities of the Guide," in *The Classics of Western Philosophy: A Reader's Guide*, ed. Jorge J. E. Gracia, Gregory M. Reichberg, and Bernard N. Schumacher (Oxford: Blackwell, 2003), p. 127.
5. Muslim thinkers attributed a work called the *Theology* to Aristotle. This work was actually an Arabic rendering of Plotinus' *Enneads*, including the doctrine of the emanation of the world from the One.

The Guide of the Perplexed (translator's notes)

1. (Propositions 19 and 20.) These two propositions serve to provide the sharpest possible conceptual formulation for the proof that there must be some first world cause which is above generation and corruption. Their point of departure is the difference between things whose existence is possible and things whose existence is necessary. The necessity of existence can be external or immanent, i.e., it may be due to external causes or to the essence of the thing itself. Things whose existence is necessitated by an external cause are essentially possessed only of possible existence, as conversely things of merely possible existence require for their existence an external cause. If there were no being whose existence is necessitated by its essence, then all things would essentially be only possibly existent. It would then be possible that none of them should exist. There must thus be a supreme cause which exists by immanent necessity, i.e. whose essence includes existence. This connection of essence and existence, which here appears as a mere postulate, is in the ontological proof for the existence of God in Western philosophy deduced from the concept of God.

2. (Propositions 21 and 22.) In these two propositions the transition is made from the necessary existence of God to His absolute simplicity and incorporeality, thus arriving at the conception of God which forms the basis of the theory of the attributes.

3. Literally: becoming.

4. This proof for the existence of God does not, as Maimonides says, derive from Aristotle (where we find, at most, some vague suggestion of such an argument) but from the Moslem philosopher Avicenna, though the latter's argumentation is rather freely adapted by Maimonides. He concludes that because it is possible for everything subject to generation and corruption to pass at some point into nonexistence, there must be some being that cannot come into being or perish because its essence excludes every change.

5. This proof derives from Aristotle himself. It is based on the principle that the series of causes cannot be infinite, but that there must be a first cause. While elsewhere the happening of the effect, which in Aristotle's system is defined as a transition from potentiality to actuality, presupposes a corresponding change in the cause, the supreme cause works without any change in itself; otherwise a further cause would be needed. Its working is not bound up with any process within it.

6. In Aristotle's system the form of all things belonging to the same species, e.g. of all human beings, is identical. That there are several beings possessing the same form is due to the fact that the same form realizes itself again and again in different matter. With incorporeal beings such plurality is impossible, there can be only one immaterial substance of any one species. With regard to God it follows that there can be only one being of necessary existence, i.e. only one God.

7. Or: prepares it for receiving shape.

8. This proof of the unity of God is an emended form of a proof advanced by the Mutakallimun. The latter had refuted the assumption that the world was the work of two Gods by pointing out that it would then be possible for the two Gods to restrain and disturb each other in their activity. In his presentation and critique of the views of the Mutakallimun, Maimonides had found fault with this refutation of dualism because it did not envisage the possibility that the different parts of the world may be the work of different creators. The argumentation of the Mutakallimun becomes in his view conclusive only if we know that the world is a homogeneous whole, all parts of which are connected. Only the unity of the world permits us to draw a cogent conclusion as to the unity of its creator. Hence he gives in another chapter of the Guide (Part I, ch. LXXII, not included in this selection) detailed proof for the unity of the world, on which he here bases his proof of the Unity of God.

9. This discussion of time is directed against the argumentation of Aristotle. The latter demonstrates first that time has no beginning, and from this concludes that movement, too, has no beginning, since time cannot exist without movement (cf. *Physics* VIII.1; *Metaph.* XII.6). Maimonides

reverses the argument. From the Aristotelian definition of time as measure of movement he concludes that the question whether time had a beginning or not depends on whether movement had a beginning or not. If the world is created, then time itself is one of the created things. The idea that the creation of the world includes the creation of time goes back to Plato (*Timaeus* 37, 38). Galen's skeptical pronouncement that we cannot understand the nature of time, mentioned earlier in the text, is in keeping with the skeptical attitude of that thinker on all problems belonging to, or touching on, metaphysics.

10. The rendering with "world" (a meaning which *olam* never has in biblical Hebrew) appears also in Targum and Talmud (Sotah 10b). Authorized Version: "the everlasting God."

11. Authorized Version (with all versions): "possessor."

12. The view that the omnipotence of God does not attain what is essentially impossible was in this form first enunciated by the Aristotle commentator Alexander of Aphrodisias (*De Fato*, ch. XXX), who also adduces similar instances. Those who asserted that matter is uncreated, saw also in the emergence of a thing without being preceded by matter an absolute impossibility. Maimonides accepts the principle as such, but distinguishes between that which is absolutely impossible, e.g. that which contains within itself a logical contradiction, and that which is in conflict with the actual laws of our universe. The creation of matter he reckons as a case of the latter kind.

13. Here the idea that the world is created but founded upon eternal matter is rejected with the same emphasis as Aristotle's idea of the eternity of the world. Later on (ch. XXV) Maimonides admits that it is not in conflict with the biblical conception of God, though he still insists on *creatio ex nihilo* because the eternity of matter cannot be proved.

14. Movement must here be understood in the widest sense, in which every change is a movement. From this conception of movement it results that there cannot be a first movement, since the emergence of movement is in itself a movement which precedes the alleged first movement; thus a *regressus ad infinitum* would arise. This argumentation goes back to Aristotle (*Physics* VIII.1), but reproduces only part of his demonstration, and that in a rather free form.

15. This proof derives from Aristotle (*Physics* I.9). It is based on Aristotle's theory, mentioned here frequently, that the generation and corruption of things is due to existing matter accepting one form instead of another. This view excludes any possibility of new matter or form themselves coming into being.

16. The idea that the immutability of God excludes a beginning of the world in time is of Neoplatonic origin. In Arabic literature it is quoted under the name of the Neoplatonic philosopher Proclus (cf. Shahrastani, *Religionspartheien und Philosophen Schulen*, trans. Theodor Haarbruecker [Halle, 1850], II.199 seq.).

17. Since prophecy is also possible on the assumption of the eternity of the world, our decision in favor of creation in time can be supported by the teachings of the prophets without moving in a vicious circle.

18. Maimonides distinguishes three stages: that which preceded the creation of the world, that of creation, and that in which the world has been since its creation. The laws valid in the world since the conclusion of the creative process have no validity either for the stage before its creation nor for the process of creation itself. The error of the philosophers consists in their attributing absolute validity to the laws valid within the world, for which reason, as mentioned in ch. XIII, they reckon *creatio ex nihilo* among the absolute impossibilities, which are not attained by the power of God.

19. Both arguments in our chapter aim at proving that action which emanates from God can have a beginning without any change taking place in God's essence and without any necessity of looking for a cause for such a change. True, it is difficult to visualize action starting without any happening within the cause, but the same difficulty also attaches to the emanation theory accepted by those who think the world eternal. This also makes the world proceed from God without anything taking place within God. The real difficulty is to think of God as cause without ascribing to Him any activity. This difficulty remains whether we take God's causality to be eternal or to have had a beginning in time.

20. Or: the world is therefore necessarily existent.

21. This principle does not derive from Aristotle, to whom the emanation theory is alien, but from the Arab Aristotelians, particularly Avicenna, who took it from Neoplatonic sources. Neither are the following three principles to be found in Aristotle, though the second and fourth actually are in harmony with his system. It has not yet been discovered from where Maimonides took them in this particular form.

22. The theory of emanation, be it in its original Neoplatonic form or in that which it was given by the Arab Aristotelians, is faced with the difficulty of explaining how the manifold forms of being can proceed from the absolutely simple ultimate cause, especially if one acknowledges the first principle, that a simple cause can only have a simple effect. The Moslem Aristotelians endeavor to account for the gradual transition from unity to plurality by saying that the thinking substances proceeding from God know not only

themselves but also their causes. Thus a plurality of intelligibles arises in their mind, which increases in proportion to their removal from the first cause. This plurality in the mind of those thinking substances is also made to explain the fact that from each of them emanates not only a further thinking substance but also a heavenly sphere (cf. Shahrastani, II.262 seq.). Against this bizarre theory Maimonides turns his criticism; a similar critique had been put forward by the Moslem theologian Algazali (1059–1111).

23. Or: any proof of (the unity of) matter.

24. The further objections of Maimonides do not refer any more to the problem of transition from unity to plurality, but are an attempt to show that the theory of emanation cannot explain why the world, and in particular the heavenly spheres emanated directly from the spiritual beings, possess the arrangement which we observe. A modern writer (Pierre Duhem, *Le Système du monde* [Paris: Hermann, 1913–1959], V.191 seq.) asserts that in this critique, too, Maimonides follows Algazali, who in turn develops ideas of the Mutakallimun. Maimonides himself occasionally points out a certain relationship between his own ideas and those of the Mutakallimun. However, he employs the points made by his Moslem predecessors in an entirely new sense. The Mutakallimun began by saying that the actual nature of things is entirely accidental; and a rose, for instance, might have any color instead of red. From this they conclude directly the necessity of a creator who selected one of those possibilities. Algazali employs this very line of thought with reference to the spheres. Maimonides does not directly deduce from the accidental character of things that they originate from a divine act of will. He merely demonstrates that their accidental character is incompatible with the theory of emanation, by which all things proceed with logical necessity from the ultimate cause of the universe. Since it has been established before that their last cause is God, we can conclude indirectly that they do not emanate from God but are a work of His will.

25. Perhaps Maimonides has here in view the opinion of Avicenna that the teaching of the creation of the world in time is nothing but a presentation, adapted to the comprehension of the masses, of the eternal emanation of the world from God.

RAMÓN LLULL

1. Llull's *Vita coaetanea*, pars. 2 and 9, in *Doctor Illuminatus: A Ramon Llull Reader*, ed. and trans. Anthony Bonner (Princeton: Princeton University Press, 1993), pp. 11, 13.

2. *Vita coaetanea*, par. 2, in Bonner, *Doctor Illuminatus*, p. 11.

3. "Art" is the standard English term for the *Ars magna*, the project that absorbed the greater part of Llull's life. But the terms *Ars magna* and "Art" are sometimes used differently, even by Llull himself. Llull uses *Ars magna* as an abbreviation for his *Ars generalis ultima*. In addition, through his translator, he uses "Art" as an abbreviation for specific works such as the *Ars brevis*. Both of these usages can be observed in the following prologue to the *Ars brevis*.

4. The Third Order is an association of laymen and laywomen dedicated to the spirituality of St. Francis of Assisi. See *Vita coaetanea*, par. 23, in Bonner, *Doctor Illuminatus*, p. 26, including note 77; and Antoni Oliver, "El Beato Ramón Llull en sus relaciones con la Escuela Franciscana de los siglos XIII–XIV," *Estudios Lulianos* 10 (1966): 54–55.

5. For details, see John R. Welch, "Apuntes sobre el pensamiento matemático de Ramón Llull," *Theoria* 4 (1989): 451–459.

6. Leibniz, *Mathematische Schriften*, ed. C. I. Gerhardt (Berlin and Halle, 1849–1863; rpt. Darmstadt: Hildesheim, 1962), vol. 7, p. 185. Emphasis in original. See also Catherine Wilson, *Leibniz's Metaphysics: A Historical and Comparative Study* (Princeton and Manchester: Princeton and Manchester University Presses, 1989), ch. 1.

Ars Brevis (translator's notes)

1. That is to say, assuming that one knows under which of the ten general questions (see Part IV below) any particular question should be classified. The point is made more clearly in the corresponding passage of the *Proemium* of the *Ars generalis ultima*.

2. These "parts" correspond exactly, which greatly facilitates crossconsultation. Note that throughout the *Ars brevis* Llull almost always refers to the *Ars generalis ultima* as the *Ars magna*.

3. Some of the MSS and all of the printed sources consulted have just "duration." These two concepts are interchangeable in this slot of Figure A, which does not mean that they are synonymous, except as an attribute of God.

4. See Part IV, n. 14 below, for the original Latin terms and their relationship to the equivalent "rules."

5. Note how this phrase is couched in terms identical with the new definition of "conjunctive middle" of Figure T, sec. 2 below.

6. *Contrahitur* could also be translated as "joined or combined with," at the same time carrying with it the idea of "contraction." Llull elsewhere opposes *contracció* to "abstraction."

7. The "predicaments" are the Aristotelian categories.

8. Combination without repetition of nine elements taken two at a time, hence

$$\binom{9}{2} = \frac{9 \cdot 8}{1 \cdot 2} = 36.$$

9. In the *Lectura super Artem inventivam et Tabulam generalem* Llull is more explicit: "Each compartment has six meanings, like the compartment of B C, which signifies Goodness, Greatness, Difference, Concordance, First and Second Rule, and like the compartment of B D, which signifies Goodness, Duration, Difference, Contrariety, First and Third Rule, and so on for the others," which is followed by a detailed interpretation of each compartment.

10. Llull is saying that with the outer wheel remaining fixed, we can place opposite the B on that wheel all the possible two-letter permutations of the remaining eight letters of his alphabet, which gives

$$\binom{8}{2} = \frac{8 \cdot 7}{1 \cdot 2} = 28$$

usable portions of the two inner wheels (i.e., without repetitions of letters). Now since in any one position we can read off nine compartments between the linked-up spokes, as it were, this gives us a total of 28 x 9 = 252 compartments. This does, however, involve repetitions; in fact, each compartment is repeated three times, since, B C D = C D B (which appears when C K are lined up under B) = D B C (which appears when I K are lined up under B). For Llull's combinatorial purposes here, however, this is unimportant. In the table in Part V he has eliminated the superfluous combinations, giving 252 ÷ 3 = 84 columns (see n. 20 below).

11. Marçal in his commentary on this passage quotes the statement from Llull's *Art amativa* that "the entire Art is contained in this Fourth Figure." *Ars brevis*, ed. Francesc Marçal (Palma de Mallorca: Rafael Moya, 1669), p. 20.

12. These definitions of the eighteen principles appear in every work of the Art, from the *Ars inventiva veritatis* on, as well as the *Tree of Science*, sometimes with extensive commentaries. For the unusual nature of these definitions, see Bonner, *Doctor Illuminatus*, pp. 292–293. Llull was aware of the reactions these definitions aroused; at the end of this section in the *Ars generalis ultima*, with uncharacteristic anger, he rails against "those who, with dog's teeth and a serpent's tongue scorn and slander these principles of mine and their definitions. The Art, however, requires one principle to assist another." This is a reference to the "mixtures" (in this case of one dignity defined in terms of the others) so essential to the Art.

13. Note the curious linking of "virtue" and "unity," ever present in these Llullian definitions.

14. These ten Rules or Questions first appeared in the *Taula general* of 1293–1294, and were reproduced almost verbatim in the *Arbre de filosofia desiderat* of 1294. From then on no work of the Art is without them, and they play an important role in the *Logica nova*. So the reader can get an idea of the original terminology, the list of rules with their corresponding questions in the *Ars generalis ultima* is as follows: B. *possibilitas—utrum?*; C. *quidditas—quid?*; D. *materialitas—de quo?*; E. *formalitas—quare?*; F. *quantitas—quantum?*; G. *qualitas—qualis?*; H. *tempus—quando?*; I. *locus—ubi?*; K-1. *modalitas—quomodo?*; K-2. *instrumentalitas—cum quo?* Note that in order to accommodate ten rules to a nine-letter alphabet, Llull had to put two rules in the last slot. It is curious to observe that Giordano Bruno in his *De lampade combinatoria lulliana* (Strasbourg: Zetzner, 1617), p. 705, refers to these ten questions as the "syncategoremata" of the Art, in opposition to the "categoremata" of Figures A and T. Marçal has an interesting *scholium* on the double nature of these questions (referring to the unknown or doubtful) and rules (referring to methods or argumentation or teaching) (*Ars brevis*, ed. Marçal, p. 44).

15. The *Ars generalis ultima* has "essentially and naturally" instead of "coessentially."

16. The different version of this last sentence in the *Ars generalis ultima* helps to explain Llull's meaning: "To which one must reply that it is composed of its own essential principles, that is to say, its intellective, intelligible and understanding. And similarly with man who is made up of his body and his soul, with a nail which is of iron, and so on."

17. This example is from the ninth rule [K-1]; cf. the corresponding part of the *Ars generalis ultima*.

18. Note the exact parallel between these four species and those of the first rule of K.

19. The *tabula* (Catalan *taula*), which is derived directly from the Fourth Figure (cf. the following note), first appeared in the *Taula general* of 1293–1294. In its full form it only reappeared in the *Ars compendiosa* of 1299 and in the *Ars generalis ultima;* the abbreviated form only appears in the *Ars brevis*.

20. As Llull says here, this table is an abbreviation or sample of the larger one in the *Ars generalis ultima*. The latter is engendered by the machinery of the Fourth Figure, but omitting the repetitions, which gives us

$$\binom{9}{3} = \frac{9 \cdot 8 \cdot 7}{1 \cdot 2 \cdot 3} = 84$$

compartments (cf. Part II, n. 10 above). For these compartments, see Giordano Bruno, *De lulliano specierum scrutinio* (Strasbourg: Zetzner, 1617), pp. 670–671, and Agrippa von Nettesheim, *Commentaria in Artem brevem Raymundi Lulli* (Cologne: Joan Soter, 1531), pp. 841–849. Llull then takes each of them and sets it at the head of a column containing further variations achieved by distinguishing the letters referring to Figure A from those referring to Figure T. If for the sake of our calculations we do this by using uppercase for the former and lowercase for the latter, instead of merely separating them by the letter T as Llull does, it will become clear that the first column, for instance, consists of all the permutations of the six letters B C D b c d taken three at a time, or

$$\binom{6}{3} = \frac{6 \cdot 5 \cdot 4}{1 \cdot 2 \cdot 3} = 20,$$

giving us the number of triads in each column. We thus have a total of 1,680 compartments. Now for the *Ars brevis*, Llull takes just 7 of the 84 columns of the larger table. He chooses them by taking the first of the 28 starting with B, the first of the 21 starting with C, etc., ending with the one starting with H (cf. the passages cited from Bruno and Agrippa; the former says that the *Ars brevis* uses the first element of each "domus").

21. The compartment of B C implies those of B B, C C, and C B, and this for the two different meanings of each letter. We therefore have four concepts, each of which can be combined with three others, or 4 × 3 = 12.

22. The *Ars generalis ultima*, whose text—with the exception of the larger table—has up to this point been very similar to that of the *Ars brevis*, now continues with examples of questions and answers from each of the thirty-six compartments of the Third Figure.

JUAN LUIS VIVES

1. Juan Luis Vives, *Juan Luis Vives against the Pseudodialecticians: A Humanist Attack on Medieval Logic*, trans., intro., and notes by Rita Guerlac (Dordrecht and Boston: D. Reidel, 1979), p. 75.

2. *De anima et vita*, Book 2, ch. 2.

3. *Summa theologiae*, Part I, questions 75–90.

4. José Ortega y Gasset, *Vives-Goethe*, in *Obras completas* (Madrid: Revista de Occidente, 1946–1983), vol. 9, p. 536.

5. Paracelsus, "the Luther of physicians," burned Galen's and Avicenna's works in front of the University of Basel in 1527.

6. Carlos G. Noreña, *Juan Luis Vives and the Emotions* (Carbondale and Edwardsville: Southern Illinois University Press, 1989), p. 161.

On the Soul and Life (translator's and editor's notes)

Bracketed text is the editor's addition.

1. [The Mayans text of *De anima et vita* reads: *motus autem de bono præsenti quod sumus assequuti, lætitia, de bono futuro, cupiditas nuncupatur, quæ intra amoris limites includitur. Opera omnia,* ed. Gregoria Mayans (Valencia: Benedict Montfort, 1782), vol. 3, p. 426. In order to avoid making Vives say that joy is about both present and future goods in the same paragraph, I depart somewhat from the translation of this passage by Carlos Noreña, which reads: "The movement of the soul about a present good which we possess is called joy. About a future good, is called desire. Joy is an emotion about a future good, an emotion which falls within the boundaries of love."]

2. In the introduction to Book 3 of *De anima et vita.*

3. Vives obviously means that a small grief is forgotten in the presence of a more severe one.

4. *De officiis* 1.4.

5. Publilius Siro, *Sententiae* v.1969.

6. *De divinis nominibus,* in *Patrologia Graeca,* vol. 3, 4.634.

7. Martial, *Epigrammata* 6.11.10. Also, Seneca, *Epistulae* 9.4.

8. The last paragraph is a confessedly free translation of a Latin text that is no great compliment to Vives' style, or, as it is well possible, has been transmitted to us in a faulty manner. Here is the Latin original: *Quod si quis non potuit opera praestare, at dedit sanum ac praesens consilium, declaravit se conari vel tentando vel manifesta indicatione affectus alicuius, qui voluntatem patefaceret.*

9. The "comedian" is Terence. The quotation was probably taken from Cicero's *De amicitia* 24.

10. The words "we love" are not found in the original but seem necessary to make any sense of it. This section of the text seems to be plagued with typographical mistakes.

11. *Epistulae* 1.18.69.

12. See Cicero, *De officiis* 3.10 and *Tusculanae disputationes* 5.22.63.

13. Luke 22:28.

14. Vives is probably referring to the friendship between Damon and Pythias. See above, note 12.

15. Although Vives uses the expression *amor concupiscentiae* to signify

self-interested love, I have decided to avoid the word "concupiscence" in the English translation as unusual and alien to most readers.

16. *Aeneid* 6.276: *malesuada fames.*

17. See Aristotle, *Historia animalium* 7.4.138.

18. *Naturalis historia, De homine,* 7, introduction.

19. Proverbs 17:22.

20. The personally revealing character of this lengthy chapter is emphasized by the fact that its contents are not backed by any reference to classical literature.

21. *Eunuchus* 2.272: *Num quidnam hic quod nolis vides?*

22. *Iliad* 2.252.

23. Dionysius stayed busy at Corinth while in exile by opening a school there. See Valerius Maximus, *Factorum et dictorum memorabilium* 6.9.6.

24. *Pro Murena* 20: *Cui dolet, meminit; cui placet, obliviscitur.*

25. *Tusculanae disputationes* 2.11.25.

26. *Ad Atticum* 9.17: *Me hebetem reddiderunt.* Vives modifies the Latin expression *hebetem reddiderunt* into the less classical form *hebetarunt.*

27. Ovid, *Metamorphoses* 6.301.

28. Psalms 148:28.

29. Suetonius, *De poetis* 120.

30. *Pharsalia* 9.108.

31. Euripides, *Hecuba,* line 1265.

32. I have not been able to verify this reference.

33. This is admittedly a strange doctrine, but the Latin text does not seem to allow any other interpretation.

34. Psalms 103:16.

35. *Rhetoric* 2.5, 1382a22.

36. Quoted by Seneca in *De ira* 2.11; and by Cicero in *De officiis* 2.7.

37. *Rhetoric* 2.5, 1382a2–24.

38. Horace's *Epistulae* 1.18.84: *Nam tua res agitur paries cum proxima ardet.*

39. Cicero's *Tusculanae disputationes* 4.8.19.

40. Livy, *Historiae* 21.4.

41. *Naturalis historia* 7.praef: *Nulli vita fragilior, rerum omnium libido maior, nulli pavor confusior, nulli rabies acrior.*

42. *De coniuratione Catilinae* 58.1.

43. Heroides, 1.67: *Utilius starent etiam nunc moenia Phoebi.*

44. Throughout this chapter Vives seems to hesitate about the power of thought and reflection to increase or to decrease fear.

45. *Aeneid* 2.12.

FRANCISCO DE VITORIA

1. The year of Vitoria's birth is highly uncertain. See Francisco de Vitoria, *Relection on Homicide and Commentary on* Summa theologiae *IIa–IIae Q. 64*, ed., trans., and intro. John P. Doyle (Milwaukee: Marquette University Press, 1997), p. 11, and Ramón Hernández Martín, *Francisco de Vitoria: Vida y pensamiento internacionalista* (Madrid: Biblioteca de Autores Cristianos, 1995), pp. 11–17.

2. James Boswell, *The Life of Samuel Johnson, LL.D.*, 2nd ed. (London: Henry Baldwin, 1793), vol. 1, p. 419. I have modernized the spelling.

3. Francisco de Vitoria, *Political Writings*, ed. and trans. Anthony Pagden and Jeremy Lawrance (Cambridge: Cambridge University Press, 1991), pp. 231–292.

4. Bartolomé de Las Casas, *In Defense of the Indians*, trans. and ed. Stafford Poole (DeKalb: Northern Illinois University Press, 1974), pp. 340–341.

5. See Hernández Martín, *Francisco de Vitoria*, pp. 291–294, 363, 366–372, and Gregory M. Reichberg, "Francisco de Vitoria, *De Indis* and *De iure belli relectiones* (1557): Philosophy Meets War," in *The Classics of Western Philosophy: A Reader's Guide*, ed. Jorge J. E. Gracia, Gregory M. Reichberg, and Bernard N. Schumacher (Oxford: Blackwell, 2003), pp. 201–202.

6. *Summa theologiae*, IIa–IIae, question 40, article 1.

7. One source is Isidore of Seville, *Etymologiae*, Book 5, ch. 6, included in this volume.

8. For a range of views, see James Brown Scott, *The Spanish Origin of International Law: Francisco de Vitoria and His Law of Nations* (Oxford: Clarendon Press and London: Humphrey Milford, 1934), pp. 164, 281–288; Bernice Hamilton, *Political Thought in Sixteenth-Century Spain: A Study of the Political Ideas of Vitoria, Soto, Suárez, and Molina* (Oxford: Clarendon Press, 1963), p. 98; Pagden and Lawrance in Vitoria, *Political Writings*, pp. xvi, xxviii; and Doyle in Vitoria, *Relection on Homicide*, pp. 14, 44 n. 51.

On the Law of War (translators' notes)

1. Relections were governed by a time-limit of two hours.

2. Vulgate reading; Authorized Version has "avenge" for "defend."

3. The texts quoted by Vitoria in this article had been traditional in disputes on war since Gratian's discussion in *Decretum* C.23; these are taken

from C.23.1 d.a.c.1. Vitoria had rehearsed the same arguments in article 1 of his 1535–1536 lecture, *De Bello: On St. Thomas Aquinas, Summa Theologica, Secunda Secundae, Question 40* (English translation in Scott, *Spanish Origins of International Law*, Appendix F).

4. Martin Luther, *Resolutiones disputationis de virtute indulgentiarum* (1518). As Maurice Barbier points out in *Leçons sur les Indiens et sur le droit de guerre* (Genève: Librairie Droz, 1966), p. 111 n., this Lutheran proposition had been explicitly condemned by Pope Leo X in the bull *Exsurge Domine* (15 June 1520). Vitoria had already developed his objections to the pacifism of the Protestant reformers in his lecture *De Bello* (Scott, *Spanish Origins of International Law*, Appendix F, cxvi).

5. This handful of influential texts by Augustine was the basis of medieval theories of the just war. See Jonathan Barnes, "The Just War," in *Cambridge History of Later Medieval Philosophy*, ed. Norman Kretzmann, Anthony Kenny, and Jan Pinborg (Cambridge: Cambridge University Press, 1982), p. 771. Here and throughout, Vitoria cites these texts from Gratian's *Decretum* C.23, using the incorrect titles *Contra Manichaeos* (= *Contra Faustum* 22.74–79), *Liber 83 quaestionum* (= *QQ. in Heptateuchum*), *De uerbis domini* (= *De ciu. dei* XIX.12), and *De puero centurionis* (= *Ep.* 138).

6. This crucial passage was quoted incorrectly by Aquinas, and "badly garbled" by Gratian (Barnes, "Just War," p. 778 n. 37). Vitoria's mistaken readings derive from the former, not the latter; they have been retained in the translation.

7. The distinction between public enemies (*hostes*) and brigands or robbers (*latrunculi uel praedones*), important in Roman and canonist discussions of *Vim ui*, is ignored by Vitoria, who blurs the lines between public and private self-defense. Aquinas denied that war could be declared by a private person, "since he can prosecute his rights in the court of a superior" (*ST* II-II.40.1; Barnes, "Just War," pp. 775–776); Vitoria further diverges from the theologians' line in going on to cite the jurists' view that anyone, even a private person, can declare war in self-defense (see also his lecture *De Bello*, in Scott, *Spanish Origins of International Law*, Appendix F, cxvi–ii).

8. St. Antonino, *ST* II.7.8, defines legitimate self-protection as that carried out "with the moderation of an irreproachable defense" (*moderamen inculpatae tutelae*). This was the standard definition of "proportionality" or "minimal force" in canon law (X.5.12.18) and in treatises such as those of John of Legnamo and Johannes Teutonicus (Barnes, "Just War," p. 780).

9. Vitoria follows closely the position of the canonists, and in particular of Innocent IV's commentary on *Olim causam quae* (*Ad* X.2.13.12),

where it is stated that self-defense made *incontinenti*, "that is before turning to any other business," does not need the authority of a prince, even for the clergy.

10. The mainstream medieval theorists of the just war all agreed on the importance of *authority* (*Decretum* C.23.1.2), conceiving such authority to be that of a sovereign "recognizing no superior" (since such a prince has no other recourse for obtaining justice). Vitoria, however, "derived authority not from sovereignty, but from the Aristotelian principle that a republic must be self-sufficient" (Barnes, "Just War," pp. 775–777).

11. Kingdoms which are part of the same crown (as Castile and Aragon were both parts of the Spanish crown) can still be "perfect" independent commonwealths (for this Aristotelian sense of "perfect" as "self-sufficing," see *Politics* 1253a1–2). In his lecture *De Bello*, Vitoria used the example of the Duke of Milan, "who may declare war if need be, because even though he is subject to the emperor, the duchy of Milan is nevertheless perfect and does not share its being with any other commonwealth" (Scott, *Spanish Origins of International Law*, Appendix F, cxvii).

12. Vitoria's argument here derives from Cajetan's commentary on *ST* II-II.40.1 §3, who also adduces the authority of "custom." The argument was accepted by most of Vitoria's followers until Suárez (*De bello* 2.2) challenged it by introducing a distinction between wars fought by the subjects of different princes, which were legitimate, and those fought by subjects of the same prince as in Vitoria's present case, which were not.

13. On this extension of "authority" through the impotence or indolence of sovereigns, see Barnes, "Just War," p. 777. Suárez drew the inevitable conclusion, that authority is in practice needed only for aggressive wars, not defensive (*De bello* 2.1–2).

14. This claim derives from Cajetan's *Summula*, *s.v.* bellum §6, which restricted the prince's authority to outsiders who had given legitimate cause for offense (*perturbatores reipublicae extrinsecos*). The argument was further developed by Vitoria's successors, notably Suárez, *De bello* 4.7.

15. "Ex omnibus supradictis": the *dubia* discussed by Vitoria in the reminder of the relection in fact concern only the points raised in Articles 3 and 4 of Question 1. The first five *dubia*, which relate to 1.3, are arranged as Question 2, and the remaining nine, which relate to 1.4, as Question 3.

16. Variant manuscripts amplify the list of innocent noncombatants in this sentence as follows: "In wars against fellow-Christians, the same argument holds true of harmless farming folk, and other peaceful civilians (*gens togata*), who are all to be presumed innocent unless there is evidence to the contrary; and also travelers or visitors who happen to be in the enemy's

territory, who are presumed innocent and are not really enemies at all." See Vitoria, *Political Writings*, ed. and trans. Pagden and Lawrance, pp. xxxiv–xxxvi, 315 n. 37.

17. The reference is to the official patents or *cartas de represalia* given by various crowns to privateers or *corsairs*, as they were known in Spain, to plunder the ships of other nations for their own profit.

18. The reference is to the massacre of Thessalonica in A.D. 390, to St. Ambrose's subsequent excommunication of Theodosius I, and to the emperor's penitent submission.

19. For this defense of the Roman Empire, compare Vitoria's *On the American Indians* 2.1, 3.7. The passages to which Vitoria refers may be identified as Augustine, *De ciuitate dei* III.10, XVIII.22; Jerome, *In Isaiam* XVII.40; Ambrose, *Epist.* 61; and Aquinas, *De regimine principum* III.4–5.

20. The legal principle that "laws should always be interpreted in the more lenient sense" is stated, for example, in *Sext* 5.12.15 and *Digest* XLVIII.19.42.

BARTOLOMÉ DE LAS CASAS

1. The theory and practice of *encomienda* should be distinguished. In theory, natives "entrusted" (*encomendados*) to Spaniards for a limited time had not only an obligation to work but rights to compensation, defense, and religious instruction. But in practice these rights were often ignored, and natives once "entrusted" frequently served for life. So even though Spanish legislation consistently treated the natives as free, *encomienda* in practice was comparable to serfdom.

2. Bartolomé de Las Casas, *Historia de las Indias*, in *Obras completas*, vol. 5 (Madrid: Alianza, 1994), Book 3, ch. 29, p. 1879.

3. Sirach (Ecclesiasticus) 34:18.

4. As newly appointed Protector of the Indians, Las Casas proposed that African slaves be used instead of Indians. Later he admitted his error: "the same reasons hold for them [the Africans] as for the Indians," and "the captivity of the blacks was just as unjust as that of the Indians." Las Casas, *Historia*, Book 3, ch. 102, p. 2191; and ch. 129, p. 2324.

5. Las Casas, *Historia*, Book 3, ch. 160, p. 2472.

6. Drafted in 1542 but not published until 1552, this work has been vilified as the source of the *leyenda negra* ("black legend") of Spanish cruelty in the New World.

7. José Luis Abellán, *Historia crítica del pensamiento español* (Madrid: Espasa-Calpe, 1986), vol. 2, pp. 485–486.

In Defense of the Indians (author's, translator's, and editor's notes)

Bracketed text is the translator's addition or clarification; bracketed text with an asterisk is the editor's.

1. 2 *Ethics*, ch. 9. 3 *Ethics*, ch. 5. 5 *Ethics* [sic], ch. 6. And 2 *Topics*. The same point is proved from the text of cc. 1–2, D. 13. The canonists note this on Gratian, c. 1, D. 14, and c. 7, C. 22, q. 4. And the lawyers on the Digests, 18, 6, 1, next to the last paragraph, and Digests, 50, 17, 20.

2. [*Summa Theologiae*,] I-II, q. 20, a. 5; q. 73, a. 8c.

3. These things are proved especially in Gratian, c. 25, D. 50; c. 28, D. 50. Decretals, 2, 1, 4, #*De Adulteriis*, 3, 46, 2. Gratian, c. 6, D. 4, and other passages. John Andrea has a very lengthy commentary on permission in his commentary on the rule *Peccatum* in the rules of law, q. 3. And the learned Master Vitoria approves our position here when he speaks about not waging war on the Indians in his second *Relectio de Indis*.

4. [Verse 13].

5. [Verse 7].

6. [Verse 53].

7. *In III Sententiarum*, d. 47, a. 3, ad 1um.

8. [22:21–23].

9. [Verse 16].

10. Exodus 23[:7].

11. According to Saint Thomas, *Quodlibetale*, 9, a. 15, and Henry of Ghent, *Quodlibetale*, 2, a. 17.

12. [*Summa Theologiae*,] II-II, q. 64, at the end of the body of a. 6.

13. [I-II], q. 100, a. 8, ad 3um.

14. Ch. 22, col. 6, at the beginning and the end.

15. On the rubric *De Constitutionibus*, col. 4.

16. *Regulae de Idiomate*, p. 231 and the following. [*The reference seems to be to Luis Gómez, *Regulae, ordinationes et constitutiones judiciales cancellariae apostolicae* (Paris, 1546).]

17. *Ethics*, Book 7.

18. *De Civitate Dei*, Book 22, ch. 20.

19. *Parallipomenon Hispaniae*, Book 7.

20. *Topics*, Book 1.

21. *Rhetoric*, Book 1, ch. 20.

22. See *Ethics*, Book 1, ch. 2.

23. *De Praeparatione Evangelica*, Book 4, ch. 7.

24. *Recognitiones ad Iacobum, Fratrem Domini*, Book 9.

25. *Divinarum Institutionum,* Book 1, ch. 21.

26. *Problemata,* p. 465 [*Roman Questions* 83].

27. Book 4, p. 299 [*History* 4.62.3].

28. *Polyhistoria,* ch. 20.

29. Book 2, ch. 1.

30. *Polyhistoria,* Book 6, fol. 190.

31. *De Situ Orbis,* Book 3.

32. See *De Rerum Inventoribus,* Book 5, ch. 8.

33. *De Civitate Dei,* Book 6, ch. 10.

34. *In 1ᵃᵐ Epistolam ad Corinthios,* homily 7.

35. At the beginning of his book *De Fide Orthodoxa.*

36. Ch. 3. See also Gregory of Nazianzen, *Theology,* col. 11; Lactantius, *Divinarum Institutionum,* Book 3, ch. 11.

37. In his book *Tusculan Questions.*

38. *De Legibus.*

39. In the first and second books of *On Heaven and Earth* and in the third book of the *Physics.*

40. *De Consolatione Philosophiae,* Book 3, prose 10.

41. *Contra Gentes,* Book 3, ch. 119.

42. *Politics,* Book 7, ch. 9.

43. *Ethics,* Book 8, ch. 10.

44. *Ethics,* Book 8, ch. 10.

45. *In IV Sententiarum,* d. 10, q. 1, a. 2c.

46. Psalms 115[:12].

47. *Ethics,* Book 4.

48. Romans 8[:18].

49. Timothy 4[:8].

50. *De Civitate Dei,* Book 10, ch. 4.

51. *Contra Gentes,* Book 3, ch. 120.

52. [*Summa Theologiae,*] II-II, q. 85, a. 1.

53. Digests, 1, 1, 2.

54. Digests, 1, 1, 1. Institutes, 2, 1, 11.

55. As Ovid mentions in *Pastores,* ch.1; Lucan in his *De Bello Civili,* Book 6, and Juvenal in the next to the last satire. I have taken the above-written argument from Saint Thomas [*Summa Theologiae,*] II-II, q. 85, a. 1, ad 1ᵘᵐ; *In IV Sententiarum,* d. 26, q. 2, a. 1, ad 1ᵘᵐ; and *Quodlibetale* II, a. 8c.

56. In the first book of *Politics,* ch. 1.

57. Saint Thomas speaks of this in the [*Summa Theologiae,*] II-II, q. 57, a. 2, ad 2ᵘᵐ; q. 60, a. 5, ad 1ᵘᵐ et 2ᵘᵐ; q. 66, a. 7c.

58. This is clear in Genesis 17 regarding the covenant and in Leviticus 1 regarding the offerings. Abulensis treats these matters in a learned way in his *Commentary on Leviticus*, q. 11 and 12; *Commentary on Exodus*, q. 9, col. 7, c. 25; and his partial *Commentary on Genesis*, ch. 15.

59. See Seneca [no specific reference given] and Saint Thomas [*Summa Theologiae*], II-II, q. 107, a. 5 and 6.

60. Book 1.

61. Ecclesiasticus 34[:24].

FRANCISCO SUÁREZ

1. *De verbo incarnato*, in Francisco Suárez, *Selections from Three Works of Francisco Suárez, S.J.*, ed. James Brown Scott (Oxford: Clarendon Press and London: Humphrey Milford, 1944), vol. 2, pp. 11a n. 2 to 12a.

2. Joseph Fichter, *Man of Spain: Francis Suarez* (New York: Macmillan, 1940), p. 327.

3. John P. Doyle, "Francisco Suárez: On Preaching the Gospel to People Like the American Indians," *Fordham International Law Journal* 15 (1991–1992): 884–886.

4. James I had Suárez's *Defensio fidei catholicae* solemnly burned in St. Paul's Cross in 1613.

5. Drawing on sources such as Aristotle's *Politics* (e.g., 4.10; 5.10, 1313a5–16; 5.11, 1314a13–29) and the Roman legal principle of *salus populi suprema lex*, Scholastic thinkers such as Aquinas, Vitoria, Alonso de la Vera Cruz, and Roberto Bellarmino had developed populist political theory before Suárez.

On Laws (translators' notes)

1. With reference to a power inherent in human nature.

2. This passage is not found in *De Amicitia*. A very similar passage is found in Cicero's *De Republica*, Bk. VI, ch. xiii, which reads: *nihil est enim illi principi deo, qui omnem hunc mundum regit, quod quidem in terris fiat, acceptius quam concilia coetusque hominum iure sociati, quae civitates appellantur* (For nothing of all that is done on earth is more pleasing to that supreme God who rules all this world than the assemblies and gatherings of men associated in justice, which are called States).

3. This would seem, in the light of the context, to be the most acceptable interpretation of Suárez's argument at this point, although the Latin text is ambiguous: *quia neque omnes sunt aliorum superiores.*

4. Suárez is apparently presenting here the arguments opposed to the very alternative which he nevertheless accepts. (See the first sentence of section 3 of this chapter.) Thus the word *videtur* (would . . . seem) should not be overlooked by the reader.

5. Suárez merely paraphrases Augustine's statement in these two passages.

6. The Latin has simply *radicaliter*.

7. Not included in these *Selections*.

8. That is to say, the law of each state and the law common to all men.

9. This is the usual English translation of the Greek title for this Dialogue, referred to in our Latin text as *Dialogo Civili, seu de Regno*.

10. I.e., the various titles to monarchical power. This enumeration extends throughout the remainder of section 2, and through the whole of sections 3 and 4.

11. I.e., the deduction "that the kingdom must be superior to the king," and the consequent inference "that the kingdom may, if it shall so choose, depose or change its kings." See the second paragraph of section 5 of this chapter.

12 *Defensio Fidei Catholicae*, in Suárez, *Selections from Three Works*, Bk. 6, ch. iv, p. 705, and in Disp. XIII of *De Bello*, in Suárez, *Selections from Three Works*, sec. viii, pp. 854–855.

13. See the first sentence of this chapter.

14. Bk. IV, ch. iii, which is not included in these *Selections*.

15. Not included in these *Selections*.

BENITO JERÓNIMO FEIJÓO

1. Gregorio Marañon, *Las ideas biológicas del Padre Feijóo*, 4th ed. (Madrid: Espasa-Calpe, 1962), pp. 273–274.

2. Angel-Raimundo Fernández González, "Introducción," in Benito Jerónimo Feijóo, *Teatro crítico universal*, 7th ed. (Madrid: Catedra, 2002), p. 21 n. 25.

3. Benito Jerónimo Feijóo, *Defensa de la mujer*, ed. Victoria Sau (Barcelona: Icaria, 1997), p. 92.

4. I. L. McClelland, *Benito Jerónimo Feijóo* (New York: Twayne Publishers, 1969), p. 2, citing *Teatro crítico universal*, vol. 5, discourse 5.

5. Fernández González, "Introducción," p. 44.

6. José Luis Abellán, *Historia crítica del pensamiento español*, vol. 3 (Madrid: Espasa-Calpe, 1981), p. 507.

7. McClelland, *Benito Jerónimo Feijóo*, p. 44.

8. G. Delpy, *Feijoo et l'Esprit Européen* (Paris: Hachette, 1936), p. 313; McClelland, *Benito Jerónimo Feijóo*, pp. 155–156, 165; Fernández González, "Introducción," pp. 56–57. A facsimile edition of a 1768 translation is available in volume 6 of *Conduct Literature for Women III, 1720–1770*, ed. Pam Morris (London: Pickering & Chatto, 2004).

9. The translation is based on the editions of "Defensa de las mujeres" in Feijóo's *Teatro crítico universal* (Madrid: Joaquin Ibarra, 1778), vol. 1, pp. 325–398; and in *Obras escogidas de Fr. Benito J. Feijoo con una advertencia preliminar* (Barcelona: Daniel Cortezo y C.ª., 1884), pp. 61–85.

A Defense of Women (author's and translator's notes)

Bracketed text is the translator's addition.

1. [Ovid, *Amores*, Book 2, Elegy 4.]

2. [In Boccaccio's *Il Corbaccio*.]

3. *Opusc. Except.* [*Opuscule ou petit traitté sceptique sur cette commune façon de parler: N'avoir pas le Sens commun* in *Œuvres* (Paris: Louis Billaine, 1669), vol. 9, p. 247.]

4. [That more women are born than men was a common belief. Feijóo refers to it again, but noncommittally, in the second paragraph of section 2.]

5. [King Roderic was the last Visigothic king of Spain. According to legend, he dishonored Florinda, the beautiful daughter of Count Julian, and Julian took revenge by bringing the Moors to Spain. Feijóo refers to Julian's daughter as "la Cava"; accordingly, she is sometimes called "Cava" in English. But Cervantes explains that "cava" comes from the Arabic for "wicked woman" (*Don Quijote*, I, ch. 41), and Feijóo's point is that Florinda was *not* wicked. Hence the term "cava" is avoided here.]

6. [In the original text of the Discourse, Feijóo simply assumed that this common opinion is true. He came to doubt it, however, and the translation reflects his emendation in a later addition.]

7. [See note 5 above.]

8. [Pliny the Elder, *Natural History*, Book 7, ch. 17.]

9. Serm. 86, *in Cant.* [Bernard of Clairvaux, Sermon 86, *In Canticum Canticorum*.]

10. ["Semiramis" was the Greek name for Sammu-ramat.]

11. [The Catholic monarch Isabel of Castile is referred to in English as Isabella; her husband Fernando, mentioned at the end of the paragraph, as Ferdinand.]

12. [Matt. 12:42, Luke 11:31.]

13. *Politics,* Book 2, ch. 7.

14. [Gen. 3:16.]

15. [Shapur II, king of Persia from 309 to 379, was said to have been crowned *in utero.*]

16. I [Feijóo] do not propose women who have taken their own lives as examples of virtue but as instances of excessive fortitude, which is sufficient to make the point at hand.

17. [Feijóo refers to Bona Lombarda (1417–1468).]

18. Seneca, *In Consolatione ad Marciam.*

MIGUEL DE UNAMUNO

1. Margaret Thomas Rudd, *The Lone Heretic: A Biography of Miguel de Unamuno y Jugo* (Austin: University of Texas Press, 1963).

2. Salvador de Madariaga, "Introduction," in *The Tragic Sense of Life in Men and Nations* (Princeton: Princeton University Press, 1972), p. xxx.

3. Hugh Thomas provides a vivid account in *The Spanish Civil War,* 3rd ed. (Middlesex: Penguin, 1984), pp. 501–503.

4. See *Del sentimiento trágico de la vida en los hombres y en los pueblos,* in *Obras completas,* vol. 7 (Madrid: Escelicer, 1967), ch. 9, pp. 234–235; and ch. 11, pp. 273–276.

5. Ibid., ch. 3, pp. 139–140, 142.

6. The work appeared in serial form in *La España moderna* beginning in December 1911.

7. *Del sentimiento trágico,* ch. 6, p. 183.

8. José Luis L. Aranguren called Unamuno "nuestro gran protestante," *Catolicismo y protestantismo como formas de existencia* (Madrid: Alianza, 1980), p. 252. Unamuno learned Danish for the express purpose of reading Kierkegaard in the original. As the following excerpt shows, he was particularly influenced by Kierkegaard's *Stages on Life's Way.*

The Tragic Sense of Life (author's, translator's, and editor's notes)

Bracketed text is the translator's addition or clarification; bracketed text with an asterisk is the editor's.

1. [Alfred Fouillée (1838–1912) was a French philosopher and sociologist who wished to reconcile traditional metaphysical thought with natural

science through his concept of the *idée-force,* i.e., that thought or mind is always behind action. His central work is *Psychologie des idées-forces* (Paris, 1893), 2 vols.]

2. Ritschl, *Geschichte des Pietismus,* Book VII, 43.

3. [Étienne Pivert de Sénancour, *Obermann,* trans. J. Anthony Barnes (London and New York, 1910, 1915), vol. 2, Letter XC, p. 252.]

4. [*The Nation* (London), vol. 11, no. 14,] July 6, 1912 [p. 504].

5. [* "Emperor of pedants" may be a reference to Otto von Bismarck, whose assertion "Wir sind nicht auf dieser Welt, um glücklich zu sein und zu genießen, sondern um unsere Schuldigkeit zu tun" is almost identical to Unamuno's German parenthesis. But Kant, whose views were similar and whose ethics is a prime example of the "[r]ational and rationalistic ethics" that Unamuno excoriates as "[p]edantry of pedantries" later on in this selection, may be the target instead (or as well).]

6. *Präludien,* I. [In the chapter "Über Friedrich Hölderlin und sein Geschick," in Wilhelm Windelband, *Präludien: Aufsätze und Reden zur Einführung in die Philosophie* (Tübingen, 1911).]

7. [Unamuno writes "'se les muera,' y no sólo 'se muera.'" The Spanish phrase is by natural usage more vivid: it conveys the intimate colloquial sense of personal loss.]

8. [An echo of Kierkegaard's three stages on life's way: aesthetic, ethical, and, the loftiest, religious.]

9. *Diálogos de la conquista del reino de Dios* (*Dial.,* III, 8).

10. [The reference here is to the clash between Unamuno and José Ortega y Gasset in 1909. When Azorín wrote his article "Collección de farsantes" for the newspaper *ABC* of September 12, 1909, to defend his country against foreign detractors, Unamuno wrote him a private letter of congratulations which found its way into the same newspaper. Unamuno referred to the "simpletons" (*papanatas*) fascinated by Europeans. "It is time," he said, "to declare that we are their equals and perhaps even better in quite a number of things." And he added: "If it were impossible for one nation to produce both a Descartes and Saint John of the Cross, I would opt for the latter." In answer, Ortega wrote his article "Unamuno y Europa, Fábula" in which he refers to St. John of the Cross as a "handsome little monk with an incandescent heart who wove lacework of ecstatic rhetoric in his cell," and calls Unamuno a "wild man" (*energúmeno*) who cannot see that without Descartes "we would remain in darkness and see nothing, certainly not the dark robe (*pardo sayal*) of Juan de Yepes (St. John of the Cross)." The article is in the *Obras completas* of José Ortega y Gasset (Madrid, 1957), vol. 1.]

11. [The ideas of the German philosopher Karl Christian Friedrich Krause (1781–1832), as propagated by Julián Sanz del Río (1814–69), had enormous influence in Spain. Sanz del Río studied in Heidelberg with disciples of Krause, and when he assumed his chair of philosophy at the Central University of Madrid, he attracted many enthusiasts to his Krausist system. Briefly, he held that it was the duty of Humanity, through rational effort, to carry out on earth God's harmonious design and to resolve all differences. The Krausists' view of God had nothing to do with dogma or revelation, or indeed even Christianity, but imbued many men with a sense of mission: e.g., Francisco Giner de los Ríos founded the independent secular Institución Libre de Enseñanza, a landmark in Spanish "idealist" educational reform. The definitive history of Krausism is to be found in vol. 1 of *La Institución Libre de Enseñanza* by Vicente Cacho Viu (Madrid, 1962). (And cf. review in English of this book in *The University Bookman*, Winter, 1964.)]

THE SCHOOL OF MADRID

1. Very little of Gaos' work has been translated into English. An exception is "Negation" in A. Robert Caponigri's *Contemporary Spanish Philosophy*, pp. 76–91. For more on Latin American philosophy, see Susana Nuccetelli and Gary Seay, eds., *Latin American Philosophy: An Introduction with Readings* (Upper Saddle River, NJ: Prentice Hall, 2003); Eduardo Mendieta, ed., *Latin American Philosophy: Currents, Issues, Debates* (Bloomington: Indiana University Press, 2003); and Jorge J. E. Gracia and Elizabeth Millán-Zaibert, eds., *Latin American Philosophy for the 21st Century: The Human Condition, Values, and the Search for Identity* (Amherst, NY: Prometheus, 2004).

JOSÉ ORTEGA Y GASSET

1. José Ortega y Gasset, *Prólogo para alemanes* in *Obras completas* (Madrid: Revista de Occidente, 1946–1983), vol. 8, ch. 2, p. 24; see also pp. 21–22.

2. Ibid., ch. 1, p. 16.

3. Ibid., ch. 5, pp. 55, 57.

4. *Meditaciones del "Quijote"* in *Obras completas*, vol. 1, p. 322.

5. *Historia como sistema*, in *Obras completas*, vol. 6, ch. 4, pp. 21–22. See also *Apuntes sobre el pensamiento: Su teurgia y su demiurgia*, in *Obras completas*, vol. 5, pp. 520ff.

6. "[S]oy *por fuerza* libre," *Historia como sistema,* ch. 7, p. 34. Ortega was calling attention to the linkage between freedom and necessity at least as early as 1934 in *Prólogo para alemanes,* ch. 3, p. 28. This was some seven years after Heidegger's *Sein und Zeit* but nine years before Sartre's claim in *L'Être et le Néant* that we are "condemned to be free."

7. *Prólogo para alemanes,* ch. 3, p. 41; *¿Qué es filosofía?* in *Obras completas,* vol. 7, Lección 7, p. 369.

History as a System (author's and editor's notes)

Bracketed text is the editor's addition.

1. *Œuvres de Descartes,* ed. Charles Adam and Paul Tannery (Paris: L. Cerf, 1897, 1931), vol. 6, p. 19.

2. In his book *On Liberty,* ch. 2, John Stuart Mill makes very opportune use of this same distinction, expressed in the same terms of "living faith" and "dead, inert faith."

3. [Just as "utopia" means "no place," *ucronismo* (the singular of Ortega's plural term) means "no time." *Ucronismos* is here translated as "achronisms." Just as a utopia can be an imagined place, an achronism (such as Loeb's) can be an imagined time.]

4. The form I first gave to this thought, in my youth, may be found in *El tema de nuestro tiempo,* 1923 (English translation by James Cleugh, 1932).

5. Bergson, the least Eleatic of thinkers, whom we must allow today to have been right on so many points, constantly uses the expression *l'être en se faisant.* But a comparison of his sense with that which I here give to the same words shows a radical difference. In Bergson the term *se faisant* is merely a synonym of *devenir.* In my text *making oneself* is not merely *becoming* but in addition the way in which human reality *becomes,* which is the effective and literal *making oneself,* a *fabricating oneself,* we might say.

6. See *Meditaciones del Quijote,* 1914. In this early book of mine it is already suggested that *I* am no more than one ingredient in that radical reality "my life," whose other ingredient is circumstance.

7. Be it recalled that the Stoics spoke of an "imagining of oneself," φαντασία ἑαυτοῦ.

8. I have already shown excessive temerity, and incurred excessive risk, in thus attacking at the gallop, like the Median warriors of old, the most fearsome themes of general ontology. Now that I have come to a point where, if I were to be moderately clear, it would be necessary to establish carefully the difference between so-called "collective or social life" and personal life, I would ask permission to renounce emphatically any intention of

so doing. Should the reader be moved to curiosity concerning my ideas on the matter or, in general, concerning the development of all that has preceded, he will find both set forth, as adequately as may be, in two books. In the first, under the title *El hombre y la gente,* I have tried faithfully to expound a sociology which does not, as in the past, avoid the truly basic problems. The second, *Sobre la razón viviente,* is an attempt at a *prima philosophia.*

9. *De Genesi ad litteram* vi.13.24 (*Patrologia Latina,* vol. 34).

10. A simple example will make clearer what I have sought, with extreme concision, to convey in these last few lines. In an excellent book recently published by Paul Hazard, *La Crise de la conscience européenne, 1680–1715,* the third chapter begins thus: *L'Europe semblait être achevée. Chacun de ses peuples avait des caractères si bien connus, et si décidément marqués, qu'il suffisait de prononcer son nom pour que surgît une série d'adjectifs qui lui appartenaient en propre, comme on dit que la neige est blanche et le soleil brûlant.*

This means that about the year 1700 one of the active ingredients of human life here in the West was the conviction felt by European peoples that they knew one another. Let us admit the facts, referred to by the author, whose collective enunciation forms this proposition. Is this enough to make the proposition true? For it happens that exactly the same proposition might be valid for the life of Europe today. Who can doubt, nonetheless, that the knowledge of one another that European peoples believe they possess today is something very different from that of two centuries ago? And different, be it clearly understood, not solely nor chiefly by its content, but in the certainty, the fullness, the daily presence, and general sense it has for us. This means, however, that as an active factor in our lives its reality is in consequence very different from the reality of two centuries ago. Hence Hazard's proposition and the concept its terms express are inadequate, since they are equivocal. If they are valid for today, they are invalid for 1700. And if they are valid for both, they will be equally valid for 1500, for it is beyond question that then, too, the nations of Europe believed they knew one another. Now, in the measure in which a concept has validity for different epochs of humanity, it is an abstraction. Yet the conception that Hazard is trying to express is of an essentially concrete order, and it escapes through the abstract meshes of his proposition. Had this been thought in terms of the reality of 1500 and of that of 1900, for example, it is evident that it would have thrown much more light on what was in fact happening in 1700. In history there come in—and once it has resolutely constituted itself historical reason, there must come in still more—abstract concepts that are valid for whole ages and even for the whole of man's past. But this is a question of concepts whose object is also an abstract moment of reality, of the same degree of abstraction as themselves. In the measure of their abstractness they are clearly formal: they do not, in themselves, think anything real but demand to be made concrete. When therefore we say that they are valid for different ages, their validity is to be understood as one of forms requiring a content, as an instrumental validity; they do not describe "historic forces." An approximate analogy may be seen in geometrical concepts, which are valid for, but do not explain, physical phenomena, because they do not represent forces.

The need to think systematically in history has many corollaries, one of which is this, that it will have to increase substantially the number of its terms and concepts. Naturalists will not take this amiss if they reflect that they possess today some millions of concepts and terms to describe the vegetable and animal species.